Born in Lancashire and educated at Oxford, best-selling biographer Anthony Holden was an award-winning journalist before becoming a prolific writer and broadcaster. He has won praise for his translations of Greek poetry and opera libretti as well as his definitive biographies of a wide range of figures, both living and historical.

Best-known for his studies of Tchaikovsky, Laurence Olivier and the Prince of Wales, Holden has also written a history of the Hollywood Oscars and *Big Deal*, an account of a year as a professional poker-player which was praised by enthusiasts from Walter Matthau and David Mamet to Salman Rushdie. He has published poetry, music and drama criticism, and polemical pamphlets advocating constitutional reform.

Anthony Holden has presented numerous TV documentaries, and continues to write regularly for a wide range of newspapers and periodicals on both sides of the Atlantic. He has recently been made a Fellow of the Centre for Scholars and Writers at the New York Public Library, where he is researching a biography of the Romantic poet and journalist Leigh Hunt.

Also by Anthony Holden

The St Albans Poisoner
Charles, Prince of Wales
Olivier
Big Deal: A Year as a Professional Poker Player
The Oscars: The Secret History of Hollywood's Academy Awards
The Tarnished Crown: Crisis in the House of Windsor
Tchaikovsky
Diana: A Life, a Legacy

JOURNALISM

Of Presidents, Prime Ministers and Princes
The Last Paragraph: The Journalism of David Blundy (ed.)

TRANSLATION

Aeschylus' Agamemnon
The Greek Anthology (contrib.)
Greek Pastoral Poetry
Mozart's Don Giovanni (with Amanda Holden)

Mr. WILLIAM
SHAKESPEARES
COMEDIES,
HISTORIES, &
TRAGEDIES.

Published according to the True Originall Copies.

LONDON
Printed by Isaac Iaggard, and Ed. Blount. 1623.

The title page of the First Folio (1623), with Martin Droeshout's portrait, the only image of Shakespeare approved by those who knew him.

WILLIAM SHAKESPEARE

His Life and Work

Anthony Holden

An *Abacus* Book

First published in Great Britain in 1999
by Little, Brown and Company
This edition published in 2000 by Abacus

A CIP catalogue record for this book
is available from the British Library.

ISBN: 0 349 11240 1

Typeset by Palimpsest Book Production Limited,
Polmont, Stirlingshire
Printed and bound in Great Britain by
Clays Ltd, St Ives PLC, Bungay, Suffolk

Abacus
A Division of
Little, Brown and Company (UK)
Brettenham House
Lancaster Place
London WC2E 7EN

For Frank Kermode

If my slight Muse do please these curious days,
The pain be mine, but thine shall be the praise.

CONTENTS

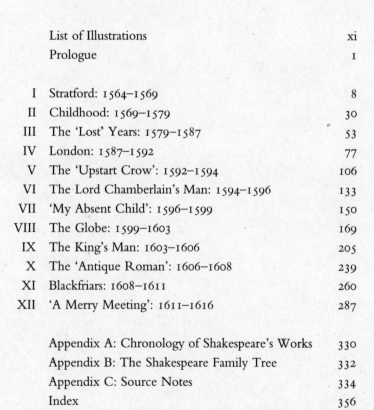

LIST OF ILLUSTRATIONS

Integrated illustrations

p. 328: Shakespeare's burial entered in the Stratford-upon-Avon parish register. [Shakespeare Birthplace Trust]

Plate section credits

Black and white

1, 2, 11: Shakespeare Birthplace Trust
3, 4, 6, 7, 8, 10, 13, 15: Mary Evans Picture Library
5: Lancaster University Photographic Unit
9: AKG Photo
12, 14: Bridgeman Art Library

Colour

1: J. Salmon Ltd
2, 3, 4, 5, 10a: Shakespeare Birthplace Trust
6, 10b, 10c: AKG Photo
7, 8: Bridgeman Art Library
9, 11a: Mary Evans Picture Library
11b: Jarrold & Sons Ltd

The man everywhere, in Shakespeare's work, is so effectively locked up and imprisoned in the artist that we but hover at the base of thick walls for a sense of him . . . There are moments when we are willing to let it pass as a mystery, but there are others when its power to torment us intellectually seems scarcely to be borne . . .

It is never to be forgotten that we are here in the presence of the human character the most magnificently endowed, in all time . . . so that of him, inevitably, it goes hardest with us to be told that we have nothing, or next to nothing . . . He slunk past in life: that was good enough for him, the contention appears to be. Why therefore should he not slink past in immortality?

The figured tapestry, the long arras that hides him, is always there, with its immensity of surface and its proportionate underside. May it not then be but a question, for the fullness of time, of the finer weapon, the sharper point, the stronger arm, the more extended lunge?

—*Henry James, introduction to* The Tempest, *1907*

PROLOGUE

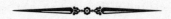

There are no great biographies of Shakespeare, according to the American scholar Harold Bloom, 'not because we do not know enough, but because there is not enough to know'. Such resonant truths have never deterred well-meaning Bardolaters, both amateur and professional, from climbing on each other's shoulders to a height where the view is now as richly detailed as at any time since Shakespeare's own. But can we, amid the named and numbered trees of the Forest of Arden, espy the man?

Somewhere in the world, it is said, a book on Shakespeare is published every day. At the turn of the twenty-first century, as he is universally voted Man of the Millennium, and wins surrogate Oscars via the writers of the film *Shakespeare in Love*, Shakespeare is bigger business than ever. As his home town is increasingly colonized by tourists, whether or not they choose to visit the theatre which bears his name, the long-suffering son of Stratford is meanwhile being picked apart by historicists, feminists, Marxists, new historicists, post-feminists, deconstructionists, anti-deconstructionists, post-modernists, cultural imperialists and post-colonialists. Perhaps it is time someone tried to put him back together again.

This attempt claims no more than what the late Anthony Burgess called 'the right of every Shakespeare-lover who has ever lived to paint his own portrait of the man'. Burgess, to my mind, made the last, best attempt at a popular, accessible, yet academically sound biography – in 1970, a generation and more ago, now distant enough to justify yet another attempt by yet another generation to re-create the poet in its own metropolitan, turn-of-another-century image.

Four hundred years after the Globe first opened, Shakespeare's theatre is back on the south bank of the Thames for the first time since his own day, staging his plays in much the way his own audiences would have seen them. Four centuries since the long, glorious reign of the first Queen Elizabeth drew towards its close, England is approaching the Golden Jubilee of the second – an age when John of Gaunt's 'sceptr'd isle' is uncertain of its own identity, with Scotland and Wales asserting their separateness within a potentially federal Europe, and Ireland still troubled, as compared with the first Elizabeth's mightily self-confident nation, pushing back the frontiers of science, culture and global exploration.

What more opportune moment to respond to Henry James's challenge by wielding 'the finer weapon, the sharper point, the stronger arm' in the pursuit of 'the more extended lunge'? My own motives and aspirations in tackling this most daunting of biographical tasks – beyond the chance to savour, in the happy phrase of my Oxford tutor, 'the apparently boundless hospitality of Shakespeare's imagination' – add up to a labour of love: an identikit portrait of a much-wanted man who appears to have spent his life and work wilfully trying to evade capture. 'We ask and ask,' as Matthew Arnold wrote of the man from Stratford. 'Thou smilest, and art still.'

In truth, as I maintain at the outset of this book, we know more about the life of Shakespeare than that of any of his literary contemporaries bar Ben Jonson. And the rest is there for all to see, in and between every line he ever wrote – as well as the order in which he wrote them. 'We do not understand Shakespeare from a single reading, and certainly not from a single play,' as T. S. Eliot sternly reminds us; but 'there is a relation between the various plays . . . taken in order'. Yes, as even Eliot concedes, there is a 'pattern in Shakespeare's carpet'.

It is one of many oft-repeated 'Bardisms', fast approaching the status of cliché, that we do not read Shakespeare; he reads us. By the same token, continuing conflicts between the various factions of the booming Shakespeare industry suggest that too many academics no longer read Shakespeare so much as rewrite him. Is the same to be said of biographers?

Perhaps. But I must part company with Harold Bloom when he asserts that 'we cannot know, by reading Shakespeare and seeing him played, whether he had any extrapoetic beliefs or disbeliefs'.

No writer, not even this *nonpareil*, can ever entirely absent himself from his work. Bloom takes G. K. Chesterton to task for suggesting that Shakespeare was a Catholic dramatist, and that Hamlet was 'more orthodox than sceptical'; yet he himself proceeds to counter-claim that 'by reading Shakespeare, I can gather that he did not like lawyers, preferred drinking to eating, and evidently lusted after both genders'.

As Bloom has also written elsewhere: 'If you read and re-read Shakespeare endlessly, you may not get to know either his character or his personality' – again, after the reading and re-reading that went into the writing of this book, I beg to differ – 'but you will certainly learn to recognise his temperament, his sensibility and his cognition.'

The arguments of both camps seem to me, as is so often the way with Shakespeare studies, equally legitimate, equally dubious. One scholar who has read this book in manuscript disagrees with some of it as violently as he 'rhapsodises' about the rest – depending, of course, on whether or not it supports his own, highly contentious point of view. Another eminent academic disapproves of the very concept of a Shakespeare biography, while a celebrated Shakespearean actor-cum-scholar generously says it has helped him to a better understanding of the works (which he knew pretty well in the first place).

To some lovers of Shakespeare, it is heresy to find biographical inferences between the lines of his poems and plays; to others, his true autobiography lies in his work. If the twain can never meet, it seems to me that there exists a middle ground through which it is relatively safe (and quite legitimate) to pick your way – a minefield, of course, sown with springes to catch not so much woodcocks as prodigal souls like mine, the blood burning, vows on the tip of the tongue, 'giving more light than heat', no doubt 'extinct in both'.

One kindred spirit who sounds like he will forgive me the attempt, *pace* the outcome, is the novelist John Updike, who recently distilled the first 'and perhaps most worthy' reason for reading literary biographies as 'the desire to prolong and extend our intimacy with the author – to partake again, from another angle, of the joys we have experienced within this author's *oeuvre*, in the presence of a voice and mind we have come to love'.

Reading these words, in the midst of my task, made me realise that one reason I was writing this book was that I wanted to read it. Shakespeare biography has recently got so bogged down in disputes about the digging of ditches and mending of hedges, payment (or non-payment) of fines and tithes, the design and logistics of Elizabethan theatres, how his contemporaries brushed their teeth, whether they had bad breath, right down to the decor of the guest bedroom of an Oxford tavern where he may or may not have bedded the landlord's wife – not to mention the perennial Fair Youths and Dark Ladies – that the man himself is too often allowed to slip away and watch from the wings, no doubt with a smirk, for whole chapters at a time. I have attempted to keep him squarely in sight, pin him firmly to the page, no matter how hard he has struggled to escape. It is fatal, I have found, to look away even for a moment. He is gone again, vanished to one of his own imaginary horizons. There follows the distant sound of cackling.

If each generation re-creates Shakespeare in its own image, my contribution is to despatch him to the Lancashire of my (and, I am convinced, his) youth. As you read of young Will 'Shakeshafte' passing in his teens from the Hoghton family to the Hesketh household, you may or may not care to know that my late father was a shopkeeper in Hoghton Street, Southport, some twenty miles from the scene of these late-sixteenth-century events, and that one of the first young women on whom I looked with all Silvius' hopeless ardour for Phebe was a Hesketh, direct descendant of the local toffs who took in the young actor-playwright in the 1580s. (Subsequently, since you ask, she married a publisher. Neither Shakespeare nor I can be expected to approve.)

Juvenilia apart, I must first acknowledge an obvious debt – spelt out in due detail in the source notes – to the four centuries of Shakespeare scholars and biographers who have gone before me, up to and including the present day. It is inevitable, in the words of a pioneer among the current crop, Ernst Honigmann, that 'everyone who writes about Shakespeare borrows from earlier writers'.

Alongside that of the late Sam Schoenbaum, greatest of twentieth-century Shakespeare archaeologists, of the buccaneering novelist-biographer Burgess, and of the iconoclastic Eric Sams, Honigmann's name heads the list of scholars whose work has helped to shape my own. (He has also been kind enough to read and evaluate a draft of my Chapters II and III.) But I have spared the reader a further list of my own extensive reading, as any Shakespeare bibliography worthy of the name would all but double the length of this book, which I have tried to keep within manageable bounds. So my research is itemised in the source notes, which offer publication details of the books I have found most rewarding. I have also chosen to spare the general reader the distraction of superscript note numbers in the text; the opening words of quotations may be found in the Source Notes, via page numbers in the running heads, to assist the reader towards original sources and further reading.

Quotations throughout the book conform primarily to the text of *The Riverside Shakespeare*, which I have found the most reliable, informative and scholarly single-volume edition of the Works. The Riverside text forms the basis of Professor Martin Spevack's computer-generated *Complete and Systematic Concordance to the Works of Shakespeare*, now abridged in the one-volume *Harvard Concordance to Shakespeare*. In all other quotations I have modernised the spelling, often with some reluctance, indulging myself by leaving an inconsistent few to retain their inalienable period charm.

The staff of the London Library and the Shakespeare Centre Library in Stratford-upon-Avon have been unfailingly helpful (as has Ben Holden, chasing down some of the more rarefied material in Oxford University's Bodleian and English faculty libraries). I am also grateful to the wide variety of academic Shakespeare specialists who have listened to and argued with me during my four years' work on this book; I will not drop their names here, as the responsibility for its contents should remain mine alone. The same goes for the many Shakespearean actors, directors and enthusiasts, both amateur and highly professional, who have shown great patience when buttonholed by the Ancient Mariner of Bardic lore into whom I have turned these last few years.

A. Alvarez, Melvyn Bragg, John Fortune and Peter O'Toole kindly read the manuscript in typescript and made many helpful suggestions. I have rarely enjoyed such profound disagreements with anyone as genially as with Eric Sams, who also took my penultimate draft to pieces, and will strenuously protest at much of what remains –

notably on such contentious issues as collaboration, 'memorial reconstruction', 'pirate' publication (with special reference to the Sonnets), right down to the spelling of the name of Shakespeare's only son. I am also grateful to Professors Richard Wilson and Richard Dutton of Lancaster University for an invitation to speak at the 'Lancastrian Shakespeare' conference in July 1999, held in part at Hoghton Tower, under the auspices of the university's Shakespeare programme; and to the many scholars present (notably Father Peter Milward, Professors Stephen Greenblatt, Eamonn Duffy, Gary Taylor and others) from whose wisdom and expertise I benefited.

The *Observer* generously gave me unlikely amounts of space to expatiate on Shakespeare in the various guises in which he continues to haunt all our lives; my thanks to its Review editor, Lisa O'Kelly, and arts editor, Jane Ferguson. Robert Butler, drama critic of the *Independent on Sunday*, kindly took me to many Shakespeare first nights, which also entailed many patient hours of argument. He of all people knows the travails that went into this book – beyond, of course, my wife and children, who have welcomed Shakespeare into our household with all the forbearance they have previously shown such long-stay guests as Laurence Olivier, Tchaikovsky and others, even the Prince of Wales.

The book would never have been written without the touching faith in my ability to do so of my friend and publisher, Alan Samson; I am equally grateful to Philippa Harrison, Andrew Gordon, Rosalie Macfarlane, Linda Silverman, Amanda Murray and all their colleagues at Little, Brown on both sides of the Atlantic. My agent, Gill Coleridge, has been her constant, supportive, inimitable self.

But my deepest debt ranges over thirty years, from my inspirational tutor in the late 1960s at Merton College, Oxford, John Jones, author of the wonderfully observed *Shakespeare at Work*, to my friend and mentor Sir Frank Kermode, whose lifetime steeped in the poetry of Shakespeare will soon result in the publication of his own, rather different study, hard on the heels of my own. Such fun did Frank and I have while simultaneously writing about our mutually beloved Bard, if in different ways and at very different levels, pooling thoughts both wonderfully insightful (his) and outrageously erratic (mine), that it is as much a pleasure as a privilege to have wrung from him his leave for the dedication.

A NOTE ON MONETARY VALUES

The computer wizardry of Robin Marris, Emeritus Professor of Economics at Birkbeck College, London, suavely picked up my gauntlet by coming up with a mercifully simple formula for the approximate conversion of Elizabethan monetary values to those of the present day. Commodities such as foods must be excluded because prices would of course fluctuate according to their scarcity value. In the case of more stable figures, such as income, expenditure and property, the Marris formula works out simply as 'multiply by 500'.

Shakespeare's purchase of New Place in 1597 for £60, for instance, would convert to £30,000 at today's prices, which seems a bargain for one of the most handsome houses at the heart of a provincial town. His annual income from the theatre, which at its peak reached some £200, would thus be the equivalent of a handsome £100,000 – rather less, I am given to believe, than the annual income of some of the leading playwrights of our own day.

I

STRATFORD

1564–1569

Both his parents were illiterate. His father, who rose to become Mayor of Stratford-upon-Avon, all his life signed his name with a mark. His mother, like most women of her day, was never taught to read or write.

There are those who believe that their eldest son was himself unable to read or write, that the collected works of William Shakespeare could not have been written by the simple son of Warwickshire whose baptism was recorded in the parish register of Stratford's Holy Trinity Church on 26 April 1564. So miraculous is Shakespeare's achievement that a thriving industry has grown up around baffled, usually snobbish attempts to deny it – to suggest that it must have been the work of more than one man, that the 'rude groom' from Stratford could only have been plagiarising, stealing or rewriting the work of others, lending his name to plays and poems which really belonged to better-educated contemporaries, also better-born.

Least logical of all, in the face of the canon's sheer scale and diversity, its breadth of observation and experience, its unparalleled combination of eloquence, learning and wisdom, are those who ascribe it all to some other individual, usually aristocratic – and also, presumably, possessed of superhuman powers. Anti-Stratfordians, as these diverse opponents of Shakespeare's authorship are collectively known, must also assume

that his friend and fellow playwright Ben Jonson, who first called him
'Swan of Avon', was in on the plot – that Jonson was, not to mince
words, lying when he wrote of Shakespeare: 'I loved the man, and do
honour his memory (on this side idolatry) as much as any. He was indeed
honest, and of an open and free nature; had an excellent fantasy, brave
notions, and gentle expressions, wherein he flowed with that facility
that sometime it was necessary he should be stopped . . .'

Was Jonson still lying in the title of his poem 'To the Memory
of My Beloved, the Author, Mr William Shakespeare, And what he
hath left us', and in its sentiments on the title page of the posthumously
published First Folio?

> Soul of the Age!
> The applause! delight! the wonder of our stage!
> My Shakespeare, rise ! . . .
> He was not of an age, but for all time!

Must the same go for the writer Robert Greene, who enviously
attacked the young Shakespeare's work in 1592; for the printer Henry
Chettle, who rapidly apologised amid a shower of personal compliments; for the Stratford mercer Richard Quiney, whose son married
Shakespeare's daughter, and who in 1598 wrote a begging letter to 'my
loving good friend and countryman'; for the anonymous author of the
so-called *Parnassus Plays*, who saluted 'sweet' Master Shakespeare as the
author of *Richard III*, *Romeo and Juliet*, *Antony and Cleopatra* and the
poem *Venus and Adonis*, a copy of which he wished to keep beneath his
pillow; for the Elizabethan scholar, critic and lawyer Gabriel Harvey,
who praised Shakespeare as the author of *Hamlet*, *Venus and Adonis* and
The Rape of Lucrece; for the comic actor Will Kemp and his satirical
reference to 'my notable Shakerags'; for his family friend Leonard
Digges, who spoke of 'thy Stratford monument'; and for numerous
other contemporaries up to and including the playwright's friends
and fellow actors John Heminges and Henry Condell, who lovingly
gathered his plays into the indispensable First Folio of 1623, seven
years after his death, to 'keep the memory of so worthy a friend and
fellow-worker alive as was our Shakespeare'?

Was King James I of England and VI of Scotland also conning
posterity when he named William Shakespeare and eight others, plus

'the rest of their associates', as the King's Men in a royal charter granted under the Great Seal of England on 17 May 1603? Of course not. Only a talent so uniquely versatile could have inspired such a perverse combination of jealous rivalry, awe-struck eulogy and affectionate remembrance.

Beyond the tedious, class-ridden distraction that its subject never existed, or could not have been the man who wrote the plays and poems attributed to him, or was even (in a tired academic joke) a different man of the same name, Shakespeare biography must chart a wary course through the encrusted myths of more than four centuries – the first being the popular delusion that there is scant documentary evidence about the life of the most remarkable poet the world has been privileged to know. Shakespeare's life is in fact documented in more detail than that of any writer of his age, except to some degree Ben Jonson, as we shall see from these (and many other) contemporary references to his work.

So another myth must be dispelled at the outset. There is no evidence, alas, to support the popular belief that William Shakespeare was born – as fifty-two years later he was to die – on 23 April, the date celebrated in England since 1222 as the feast day of dragon-slaying St George. As the poet's posthumous fame grew, securing a unique niche for his country in the cultural history of the world, it was a natural enough temptation for posterity to unite the birthday of England's national poet with that of its patron saint. But the tradition is based on a false assumption, that Elizabethan baptisms invariably took place three days after the birth.

The instruction given to parents in the 1559 Prayer Book, published five years before Shakespeare's birth, was to have the christening performed before the first Sunday or holy day following the birth 'unless upon a great and reasonable cause declared to the curate and by him approved'. In 1564 the 23rd day of April happened to fall on a Sunday, four days after the feast day of St Alphege and two before that of St Mark – traditionally an unlucky day, so the curate's permission to avoid it may well have been forthcoming. But the contemporary inscription on Shakespeare's tomb in Holy Trinity – that same church where he was christened on 26 April by the vicar of the parish, John Bretchgirdle – reads that he died in his fifty-third year ('*obiit anno . . . aetatis 53*'). We know that he died on St George's Day, 23 April, so this

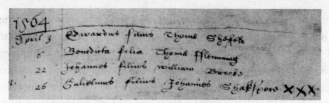

Shakespeare's baptism on 26 April 1564 entered in the
Stratford-upon-Avon parish register.

would seem to imply that he was born before it, however marginally. There are few more satisfactory resolutions of this problem than that of the poet Thomas de Quincey, who suggested that Shakespeare's granddaughter Elizabeth Hall married on 22 April 1626 'in honour of her famous relation' – choosing the sixty-second anniversary of his birth, in other words, rather than the tenth of his death.

William Shakespeare of Stratford-upon-Avon was to bring lasting lustre to a surname long held to be an embarrassment. In 1487, on becoming a celibate don at Merton College, Oxford, one Hugh Shakespeare had changed his name to Hugh Sawnders. '*Mutatum est istud nomen eius, quia vile reputatum est,*' records the College register: 'He changed that name of his, because of its base repute.'

For all its ripe phallic imagery, shared with similar names like Shakestaff and Wagstaff, Shakespeare survived as a fairly common surname (in all manner of different spellings) in Warwickshire and its environs throughout the late Middle Ages, particularly in the thriving city of Coventry and a cluster of villages in what was then the Forest of Arden, a dozen miles north of Stratford-upon-Avon. In 1284 a William Sakspere of Clopton, Gloucestershire, was hanged for theft; a century later, in 1385, another William Shakespeare served on a coroner's jury in Balsall.

Between 1530 and 1550 tenant farmers called Richard Shakspere, Shakespere, Shakkespere, Shaxpere and Shakstaff were penalised on numerous occasions for non-attendance at the manor court at Warwick, choosing to pay the 2d fine rather than lose a day's work making the six-mile walk each way. In fact, of course, they were all the same man: the poet's grandfather.

From 1529 to his death in 1561, Richard Shakespeare was a tenant farmer in the village of Snitterfield, four miles north-east of Stratford

on the main Warwick road. We can conjure a picture of his worka-
day life from its petty irritants, still preserved in Stratford amid the
legal records of the day: penalised in 1535 for overburdening the
common pasture with his animals; ordered in 1538 to mend the
hedges dividing his land from that of one Thomas Palmer; fined
in 1560 for not yoking or ringing his pigs, and letting his livestock
run wild on the public meadow. In October that year, only months
before his death, the collegiate church of St Mary, Warwick, gave
all its tenants a two-week deadline to create a hedge and dig a ditch
between 'the end of Richard Shakespeare's lane' and 'the hedge called
Dawkins hedge'.

Evidently, Richard Shakespeare had become a senior citizen of
Snitterfield over a life long by the standards of his day. Several times
he was chosen to take responsibility for valuing the estates of deceased
friends and neighbours. In 1560, when Sir Thomas Lucy held an
'inquisition' in Warwick into the estates of Sir Robert Throckmorton,
Richard 'Shakyspere' was a member of the jury. At the time of his
death in February 1561, he owned the land between his house on
the High Street and the stream which flowed through the centre of
Snitterfield. His estate was valued at £38 17s – a not insubstantial sum,
when compared with the £34 left three years earlier by the vicar of the
parish, Sir Thomas Hargrave.

Richard Shakespeare's landlord was Robert Arden, of the nearby
village of Wilmcote, in the parish of Aston Cantlow, whose daughter
Mary would marry Shakespeare's son John in 1557. John was the
second, perhaps the third of Richard's sons. The parish records
mention a Thomas Shakespeare, whose £4 rent was the largest of
all Snitterfield tenants, but not his parentage. But Henry Shakespeare,
a colourful character in constant trouble with the law, certainly was
Richard's son, John's younger brother, the future poet's uncle – and
the black sheep of the family.

A tenant farmer like his father, with land at nearby Ingon, Henry
appears to have inherited the Shakespeare indifference to keeping his
fences and ditches in good repair, or playing his communal part in the
maintenance of the Queen's highway. More reckless than his father,
Henry served frequent prison terms for trespass and debt, and was
temporarily excommunicated for refusing to pay his tithes. In 1574
he 'drew blood' in a fight with one Edward Cornwell – also, later, to

become William's uncle, as the second husband of his mother's sister Margaret; having failed to turn up in court, Henry was fined *in absentia*. Nine years later, in 1583, he and two friends were also fined for the curiously provocative act of attending church in hats, rather than caps – in defiance of the Statute of Caps, a recent measure designed to assist the ailing cap-making industry. For all the attraction of seeing this as a gesture of religious protest – there was widespread Puritan opposition to the statute – it was more likely just another roguish act of defiance from a man impatient with authority all his life.

Henry also pioneered the Shakespeare trait of not repaying debts until sorely pressed; once, as he languished in Stratford jail for non-payment, his surety, William Rounde, took the chance to reclaim two oxen which Henry had bought but not yet paid for. Though still in debt when he died in December 1596, the poet's Uncle 'Harry' left corn and hay 'of great value' in his barn, and a mare in the stable.

Henry's younger brother John, the poet's father, was a Shakespeare of quite another stamp. Born in 1529, he was dubbed *agricola*, or husbandman, in documents relating to his father's estate; but by then, the early 1560s, he had long forsaken the traditional Shakespeare life on the land for what he saw as more prosperous urban pastures. Though raised in the family business of tenant-farming, John had set his sights higher from early youth, migrating to the thriving market town of Stratford by the mid-point of the century.

Settled in a lush, wooded valley, by then a decent-sized town of some 1,500 souls, Stratford-upon-Avon originally took its name from the point where a Roman road (or 'straet') crossed (or 'forded') the elegant river flowing through its heart. One of the oldest settlements in Christian England, Stratford is mentioned in the Domesday Book as the personal fiefdom of the Bishops of Worcester; by Shakespeare's day its agricultural tenants had won their emancipation, and formed the nucleus of a thriving mercantile community, with artisans and shopkeepers displaying their wares on market days alongside the usual livestock and country produce. Already the Avon (Welsh for 'river') was spanned, as still it is, by a handsome stone bridge built by Sir Hugh Clopton, a wealthy local mercer who had risen to become Lord Mayor of London. In the heart of Stratford, in the last decade of the fifteenth century, Clopton built himself the biggest house in town, which he called New Place. It was one measure of the subsequent success in London of another son of Stratford, the glover's boy William Shakespeare, that eventually he in turn would become the proud owner of New Place.

A hundred miles from the capital, but handily close to the major Midlands townships of Worcester and Warwick, Banbury and Oxford, Stratford was described by a contemporary map-maker as '*emporium non inelegans*' – a market town not without its charms, already boasting the handsome thirteenth-century parish church of Holy Trinity, and the smaller but even older, equally finely detailed chapel of the Guild of the Holy Cross. Both would play significant roles in the life of John Shakespeare, and make cameo appearances in the works of his son. Beside the parish church, on the banks of the Avon, stood a charnel-house crammed to overflowing with the bones of the dug-up dead; the young William's religious dread of it, as he played in the churchyard as a child, finds apparent echoes in Macbeth's horror at Banquo's ghost and Juliet's feverish protests to Friar Laurence about marrying anyone other than Romeo:

> O, bid me leap, rather than marry Paris,
> From off the battlements of any tower,
> Or walk in thievish ways, or bid me lurk
> Where serpents are; chain me with roaring bears,
> Or hide me nightly in a charnel-house,
> O'er-cover'd quite with dead men's rattling bones,
> With reeky shanks and yellow chapless skulls . . .

We know that by 1552 John Shakespeare was living on the north-eastern side of town, in Henley Street, thanks to his ignominious debut in the town records on 29 April: fined a shilling, along with Humphrey Reynolds and Adrian Quiney, for making an unauthorised dunghill – *sterquinarium*, or midden heap – in front of the house of a neighbour, the wheelwright William Chambers. In those days of the plague, a fine equivalent to two days' pay for an artisan was a suitably stern judgement on those too idle to use the communal muck-hill at the rural end of the street. In a rare defiance of the family tradition (and his own later practice), John Shakespeare paid his fine promptly. Already, it seems, he had it in mind to become not just a worthy citizen of Stratford, but a civic eminence. This early misdemeanour appears to have proved no bar to his upward mobility.

John Shakespeare and others fined for making an unauthorised dung-hill in Henley Street, Stratford-upon-Avon, 29 April 1552.

After serving (we can but assume) the statutory seven-year apprenticeship, Shakespeare's father had entered trade as a glover and whittawer: a dresser of 'whitleather', soft light-coloured leather. Between 1556 and 1592 various legal documents concerning unpaid debts and bail sureties unambiguously describe Johannes Shakyspere, or Shakspere, or Shackspeare, as a 'glover'. His craft involved the 'tawing' of hides and skins – of deer and horses, goats and sheep, but not of protected livestock such as cattle or pigs – by soaking them in a solution of salt and alum (aluminium sulphate). The resulting leathers he fashioned not only into gloves, but belts, purses, aprons – whatever he could sell in his shop, or in the glovers' stall given prime position on market days beneath the clock of Stratford's Market Cross, today the traffic island at the junction of the High Street, Bridge Street and Henley Street, which leads to the Shakespeare Memorial Theatre.

The seventeenth-century diarist John Aubrey, one of the first to visit Stratford in search of Shakespeare evidence, reported unequivocally that the poet's father was a butcher. Aubrey is never the most reliable of witnesses, but it does seem plausible, in the light of later events, that there was a period in John Shakespeare's life when he might have defied the regulations strictly separating the otherwise allied professions of whittawer and butcher. He certainly traded openly in the wool of sheep slaughtered for their skins. The eastern wing of the Henley Street house which doubled as his leather goods store was known as 'the Woolshop'; when the floor was relaid in the nineteenth century, after the house had become an inn, the landlord testified to finding beneath the floorboards 'the remnants of wool, and the refuse of wool-combing . . . imbedded with the earth of the foundation'.

So why not their meat as well, if under-the-counter, hugger-mugger? According to Aubrey, the young William himself would kill a calf 'in a high style, & make a speech'; and there are plenty of expert references to the art of butchery in the plays – not least to the expertise of the human butcher, or hangman, who performed the drawing and quartering which followed the half-hanging of convicted felons from cutpurses to Romanist recusants. Theirs are the hands of which Macbeth is thinking, thick with blood and entrails from a human belly, when he shudders at his own 'hangman's hands' after murdering Duncan.

'Is it not parchment made of sheep-skins?' Hamlet asks Horatio, who replies, 'Ay, my lord, and of calves'-skins too.' A Warwickshire antiquary has devotedly catalogued copious Shakespeare references to 'the hides of oxen and horses, to calf-skin, sheep-skin, lamb-skin, fox-skin and dog-skin, deer-skin and cheveril'. The poet knew that neat's-leather was used for shoes, sheep's leather for a bridle, that tanned leather could keep out water, and that deer's hide was the keeper's perquisite. 'He notices leathern aprons, jerkins and bottles, the "sow-skin bowget" or bag carried by tinkers.' He makes frequent reference to cheveril, or kid-skin, whose softness and flexibility suited it to the making of fine gloves – and thus, also, of fine Shakespearean metaphors. Mercutio jokes about Romeo's 'wit of cheveril, that stretches from an inch narrow to an ell broad', and Viola's clown about a sentence that 'is but a chev'ril glove to a good wit. How quickly the wrong side may be turn'd outward!' At the end of his writing career, in *Henry VIII*, the poet has a wise old lady speak of Anne Bullen's 'soft cheveril conscience', that would receive gifts if she might 'please to stretch it'. Calf-skins make an especially telling appearance in *King John*, when the Bastard Faulconbridge defiantly repeats an insult to the Duke of Austria: 'And hang a calf's-skin on those recreant limbs.' But the trade of Shakespeare's father is nowhere, perhaps, more authentically recalled than in Mistress Quickly's description of Master Slender in *The Merry Wives of Windsor*: 'Does he not wear a great round beard, like a glover's paring knife?'

Other legal documents, the key pieces of our jigsaw for this period, involve John Shakespeare in suits concerning the sale and purchase of timber, and barley, whose sole commercial use was for the manufacture of beer and ale. Clearly he was something of an entrepreneur, a jack of all trades – a '*Johannes factotum*', as his son was enviously to be mocked, during his father's lifetime. John Shakespeare, again like his son after him, was also something of a property dealer.

If by 1552 Shakespeare's father owned or rented all or part of the Henley Street house still held sacred (despite scant evidence) as The Birthplace, he soon added to his property portfolio with the purchase in 1556 of a freehold estate with garden and croft, *tenementum cum gardino et crofto*, in Greenhill Street (later to become known as More Towns End). The business must have been thriving, for that same year also saw him buy an adjacent house in Henley Street, complete with garden, which would become the east wing or Woolshop when the two properties were joined together as a handsome, three-gabled dwelling.

More than forty years on, in 1597, the Stratford records show John selling off a narrow strip of land alongside this property to a draper named George Badger, for the purpose of building a wall, and another small parcel to Edward Willis of King's Norton, who proposed to open an inn called the Bell. Thus we can be reasonably sure that Henley Street remained the Shakespeare family home, through many vicissitudes for its paterfamilias, over half a century and more. It was still in the family 150 years later.

In 1553, soon after John Shakespeare had settled there, the borough of Stratford-upon-Avon had received its formal charter of incorporation from the Crown. Subject to the whims of the lord of the manor – in this case the Earl of Warwick, who still nominated the vicar and schoolmaster, and had power of veto over the borough's choice of bailiff, or mayor – this afforded a large degree of self-government to an elected council of aldermen and burgesses, who themselves appointed lesser functionaries. As luck would have it, the ambitious glover had arrived in the right town at the right time, the perfect moment to establish a mercantile foothold in the community while answering its new need for civic leaders. Nor, presumably, would a badge of office – and thus local respectability – be all that bad for business.

John's first recognition came in September 1556, within three years of the borough's incorporation, when he was chosen as one of its two ale-tasters – an office for 'able persons and discreet', whose duties were to check that bakers made loaves of regulation weight, and brewers 'wholesome' ales and beers at regulation prices. The ale-taster's powers were considerable: those he found in breach of the regulations were liable to appear before the twice-yearly manorial court, or 'leet', which had the power to inflict punishments from fines to a whipping, a sojourn in the stocks or pillory, or even worse public humiliation in the 'cucking stool' – a chair in the shape of a giant chamber-pot, in which the offender was ducked in the river to the delighted derision of his clientele.

Within nine months of his appointment, in June 1557, the new ale-taster found himself on the wrong side of the law, blotting his copybook by failing to attend three sittings of the Court of Record in his official capacity. The 8d fine he paid seems to have been worth it, for that spring saw John Shakespeare with other priorities to take his mind off his duties.

The journey back and forth to Wilmcote, presumably after hours, would have taken its toll on John's extra-curricular activities. Having established a secure base in the heart of Stratford, he returned to his rural roots for his bride, while still intent on social advancement. Mary Arden was not just the daughter of a prosperous farmer, his father's landlord; hers was one of Warwickshire's most prominent families, tracing its ancestry back beyond the Norman Conquest to the Domesday Book, fully four columns of which were filled by the landholdings of Turchill of Arden – more than any other individual.

Mary was the youngest of eight daughters of the widowed Robert Arden, whose second marriage in April 1548 (to Agnes Hill, née Webbe, widow of another prosperous farmer) added four stepchildren to the substantial brood already crammed into the two-storey Wilmcote farmstead. Whether it was the timber-frame house in Featherbed Lane identified in the late eighteenth century, and today visited by flocks of tourists, as 'Mary Arden's home', we cannot be sure – any more than we can be sure that her son William was born in the Henley Street manse today known as The Birthplace. But it would have been very similar, with its stone foundation and gabled dormers, timbered ceilings and rough-hewn oak beams, stone hearths and inglenooks, its main walls bedecked with painted hangings which would pass from the playwright's childhood memory into his first play to be performed, *The First Part of the Contention betwixt the two famous Houses of York and Lancaster* (later known as *Henry VI Part 2*):

Like rich hangings in a homely house,
So was his will in his old feeble body.

So powerful an impression was left by the biblical and mythological
scenes dominating the main rooms of his mother's family home that
William remained wide-eyed at the age of thirty, when he published
his poem *The Rape of Lucrece*:

Who fears a sentence or an old man's saw
Shall by a painted cloth be kept in awe.

No record survives of John Shakespeare's marriage to Mary Arden,
but it must have taken place – presumably in the parish church of St
John the Baptist, Aston Cantlow, where no register was yet kept –
towards the end of 1557. Their first child was born in the ninth month
of 1558; but Mary would not have married during 1556, as her father lay
dying. On 24 November that year Robert Arden made his will, whose
terms suggest that his youngest daughter was, like King Lear's, also his
favourite. Beyond the customary ten marks, Mary's father left her his
most valuable possession in its entirety: the Arden estate in Wilmcote,
named Asbies, 'and the crop upon the ground sown and tilled as it is'.

Such was the handsome dowry Mary Arden brought to her marriage
to the Stratford glover, by whom she would bear eight children in all
– four sons and four daughters – over twenty years. A decade or so
older than his wife, John would live into his seventies, well beyond
the average span of his day, and Mary would outlive him by some
seven years.

William was the third of their children to be born, but the first to
live beyond childhood. A daughter, Joan, had been christened on 15
September 1558 by Roger Dyos, a Catholic priest driven from his post
soon after Queen Elizabeth succeeded her Catholic half-sister Mary
on the throne later that year. No record has been found of poor
Joan's death or burial; but the fact that the Shakespeares christened
another daughter by the same name eleven years later, on 15 April
1569, amounts to melancholy proof that the first Joan did not survive
childhood, probably dying at the age of only one or two, as the register

for the years 1559–60 is particularly sketchy. A second daughter, Margaret, was baptised on 2 December 1562 by the newly arrived Anglican priest, John Bretchgirdle, who also performed her funeral only four months later, in April 1563.

The Shakespeares' third child was himself lucky to survive infancy. William was less than three months old when the plague struck Stratford, imported from the slums of London by itinerant traders and vagabonds. '*Hic incepit pestis*' reads the dread entry in the burial register for 11 July 1564, beside the name of Oliver Gunne, an apprentice – only the twentieth person to be interred since 1 January, compared with 240 during the remaining five months of the year. It is a fair estimate that more than 200 souls – or one in seven of Stratford's population – were carried off by the grim disease, those most at risk being the community's youngest and oldest members. The records show that the plague claimed all four children of the Green family, neighbours of the Shakespeares in Henley Street. It seems highly likely that Mary, having already lost two daughters in their infancy, would have evacuated her firstborn son to the safety of her family home at Wilmcote, still occupied by her widowed stepmother, for the duration.

Already a burgess, an elected member of the council, her husband attended an emergency meeting that August, held alfresco to avoid the dangers of contagion. John Shakespeare contributed three shillings to a fund to assist victims of the plague, which did not abate until December, with the onset of the midwinter cold. By then, the turn of the year 1564–65, Shakespeare's father was a rising star of the Stratford council chamber.

On 30 September 1558, two weeks after the birth of his first child, the well-married glover had been sworn in (with Humphrey Plymley, Roger Sadler and John Taylor) as one of the borough's four constables, 'able-bodied citizens charged with preserving the peace'. Although proverbially stupid – an Elizabethan tradition his son would immortalise in the characters of Constables Dogberry and Dull – these local worthies, guardians of law and order, took on unenviable responsibilities in these unruly times. John Shakespeare would often have been called upon to break up drunken brawls, confiscate weapons from men made menacing by liquor, and give evidence against them in court. He was also responsible for policing the town's precautions against the ever-present threat of fire, and reporting to the church authorities any malingerers caught 'bowling, gaming or tippling' when they should have been at divine worship.

For a year Shakespeare's father evidently performed these duties efficiently enough, for 6 October 1559 saw him reappointed 'petty constable' – despite a fine that April for 'failing to keep his gutter clean' – and promoted to the equally unpopular role of *'affeeror'*, or 'assessor', the civic functionary responsible for assessing fines not laid down by statute. It was not long before his upward progress reached its first plateau, with his election as one of Stratford's fourteen burgesses, the bulk of the town council responsible for all administration, who met in the Guild Hall every morning at 9 AM.

John Shakespeare makes his mark as 'affeeror' of the 'leet', 4 May 1561.

Whatever the effect of his public duties on the conduct of his business, John Shakespeare's fluctuating financial fortunes seem at first to have had little impact on his civic standing. His three-shilling contribution to the plague fund in the August following William's birth was followed by only sixpence the following month, at the end of which his name enters the municipal lists as a witness to a corporation order. Already he was the borough treasurer, a regular attender of council meetings, who presented Stratford's annual accounts for 1564 at a plenary meeting held on 1 March 1565. By July he had been elevated to alderman – unembarrassed, it seems, by an order shortly thereafter to pay £3 2s 7d 'for restitution of an old debt'. In mid-February 1566 the records show him again presenting the annual accounts, a citizen solid enough to stand bail that September for one Richard Hathaway – father, as it happens, of his son's future bride. Each time he 'signed' the borough accounts, Shakespeare's father used as his mark an elegantly drawn pair of compasses, one of the tools of his trade.

As an alderman, John was entitled to attend church and all other public occasions in a black cloth gown trimmed with fur. He would also have sported a ring which evidently made a lasting impression on his observant young son. 'When I was about thy years, Hal,' brags Sir John Falstaff in *1 Henry IV*, 'I could have crept into any alderman's thumb-ring.' The ring surfaces again in Act 1 of *Romeo and Juliet*, in Mercutio's resounding Queen Mab speech:

> She is the fairies' midwife, and she comes
> In shape no bigger than an agate stone
> On the forefinger of an alderman.

As the Shakespeare family prospered, so it grew. A second son, Gilbert, was christened on 13 October 1566; like William he managed to survive infancy, living until 1612. Named after John Shakespeare's friend Gilbert Bradley, a fellow glover and council member, Gilbert Shakespeare appears to have followed his brother to London, where he is described in 1597 as a haberdasher of St Bride's, before returning to Stratford, where he seems to have fallen into undesirable company and occasionally foul of the law. The record of his burial, on 3 February 1612, four years before William, shows that he died *adolescens*, or unmarried.

In September 1567 we find their father being addressed for the first time as 'Mr Shakespeyr', a title of some considerable dignity. Another year, and he has been elected bailiff, or mayor, in his mid-thirties, in a three-way contest with Robert Perrot and Robert Salisbury held on 4 September 1568. On 1 October John presided over his first council meeting as bailiff, and five days later over his first Court of Record.

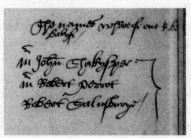

John Shakespeare stands as a candidate for bailiff, 4 September 1568.

As an impressionable four-year-old, Shakespeare would now have seen a po-faced clutch of mace-bearing sergeants arrive at Henley Street early each day to escort his fur-trimmed father, with great ceremony, in a procession through the streets of Stratford to preside over the morning meetings at the Guild Hall. On Thursdays and fair-days the same parade would snake through the market and the fair, and on Sundays process solemnly to church, where the Shakespeare family now sat in the front pew. As bailiff, John Shakespeare shared with one other senior alderman the duties of Justice of the Peace: issuing warrants, hearing cases of debt and local by-law violations, negotiating with the lord of the manor. On Thursdays, after market, he would set the price of corn, and thus of bread and ale, for the following week, amid furious lobbying from bakers and brewers.

In 1569, midway through John Shakespeare's year in office as 'the Queen's officer & chief of the town', there occurs the first recorded visit to Stratford by a travelling troupe of players. 'Can this be mere coincidence?' it has rightly been asked. 'The substantial sums payable to players had to be authorised and disbursed by the local council; and the father of a great playwright may well have evinced a special interest in and feeling for staged entertainment.' By virtue of his role as censor, moreover, the mayor – and no doubt his family – enjoyed the privilege of a private performance by the Queen's Players.

With civic honours came further commercial prosperity. On 4 November 1568 Mayor Shakespeare sold five hundredweight of wool to John Walford of Marlborough – a debt he was still to be found pursuing more than thirty years later; and in 1568–70 he was recorded as the tenant of Ingon Meadow, a fourteen-acre estate two miles north-east of Stratford, in the parish of Hampton Lucy.

As his worldly success spread to the countryside of his and Mary's roots, to the very land farmed by his wayward brother Harry, John stepped down from Stratford's top job, choosing not to exercise his right to run for another term of office. Most likely, having achieved all he could by way of civic eminence, he deemed it more than time to return his attention to the family business. But he remained a respected elder of Stratford, his advice valued by the corporation, who in September 1571 elected him Chief Alderman and Justice of the Peace for the coming year, and ex-officio deputy to the new bailiff, his old friend and Henley Street neighbour Adrian Quiney, a mercer. In January 1572 the two rode together to London as ambassadors for the borough, deputed by their fellow councillors to report on parliamentary affairs affecting Stratford and represent its interests 'according to their discretions'.

During 1569, the year of the birth of the second Joan, John Shakespeare had mustered all his confidence to describe himself as 'Bailiff, Justice of the Peace, the Queen's Officer and Chief of the Town of Stratford' in his formal application to the College of Arms for the ultimate in self-made respectability: a coat of arms. This outward sign of his worldly success would set the seal, literally, on two decades of solid achievement.

But it was not to be – not, at any rate, for another quarter of a century, until his increasingly successful playwright son reapplied on his father's behalf in 1596 to the College of Arms, then as now on the banks of the Thames at Blackfriars, directly opposite the Globe theatre. Then, at last, the Clarenceux King-of-Arms duly noted that John Shakespeare 'was a magistrate in Stratford upon Avon. A justice of the peace, he married a daughter and heir of Arden, and was good of substance and habileté.' But this first application in 1569 was declined by the authorities in London – for reasons which are nowhere documented, if not difficult to surmise.

John Shakespeare's eldest son had been born in dangerous times. It was less than half a century since the Queen's father, King Henry VIII, had broken with Rome, despoiled and looted church landholdings and shrines, executed notables from Sir Thomas More to two of his own wives, including Elizabeth's mother.

The Elizabethan era was fast approaching its apogee – a sustained period of military, political, scientific and cultural achievement without parallel in British history. But it was also an age of ferocious religious persecution. Herself a deeply devout and civilised woman, Elizabeth presided with apparent reluctance over the pursuit, torture and execution of papists, in sporadic purges of varying intensity. But it was a time for followers of the 'old' faith to tread carefully, to worship in corners – for some, if necessary, to deny their faith or at the least 'equivocate'.

In 1757, a century and a half after John Shakespeare's death, a document of great significance was found hidden in the rafters of the family house in Henley Street – by then occupied by Thomas Hart, a direct lineal descendant of William's sister Joan. Retiling Hart's roof was a team of workmen led by Joseph Moseley, a master-builder described as 'very honest, sober, industrious', who on 29 April came upon a small 'paper-book', or pamphlet, tucked between the old tiling and the rafters. Its six stitched leaves turned out to contain fourteen articles amounting to a profession of Roman Catholic faith.

The document, which has become known as John Shakespeare's Spiritual Last Will and Testament, passed from Hart and Moseley to a local alderman, on to the eighteenth-century Shakespeare reliquary John Jordan and eventually (via the vicar of Stratford, James Davenport) to Shakespeare's eighteenth-century biographer, Edmund Malone. Having satisfied himself that it was genuine, though by now lacking its first page, Malone duly published it as an appendix to his 1790 edition of the Works.

The document has since vanished – 'a pity', in the understatement of one of the outstanding twentieth-century Shakespeare biographers, Samuel Schoenbaum, for the advanced techniques of modern scholarship might have answered 'several intriguing questions' regarding the script, the paper, the watermark, the handwriting and, of course, John Shakespeare's signature. Was it a cross or his characteristic mark of the glover's compass? Malone subsequently recanted his conviction that the document was genuine, and the hapless Jordan was accused of forgery; it took until 1923 for a diligent Jesuit scholar, burrowing around the British Museum, to come up with an uncannily similar Italian document, also dating from the sixteenth century.

This was the 'last testament' of Saint Carlo Borromeo, the Cardinal Archbishop of Milan, who died in 1584 and was canonized in 1610. Borromeo's 'Last Will of the Soul, made in health for the Christian to secure himself from the temptations of the devil at the hour of death' was composed during a virulent bout of the plague in Milan in the 1570s, said to have claimed 17,000 Catholic lives. His Testament, which became a mantra of the Counter-Reformation, was clearly the original of the English translation found hidden in what had once been John Shakespeare's roof.

How did it get there? In 1580 Borromeo was visited in Milan by a group of Jesuit missionaries, led by Father Edmund Campion, an English recusant who two years later would be tried and gruesomely executed for treason. Campion and his colleagues brought back with them to England numerous copies of Borromeo's testament, which was now circulating around Catholic Europe in huge quantities. 'Three or four thousand or more of the Testaments' were ordered from Rome by Campion and his colleagues, 'for many persons desire to have them.' Once back in England, Campion passed through the Midlands

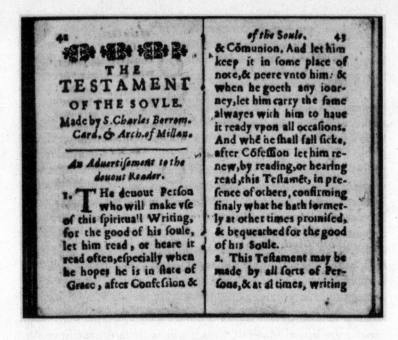

Title page of Cardinal Borromeo's Testament of the Soul.

– specifically Lapworth, just twelve miles from Stratford – en route to Lancashire, where he was again to play a significant role in the life of young William Shakespeare.

Campion's host at Lapworth was Sir William Catesby, a relative by marriage of the Ardens, who was arrested and imprisoned in the Fleet for his pains. In Elizabethan England, Catholics literally risked their lives by admitting popish priests into their houses, whether to take their confession and celebrate Mass or merely to indulge in theological discussion. Policed by the Privy Council, who conducted periodic raids on secret strongholds of recusancy all over the country, adherence to the 'old' faith was a crime amounting to treason, and punishable by death. Elizabeth's reign saw almost 200 Catholics meet excruciating ends on the public scaffold. Just two years after her own death, Catholic apostasy reached its celebrated climax in the 1605 'Powder Treason', now better known as the 'Gunpowder Plot' – whose leader was not Guy Fawkes, as legend would have it, but Robert Catesby, son of that same Sir William who invited Edmund Campion to visit Warwickshire in 1580.

An English translation of Borromeo's Testament, which finally came to light as recently as 1966, proved that the document faithfully attested by John Shakespeare was thus formulaic, but genuine beyond all doubt. A lifelong recusant – as witnessed by his subsequent fines for non-attendance of church, even while still a prominent member of the Stratford community – Shakespeare's father might well have been one of the furtive souls invited by Catesby, his Catholic wife's Catholic kinsman, to meet Campion at Lapworth, and to carry away one of the secretly made English translations imported by the thousand from Rome. If not, it was probably passed to him by John Cottom, then the Stratford schoolmaster, whose recusant brother Thomas was one of Campion's travelling companions.

Three years later, a new round of raids and persecution dogged Warwickshire Catholics after a rash attempt by a local fundamentalist, John Somerville, to assassinate the Queen. As the authorities descended in search of vengeance, the clerk of the council, Thomas Wilkes, bore witness to the urgent efforts of local recusants to 'clear their houses of all show of suspicion'. Somerville, who was captured and hanged en route to London, was married to Margaret Arden, a Catholic cousin of Shakespeare's mother. Perhaps this was the moment her husband felt it prudent to hide his copy of the Spiritual Testament up in the roof?

Aged seventeen when the Testament came into the family home, and twenty by the time his father felt obliged to hide it, the precocious William certainly seems to have absorbed its contents, whatever his personal reaction to them. The Testament's Item I acknowledged the possibility of being 'cut off in the blossom of my sins', a terrifying prospect catered for in Item IV: 'I, John Shakespeare, do protest that I will also pass out of this life, armed with the last sacrament of extreme unction: the which if through any let or hindrance I shall not be able to have, I do now also for that time demand and crave the same.' The words of the English translation find a direct echo in those of the Ghost of Hamlet's Father, written within a year of the death of the poet's:

> Cut off even in the blossoms of my sin,
> Unhous'led, disappointed, unanel'd,
> No reck'ning made, but sent to my account

With all my imperfections on my head.
O, horrible, O, horrible, most horrible!

So appalled was John Shakespeare's son, in life as in art, by the fate of those who met their maker 'unaneled' that Hamlet even spares his father's murderer, his hated stepfather Claudius, when presented with the chance to kill him while at prayer. 'No!' he cries,

Up sword, and know thou a more horrid hent:
When he is . . .
                                        . . . about some act
That has no relish of salvation in't . . .
. . . that his soul may be as damn'd and black
As hell, whereto it goes.

No shriving time allowed, the Ghost of Hamlet's Father occupies an authentically Catholic version of Purgatory:

My hour is almost come
When I to sulph'rous and tormenting flames
Must render up myself . . .
Doomed for a certain term to walk the night,
And for the day confined to fast in fires,
Till the foul crimes done in my days of nature
Are burnt and purged away.

So soon after his own father's death, Shakespeare clearly shares Hamlet's sense of horror that his father's 'canonised bones, hearséd in death / Have burst their cerements'. The fate of unburied bones haunts his work to the terminal point of his own stark epitaph, still there today to chill the heart of the visitor to Stratford's Holy Trinity church, with its curse on him that 'moves my bones'.

Shakespeare's Catholic indoctrination in childhood ran deep, whatever the subsequent falling-off in his beliefs. For both father and son, throughout the poet's youth, the 'equivocation' so dear to the heart of the Porter in *Macbeth* was a necessary evil to survive amid the religious McCarthyism then dogging Warwickshire dissenters.

By the time he felt obliged to hide his Catholic Testament in the roof at Henley Street, Shakespeare's father was retired from active local politics, and celebrating the birth of his first grandchild by his son William. How it must have pained him, twenty years earlier, to fulfil his duties as Stratford's chamberlain by authorising the payment of two shillings to workmen charged with the task of 'defacing images in the chapel' – Stratford's Guild Chapel, embellished with papist murals of the murder of Thomas à Becket, St Helena's Dream and the Day of Judgement – and hitherto protected by the most powerful man in town, William Clopton, and his son, both Catholics.

But Clopton senior had died in 1560, and now his son had taken himself abroad. Given the political climate, the local council seized the moment to mutilate the heretical frescoes, in danger of bringing into disrepute a town so recently granted its royal charter. Two years later the council spent a further two shillings on the cost of dismantling the chapel's rood loft. And in 1571, John Shakespeare was present when his friend and successor as bailiff, Adrian Quiney, ordered the replacement of the chapel's stained-glass windows with clear panes, and the disposal of the popish capes and vestments still preserved in the chapel, if long since disused.

John Shakespeare may have disguised his religion well enough during his rise to civic eminence, like many fellow Catholics at that time of persecution. But this was an age of informers, well paid for their pains, who helped the authorities keep a close eye on countless pockets of papist defiance throughout the land. John's semi-concealed religious sympathies may well have been responsible for the College of Arms's otherwise mysterious refusal to grant him a coat of arms in 1569. They may also have played a role in the sudden, unwelcome development – eventually to cut short the education of his five-year-old schoolboy son William – that over the next few years, after two decades of sustained success, the former Mayor of Stratford's fortunes went into an abrupt and quite unexpected decline.

II

CHILDHOOD

1569–1579

Ben Jonson famously said that his friend Will Shakespeare had 'small Latin and less Greek'. By the standards of our day, if not his own, Jonson was wrong about the Latin; but the myth persists that this particular poet, because he did not enjoy the university education of his literary contemporaries, 'wanted art' (Jonson again), that he was 'untaught, unpractised' (Dryden), that he was 'fancy's child' warbling his 'native woodnotes wild' (Milton). 'How far sometimes a mortal man may go,' mused the playwright Francis Beaumont, in the year before Shakespeare's death, 'by the dim light of Nature.' In Sonnet 78, even the mock-modest poet himself appears to protest 'my rude ignorance'.

There is no documentary evidence that Shakespeare attended Stratford's grammar school, the institution traditionally held to be his *alma mater*; the registers for the period, unsurprisingly, have not survived. But we have the word of his first biographer, Nicholas Rowe, that John Shakespeare installed his son 'for some time at a Free-School'; and only one such was available to the son of a civic eminence, the King's New School in Church Street, behind the Guild Chapel, only a few hundred yards' trudge from the family home in Henley Street. With the granting of its borough charter in 1553, amid the post-Reformation zeal for learning, Stratford had been as swift as other new townships to establish a school of the highest standards, run by a master whose qualifications entitled him to a grace-and-favour house in the Guild precincts and the handsome stipend – more than Eton paid – of £20 a year.

Seven was the all-male school's minimum age of entry, but pupils as young as four or five began their studies at the adjacent 'petty school', under the wing of an '*abecedarius*' (or usher) appointed and paid by the Master. With the birth of the second Joan in the summer of 1569, amid the seemingly unstoppable upward mobility of John Shakespeare, we may thus envisage a reluctant five-year-old William buckling down to an arduous school routine at the behest of his impatient, ambitious father. The long school day ran from 6 AM to 6 PM, beginning and ending with Protestant devotions, with only a two-hour lunch break at 11 otherwise interrupting fully ten hours of lessons every day, six days a week, every week of the year, except holy days – a very different thing from holidays, which were a concept alien to the Elizabethan schoolboy.

'Monsieur, are you not lett'red?' Armado asks the pedant Holofernes in *Love's Labour's Lost*, to which Moth replies: 'Yes, yes, he teaches boys the horn-book.' Like Shakespeare's many other references to the dull drudgery of school-work, this was written more than two decades later with a combination of rueful resentment and gently affectionate nostalgia. The 'horn-book' was the indispensable item in every novice schoolboy's armoury: a sheet of paper, or parchment, framed in wood, protected by a thin overlay of transparent horn. On it were inscribed the Lord's Prayer and the letters of the alphabet, both small and capital, plus sundry permutations of the five vowels with the first three consonants, *b*, *c* and *d*, to teach the rudiments of constructing syllables. Preceded as it was by the mark of the cross, the alphabet was known as 'Christ cross row' – as witnessed by George, Duke of Clarence, confiding to the future Richard III his alarm about the neurotic superstitions of their brother, King Edward IV:

> He hearkens after prophecies and dreams,
> And from the cross-row plucks the letter G,
> And says a wizard told him that by G
> His issue disinherited should be;

And, for my name of George begins with G,
It follows in his thought that I am he.

Once the alphabet was mastered, the horn-book was supplemented by *The ABC With the Catechism*, which added the catechism from the Book of Common Prayer and some mealtime graces. 'That is question now,' muses Philip the Bastard in *King John*, 'and then comes answer like the Absey book.' The third and most advanced of the standard textbooks was *The Primer and Catechism*, which featured the Calendar and Almanac, plus the seven penitential psalms and other religious texts. Thus were schoolboys scarce out of infancy weaned on *prosodia* (the 'pronouncing of letters, syllables, and words with the mouth') and *orthographia* (the 'writing of them with the hands'). Spelling, of course, was not yet considered a necessary skill; in the absence of any orthodoxy, spelling remained 'gloriously impressionistic', as Anthony Burgess noted with typical exuberance: 'To learne to wrytte doune Ingglisshe wourdes in Chaxper's daie was notte dificulte.'

These basic skills, plus perhaps the fundamentals of numeracy, would thus have been mastered by the time the seven-year-old Shakespeare graduated to the grammar school proper in 1571, the year his father was nominated Stratford's Chief Alderman. Now William's education would be in the hands of a succession of eminently qualified if pedantic pedagogues, by turns bookish and pious, all Oxford men of apparently unflinching rectitude. The pattern had been set in 1565, the year after Shakespeare's birth, by a devout friend of Vicar Bretchgirdle named John Brownsword, briefly followed in 1568 by John Acton, a scholar of Brasenose College, Oxford. Another Oxford college, Corpus Christi, supplied his successor, the Lancastrian Walter Roche, who lasted only two years – probably those William spent at the petty school, hunched over his 'Absey' book and catechism – before departing to make more money as a lawyer.

In 1571, the year of William's arrival in the senior school, Roche was succeeded as Master by Simon Hunt, who four years later matriculated at the Catholic University of Douai, became a Jesuit in 1578 and then penitentiary at St Peter's in Rome, where he died in 1585. Whatever impact he had on the young William, and whatever bonds he forged with his recusant father, Hunt moved on to self-imposed religious exile after just four years, having supervised the poet's education between the impressionable ages of seven and eleven. His successor turned out to be an equally significant childhood mentor, the self-made scholar–cleric Thomas Jenkins, who arrived as Master from Warwick grammar school. Son of an 'old servant' to Sir Thomas White, founder of St John's College, Oxford, Jenkins *fils* took his degree there, going on to become a Fellow of sufficient stature to be granted the lease of Chaucer's house at Woodstock.

Though Jenkins was a Londoner, his very name appears to have inspired the affectionate parody of a Welsh pedagogue in *The Merry Wives of Windsor*, in which Falstaff scorns Sir Hugh Evans for speaking 'Welsh flannel' and making 'fritters of English'. It can also be no coincidence that the name of Evans's pupil is William (one of only two characters in the canon to whom the playwright gave his own name). When Mistress Page complains to Sir Hugh that 'my husband says my son profits nothing in the world at his book', Evans attempts to prove her wrong by putting young William through his paces.

> *Evans:* Well, what is your accusative case?
> *William:* *Accusativo, hinc.*
> *Evans:* I pray you, have your remembrance, child. *Accusativo, hung, hang, hog.*
> *Quickly:* 'Hang-hog' is Latin for bacon, I warrant you.
> *Evans:* Leave your prabbles, oman. What is the focative case, William?
> *William:* *O—vocativo, O.*
> *Evans:* Remember, William: focative is *caret*.
> *Quickly:* And that's a good root.
> *Evans:* Oman, forbear.
> *Mrs Page:* Peace!
> *Evans:* What is your genitive case plural, William?
> *William:* Genitive case?
> *Evans:* Ay.
> *William:* *Genitivo: horum, harum, horum.*
> *Quickly:* Vengeance of Jinny's case! Fie on her! Never name her, child, if she be a whore.

This halting exchange is almost verbatim mimicry of the standard Latin primer of the day, William Lily's *Short Introduction of Grammar*, clearly so imprinted on the mind of this other William as to remain embedded there more than twenty years later. Latin, *pace* Jonson, was the very core of the grammar school curriculum. Apart from Lily, with his declension and conjugations, and sample set texts for learning by rote, the seven-year-olds were force-fed such other Latin anthologies as Erasmus's *Cato* and the *Sententiae Pueriles* of Leonard Cullmann. They were introduced to Aesop's *Fables* via a Latin translation, and to the works of Terence and Plautus, scenes from whose comedies they regularly acted out. That Shakespeare's earliest comedies were to draw so heavily on Plautus, setting a lifelong pattern by adopting the five-act structure of classical comedy, is surely as much of a tribute to Jenkins's pedagogic powers as his being rendered immortal for the passing amusement of a queen.

'Ah, good old Mantuan!' enthuses Holofernes in *Love's Labour's Lost*, quoting the opening lines of Baptista Spagnuoli's 'Bucolica':

> I may speak of thee as the traveller doth of Venice:
>> *Venechia, Venechia,*
>> *Che non te vede, non te prechia.*
> Old Mantuan, old Mantuan! Who understandeth
> thee not, loves thee not.

'Mantuanus', the Mantua-born Carmelite who beguiled his retirement with bucolic eclogues, was among the authors studied by boys in their third year, aged nine or ten, along with other 'modern' Latin moral poets such as Palingenius, whose *Zodiacus Vitae* acquainted young William with 'the great commonplace' (in one of Samuel Schoenbaum's boldest throwaway lines) 'that all the world's a stage'. That he put praise of the Mantuan in the mouth of a pedant may well suggest (as it does to the mischievous Schoenbaum) that Shakespeare 'never got beyond the first eclogue'. Or it may rather, with its wry, ironic tone of voice, betoken a lasting affinity with the ancient authors who first whetted this particular pupil's appetite for poetry – despite the basic drudgeries familiar to all such schoolboys through the ages, before and ever since. Armed with a dictionary, the boys

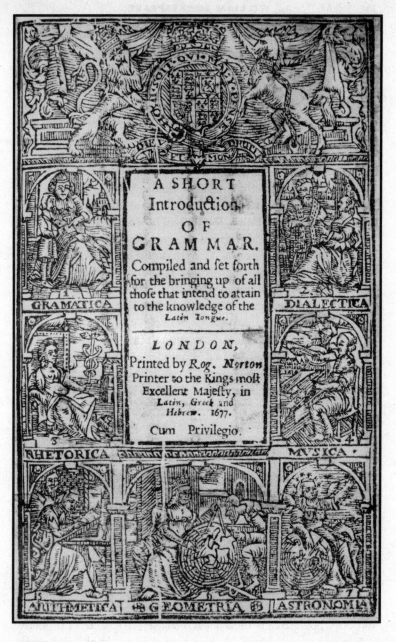

The title page of William Lily's *Short Introduction of Grammar (1540)*, used at school by Shakespeare.

of Stratford grammar school were already mastering the disciplines of written Latin by translating passages from the Geneva Bible, and spoken Latin via the colloquies of Corderius, Gallus or Vives, and the dialogues of Erasmus.

At the age of eleven, as schoolmaster Jenkins arrived in 1575, the young Shakespeare would have graduated to Cicero, Susenbrotus, Quintilian and Erasmus' *De Copia* as rhetoric and logic entered the senior-school syllabus. These were the springboard for both written epistles and spoken orations. They were also the gateway to Virgil, Horace and Ovid, all of whom won a lasting place in Shakespeare's heart, above all Ovid's *Metamorphoses*, a prime source for so many poetic motifs. An affection for Juvenal is also heard in Hamlet's 'satirical rogue', though there are few such fond records of Persius, or the historians Sallust and Caesar, or Cicero's *De Officiis*, the standard school introduction to moral philosophy. 'Small Latin' to Ben Jonson, perhaps – but to one latter-day authority, Shakespeare would have left Stratford grammar school 'as well qualified in Latin as a modern classics graduate'.

'Less Greek' we may allow; Shakespeare's studies would have progressed barely, if at all, beyond some elementary dabbling in the baffling hieroglyphics of a Greek New Testament. As for lack of university 'polish': the universities of the day added little such gloss to a schoolboy's studies of classical literature or logic, rhetoric or moral philosophy, existing more as training grounds for professions such as the law, medicine or divinity. The man of letters was not then regarded as having entered a profession. It seems significant that of the twenty-six male children registered as having been christened in Stratford in the year of Shakespeare's birth, only one went on to university – another William, surnamed Smith, who matriculated at Exeter College, Oxford, in 1583 – at the unusually late age of nineteen. Smith ended up, with seeming inevitability, as a schoolmaster, rather proving the brutal aside given by his schoolmate to Berowne, again in *Love's Labour's Lost*:

> Small have continuous plodders ever won
> Save base authority from others' books.

Item 41 of the Injunctions issued in the Queen's name in 1559 decreed 'that all teachers of children, shall stir and move them to the love and due reverence of God's true religion, now truly set forth by public authority'. The Act of Uniformity stipulated the use of Elizabeth's Book of Common Prayer in churches throughout the land, as well as 'the new Kalendar, a Psalter, the English Bible in the largest volume, the two tomes of the Homilies and the Paraphrases of Erasmus translated into English'. These Homilies were to be read 'distinctly and plainly', whether or not the vicar chose to add an address of his own. They were, in effect, sermons approved by the legal authorities, 'for the better understanding of the simple people' on themes such as the virtues of obedience or the perils of rebellion. As they duly instilled fear and conformity into potentially recusant souls, so their rhythms and imagery were absorbed into the young Shakespeare's poetic imagination, leaving his rational mind to roam free. His early attendance of Sunday school at Holy Trinity is attested by Malvolio's notorious dress sense: 'Cross garter'd . . . like a pedant that keeps a school i' the church.'

Was the Protestant church dressing the young Shakespeare, like his father, in borrowed robes? 'Though honesty be no puritan,' jests the clown Lavache in *All's Well That Ends Well*, 'yet it will do no hurt; it will wear the surplice of humility over the black gown of a big heart.' As Calvinist ministers outwardly conformed to the law, by wearing the surplice above their black Geneva gown, so the young Shakespeare learned to disguise the truth of his family's Roman leanings, while his eager mind became steeped in the rituals and sacred texts of both orthodoxy and heterodoxy. As both a pupil of the grammar school and the son of a rising council member, William would have received instruction in his catechism from the parish priest, and regularly attended matins, evensong and communion. Churchgoing was enforced by law, with stiff fines for non-attendance or other breaches of the observance of the Sabbath.

Shakespeare 'died a papist', testified Richard Davies, sometime chaplain of Corpus Christi College, Oxford, some seventy years after the poet's death. The most persuasive subsequent evidence also suggests that Shakespeare's father brought him up a secret Catholic, obliged to conform outwardly to Protestant orthodoxy, as was John Shakespeare himself as a member of the Stratford council. The young

William would continue a furtive papist for some years yet, as we shall see; but he was meanwhile steeped in Protestant orthodoxy throughout his schooldays, absorbing texts and tenets which echo through his work.

Quotations from or references to no fewer than forty-two books of the Bible – eighteen each from the Old and the New Testaments, and six from the Apocrypha – have been identified throughout the plays and non-dramatic poems. The New Testament (with the exception of Revelation) was read in its entirety three times during the course of a church year, the Gospels and Acts at Matins and the Epistles at Evensong. Shakespeare appears to have been especially impressed by the Books of Genesis and Matthew, Job and the apocryphal Ecclesiasticus. The story of Cain struck deep; he refers to it more than twenty-five times. Of Adam and Eve, there is 'hardly a phrase of the story that has been missed'. So frequent are his allusions to Genesis and Matthew that it seems logical to deduce these were the first books he studied; that he often quoted from memory, and thus made mistakes, is suggested by the repeated error in *Richard II* of putting the words 'All hail' in the mouth of Judas as he betrays Christ; in the gospel, they are spoken only by Jesus himself.

Of the holy texts available, the Bishops' Bible of 1568 (a revision of the Great Bible of 1539–41) was that stipulated by the episcopate; but it never claimed the same affection in the hearts of the 'simple people', or the mind of the young poet, as the more widely available Geneva Bible. Like most well-to-do families, even the illiterate Shakespeares would have owned a copy, which William evidently absorbed. The revised Geneva Bible of 1595 translated Ecclesiastes 5:11 as 'The sleep of him that travelleth is sweet' – of which we hear a clear echo in the Provost's description of the drunken jailbird Barnardine in *Measure for Measure*:

> As fast lock'd up in sleep as guiltless labour
> When it lies starkly in the traveller's bones.

In the poet's mind, inevitably, these resonant sources could also merge. In the Geneva Bible's 'We have spent our years as a thought', we can perhaps discern the seeds of Prospero's

> We are such stuff
> As dreams are made on; and our little life
> Is rounded with a sleep.

Likewise, in the psalmist's 'We bring our years to an end, as it were a tale that is told . . .', we can hear the makings of Macbeth's nihilistic ruminations on hearing of his wife's death.

Just as there is no record of William Shakespeare's entry to Stratford grammar school, so there is no record of his leaving it. After a decade and more of intensive schooling, those few boys talented enough for university moved on around the age of fifteen, when the rest would have to start earning their living. In Shakespeare's case, there is reason to believe that he left school even earlier.

William was only thirteen when his father's professional fortunes entered their sudden decline; the Stratford records show that the council meeting of 5 September 1576 was the last attended by the former bailiff, now Chief Alderman, for some years. Financial difficulties were not easy to conceal; a five-year-old suit for a debt of £30, pressed again in 1578 by Henry Higford of Solihull, is as conspicuous in the Stratford records as John Shakespeare's unexplained absence throughout 1557–78 from the deliberations of the council he had recently chaired.

That its members continued to hold him in affectionate regard, whatever the problems that kept him from their midst, is evidenced by several exemptions from the regular financial obligations incumbent on civic elders. The records for 29 January 1578 name John Shakespeare among several to be spared the statutory aldermanic payment towards the maintenance of three borough pikemen, two billmen and one archer. On 19 November he is again exempted from the weekly tax for the poor levied on all aldermen. Only the previous week,

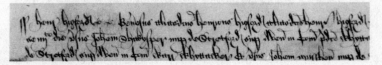

Court of Common Pleas: action by Henry Higford against John Shakespeare and John Musshen for debt, 1573 and 1578.

ominously, John and his wife are recorded to have sold 'seventy acres of land to Thomas Webbe and Humphrey Hooper'. This was part of Mary Arden's dowry. The family fortunes were indeed in trouble.

''Twere pity they should lose their father's lands,' says King Edward in one of Shakespeare's first plays, *3 Henry VI*. The poet is still mindful of such priorities more than a decade later, soon after his own father's death, when paternal responsibility is stressed twice in close proximity in *Hamlet* as a good enough reason to go to war:

> But to recover of us, by strong hand
> And terms compulsatory, those foresaid lands
> So by his father lost.

Horatio's explanation of young Fortinbras' motives is echoed almost immediately by Claudius, whom he has been 'pestering' about the surrender of those lands 'lost by his father'.

In such a crisis, what more natural than for proud John Shakespeare to remove his eldest son from school to make an early start at his father's side in the glover's shop and his mother's at the domestic hearth? Barely a century later, in 1701, Rowe suggested that 'the narrowness of his circumstances, and the want of his assistance at home, forced his father to withdraw him from thence' – to wit, the free-school. As early as 1577, the first year of John Shakespeare's reversals, John Aubrey has thirteen-year-old William working beside his father as 'a butcher'. Just as Aubrey has the glover's son killing a calf 'in high style' – to an impressionable young boy, perhaps 'the unkindest cut of all' – so Hamlet puns in high style on Polonius' fate when playing Julius Caesar:

> I was kill'd i' th' Capitol; Brutus kill'd me.
> It was a brute part of him to kill so capital a calf there.

Conveyance of property in Wilmcote between John and Mary Shakespeare, George Gibbs, Thomas Webbe and Humphrey Hooper.

Shakespeare was certainly familiar with the 'uncleanly savours of the slaughter-house' (*King John*). There are more references to the butcher's trade in one of his first plays, *2 Henry VI*, than in any other, including an evocation of the abbatoir so vivid as to seem poignantly first-hand:

> And as the butcher takes away the calf,
> And binds the wretch, and beats it when it strays,
> Bearing it to the bloody slaughter-house . . .
> And as the dam runs lowing up and down,
> Looking the way her harmless young one went,
> And can do naught but wail her darling's loss . . .

It is also likely that the young Shakespeare, as would befit the bailiff's son, himself donned butcher's apron and wielded the fatal knife — making that speech of Aubrey's 'in a high style'? — while taking part in the traditional Christmas mumming play, *The Killing of the Calf*. Throughout his works he displays a detailed technical knowledge of butchery, and the properties of its prime consequence, blood, which permeates so many of the plays: how it can form into 'gouts' (*Macbeth*), 'spout' in a trumpeter's eyes (*Troilus and Cressida*) or 'like a fountain' (*Julius Caesar*), or drips 'drop by drop' (*1 Henry VI*); how it follows the withdrawn knife (*Julius Caesar*), can 'temper clay' (*2 Henry VI*) or make a 'paste' (*Titus Andronicus*) or 'manure' the battlefield (*Richard II*), even how it grows dark as it coagulates, and a 'watery rigol' or clear serum 'separates from the black clot' (*The Rape of Lucrece*).

So Shakespeare knew his butchery. In the ensuing four centuries, many other gossips and scholars have enlisted him in as many other trades besides, transfixed by the expertise of his many references to the law, medicine, the military, the navy, the court and the countryside — which can only have been deployed, it has been held, by a trained lawyer, doctor, soldier, sailor, nobleman, falconer and/or scholar-gardener. For the plain fact is that, between his baptism in 1564, his marriage in 1582, the births of his children in 1583–85 and the first mention of him as a London playwright in 1592, there is not one documented reference to William Shakespeare of Stratford-upon-Avon. It is, to be brutally honest, no more than a plausible assumption that he went to school at all.

However much he absorbed from the syllabus of the day, and however well it served him in later life, the playwright pleased his audience by affecting, however genially, the conventional distaste of schoolboys for their labours. Four centuries of schoolchildren have recognised themselves in Jaques's 'whining' schoolboy,

> with his satchel
> And shining morning face, creeping like snail
> Unwillingly to school.

In *2 Henry VI*, Jack Cade condemns Lord Say to summary death for having 'most traitorously corrupted the youth of the realm in erecting a grammar school'. In *The Taming of the Shrew* Gremio leaves Petruchio's wedding 'As willingly as e'er I came from school.' Sighs Romeo beneath Juliet's balcony:

> Love goes toward love as school-boys from their books
> But love from love, toward school with heavy looks.

Whether from school untimely ripped, or mercifully released, the teenage Shakespeare seems to have been a lad mature beyond his years, taking due pride in the faith shown in him by his sorely pressed father. 'Upon his leaving school,' according to Rowe, 'he seems to have given entirely into that way of living which his father proposed for him.'

As an extra pair of hands in his father's shop, both out back and up front, his spare time spiced with some illicit butchery, he would soon have felt the need to spread his wings yet wider. The family's cashflow problems, though stabilized by selling off land and other assets, showed no signs of improvement. As anxious to broaden his own experience as to help his father, might Will have clerked for the Stratford lawyer handling John Shakespeare's ceaseless litigation? Might he have smuggled home shanks of meat for his mother from the animals whose hides furnished his father's wares? Might he even have tried to help his family through these straitened times, seeing it as his duty as the eldest son, with a little deer-poaching?

All these theories and more, many more, have been canvassed by four centuries of admirers, both amateur and professional, seeking to fill the troublesome gap between the end of Shakespeare's schooldays and his arrival in London. All we know for sure about that decade is that he married and fathered three children. The rest was, and will always remain, fertile territory for the literary gumshoe.

Shakespeare's most influential early biographer, Edmund Malone, suggested in 1790 that he had been employed 'while yet he remained at Stratford, in the office of some county attorney, who was at the same time a petty conveyancer, and perhaps also the Seneschal of some manor-court'. Malone was himself a barrister-turned-scholar. Legal clerking may seem unlikely at so young an age, and is dependent on no evidence beyond the remarkably wide range of legal terms expertly deployed throughout his work; with so much litigation dogging his father's life, and later his own, Shakespeare must have developed an intimate acquaintance with a veritable raft of lawyers, and absorbed the technical terms of their trade with the due relish of a born writer. He may, after his arrival in London, have spent some time in a lawyer's office, learning at least the art of the scrivener, or lawyer's copy-clerk.

As young as thirteen, according to one daydreamer, Shakespeare ran away to sea aboard Drake's *Golden Hind*, circumnavigating the globe prior to active service eleven years later against the Spanish Armada. Others have despatched him to Germany and Italy, especially the latter, as conjured in such plays as *Romeo and Juliet*, *The Merchant of Venice* and *The Taming of the Shrew*: 'The whole charm of Italy and its sky unconsciously guided his pen.' Even the usually sober Schoenbaum seems to believe (or want to believe) that the Italian scholar John Florio, secretary to his patron the Earl of Southampton, took Shakespeare off on a guided tour of Italy during the enforced closure of the theatres because of the bubonic plague. If he 'explored the inland waterways of Northern Italy, finding his way from Ferrara on the River Po to the marshy territories of the Venetian Republic', that would account for 'his knowledge of Italian customs, ceremonials and characteristics, and of the topography of the northern towns', as well as his 'smattering of the language', enabling him to conjure up 'the atmosphere and fragrance of Italy – of Venice and Verona, of fair Padua . . . in a series of plays rich in local colour'.

There is no reason, as has been observed, to demand 'geographical accuracy' of a playwright who elsewhere gives Bohemia a sea coast (in *The Winter's Tale*), just as he makes ports of Milan (*The Tempest*) and Verona (*The Two Gentlemen of Verona*), and gives Padua a ferry to Venice (*The Merchant of Venice*) – where, indeed, he sets two plays without once making any mention of water in the streets.

In our own century Sir Duff Cooper, the British soldier and diplomat, noted that 'the author who . . . makes a character depend on the tide in order to sail by sea from Verona to Milan was not a great traveller'. Undeterred, Cooper himself boldly despatched 'Sergeant Shakespeare' to the Low Countries under the banner of the Earl of Leicester, whose principal seat was close to Stratford at Kenilworth, and in whose acting troupe Shakespeare might eventually have fetched up in the capital.

Like so many others, before and after him, Cooper was driven to his conclusions by exasperated amazement at the poet's effortless displays of detailed technical knowledge. Himself a British officer serving near the front line in France in the First World War, Cooper settled down in the trenches to read *Love's Labour's Lost*, and found himself surprised (not, in the circumstances, altogether pleasantly) by its constant military references. Only a few days before, he had heard a musketry instructor 'expounding to his squad, at what seemed to me inordinate length, the very obvious undesirability of firing with the sun in their eyes'. With what wild surmise, therefore, did he now read Berowne's advice to his fellow lords, sworn to misogyny, before meeting the princess and her ladies:

> Advance your standards, and upon them, lords;
> Pell-mell, down with them! but be first advised,
> In conflict, that you get the sun of them.

One might as well smell a battle-hardened poet in Jaques's reference to ambitious young men 'seeking the bubble reputation / Even in the cannon's mouth'. Cooper duly does, adding that another of the earliest works, *1 Henry VI*, positively 'reeks' of camp: 'A fight either takes place or is described in nearly every scene of it . . . The reader receives very strongly the impression that the writer of it has been in the army.' Although touchingly couched in the form of an extended letter to his wife, who had begged leave to doubt his engaging theory, Cooper's monograph rests on a cheveril-thin thesis: 'If we can discover military matters running through the works of Shakespeare, if it is more frequent in the earlier than the later ones, and if there is nothing in the known facts of his life that renders it improbable, may we not conclude that he served in the army?'

No, not at all. Far more convincing (not to say endearing) is the time-honoured thesis that the young Shakespeare fell foul of the local squire, Sir Thomas Lucy, for stealing his deer. Young Will the deer-poacher is part of the Shakespeare story that his biographers want to believe almost as much as their readers; and there is plenty of encouraging evidence.

The tale took root as early as 1709, again with Nicholas Rowe, who has the newly married poet falling foul of Lucy for poaching in his park at Charlecote:

> He had, by a misfortune common enough to young fellows, fallen into ill company; and amongst them, some that made frequent practice of deer-stealing, engaged him with them more than once in robbing a park that belonged to Sir Thomas Lucy of Charlecote, near Stratford. For this he was prosecuted by that gentleman, as he thought, somewhat too severely; and in order to revenge that ill usage, he made a ballad upon him. And though this, probably the first essay of his poetry, be lost, yet it is said to have been so very bitter, that it redoubled the prosecution against him to that degree, that he was obliged to leave his business and family in Warwickshire, for some time, and shelter himself in London.

The deer-stealing Shakespeare swiftly established a firm hold on literary imaginations, not least because the playwright devotes a hundred lines to the subject at the beginning of *The Merry Wives of Windsor*, in which Justice Shallow has been seen as a caricature of Sir Thomas Lucy. Shallow's cousin Slender even specifies a dozen white 'luces' (or 'louses' to the Welsh parson Sir Hugh Evans) in Shallow's coat of arms. Lucy was indeed the local magistrate – quite prepared to sit in judgement on a poacher caught on his own estates – and his family's coat of arms did indeed bear three punning luces, or pike, which when quartered (as on one of their Warwickshire tombs) would add up to the twelve mentioned by Slender.

Richard Davies, the seventeenth-century clergyman of Corpus Christi College, Oxford, embellished local lore with the intelligence that Shakespeare was 'much given to all unluckiness in stealing venison and rabbits, particularly from Sir—Lucy, who had him oft whipped and sometimes imprisoned and at last made him fly his native country'. By the end of the eighteenth century, another biographer had even come up with the text of the satirical 'ballad' to which Rowe refers:

> Sir Thomas was too covetous,
>   To covet so much deer,
> When horns enough upon his head
>   Most plainly did appear.
>
> Had not his worship one deer left?
>   What then? He had a wife
> Took pains enough to find him horns
>   Should last him during life.

Was this one of the high-spirited young Shakespeare's earliest verses, roguishly pinned to the gates of Charlecote to revenge himself for punishments at Lucy's hands? According to a manuscript, *History of the Stage*, written between 1727 and 1730 (but said in its own time to be 'full of forgeries and falsehoods of various kinds'), a Cambridge Greek scholar named Joshua Barnes claimed to have heard these stanzas sung by an old woman in a Stratford inn some forty years earlier. 'Such was his respect for Mr Shakespeare's genius' that Barnes gave her a new gown for these two stanzas, 'and, could she have said it all, he would (as he often said in company, when any discourse has casually arose about him) have given her ten guineas.'

Other versions of the ballad appeared during the eighteenth century, along with reports from the likes of one Thomas Jones of a village near Stratford named Tarbick, who died in his nineties in 1703, that 'several old people at Stratford' told 'the story of

Shakespeare's robbing Sir Thomas Lucy's park', complete with the first stanza of a different version of the ballad 'stuck [by Shakespeare] upon [Lucy's] park gate, which exasperated the knight to apply to a lawyer at Warwick to proceed against him':

> A parliament member, a justice of peace,
> At home a poor scarecrow, at London an ass,
> If lousy is Lucy, as some folk miscall it,
> Then Lucy is lousy whatever befall it:
> > He thinks himself great,
> > Yet an ass in his state,
> We allow by his ears but with asses to mate.
> > If Lucy is lousy, as some folk miscall it,
> Sing lousy Lucy, whatever befall it.

By 1763, the deer-poaching story had attained the respectability of a mention in the entry on Shakespeare in the *Biographica Britannica*, which spoke of continuing hostilities between the former bailiff's son and the indignant squire to the point where Lucy's anger drove Shakespeare 'to the extreme end of ruin, where he was forced to a very low degree of drudgery for a support. How long the knight continued inexorable is not known; but it is certain that Shakespeare owed his release at last to the Queen's kindness.'

Four miles upstream from Stratford on the banks of the Avon, and thus a mere two miles from the Snitterfield farm of Shakespeare's uncle, the Lucy estate at Charlecote boasted the first Elizabethan mansion in Warwickshire, completed in 1558, six years before Shakespeare's birth. In his lifetime, there was no park as such at Charlecote; it was not until 1618, two years after the poet's death, that the Lucy family applied for a royal licence to create one. In the mid-1580s, when young Will and his pals might well have been up to nocturnal larks, probably fortified by too much ale, Lucy's lands would have consisted merely of a 'free-warren' teeming with rabbits, hares and foxes, wood-pigeon, pheasants and other beasts and fowls ripe for poaching. So why not deer as well, fallow or otherwise?

Late-eighteenth-century Bardolaters buttressed the legend by transferring its location across the river, and two miles north, to

Fulbrook, midway between Stratford and Warwick – one of the sites visited in 1795 by Samuel Ireland for his *Picturesque Views on the Upper, or Warwickshire Avon*:

> Within this park is now standing a spot called Daisy Hill, a farm house, which was anciently their keeper's lodge. To this lodge it is reported our Shakespeare was conveyed, and there confined at the time of the charge, which is supposed to have been brought against him. This supposition, however slight soever the foundation of it may be, I yet thought sufficient to give an interest to the spot in which it is presumed to have passed.

When Sir Walter Scott stayed with the Lucys in April 1828, he noted in his journal that his hosts themselves disowned the Charlecote legend, shifting the young Shakespeare's deer-poaching to Fulbrook: 'The tradition went that they hid the buck in a barn, part of which was standing a few years ago but now totally decayed.' Custody of the sometime royal park at Fulbrook had indeed been granted to the Lucys during the reign of Henry VIII, but by 1557 it had been 'disparked' and allowed to fall into disrepair – a wilderness of weeds where local sportsmen would justifiably (and legally) have regarded the occasional surviving deer as 'fair game'.

Or, to put it another way, 'Lucy thought papists fair game; and no doubt that was how they, from their side of the fence, saw the Lucy venison.' Investigation of Sir Thomas Lucy suggests that he was a more menacing figure than the 'enlightened and benevolent' squire of twentieth-century scholarship, 'feared and respected' throughout Warwickshire for his remorseless pursuit of Catholic recusants, if amiable enough (when it suited him) to have played peacemaker in a legal dispute between one of his servants and Shakespeare's friend Hamnet Sadler.

Tutored by the Puritan John Foxe, whose *Book of Martyrs* (1563) was studied by Shakespeare, Lucy is known to have been an especially vigorous persecutor of Warwickshire Catholics – not least those Ardens, close relatives of Shakespeare's mother, condemned and executed in 1583. Appointed to 'put down abuses in religion', Lucy capitalised on his election as Member of Parliament for

Warwickshire the following year to campaign for the execution of a fellow MP named Parry, who had questioned the severity of the anti-Catholic legislation. There were no half-measures for Lucy as he called on Parliament to devise custom-built punishments for so dastardly a traitor:

> Forasmuch as that villainous traitor Parry was a member of this house in the time of some of his most monstrous, horrible and traitorous conspiracies that Her Majesty vouchsafe to give licence to this house to proceed to the devising and making of some law for his execution and his conviction as may be thought fittest for his so extraordinary and most horrible kind of treason.

In like vein, in perhaps the first play Shakespeare wrote, no half-measures were good enough for the ghastly Gloucester, in the eyes of the interrogating Cardinal: 'Did he not, contrary to the form of law, / Devise strange deaths for small offences done?' Soon York takes up the same theme: 'You did devise / Strange torments for offenders, never heard of . . .' (2 Henry VI).

In vain was his innocence protested by Parry, whose conviction Lucy had so boldly pre-empted; his parliamentary privileges were promptly suspended, and he was eventually put to death in Westminster in March 1585. By 1592, some five years after Shakespeare had left Stratford for London, Lucy instigated two indictments against John Shakespeare for failing to attend the prescribed Protestant church services.

So Sir Thomas haunted the lives of both Shakespeares, father and son. There is no evidence that Lucy's wife – handsomely praised by her husband as 'most Godly' in the inscription on their tomb in St Leonard's, Charlecote – rendered him the cuckold of the ballad; and it is intriguing to note that Shakespeare treats his ancestor Sir William Lucy most respectfully in 1 Henry VI. But the deer-poaching Shakespeare is memorialised to this day in a clutch of nineteenth-century dwellings named Deer Barn Cottages, on the site of the land enclosed by the Lucys in the year before Shakespeare's death. Five years earlier, in 1610, when he was back in Stratford contemplating retirement, memories of the poet's youth would have been stirred by the Star Chamber suit brought by another Sir Thomas Lucy against poachers who killed deer in his park at Sutton, and 'afterwards made an ale-house boast about their depredation'.

After reading *Venus and Adonis*, the journalist and constitutional historian Walter Bagehot felt moved to assert: 'It is absurd to say we know *nothing* about the man who wrote that; we know that he had been after a hare.' In *Titus Andronicus*, another of Shakespeare's earliest plays, Demetrius asks his brother Chiron:

> What, hast thou not full often strook a doe
> And borne her cleanly by the keeper's nose?

There is also a note of personal nostalgia in Bassanio's childhood memories as he offers solace – ingenious to the point of archness – to his friend Antonio, the Merchant of Venice, as he frets about his argosy:

> In my schooldays, when I had lost one shaft,
> I shot his fellow of the self-same flight
> The self-same way, with more adviséd watch,
> To find the other forth; and by adventuring both,
> I oft found both. I urge this childhood proof . . .

As recently as 1958 the late Alice Fairfax-Lucy (mother of Charlecote's present occupant, Sir Edmund Cameron-Ramsay-Fairfax-Lucy RA) waxed lyrical about the thought of such high jinks on her ancestors' estate:

> The portraits of Shakespeare are few and of debatable authenticity. In the shadowy throng of the Great he cuts an uninspiring figure. But set him against the background of Charlecote warren or Fulbroke park some night near dawn, with dangerous moonlight whitening the turf, and there you have reality. Theft, capture, punishment, flight – these are all within the compass of ordinary experience.

It is on the date of this centuries-old story that Duff Cooper based his military thesis. In 1585, he argued, Shakespeare 'was in some trouble with the authorities [while] England was at war, and the press-gang was out'. As in so many similar cases, romantic longings proceed to overwhelm considerable scholarship: 'In time of private trouble a young man's thoughts naturally turn to the army; in time of foreign war a patriot's duty impels him in the same direction. Shakespeare was a young man in trouble and he was a patriot.' All too soon Cooper is grasping at straws: 'Among Leicester's troops was his nephew, the poet Sir Philip Sidney, who wrote to a friend in March 1586, six months before his death: "I wrote to you a letter by Will, my Lord of Leicester's jesting player" . . . The following year Leicester needed a messenger to go to London. Who better than the jesting player . . . [who] did not return?'

It is a charming way of solving the perennial problem of Shakespeare's all-but-complete disappearance from the public record between his schooldays and his unrecorded arrival in London. The problem is that 1585 marks one of the few exceptions, being the year in which his wife Anne gave birth to twins, whose baptism is recorded in the Stratford register on 2 February. So he could hardly have been on active service in the Low Countries nine months earlier. Even the most imaginative biographers have yet to suggest that Shakespeare was not the father of his own children.

The year 1585, when 21-year-old Shakespeare again vanishes from the public record until his name is first mentioned as a London-based playwright seven years later, has become generally accepted as the starting-date for the so-called 'lost' years – when biographers can (and do) let their imaginations run riot. One twentieth-century scholar prefers to regard the lost years as dating from his birth in 1564 – for, 'excepting the three dates 1582, 1583 and 1585 [his marriage and the baptisms of his three children], we have no certain knowledge of his activities or whereabouts during those 28 years'.

If Shakespeare stayed at school until the age of fifteen or sixteen, when boys 'normally went to university', the 'lost' years would in fact seem best defined as the period from 1579 to 1592. But he may well have left school, as we have seen, even younger. So how (and where) did Shakespeare spend his teens? Did he, as has been argued by a vociferous minority, begin his theatrical career much earlier than has been suspected? How else, it is often asked, could he have passed these years?

How indeed?

III

THE 'LOST' YEARS

1579–1587

Dated 3 August 1581, and proved soon after his death the following month, the will of Alexander Hoghton Esq. of Lea, Lancashire, bequeathed to his half-brother Thomas all his musical instruments and his stock of 'play clothes', or costumes, 'if he be minded to keep & do keep players'. If Thomas were not so minded, the instruments and costumes were to pass to Alexander's neighbour and friend Sir Thomas Hesketh, kinsman of his second wife Elizabeth (*née* Hesketh), along with two players about whom the dying man added an earnest petition:

> And I most heartily require the said Sir Thomas to be friendly unto Fulk Gyllome and William Shakeshafte now dwelling with me and either to take them unto his service or else to help them to some good master, as my trust is he will.

William Shakeshafte is mentioned again later in the will, as one of eleven servants left an annuity of £2, on top of the year's wages bequeathed all Hoghton's staff. Four hundred years on, it now seems clear that this 'Shakeshafte' was in fact fifteen-year-old William Shakespeare – youthful tutor-turned-actor in a noble, wealthy and illicitly Catholic household in Lancashire.

'In his younger years,' testified John Aubrey, Shakespeare was 'a schoolmaster in the country'. Although this confident assertion appears on the same page as the dubious 'His father was a butcher', it is (unusually) buttressed by a marginal note: 'from Mr Beeston'. Aubrey's information came first-hand, in other words, from William Beeston, son of the celebrated actor Christopher Beeston, one of Shakespeare's colleagues in the Lord Chamberlain's company. Young Beeston would have heard his father reminisce about Shakespeare, with whom he would have had long hours to kill backstage, on tour and in sundry inns.

Given the status of sixteenth-century surnames – infinitely flexible, as we have seen – there is scant cause for surprise in the change in name from Shakespeare to Shakeshafte. It can scarcely be called an alias, to cover a young Warwickshire Catholic's tentative tracks amid the network of informers then riddling boldly recusant Lancashire; but it perhaps had its uses as a variant. Shakespeare's grandfather Richard appears as Shakstaff and Shakeschafte as well as Shakspere in the Snitterfield records; in Lancashire, at the time, the familiar local variant was Shakeshafte – a natural enough name for an out-of-county man to assimilate, or an equally natural lapse on the part of the scrivener drawing up Hoghton's will.

Another such variant was 'Cotham' for Cottom. A Lancashire neighbour, friend and fellow recusant named John Cotham was another beneficiary named in Alexander Hoghton's will; and that same John Cottom (in his own preferred spelling) just happened to be the teacher who took over as Master of Stratford grammar school in 1579. A Lancastrian, late of London, and a graduate of Brasenose College, Oxford, Cottom was Thomas Jenkins's personal choice as his successor. Apart from the London-born Welshman Jenkins, every one of the five Masters of the Stratford school from 1569 to 1624 happened to be a Lancashire man.

It would thus seem no coincidence that Jenkins's predecessor, that other Lancastrian Simon Hunt, took himself off to Douai University before turning Jesuit and devoting himself to Rome. Among Douai's wealthy benefactors was Thomas Hoghton, Alexander's older brother, whose estate constituted the contents of the will in which Shakeshafte was remembered. The son of Sir Richard de Hoghton (1498–1559), Thomas was a recusant so unrepentant, and indeed so prominent, as to be forced to opt for permanent exile from England in 1569, dying eleven years later in Liège, where his elaborate tomb in the Church of Gervais can be visited to this day.

The sixteenth-century Hoghtons have been described as 'one of the premier families of Lancashire', descended directly from one of William the Conqueror's companions, and through the female line from the legendary Lady Godiva of Coventry, wife of Leofric, Earl of Mercia. While still in Lancashire, in charge of the family fortunes, Thomas had rebuilt the family seat, Hoghton Tower, on a ridge six miles south-east of Preston – where still it stands, housing his descendants (who co-host a Shakespeare Study Centre with the nearby Lancaster University).

Although inevitably neglected after Thomas's departure in 1569, the Hoghton estate remained substantial at the time of his death in 1580. As a priest his son was debarred from succeeding, so it passed to his younger brother Alexander, who died childless the following year. Now the estate passed to his half-brother, another Thomas, who faithfully carried out Alexander's instructions. The name of Fulke Gyllome, so closely linked with Shakeshafte's in the Hoghton will, appears twice in subsequent Hesketh records, as witness to legal documents in 1591 and 1608.

So Thomas Hoghton was not, it seems, minded to keep players, with or without their instruments and costumes – and they did indeed pass, as Alexander had wished, to his noble and even wealthier friend Hesketh. Even the musical instruments are mentioned in subsequent Hesketh inventories. Both they and the two Hoghton players, Gyllome and Shakeshafte, would have been pressed into service when plays were laid on for significant visitors.

Lancashire was a hotbed of recusancy at a time when Elizabeth's government was intensifying its periodic purges on Roman Catholics, many of whom were at the least fined or imprisoned, at worst tortured and publicly executed. New legislation 'to retain the Queen's Majesty's subjects in due obedience' received the royal assent on 18 March 1581, only months before Alexander made his will. Hoghton Tower was one of many safe havens for papists in Lancashire under constant surveillance by both covert informers and authorised agents of the Privy Council, in whose name frequent raids were mounted. Many leading Lancashire families, including the Hoghtons, made a public show of 'conforming' while secretly harbouring priests in their households.

One such was Thomas Cottom, younger brother of the Stratford schoolmaster John, a friend and associate of the Jesuit Edmund Campion, who visited the Hoghton household 'between Easter and Whitsuntide' 1581. Campion was arrested that July, and arraigned on 12 November, two days before Cottom (who had been arrested on his return to England from Italy in June 1580 and held in the Marshalsea). Among the evidence against Campion was that he had been staying with leading Catholic families in Lancashire, whose houses had been searched by order of the Privy Council – 'especially', according to its records, 'the house of Richard Hoghton', in whose safekeeping he had left his books. After torture on the rack, Cottom and Campion were publicly executed as traitors – or Roman Catholic martyrs – on 1 December 1581 and 13 May 1582 respectively.

Campion was the source of the copy of the testament lurking in the Shakespeare home in Stratford, if not yet hidden in the roof. Can it be mere coincidence that John Cottom resigned his Stratford post in 1581, while his brother languished in the Marshalsea, and returned to Lancashire, to his father's estate at Tarnacre, hard by the Hoghton property of Alston Hall, ten miles from the family seat at Lea? Between his return and his death in 1616, Cottom inherited his father's property and openly acknowledged his Catholicism. Less belligerent than his martyred brother, he was regarded by the authorities as less dangerous; faced with recusant fines rather than arrest and torture, he avoided his brother's grim fate by paying up.

At the time of John Cottom's arrival in Stratford in 1579, Shakespeare was fifteen years old and his father's affairs in ever more rapid decline. This was an *annus horribilis* for the Shakespeare family, who that April buried another child, William's eight-year-old sister Anne. The previous month, John Shakespeare's levy of 3s 4d for arms had gone 'unpaid and unaccounted for'; by Easter he was raising £40 by the drastic move of mortgaging what was left of his wife's dowry, Asbies, comprising a house and sixty acres in Wilmcote, to his brother-in-law Edmund Lambert, husband of Mary's sister Joan.

*Conveyance of property in Aston Cantlow by John and Mary
Shakespeare to Edmund Lambert, 1579.*

The wealthy Lambert lived fifteen miles south of Stratford in the
small village of Barton-on-the-Heath, apparently as familiar to the
young William as the inn at Wilmcote, or Wincot, half-way between
the two. In the Induction to *The Taming of the Shrew*, Christopher
Sly proclaims himself 'old Sly's son of Burton Heath' and urges his
interlocutors:

> Ask Marian Hacket, the fat ale-wife of Wincot, if she know me
> not. If she say I am not fourteen pence on the score for sheer
> ale, score me up for the lying'st knave in Christendom.

The previous autumn, Lambert had also been named in the will of
Roger Sadler, a baker of Stratford High Street, as surety for '£5, the
debt of Mr John Shakspere'. Clearly the glover was growing deep in
debt to his brother-in-law. When the £40 borrowed in 1579 fell due
the following year, John was unable to repay it; so Lambert held on
to the estate, of which he was still in possession when he died seven
years later. There followed protracted litigation in the High Court as
John Shakespeare tried to recover the property from Lambert's son
and heir, his nephew John, who counter-sued on the grounds that
further debts were due. The Asbies estate would never be recovered
by the Shakespeares.

Worse was to follow in October 1579, when John was forced
to sell off more of his children's potential inheritance; John and
Mary Shakespeare's joint interest in two 'messuages' at Snitterfield
– Mary's one-ninth share of her father's property, comprising two
houses and 100 acres of land – was sold to another relative, Robert
Webbe, for a mere £4. 'Yeoman' John Shakespeare and his wife
both made their usual marks by way of signing the deed of sale.

Throughout 1579 Stratford's former bailiff was still absent from all its recorded council meetings. With another child on the way – a third son, Edmund, named after their obliging relative Lambert, would be born the following April – William had become simply another mouth to feed. It was time for him to set about earning his own living. That same year, the record shows, his schoolfriend Richard Field, son of the Stratford tanner Henry Field, began a seven-year apprenticeship to a London printer. 'Being taken from school by their parents,' according to Sir Thomas Elyot's 1531 manual on the education of the governing classes, the 'aptest and most proper scholars . . . either be brought to court, and made lackeys or pages, or else are bounden prentices.'

Old for his age, watching his friends and contemporaries leave home to get on with their adult lives, fifteen-year-old William (like Petruchio in *The Taming of the Shrew*) was feeling on his collar

> Such wind as scatters young men through the world
> To seek their fortunes farther than at home,
> Where small experience grows.

Given a secret Catholic bond between the Shakespeare family and the newly arrived schoolmaster John Cottom, what could be more natural than accepting his help in sending William to an enviable job – perhaps even to train as a seminarist – a hundred miles away in Lancashire? There was reason enough in the unenviable doom then being pronounced by the Queen's Lord Chief Justice on scores of Roman Catholic apostates (soon to include Cottom's own brother) every month:

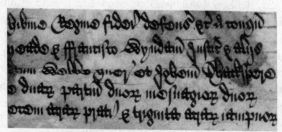

Conveyance of property in Snitterfield by John and Mary Shakespeare to Robert Webbe.

You shall be taken to the place from whence you came,
there to remain until ye shall be drawn through the open
city of London upon hurdles to the place of execution, and
there hanged and let down alive, and your privy parts cut off,
and your entrails taken out and burnt in your sight; then your
heads to be cut off and your bodies divided into four parts,
to be disposed of at Her Majesty's pleasure.

Alexander Hoghton was landlord to John Cottom's father at
Tarnacre. His own secret links with the other Cottom son, coupled
with the benevolence evident in his will, would have seen Hoghton
readily agree to take in one of Stratford grammar school's most
brilliant recent pupils – a kindred spirit in more ways than one
– as tutor to his own children, or those of his staff, while pursuing
his religious instruction.

It is 'highly unlikely', according to E. A. J. Honigmann, a leading
twentieth-century champion of Shakespeare's Lancashire connection,
that a family like the Hoghtons would have employed, at a time so
dangerous for recusants, 'a servant who was not a practising Catholic'.
There was nothing unusual about fifteen-year-old tutors, or 'unlicensed'
(or indeed Catholic) schoolmasters, in such households as Hoghton
Tower – nor indeed about tutors doubling as actors and musicians, as
the wealthy Baptista of Padua testifies, also in *The Taming of the Shrew*:

And for I know she taketh most delight
In music, instruments and poetry
Schoolmasters will I keep within my house,
Fit to instruct her youth.

It is further intriguing that the playwright has the young suitor who
applies for the job, 'well seen in music, to instruct Bianca', do so
'disguised'.

Shakespeare would have been a Hoghton hireling for at least a
year, more like two, by the time he moved on to Hesketh's employ
ten miles south-east at Rufford Old Hall in the latter part of 1581.
The Rufford connection will reappear in his life nearly twenty
years later, when the wealthy London goldsmith Thomas Savage,

one of two London merchants who help with the legal details of his purchase of an interest in the Globe theatre, turns out to be a native of Rufford. The Tudor tapestry in Rufford Old Hall, depicting the Fall of Troy, also bears tantalising comparison with the description of the same scene in 'a skilful piece of painting' in *The Rape of Lucrece*.

Seventeen and eager to please, Shakespeare had clearly impressed his first employer more as a player than a potential priest. Now he would have a real chance to shine onstage, as the grander Hesketh household at Rufford regularly received visiting troupes of actors – including such leading groups as the Earl of Derby's Players, later those of his son and heir Ferdinando, Lord Strange, and eventually a source of recruitment for the Lord Chamberlain's Men.

That same year, 1581, saw Sir Thomas Hesketh's arrest as 'a disaffected papist'. Contemporary documents suggest that he was soon released, on an undertaking to 'reform' his household by way of suppressing Catholic worship. Although briefly arrested again three years later, Hesketh seems otherwise to have managed to satisfy the authorities that Rufford Old Hall was no longer a hotbed of papist sedition – even though, intriguingly, repairs to the Great Hall uncovered a secret chamber or 'priest's hole' in the west gable as recently as 1939.

Forty-six feet long, twenty-two feet wide and eighteen feet high, that same Great Hall would have been the site of performances by Sir Thomas Hesketh's *ad hoc* group of resident players, and those of visiting troupes such as those of his friend Henry Stanley, Earl of Derby. The close connection between the noble houses of Hesketh and Stanley/Derby is amply documented, with regular visits between them recorded throughout this period in the *Derby Household Book*.

Robert Hesketh, Sir Thomas's son and heir, married Mary Stanley, daughter of Sir George Stanley, a cousin of the Earl of Derby. Outwardly more conformist than his recusant brother Thomas, Robert bred three militantly papist sons – at least one of whom, Richard Hesketh, later fought alongside the Stanleys in Flanders, taking the Spanish part against the English and their allies. On Derby's death in 1593, Hesketh was persuaded by Jesuits to return to England on a dangerous secret mission: to offer Spanish support to the earl's son and heir, Ferdinando, Lord Strange, were he to exploit his mother's descent from Henry VII to claim Elizabeth's crown. Far from averse to the offer, the new earl lost his nerve when government spies uncovered the conspiracy. To save his own skin he betrayed Hesketh, who was tried and executed at St Albans that November.

By then Shakespeare would be an established actor and playwright in London, who had recently made his name with an unprecedented historical tetralogy, celebrating the Stanleys' role in the reigns of Henry VI and Richard III. Back in the early 1580s, a precocious seventeen-year-old adrift in recusant Lancashire, he was already surrounded by themes which would recur throughout his work. His first patrons, Alexander Hoghton and Sir Thomas Hesketh, had both fathered numerous bastards, as indeed had Lord Derby; and all made unashamed and handsome provision for them in their wills, to wit: 'Thomas Hesketh, my bastard son, whom I acknowledge to be my real son, whatsoever the laws of this land do adjudge or deem to the contrary . . .' The plight of religious dissidents, Catholic or otherwise, would constantly recur in Shakespeare's writing, long after his own belief had faded. In temporal terms, meanwhile, the Stanleys were deemed worthy of his undying gratitude.

It seems unlikely that William stayed long in the employ, however enlightened, of Sir Thomas Hesketh – but long enough to gain a glimpse of life under Lord Derby, whose professional troupe of actors toured the country while Hesketh merely laid on occasional entertainments provided by members of his staff, who doubled as tutors and musicians more than players. Nor was the Hesketh household as openly Catholic as Hoghton's. Shakespeare, or Shakeshafte, would soon have felt under-employed, perhaps even out of place, at Rufford Old Hall. Might his new patron Hesketh, by all accounts a benevolent employer, have heeded the words of his late friend Alexander Hoghton, and seen it as his duty to 'help' this talented young man to some other 'good master'? If so, who more obvious – and close to hand – than his friend Lord Derby, a close friend of the Queen with his own troupe of players?

At least one of the great pioneers among twentieth-century Shakespeare biographers has thought so, however tentatively. 'If William Shakeshafte passed from the service of Alexander Hoghton into that of either Thomas Hoghton or Sir Thomas Hesketh, he might very easily have gone on into that of Lord Strange, and so later into the London theatrical world.' Since this was written during the Second World War, much more evidence has emerged to link Shakespeare to the Derbys via the Lancashire households of Hoghton and Hesketh.

But Shakespeare could not have gone straight to London with the Earl of Derby's Players in 1581, as has been suggested. However sketchy our knowledge of Shakespeare's late teens, we know one thing for sure. By the following summer, certainly by August 1582, he was back home in Stratford-upon-Avon.

The fortunes of Shakespeare's father had not improved during William's absence. In 1580 John had been fined £20 for his failure to appear in the Court of the Queen's Bench with a guarantee to keep the Queen's peace, and a further £20 by the same court as a result of his surety on the same grounds on behalf of a Nottingham hatmaker, John Audeley. No record survives to show that he actually paid these fines; but between them, they would have wiped out the £40 mortgage borrowed from his brother-in-law, Lambert. John Shakespeare seemed to have been paying the price for his somewhat indiscriminate choice of friends in more prosperous times, when he appears to have bailed out all and sundry; now he forfeited his bond of £10 of a debt of £22 incurred by his wayward brother Henry, and the bail he had stood for Michael Price, the skulduggerous Stratford tinker – a likely prototype for young Christopher Sly in *The Taming of the Shrew*, 'by birth a pedlar, by education a cardmaker, by transmutation a bearherd and now by present profession a tinker'. Only by begging his friend Alderman Hill to stand bail on his own behalf did John avoid the ultimate indignity of incarceration.

The records for 1581 show that John Shakespeare still failed to attend a single council meeting, though the year appears mercifully free of further financial transactions. We can only assume that John and Mary Shakespeare were pleased to see their eldest son returned from his lengthy sojourn up north, if less than ecstatic about his excited talk of a life in the theatre. John had troubles of his own that summer, falling out seriously enough with four old friends – William Russell, Thomas Logginge, Robert Young and the butcher

Ralph Cawdrey, then bailiff – to petition for sureties of the peace against them 'for fear of death and mutilation of his limbs'. The last thing John needed was the trouble young William was about to cause.

Sometime that August, after wandering the mile or so west down the rural footpath to the tiny village of Shottery, the worldly eighteen-year-old committed an indiscretion which would profoundly affect the rest of his life. Was it a careless roll in the hay of a summer evening, as celebrated in *As You Like It*?

> Between the acres of the rye,
> With a hey, and a ho, and a hey nonino,
> These pretty country folks would lie,
> In spring time . . .

Spring time, 'the only pretty ring time' – as, of course, in wedding rings. It is hard to believe that this ambitious young dreamer, already aware there was a world elsewhere, way beyond rural

John Shakespeare fined for non-appearance and for failing to bring into court John Audeley of Nottingham, for whom he had stood surety.

Warwickshire, was so enamoured of a homely wench eight years his senior – the same age as Juliet's mother, who is already impatient for grandchildren – as to want to marry her. Or did the local farmer's 26-year-old daughter, only a month after her father's death, set out to catch herself a much younger husband by seducing him? Either way, the autumn of 1582 saw Anne Hathaway telling her late father's friends that she was pregnant by young Will Shakespeare, the teenage son of the Stratford alderman.

There is no extant record of Anne Hathaway's birth or christening, as she was born before baptismal registers commenced in 1558. The brass plate on her tomb in Stratford's Holy Trinity church testifies that she 'departed this life' on 6 August 1623, 'being of the age of 67 years'. So she would have been born in 1556, eight years before her future husband. By her mid-twenties, life at Hewland's farm cannot have been easy for Anne – a displaced person since her father's death, living with a stepmother and three stepbrothers, probably as eager to marry her off as was she herself to escape them.

Was Shakespeare trapped into a reluctant marriage by a desperate woman eight years his senior, scared of being left on the shelf in a home no longer her own? Or was this a genuine love-match? 'Let still the woman take an elder than herself' is the heartfelt advice of Orsino, Duke of Illyria, to Cesario (alias Viola) in *Twelfth Night*:

> ... so wears she to him;
> So sways she level in her husband's heart ...
> Our fancies are more giddy and unfirm,
> More longing, wavering, sooner lost and worn
> Than women's are ...
> Then let thy love be younger than thyself,
> Or thy affection cannot hold the bent.

'For women,' he concludes, 'are as roses, whose fair flow'r / Being once display'd, doth fall that very hour.'

This last couplet hangs in the air with particular resonance as one attempts to conjure young William's feelings about the solemn consequences of his brief moment of summer pleasure. 'The course of true love never did run smooth,' as Lysander tells Hermia in *A Midsummer Night's Dream*, citing couples 'misgraffed in respect of years', to which the poet has her reply: 'O spite! too old to be engag'd to young.' Whatever Will's feelings, two of the late Farmer Hathaway's close friends, Fulke Sandells and John Richardson, came knocking on the door of the Shakespeare home in Henley Street that autumn, demanding that the son of the house do the right thing by their deceased friend's homely daughter.

Or so we may surmise. Sandells was named in Richard Hathaway's will as one of his two trustees, or executors; Richardson made his mark as a witness. The distinct impression given by the bare documentation of subsequent events is that these two worthies strong-armed young William over to the consistory court at Worcester, some twenty miles from Stratford, before he could flee his obligations. He was, after all, a minor, and his bride-to-be was pregnant. These two irregular circumstances required the official scrutiny of the diocesan court, rather than the mere reading of the banns on three consecutive Sundays which was then the only requirement for most marriage ceremonies to be legally binding. Because of his youth and her condition, Shakespeare's wedding to Anne Hathaway required a special licence; and Sandells and Richardson travelled to the Worcester diocese of John Whitgift (the future Archbishop of Canterbury) to obtain it. Whether Shakespeare actually accompanied them is uncertain; as a minor he could anyway have played no role in the legal formalities.

It has even been suggested that Sandells and Richardson obtained the licence on their own initiative, with or without the knowledge of Shakespeare's father, to ensure that the father of Anne Hathaway's future child duly became her husband. If so, they were willing to pledge the huge sum of £40 between them to guarantee the marriage, which was duly authorised in a document dated 28 November 1582, authorising the union (after only one reading of the banns) between 'William Shagspere' and 'Anne Hathwey of Stratford in the diocese of Worcester, maiden'. It was also, presumably, the loyal Sandells and Richardson who testified to Anne's dubious standing as a 'maiden'; the clergy of the day were broad-minded enough to be prepared to substitute 'single-woman' where, as in this case, appropriate.

The marriage licence of William Shakespeare and Anne Hathaway
(1582).

Anne Hathaway's name may now echo through literary history, not
least as attached to the cottage still visited today by 200,000 tourists a
year, but she was actually born with the name of Agnes. That much
is clear from her father's will, made the previous summer, in which
he details bequests for his four sons and three daughters, including ten
marks to be paid to his daughter Agnes on her wedding day. It seems
that the names Agnes and Anne, like Shaxpere and Shakespeare, were
virtually interchangeable.

Agnes/Anne Hathaway's role in Shakespeare's life is further complicated by another entry in the Worcester diocesan records, dated
the previous day, 27 November 1582, granting a licence for William
Shaxpere of Stratford to marry one 'Anne Whateley of Temple
Grafton'. This Anne Whateley appears in no other contemporary
document yet discovered, certainly none relating to our poet. Who
could she have been? Reluctant to accept the dull but probable answer
– that she is the Elizabethan equivalent of a typing error – Shakespeare
biographers have had a 400-year field day with Ms Whateley, none
more so than Anthony Burgess.

Not only in his stylish biographical novel, *Nothing Like the Sun*
(1964), but also in his marginally more sober narrative biography
Shakespeare (1970), Burgess posited the notion of a poignantly lost
love, the chaste young beauty Anne Whateley, forlornly left behind
when her dashing young beau is trapped into impregnating the ageing
hag of Shottery, who had otherwise been destined to rest for ever on
the shelf. In Burgess's imaginative scheme of things, his 'lovely boy',
eighteen-year-old Will, is exercised by 'love for the one and lust for
the other'. Blessed with 'auburn hair, melting eyes, ready tongue, tags

of Latin poetry', Will has already 'tasted' Anne's body in the spring, and run a mile once she mentions marital bliss, or 'the advantages of love in an indentured bed, away from cowpats and the prickling of stubble in a field'. He falls in love with the younger, more beauteous Anne, 'sweet as May and shy as a fawn'; but is back on the run when she too mentions marriage, without being 'wanton and forward' enough to give him a similar foretaste of her own physical charms. His libido 'pricking hard', Will heads back from Temple Grafton to Shottery, and 'a bout of lust in the August fields' with the guaranteed delights of Ms Hathaway. The consequences are predictably disastrous, as Sandells and Richardson are despatched to Stratford, ready to deploy their 'brawny

Shakespeare's Consort, *an early eighteenth-century impression by Sir Nathaniel Curzon.*

yeoman's fists in threat' by way of demonstrating that Anne of Shottery 'hath a way'.

This dire pun – Burgess's homage to James Joyce, who uses it in *Ulysses* – in fact has a very respectable pedigree. Its genesis lies in the closing couplet of Shakespeare's Sonnet 145, which appears to suggest that the young poet actually carried quite a torch – before marriage, anyway – for Ms Hathaway:

> Those lips that Love's own hand did make
> Breath'd forth the sound that said 'I hate'
> To me that languish'd for her sake;
> But when she saw my woeful state,
> Straight in her heart did mercy come,
> Chiding that tongue that, ever sweet,
> Was us'd in giving gentle doom;
> And taught it thus anew to greet;
> 'I hate' she alter'd with an end
> That follow'd it as gentle day
> Doth follow night, who like a fiend
> From heaven to hell is flown away:
> > 'I hate' from hate away she threw,
> > And sav'd my life, saying 'not you'.

The name Hathaway appears elsewhere as 'Hattaway'. Shakespeare's pun buttresses evidence that the middle 'h' of Hathaway would have been elided in the rural Warwickshire dialect of the day. The only octosyllabic Sonnet, so primitive in style and phrasing as to have been rejected as 'inauthentic', this might well qualify as Shakespeare's earliest surviving poem – discounting, that is, the doggerel attached by legend to Sir Thomas Lucy's gates. If he were already writing pastoral juvenilia, it is entirely plausible to date at least two other poems to this period, numbers 12 ('Crabbed age and youth cannot live together') and 18 ('When as thine eye hath chose the dame / And stalled the deer that thou shouldst strike') of *The Passionate Pilgrim,* as well as the lovesick shepherd's lament in number 17 ('My flocks feed not, my ewes breed not / My rams speed not . . .').

As to the mysterious Anne Whateley: for all Burgess's infectious exuberance, his lurid scenario is scarcely more credible than the desperate explanation of some Shakespeare biographers, the magisterial Sir Sidney Lee among them, that there was another William Shakespeare of Stratford who was granted a licence in Worcester to marry an Anne Whateley of Temple Grafton at much the same time as his namesake wed Anne Hathaway of Shottery.

The same Worcester clerk, it has been observed, was slapdash enough to write 'Baker' for 'Barbar', 'Darby' for 'Bradeley', and 'Edgcock' for 'Elcock'. 'Whateley' for 'Hathaway' is a transformation of quite a different order; but a likely explanation lies close at hand. On the day the Hathaway licence was issued, the Worcester court dealt with no fewer than forty cases, including that of the vicar of Crowle, one William Whateley, pursuing non-payment of tithes from Arnold Leight. This Whateley appears to have been a regular litigant, his name occurring frequently in the court records for 1582–83. For a clerk in a hurry to substitute his name for that of Wm Shaxpere's intended seems understandable. Exit, alas, the lost love of Anthony Burgess's (and his young Shaxpere's) dreams.

The mention of Temple Grafton, by contrast, adds intriguingly to the case for the continuing recusancy of young William. Its vicar, John Frith, is described in a Puritan survey of the ministry in Warwickshire as 'an old priest and unsound in religion; he can neither preach nor read well, his chiefest trade is to cure hawks that are hurt or diseased, for which purpose many do usually repair to him'. Just the man to keep the Shakespeare family happy by performing an 'unsound' wedding ceremony steeped in the old religion. In the absence of any record of the wedding – as was common, for obvious reasons, in the case of Catholic ceremonies – Temple Grafton (five miles west of Stratford) has come to rival the nearby village of Luddington (three miles west) as its venue.

William's apparent reluctance to marry a woman eight years his senior, the spectre of Anne Whateley, and a scouring of the canon for stern imprecations not to indulge in sex before marriage, have combined to lead Shakespeare mythology to fill the poet with a lifetime of regret about the early indiscretion which landed him with a wife he subsequently spent a great deal of time avoiding. Scholars who should know better hear Shakespeare nodding moral approval as Romeo and Juliet bring to their one night together – after their secret marriage – 'a pair of stainless maidenhoods'.

Hermia gives Lysander short shrift when he tries his Midsummer Night's luck: 'One turf shall serve as pillow for us both . . .'

> Nay, good Lysander; for my sake, my dear,
> Lie further off yet; do not lie so near . . .
> Such separation as may well be said
> Becomes a virtuous bachelor and a maid,
> So far be distant; and good night, sweet friend.

In *The Winter's Tale* Florizel, too, takes pride that his 'desires run not before mine honour, nor my lusts / Burn hotter than my faith'. But it is Prospero, not Shakespeare, who warns his prospective son-in-law, Ferdinand, of the dire consequences of precipitate action:

> If thou dost break her virgin-knot before
> All sanctimonious ceremonies may
> With full and holy rite be minist'red
> No sweet aspersion shall the heavens let fall
> To make this contract grow; but barren hate,
> Sour-ey'd disdain, and discord shall bestrew
> The union of your bed with weeds so loathly
> That you shall hate it both.

Shakespeare's early poem *Venus and Adonis* depicts the attempts of an ageing woman to ensnare a handsome young man of whom she is enamoured. But the youth evades her advances; not yet ready for love, he prefers to go hunting – chasing wild boar, with fatal consequences, as the young Shakespeare chased Sir Thomas Lucy's deer. The canon is full of whirlwind romances, pregnant brides and hastily arranged marriages. There are whirlwind courtships in each of such early works as *1 Henry VI*, *Titus Andronicus* and *The Taming of the Shrew*. For all their apparent biographical significance, however, we must remain ever vigilant against too readily reading the poet's own sentiments into those of his characters. These were issues ever-present in Shakespeare's life, as in his work; but we cannot necessarily conclude that the poet himself thought, with Parolles, that 'a young man married is a man that's marr'd'.

*   *   *

On 26 May 1583, Trinity Sunday, the Reverend Henry Heicroft christened the child of the six-months-married William and Anne Shakespeare with the uncommon and resoundingly Puritan name of Susanna. Was it a consciously ironical choice? Or were Shakespeare's religious beliefs already on the wane?

Now nineteen, but yet to find regular employment, he would have taken his bride to live with his parents at the capacious, double-fronted family home in Henley Street. They could not afford a home of their own; in cashflow terms Anne's dowry was small, only £6 13s 14d – 'to be paid unto her', according to the terms of her father's will, 'at the day of her marriage'. Her mother-in-law would no doubt have delighted in having her first grandchild under her own roof, and enjoyed sharing the considerable burden of childcare – William's brother Edmund was, after all, only two years older than his newborn niece; Gilbert, Joan and Richard were respectively sixteen, thirteen and eight. Would an aspirant young poet, however, have relished life in such a household as much as his wife and mother?

Within two years, Anne would bear him two more children, twins named Hamnet and Judith after their friends Judith and Hamnet Sadler, who lived next to the Corn Market, on the corner of High Street and Sheep Street; when the Sadlers produced their own son thirteen years later, they returned the compliment by christening him William.

With Anne housebound, what did life hold for the restless young Shakespeare? After the excitements of Lancashire, it must have been a desperate anti-climax to return to his father's side in the glover's shop. Already, as we have seen, he was showing an early flair for the *pièce d'occasion*, in the shape of an ingeniously turned sonnet. If he took the chance to broaden his reading, and to make the acquaintance of the troupes of players regularly passing through Stratford, he also got involved in the routine scrapes enjoyed by most young men in their late teens as they discover life's extra-curricular pleasures.

Another version of the deer-stealing Shakespeare recurs in one nineteenth-century suggestion that he stole Sir Thomas Lucy's buck 'to celebrate his wedding-day'. It is possible, as we shall see, that Shakespeare fled Stratford in the immediate wake of his marriage,

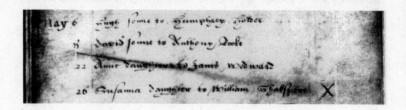

*Entries in the Stratford parish register recording the baptisms of
Shakespeare's children, Susanna (above) on 26 May 1583, and the twins
Hamnet and Judith on 2 February 1585.*

pleading the need to seek his fortune in London, with the reassurance
that he would return regularly as a travelling player; more likely, he spent
two more years leading a reluctantly humdrum life in Stratford, playing
the dutiful husband and father in town while getting up to no good (and
gathering more of the natural poet's raw material) in the Warwickshire
countryside which permeates his work, whatever its apparent setting.
Sex he had already discovered, at a price; now, as both logic and human
nature would suggest, he learned how to drown his sorrows.

Wilmcote, the nearby village whose 'fat ale-wife' earns that affectionate mention at the start of *The Taming of the Shrew*, was visited
two centuries later by the Radcliffe librarian at Oxford, Francis Wise,
in search of Shakespeare anecdote. His gleanings provided Oxford's
Professor of Poetry, Thomas Warton, with a note for his glossary in
Sir Thomas Hanmer's 1770 edition of the Works:

> Wilmcote is a village in Warwickshire, with which Shakespeare
> was well acquainted, near Stratford. The house kept by our
> genial hostess still remains, but is at present a mill.

Wise may also have been the anonymous author of a 'Letter from the
Place of Shakespeare's Nativity', published in the *British Magazine* in
1762. While staying in Stratford at the White Lion Inn, near the

top of Henley Street, he writes, his 'chearful' landlord first escorted him to the poet's birthplace. Then he took him to visit 'two young women, lineal descendants of our great dramatic poet', who kept 'a little ale-house, some distance from Stratford'.

> On the road thither, at a place called Bidford, he shewed me, in the hedge, a crab-tree, called Shakespeare's canopy, because under it our poet slept one night; for he, as well as Ben Jonson, loved a glass for the pleasure of society; and he having heard much of the men of that village as deep drinkers and merry fellows, one day went over to Bidford, to take a cup with them. He enquired of a shepherd for the Bidford drinkers; who replied, they were absent; but the Bidford sippers were at home; and I suppose, continued the sheep-keeper, they will be sufficient for you; and so indeed they were . . .

Shakespeare 'was forced to take his lodging under that tree for some hours'. The morning after was described by John Jordan, a tireless eighteenth-century collector of Bardic folklore, who took up the story eight years after Wise. The poet's companions, according to Jordan, awoke him and urged him to renew the drinking contest. Admitting defeat, Shakespeare chose instead to look around him at the view of the surrounding hamlets, and compensate his disappointed companions with a piece of extempore, hung-over doggerel. Now, he announced, he had drunk with

Piping Pebworth, Dancing Marston,
Haunted Hillborough, Hungry Grafton,
Dadgeing Exhall, Papist Wicksford,
Beggarly Broom, and Drunken Bidford.

'Shakespeare's Crab', as local legend subsequently dubbed the tree, was further immortalised in 1795 in Samuel Ireland's *Picturesque Views on the Upper, or Warwickshire Avon*. As sure as the tree bore the Bard's name, Ireland testified, all the local villages named in his morning-after verse still bore the epithets he had given them: 'The people of Pebworth are still famed for their skill on the pipe and tabor; Hillborough is now called Haunted Hillborough; and Grafton is notorious for the poverty of its soil.' Eventually, and inevitably, the tree fell prey to souvenir-hunters; what was left of it was dug up in 1824 and removed by the Reverend Henry Holyoakes of Bidford Grange. By then 'the branches had entirely vanished from the depradations of pious votaries; & the stock had mouldered to touchwood, the roots were rotten, & the timeworn remains totally useless'. To today's Bardolaters, the exact site of 'Shakespeare's Crab' remains a matter of fevered speculation.

The twins, Hamnet and Judith, were christened on 2 February 1585 by Heicroft's successor as vicar of Stratford, Richard Barton of Coventry – a 'learned, zealous and godly' minister, by one Puritan report. Approaching his twenty-first birthday, Shakespeare was still living at home with his parents. Already he had enjoyed a taste of the world beyond Stratford; already he would have listened in local taverns to travellers' tales about London and its cosmopolitan excitements. Already forming in his mind were the heartfelt sentiments of one of his *Two Gentlemen of Verona*, in the second line of what the Oxford editors boldly adjudge the first theatrical speech Shakespeare ever wrote. 'Home-keeping youth have ever homely wits,' says Valentine, on setting off 'to see the wonders of the world abroad.'

Aubrey insists that Shakespeare left for London as early as 1582, the year of his marriage, perhaps on the run from the law after some deer-stealing. He is still endorsed by modern scholars such as Eric Sams, who suggests 'close causal links among deer-stealing, pregnancy and marriage, namely mouths to feed and trades to pursue'. Burgess throws in a nagging wife: 'When was she to have a house of her own . . . What would he have to leave to his children?' Anne's alleged complaints find an early echo in *The Comedy of Errors*, as the Abbess rebukes Adriana:

> The venom clamours of a jealous woman
> Poisons more deadly than a mad dog's tooth.
> It seems his sleeps were hinder'd by thy railing,
> And thereof comes it that his head is light.
> Thou say'st his meat was sauc'd with thy upbraidings:
> Unquiet meals make ill digestions . . .

The Stratford records show that Lord Strange's Men were paid for a performance in the town on 11 February 1579. There is a growing school of thought that the boy Shakespeare hitched a ride with them to Lancashire, two months before his fifteenth birthday, with a letter of introduction in his pocket to Alexander Hoghton from the schoolmaster John Cottom. If so, he must have abandoned them for a prolonged period in his late teens, when he returned to Stratford long enough to marry and father three children.

So when did Shakespeare finally leave Stratford for London, to seek his fortune as an actor-playwright? He may have left us a clue in the words of a wise old Shepherd in one of his last plays, *The Winter's Tale*:

> I would there were no age between ten and three-and-twenty,
> or that youth would sleep out the rest; for there is nothing
> in between but getting wenches with child, wronging the
> ancientry, stealing, fighting.

As the mature Shakespeare looks back over his life, which had by this stage included its share of the youthful adventures he catalogues, twenty-three seems a very specific age to choose. Uniquely, the number crops up twice more in the same play. In 1587, the year Shakespeare turned twenty-three, Stratford enjoyed a visit from the leading theatrical troupe of the moment – the Queen's Men, handpicked for Elizabeth four years earlier by the Master of the Revels, clad in royal scarlet, and starring Richard Tarleton, the leading clown of his day (and forerunner of Yorick).

Before reaching Stratford, the Queen's Men played Abingdon, where the clamour to see them provoked a small riot; and Thame, where their performance on 13 June was followed by an incident which may have altered Shakespeare's life. That night, between the hours of 9 and 10 PM, a drunken quarrel broke out between two of the players, John Towne of Shoreditch and William Knell (probably the original Prince Hal in the anonymous *Famous Victories of Henry the Fifth*). In a close known as White Hound, Knell drew his sword and came at Towne, who found himself cornered. Drawing his own weapon, he plunged it into the neck of the advancing Knell, who died on the spot within half an hour. Pleading self-defence, Towne was spared by the local coroner and eventually pardoned by the Queen herself.

Within a year Knell's widow was remarried – to another actor,

John Heminges, who would become a close friend of Shakespeare, a beneficiary of his will, and one of the editors of the indispensable First Folio of his collected plays. At the time, it was probably within a few days that the Queen's Men arrived in Stratford – one player short. Did they find a willing volunteer in 23-year-old William Shakespeare, indigent father-of-three, son of a troubled father, anxious for steady work and prepared to travel? Was it with the Queen's Men, as their newest and most junior recruit, that the future playwright first found his way to London? In the light of subsequent events, it seems the most convincing available scenario.

IV

LONDON

1587–1592

In the summer of 1575 the Earl of Leicester entertained Queen Elizabeth I for almost three weeks at his castle at Kenilworth, twelve miles north-east of Stratford. 'When it pleaseth her in the summer season to recreate herself abroad, and view the estate of the country,' in the words of one contemporary observer, 'every nobleman's house is her palace.' Elizabeth was renowned for her ever-changing roll of favourites, from the Earl of Arundel to the Earl of Essex, but Robert Dudley, Earl of Leicester, was known at the time to be her 'favourite favourite'.

From miles around the Queen's loyal subjects flocked to glimpse their sovereign in her birthday splendour, to watch with wide eyes the afternoon revels and the lavish night-time firework displays. The highlight was a water-pageant on the lake in the castle grounds on 18 July, featuring Arion riding on the back of a dolphin – a decorated boat with oars for fins – and singing 'a delectable ditty of a song' to the accompaniment of instrumentalists hidden in the dolphin's belly.

Did alderman John Shakespeare, the Stratford glover, take his eleven-year-old son William to glimpse his Queen and share her wonder at the entertainment? 'Like Arion on the dolphin's back,' says the Captain in *Twelfth Night* of Viola's brother, 'I saw him hold acquaintance with the waves / So long as I could see.' In *A Midsummer*

Night's Dream, Oberon seems to depict a firework display, with stars shooting 'madly from their spheres', as he reminds Puck:

> Thou rememb'rest,
> . . . once I sat upon a promontory
> And heard a mermaid on a dolphin's back
> Uttering such dulcet and harmonious breath
> That the rude sea grew civil at her song,
> And certain stars shot madly from their spheres
> To hear the sea-maid's music.

And Cleopatra vividly says of Antony:

> His delights
> Were dolphin-like, they show'd his back above
> The element they liv'd in.

How else could Shakespeare ever have seen a dolphin, or the memory haunt him to such eloquent effect? If Leicester's royal pageant gave him his richest taste of the mysteries and glories of stagecraft, there had already been plenty of spectacles throughout his childhood to whet his appetite for the theatre. The records show that since 1569, when Shakespeare was five, touring troupes of players had been regularly visiting Stratford in hope of hire and salary, in much the same way that Hamlet's old friends fetch up at Elsinore.

As the bailiff's son, the young William would likewise have had a seat on the front bench in the Guild Hall for the performance by the Queen's Men that August – of what play, we do not know. Leicester's Men, led by James Burbage, followed in 1573, earning a mere 1s compared with the munificent 9s paid the Queen's Men. By August 1575 the fee had gone up to 17s for Warwick's Men, at a time when the theatrical profession was still rudimentary; no theatre, as such, had yet been built, although Burbage was soon to do something about that. Over the decade comprising Shakespeare's teens, no fewer than ten different troupes – the Queen's Men and Leicester's, Stafford's and Strange's, Derby's and Berkeley's, Oxford's and Chandos's, Warwick's and Worcester's – made some seventeen visits to Stratford.

Local pageants were also commonplace, written and performed by members of the community, but often including scenes from traditional plays. At Whitsun 1583, for instance, when Shakespeare had just turned nineteen, the surprisingly large sum of 13s 4d was paid by Stratford council to the 'local' acting troupe of 'Davi Jones and his co'. Did a stage-struck William take part, and get a taste for his share of the proceeds? In one of his earliest plays, *The Two Gentlemen of Verona*, he has a character speak in authentic tones of such amateur – and secular – entertainments:

> At Pentecost
> When all our pageants of delight were play'd,
> Our youth got me to play the woman's part
> And I was trimm'd in Madam Julia's gown . . .
> And at that time I made her weep a-good,
> For I did play a lamentable part.

Such entertainments are also recalled throughout the canon in the dumb shows (as in *Hamlet*) and parades of past and future souls (as in *Richard III* and *Macbeth*), not to mention the 'Parade of the Worthies' in *Love's Labour's Lost* and the 'ritual shooting of arrows with messages' in *Titus Andronicus*.

During 1586–87 Stratford was visited by most of the leading troupes of the day, but the undoubted climax was the arrival that summer of the stars of the circuit, the Queen's Men. The accounts of the Chamberlain for 1587, 'anno xxix Elizabeth Regine', show that the corporation paid the Queen's players a larger fee than it had previously paid any visiting troupe, the handsome sum of 20s. The expenditure of a further 16d was required to repair a broken bench, which makes it sound like Elizabeth's men gave value for money. This was the occasion on which it may be surmised that 23-year-old William, son of the glover who had seen better times, volunteered his services, bid a fond farewell to his parents, wife and three small children, and threw in his lot with the players, setting forth to seek his fortune in London.

Aldgate to the east; Bishopsgate, Moorgate, Cripplegate and Aldersgate to the north, Newgate and Ludgate to the west: today only the names survive of the seven entrances to the Elizabethan city of London set along the two-mile wall enclosing it on three sides, the fourth consisting of the wharves and warehouses of the thriving port along the sprawling River Thames. Compared with the sweetly flowing waters of the rural Avon, those of the Thames were pestilentially filthy, thick with excrement and carrion, nourishing rats and breeding disease.

Upon its silvery surface, undeterred, a bustling water-traffic vied for space with elegant, three-masted schooners disgorging their cargo for sale at Billingsgate and other markets. With London Bridge the only way to cross the river by foot – and that crowded by the shops and dwellings of prosperous merchants, every inch of its eight hundred feet a vision of Shylock's Rialto – water-taxis plied a busy trade. With cries of 'Eastward Ho!' or 'Westward Ho!' they picked their way between the splendid private barges of the wealthy, not least the Queen herself, who liked to spend the occasional festive evening leading a flotilla of small craft up and down the river amid music and fireworks.

To the west, then as now, the London skyline was dominated by St Paul's, even pre-Wren one of England's largest and most splendid cathedrals, yet still as much a place of commerce as of worship. It was some time since couriers had been barred from leading their mules down the central aisle on a short cut to Fleet Street. But its nave remained a ready rendezvous (even during services) for lawyers and their clients, servants looking for new masters, gallants looking for action – a seething tide of humanity offering pickings as rich for cutpurses and whores as for sharp-eyed poets and playwrights drawn there by the stalls of the publishers in the adjacent churchyard. At the sign of the Red Lion, or the White Horse, or divers others, the stationers living in the cathedral environs set out their stalls with the latest sermons, poems and play-texts. Of Shakespeare's works to be published in his lifetime, most would bear the imprint of St Paul's churchyard; later, the poet himself would live nearby, in Cripplegate.

To the east lay the rather more secular, brooding presence of the Tower of London, whose dark and blood-stained mysteries haunt so many of his plays, as indeed the lives of his friends and contemporaries. Just beyond, beneath St Katharine's Hospital at

1. The Market House, site of the Market Cross, Stratford-upon-Avon.

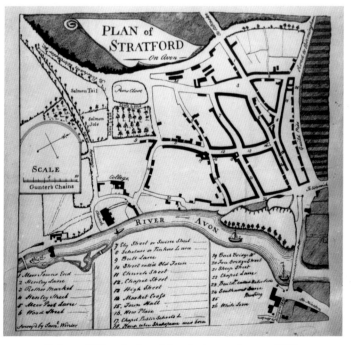

2. Samuel Winter's plan of Stratford-upon-Avon, *c.* 1759.

3. The Shakespeare family home in Henley Street, called 'The Birthplace', in the mid-nineteenth century.

4. Stratford Grammar School: an Elizabethan view.

5. Hoghton Tower, Lancashire, where William 'Shakeshafte' served as a tutor and part-time actor, and (*below*) the Great Hall, where he may have first learned to perform.

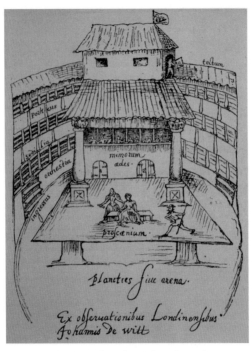

6. The Swan Theatre, London, drawn by Johann de Witt, *c.* 1596,
and (*below*) the Globe Theatre, Bankside, 1612.

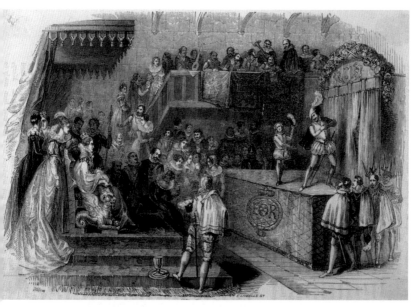

7. Queen Elizabeth I watches a play in one of her palaces, *c.* 1590.

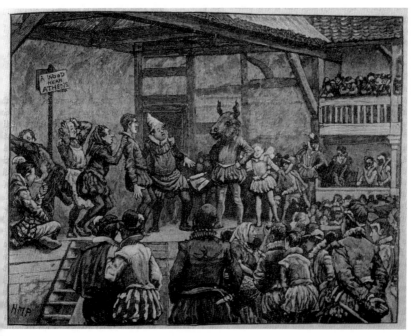

8. A performance of *A Midsummer Night's Dream* in an Elizabethan playhouse.

9. Robert Devereux, Earl of Essex
(1566–1601).

10. Sir William Cecil, Lord Burghley
(1520–98).

NON SANZ DROICT

11. Shakespeare's coat of arms.

12. Ben Jonson (1572–1637).

13. Michael Drayton (1563–1631).

14. Christopher ('Kit') Marlowe (1564–93).

15. Engraving by H. Gravelot of Shakespeare's monument in Westminster Abbey.

Wapping, lay the river's low-water mark, where dead pirates and live felons were pinioned to be washed by the fetid tide. Nearby, along the riverbank, stood Baynard's Castle, where Shakespeare's Richard, Duke of Gloucester stages his mock-reluctance to accept the crown. The strawberries favoured by Richard grew to the north in Ely Place, near the city's north-east boundary of Clerkenwell, thick with the rackety brothels frequented by the young Justice Shallow and other gallants of the Inns of Court. Beyond lay open countryside – apart from the fledgling hamlet of Islington, first stop on the Roman road to St Albans, past the lush forests of Hampstead hills. To the west and south, beyond the city limits, lay the rural villages of St Pancras and Charing Cross.

Within the city walls, crammed into a maze of passages and alleyways, lived a population fast approaching 200,000 – almost a tenth of all England. The further 'out' the parish – St Giles or St Leonard's, Cripplegate or Shoreditch – the poorer its inhabitants, squeezing into slum tenements held together by congealed mud, their upper storeys blocking out the daylight in streets too narrow for coaches. Here London life was at its most cosmopolitan, coloured by countless refugees from religious persecution all over Europe. The whole city was a babble of tongues, amid which many such immigrants prospered. *Twelfth Night*'s Antonio recommends to Sebastian as 'best to lodge' the Elephant 'in the south suburbs' – a likely reference to the Oliphant, an Italian inn in Bankside well known to Shakespeare. Was he as partial to Italian cuisine as Italian settings for his plays? In Hart Street, in the parish of St Olave's, one Paolo Marcho Lucchese served good Italian food; in Act I of *Othello*, as the Venetian elders convene in emergency session, Shakespeare's Doge asks: 'Marcus Luccicos, is he not in town?' Fond of mocking such 'potent, grave and reverend signiors', a well-fed poet seems to have been offering a sly nod to one of his favourite restaurateurs.

Most immigrants were less fortunate, confined to the 'multitudes of base tenements and houses of unlawful and disorderly resort in the suburbs' deplored in a mid-1590s report from the Privy Council, which called for tougher action from the Middlesex magistrates against the 'great number of dissolute, loose, and insolent people harboured in such and the like noisome and disorderly houses, as namely poor cottages, and habitations of beggars and people without trade, stables, inns, alehouses, taverns, garden-houses converted to dwellings, ordinaries, dicing-houses, bowling allies and brothel houses'. In such conditions, as the authorities were all too aware, pestilence thrived.

Some visitors praised the cleanliness of London's streets and the glories of its artisan areas, such as the passage 'named from the goldsmiths who inhabit it', noted for its 'gilt tower, with a fountain that plays'. Like most tourists through the ages, such travel-writers failed to wander beyond the golden fountains to the squalid, rubbish-strewn slums, their streets awash with excrement and urine, a rich breeding-ground for the black rat and its deadly parasite, the flea that carried and transmitted the bubonic plague. With no effective sewage system, it was said that London could be smelled from twenty miles away.

The regular outbreaks of plague in the capital would play as significant a role in Shakespeare's work as the other events crowding his life and Catholic times – most recently the execution of Mary, Queen of Scots, in February 1587, shortly before his arrival in a capital readying itself for war with Spain. Within a year came the defeat of Philip's Armada, inspired by the Queen's memorable lines at Tilbury – worthy of Shakespeare's *Henry V* at Agincourt – that within 'the body of a weak and feeble woman' lay 'the heart and stomach of a king, and a king of England too'. It was a high time to be English, an inspirational time to be a writer arriving at the heart of an unfolding political drama. The mood of national confidence was ripe for reflection in the arts. Drama was no longer 'a commodity to beguile the boredom of a country town, the little occasional treat of Stratford's Guildhall'. It was 'an aspect of the great world'.

With Catholic purges renewed, and more Jesuit equivocators executed, Shakespeare seems wisely to have kept his own counsel about his religion – if, indeed, it still meant much to him. As an 'uneducated' country boy, newly arrived in a city full of smart, self-satisfied university graduates, he would now have to learn to pick his way through other forms of prejudice and intrigue. His arrival on the London theatrical scene coincided with the flowering of the self-styled 'University Wits', most of whom would offer a cool welcome to the 'rude' Stratford *parvenu* with ideas above his station –

an indifferent actor, it would soon transpire, with the nerve to turn playwright.

Primus inter pares – before Shakespeare's arrival – was Christopher ('Kit') Marlowe, born the same year as the Stratford man, the son of a Canterbury shoemaker who had won himself a place at Corpus Christi College, Cambridge. Already, as Shakespeare arrived in London, Marlowe's *Tamburlaine* was holding the stage; over the next five years, before his violent and premature death in 1593, Marlowe would follow up with *Dr Faustus*, *The Jew of Malta* and *Edward II*.

Jockeying for equal billing were such lesser talents as Robert Greene, Thomas Nashe, George Peele, Thomas Lodge, John Lyly – young Oxbridge graduates all, often joining forces as much as blazing their own trails in churning out box-office fodder as fast as the acting troupes could stage it. Rivals on whom they looked down, like Shakespeare's fellow grammar-school boy Thomas Kyd, whose *Spanish Tragedy* would prove such a success, were sneered at in ruthless satires. Mocking an early play by an anonymous hand (or hands), Lodge wrote in his *Wit's Miserie* about a devil 'as pale as the vizard of the ghost who cried so miserably at the Theatre, like an oyster-wife, *Hamlet, revenge!*' In 1588, within a year of Shakespeare's arrival in London, Nashe launched an attack on certain unnamed translators and writers as having only 'a little country grammar knowledge'. Rather more specific was the object of Peele's angst in his *Edward I*, written the following year:

> Shake thy speres, in honour of his name
> Under whose royalty thou wearst the same.

Marlowe was a case apart; an elegant and civilised talent, admired, aped and mourned by Shakespeare, he was largely diverted from the theatrical in-fighting by his work as a spy in the service of the Queen's elder statesman, Sir Francis Walsingham. Shakespeare probably knew Marlowe, and enjoyed his lively company – we cannot, with any confidence, assume much more – and he would pay him posthumous homage as the dead shepherd in *As You Like It*, putting a line from Marlowe's *Hero and Leander* in the mouth of the shepherdess Phebe:

> Dead shepherd, now I find thy saw of might
> 'Who ever lov'd that lov'd not at first sight?'

The rest of the 'University Wits' preened themselves in ornate, erudite poetry and polemical pamphlets, stooping to the writing of plays merely as a handy new way, if somewhat beneath their dignity, of making money.

It was barely a decade before Shakespeare's arrival in London, in 1576, that the same James Burbage who had passed through Stratford as a player – like Snug, he was a joiner-turned-actor – had the bright idea that 'continual great profit' might accrue from the erection of a building designed purely for the presentation of plays.

A 'playhouse' was a wholly original notion; hitherto, the dramatic art had flourished in the courtyards of inns converted into makeshift theatres – the Boar's Head in Aldgate, the Bull in Bishopsgate Street, the Bel Savage on Ludgate Hill, the Bell and the Cross Keys in Gracechurch Street; the Boar's Head in Whitechapel, also the home of Burbage's prototype, the Red Lion, built in 1567 by his brother-in-law John Brayne, but now defunct. With a hefty loan from Brayne, a prosperous grocer, Burbage took a twenty-one-year lease on a patch of waste land in Shoreditch, beside the Finsbury Fields at Holywell, only half a mile outside the Bishopsgate entrance to the city. Near what is today Liverpool Street Station, on a derelict site rank with weeds, bones and all manner of detritus, he duly constructed the world's first custom-built playhouse, which he proudly christened the 'Theatre' (from the Greek *theatron*).

Like the imitators it soon spawned, Burbage's Theatre was modelled on the design of the inn-yards which had hitherto served the turns of theatrical troupes so well: a circular auditorium, with tiered galleries offering better, drier and more expensive seats for the gentry, and food and drink available for the 'groundlings' who paid a penny each to stand beneath the elements, crowding forward towards an elevated, rectangular stage, flanked by two columns supporting a protective canopy known as the 'heavens'. On each side of the stage was a door for exits and entrances, at the back a curtained recess suitable for more intimate scenes.

This was the basic design that, for most of Shakespeare's working life, shaped his drama, large-scale or small. Above the 'heavens' was a thatched loft or 'attic' with openings available for use as upstairs windows, as in Juliet's balcony scene; later, this housed the equipment for 'flying' effects, such as the descent of Jupiter in *Cymbeline*. From its roof flew a flag bearing the theatre company's symbol, raised as an advertisement before and during a performance, whose start was signalled by a liveried trumpeter at 2 PM sharp.

Below the stage, via a trap-door, was a storage area known as 'hell', convenient for such occasional use as the 'cellarage' haunted by the Ghost of Hamlet's Father. Behind the entire edifice, invisible to the audience, was the tiring-house (or dressing-room), a cramped space for actors to change their costumes and properties to be stored. Scenery, apart from the occasional bench, was minimal; the painting of scenes was in those days the job of the playwright.

Soon Burbage's prototype Theatre naturally lent its name to the type of building it fostered, and eventually to the activity it housed.

> As in a theatre the eyes of men,
> After a well-graced actor leaves the stage,
> Are idly bent on him that enters next,
> Thinking his prattle to be tedious . . .

The Duke of York's extended simile in Shakespeare's *Richard II* (*circa* 1596) is the first recorded use of the word 'theatre' as the generic term universally used ever since.

Within months of the Theatre's opening, early in 1577, another playhouse arose just two hundred yards to the south, also on Holywell Lane, in a dingy alley called Curtain Close. The Curtain was built not by a player, but a gentleman of means named Henry Laneman. For all Laneman's respectability, the sudden emergence of two such places of entertainment moved London churchmen to splutters of indignation. 'Behold these sumptuous houses, a continual monument of London's prodigality and folly!' preached Thomas White, vicar of St Dunstan's-in-the-West, at Paul's Cross in November 1577. 'It is an evident token of a wicked time,' thundered William Harrison, canon of Windsor, 'when players wax so rich that they can build such houses.'

For whatever reason – perhaps because it was run by actors, with a keener sense of what the public wanted – Burbage's Theatre fared better than Laneman's Curtain, which was forced by 1579 to resort to staging bouts of fencing. By 1585 the two impresarios had agreed to pool their resources, and the Curtain became an 'easer', or annexe, to the Theatre. By then, however, the centre of theatrical gravity was already shifting south of the river, to the Paris (short for 'Paradise') Garden – an unruly area around Bankside, where a large open meadow was the setting for running and wrestling, bowling and archery alongside the bearpits and brothels lining the riverbank. Here, in 1587, on the site of a former rose-garden, an entrepreneur named Philip Henslowe built a third playhouse, the Rose, in partnership with a wealthy grocer, John Cholmley. Also a pawnbroker and brothel-keeper, Henslowe went on to become the great theatrical impresario of his day. His account-books, an engagingly candid log of his expenditure and box-office receipts, are an invaluable source of information about the dates and venues of numerous plays by Shakespeare and others.

Soon would follow one more playhouse, the Swan, opened in 1596, also on the river's edge at the western end of Bankside, capable of holding all of 3,000 paying customers. At the time of Shakespeare's arrival in London, however, there were just the three more-or-less thriving theatres, all standing symbolically outside the city boundaries in areas aptly known as 'liberties'. Completed in February 1592 at a total cost of £100, the Rose became the home of Lord Strange's Men, now merged with the Admiral's Men, and led by the most admired actor of the day, Edward ('Ned') Alleyn. Shakespeare may already have met Alleyn on his visits to Stratford, perhaps earlier in Lancashire. Already renowned for his Tamburlaine, he would be rivalled only by Richard Burbage as the leading tragedian on the Elizabethan stage; in partnership with Henslowe, whose stepdaughter he married in 1592, Alleyn grew rich enough to found Dulwich College, where his letters and Henslowe's account-books were unearthed by Malone in 1790. 'Others speak, but only thou dost act,' said Ben Jonson of Alleyn, whom Nashe declared the best actor 'since before Christ was born'.

But Shakespeare's first London patron was James Burbage, who had been leading theatrical troupes to Stratford as long before as 1573, when his new recruit was just nine years old. The father of Richard, the actor who would create many of the great Shakespearean roles, this genial impresario was the kind to have befriended the stagestruck son of the former mayor, inviting him to look him up if ever he fetched up in London in need of work. It was at Burbage's Shoreditch Theatre, we know, that Shakespeare the actor would eventually play the Ghost in a production of his own *Hamlet*. But how did he make his start in the theatre?

Since 1583 Burbage's Theatre had been the London base of the Queen's Men, with whom we have seen Shakespeare arrive in London. Next door, it has been pointed out, was a slaughter-house, 'where a butcher's apprentice would be useful'. All the traditions stress that the newlywed father was 'poor', 'without money and friends', at the 'extreme end of ruin', forced to endure a 'very low degree of drudgery'. According to an early-eighteenth-century biographer, he was 'received into the company then in being, at first in a very mean rank; but his admirable wit, and the natural turn of it to the stage, soon distinguished him, if not as an extraordinary actor, yet as an excellent writer'.

Ten years earlier, at the end of the century in which Shakespeare died, another memoirist recorded that he was 'first received into the playhouse as a serviture'. But in what role, exactly? Later references to the playwright as a 'rude groom' appear to confirm the intriguing tradition that Shakespeare first found employment by combining the role of ostler (or stableman) with part-time actor and backstage factotum.

So says, for instance, no less an authority than Samuel Johnson. 'In the time of Elizabeth,' writes Johnson in his 1765 edition of Shakespeare, 'coaches being yet uncommon, and hired coaches not at all in use, those who were too proud, too tender, or too idle to walk, went on horseback to any distant business or diversion. Many came on horseback to the play . . .' Convinced that the young deer-poacher had slunk south to avoid the wrath of Sir Thomas Lucy, Johnson continues:

> When Shakespeare fled to London . . . his first expedient was to wait at the door of the playhouse, and hold the horses of those that had no servants, that they might be ready again after the performance. In this office he became so conspicuous for his care and readiness, that in a short time every man as he alighted called

for Will. Shakespeare, and scarcely any other waiter was trusted
with a horse while Will. Shakespeare could be had. This was the
first dawn of better fortune. Shakespeare finding more horses
put into his hand than he could hold, hired boys to wait under
his inspection, who, when Will. Shakespeare was summoned,
were immediately to present themselves, I am Shakespeare's
boy, Sir. In time Shakespeare found higher employment, but
as long as the practice of riding to the playhouse continued,
the waiters that held the horses retained the appellation of
Shakespeare's Boys.

Johnson got the idea from his amanuensis Robert Shiels, whom he
identified to his biographer Boswell as the true 'Mr Cibber', author
of *The Lives of the Poets of Great Britain and Ireland* (1753). Shiels, in
turn, traced the story back to the seventeenth-century poet laureate
Sir William Davenant, Shakespeare's godson, whom we shall meet
again in yet more intriguing guise. A degree of plausibility is added
to the legend by the fact that the Theatre and the Curtain, north of
the river, were the only playhouses accessible on horseback.

'Out ye rogue!' Prince Hal rebukes Falstaff in *1 Henry IV*. 'Shall I be
your ostler?' This has the ring of another backstage in-joke, reminding
the playwright's fellow-actors of his humble 'front-of-house' beginnings. That Shakespeare knew his horses, with an expert, admiring
eye for their breeds and breeding, cannot be doubted from copious
references throughout the canon:

> Round-hoof'd, short-jointed, fetlocks shag and long,
> Broad breast, full eye, small head and nostril wide,
> High crest, short ears, straight legs and passing strong,
> Thin mane, thick tail, broad buttock, tender hide,
> > Look what a horse should have he did not lack,
> > Save a proud rider on so proud a back.

The 'breeding jennet' worth a dozen verses of *Venus and Adonis*
prefigures not merely an expert knowledge of horses – Falstaff's 'frets
like a gumm'd velvet', while Petruchio's poor nag is afflicted with
'glanders', 'lampass', 'windgalls', 'spavins' and 'the staggers' – but also
many an equine metaphor throughout the plays. 'Deal mildly with

his youth,' York advises Richard II's mother, 'For young hot colts being raged, do rage the more.' After *Henry V*'s Prologue has asked us to imagine horses 'printing their proud hoofs i' th' receiving earth', the 'pure air and fire' of the Dauphin's Pegasus seems to echo even Shakespeare's image for his own calling: 'the poet's eye in a fine frenzy rolling' as it glances 'from heaven to earth, from earth to heaven'.

If Shakespeare invented a lucrative sixteenth-century version of valet parking, he seems also to have moonlighted backstage during performances, while his 'boys' tended the horses, as an apprentice prompter. According to his first biographer, Rowe, Shakespeare's 'first office in the theatre was that of prompter's attendant, whose employment it is to give the performers notice to be ready to enter, as often as the business of the play requires their appearance on the stage'. More likely, this was promotion for the ostler – bringing him inside the theatre, where he really wanted to be, if as yet backstage. The 'house call-boy' would have been 'a perfect post for the aspiring young actor-playwright', as has been observed. 'It offers priceless experience in the management of exits and entrances and the learning of lines.' Perhaps, suggests the same recent authority, 'the favourite device of ending a scene with a rhymed couplet, which would serve to alert an actor to an imminent entrance, was the young Shakespeare's idea?'

The role of prompter would have been a handy start, not least at rehearsals, when Shakespeare would have been required to 'stand in' from time to time, and given a chance to show off what talents he had as an actor. From there, it was but a short step to minor roles, even understudying bigger ones. Given his apparent limitations as a performer, it was only natural that the rural poet, the Plautus of his schooldays still fresh in his mind, would also turn his hand to writing. A jobbing playwright who could fill in onstage, taking on the occasional minor role, would seem a very useful acquisition to any troupe. To Shakespeare, for his part, membership of the Queen's Players was the perfect start to his career – with the leading company of the moment, regularly commanded to perform at court.

The Queen's troupe, recruited at Elizabeth's personal command, appeared frequently at court during the first season of its existence, 1583–84, while earning its keep before paying audiences at Burbage's Theatre. Precisely when Shakespeare signed on is unknown; his name is not among the dozen licensed by the City Corporation in November 1583 to play 'at the sign of the Bull in Bishopsgate Street and the sign of the Bull in Gracechurch Street and nowhere else within this city'. Among those who were was the star comedian of the moment, Richard Tarleton, whose memory lingered fondly with Shakespeare when he conjured Hamlet's touching memories of Yorick. So Tarleton's death in 1588 suggests that the poet had joined the Queen's Men by that date; the mention of his name in an early-eighteenth-century woodcut as 'one of the first actors in Shakespeare's plays' further suggests that the new recruit was already contributing new or revised dramas to the company's repertoire.

Shakespeare's first known London address was in Westminster, nearer the court than the playhouses. The Folger Library in Washington DC possesses a copy of a legal textbook entitled *Archaionomia*, edited by William Lambarde and published in 1568, on which is inscribed the name 'Wm Shakespeare'. In the same volume appears a note, presumably added by a later owner: 'Mr Wm Shakespeare lived at No 1 Little Crown St Westminster NB near Dorset Steps, St James's Park'.

Why was Shakespeare living so far from the theatrical action? The rent may, perhaps, have been cheaper; but legal records show that in early 1589 he and his parents were pursuing through a Westminster law-court their continuing claim against his cousin John Lambert for restoration of their rights in the Asbies estate. They would eventually lose their suit, and thus his patrimony; but in the process he appears to have mastered the art of the scrivener, or lawyer's copy-clerk. The handwriting of Shakespeare's signature on the book suggests as much, according to an early-twentieth-century authority; and we have the word of a contemporary, Nashe, that some playwrights of the day lived some distance from the literary heart of London, making 'a peripatetical path' to the playhouses and booksellers in the 'inner parts of the city'.

Was Shakespeare sharing digs with his fellow grammar-school boy, Thomas Kyd, chuckling defiantly over the envious attacks of the university-educated Nashe (whom he would later lampoon as the diminutive Moth in *Love's Labour's Lost*)? Were the two country hicks cobbling together a crude revenge tragedy about a Danish prince called Hamlet – now lost, but known to have enjoyed a certain success in the late 1580s? Both would have admired (and learnt, if not indeed stolen, from) Marlowe's *Tamburlaine*. As for the rest of the 'University Wits', it would seem in character for Shakespeare to come home from the Theatre, well lubricated with ale, and mock the clunking lines declaimed around him that afternoon, vowing to improve on them in his own work-in-progress.

As a member of the Queen's Men, both on the road and in town, he would have become familiar with several anonymous plays then in their repertoire which would later echo, in revised and vastly refined form, through his own. Apart from *The Troublesome Reign of King John*, *The Famous Victories of Henry the Fifth* and *The True Chronicle of King Leir, and his three daughters* – three works of unknown authorship in which Shakespeare may well have had a hand – the Queen's Men did good business with a play called *Felix and Philomena*, first performed before their patron, the Queen herself, at Greenwich in January 1585. The text they played – no doubt cobbled together by the cast, as was often the case before they acquired their own in-house playwright – was based on a work of Montemayor written in Spanish in 1542, translated into French in 1578, entitled *Felix and Felismena*. This was clearly one of Shakespeare's prime sources for his own early comedy, *The Two Gentlemen of Verona*.

But comedy could wait, as indeed could tragedy. *Titus Andronicus* is undoubtedly an early work, placed by some scholars at the very start of his play-writing career, but now broadly accepted as later than the ostler's first, at times primitive forays into stagecraft. That early version of a play called *Hamlet*, known to literary history as the ur-*Hamlet*, was also in the repertoire of the Queen's Men at this time; and there is no great reason to disbelieve that this primitive draft of a later masterpiece was the work of the young Shakespeare as much as his fellow 'grammarian' Kyd, to whom it is usually credited. But history plays were the box-office phenomenon of the moment; and it was with a history cycle quite without precedent that Shakespeare appears first to have proposed himself to his fellows as a better writer than actor.

The Queen's Men, it seems, had yet to be convinced, moving Shakespeare the writer – if not the actor – to turn freelance. They would later, of course, perform his plays regularly, as would all the troupes who could lay their hands on them; but his first efforts found their real success in the version staged by the players employed by the Derby family, with whom he had first made that early connection in Lancashire – and whose recent ancestors, craftily enough, it glorified.

'How it would have joyed brave Talbot (the terror of the French),' wrote Nashe in 1592, 'to think that after he had lain two hundred years in the tomb, he should triumph again on the stage, and have his bones embalmed with the tears of ten thousand spectators at least (at several times), who, in the tragedian who represents his person, behold him fresh bleeding.' Unless he is to be taken at face value, the envious Nashe may have been drawing ironic attention to Shakespeare's rewriting of history in the aggrandisement of the role of the House of Derby in the Wars of the Roses; if so, he missed a trick by failing to point out that the young playwright, comparatively fresh from Stratford, was also making his proxy peace with the Lucy family, by putting Talbot's lavish obsequies into the mouth of the local magistrate's ancestor Sir William:

> . . . the great Alcides of the field,
> Valiant Lord Talbot, Earl of Shrewsbury,
> Created for his rare success in arms
> Great Earl of Washford, Waterford and Valence,
> Lord Talbot of Goodrig and Urchinfield,
> Lord Strange of Blackmere, Lord Verdun of Alton,
> Lord Cromwell of Wingfield, Lord Furnival of Sheffield,
> The thrice victorious Lord of Falconbridge,
> Knight of the noble Order of Saint George,
> Worthy Saint Michael and the Golden Fleece,
> Great Marshal to Henry the Sixth
> Of all his wars within the realm of France.

So reverential a litany of a previous Lord Strange's titles, as he dies cradled in the arms of his son and heir, is enough to make posterity wonder whether the plays might not have been commissioned by his latest descendant, acquainted with Shakespeare since his Lancashire days, for performance by his own players. The lack of a performance history before 1592 permits no more than such tantalised speculation. What records there are, however, demonstrate beyond peradventure that it was Strange's players who brought the *Henry VI* cycle its biggest triumph, establishing the actor-turned-playwright as a force on the London stage.

On Saturday 19 February the 1592 Rose season of Lord Strange's Men, led by Alleyn, got off to a mediocre start. Robert Greene's comedy, *Friar Bacon and Friar Bungay*, only half-filled the theatre, as did that week's cycle of anonymous plays: *Muly Mulocco, The Spanish Comedy of Don Horatio, Sir John Mandeville* and *Harry of Cornwall*. The following Saturday, 26 February, business picked up with a packed house for Marlowe's *The Jew of Malta*. But even that was surpassed by a history play first performed the following Friday, 3 March, which proved the best box-office draw of the season. 'Harey the vj £3.16.8.' recorded Henslowe in his account-book.

According to Nashe, more than ten thousand people saw Shakespeare's first full history cycle at the Rose that summer. 'The takings continue high,' purrs Henslowe's diary for 5 April, after further performances on 7, 11, 16 and 28 March; so he scheduled fourteen more during April, May and June. The various rival theatrical troupes had been living through turbulent times, making it hard for posterity to track the stage provenance of Shakespeare's early works. From the title-page of a published version of *3 Henry VI*, we know that it had been 'oft enacted' by the Earl of Pembroke's Men, who also had *Titus Andronicus* in their repertoire. But this does not tell us much. Copyright in plays rested not with the playwright but the company who commissioned them; pirate versions abounded, even in print; there is a widely-held theory (strenuously contested in some quarters) that actors who defected to other companies were required to come up with 'memorial reconstructions', inevitably defective versions put together from their memory of other parts as well as their own – thus combining with the mistakes and improvisations of compositors to bequeath the Shakespeare industry a bottomless pit of textual problems to argue over till doomsday.

In 1590, we do know, Strange's servants and the Admiral's Men merged under the leadership of Alleyn, using the two Shoreditch playhouses, Burbage's Theatre and its annexe, the Curtain. In May

1591, for some reason, Alleyn fell out with Burbage, boldly leading his troupe across the river to Henslowe's Rose, where they found a new lease of life as Lord Strange's Men. But not all of Alleyn's colleagues followed him; seeing himself as a rival to Alleyn's thespian laurels, Burbage's son Richard persuaded some players to stay behind with him in Shoreditch, where they formed a new company under the patronage of the Earl of Pembroke. Then aged twenty-three, four years younger than Shakespeare, Richard Burbage would in time create the roles of Richard III, Hamlet, Othello and Lear; he it was, more than Shakespeare, who would maintain a lifelong association with Pembroke, ended only by the actor's death in 1619, after which the theatre-loving earl could no longer bring himself to visit the playhouse where his 'old acquaintance' had trod the boards.

Shakespeare's own connections with Pembroke – believed by some to be the 'fair youth' of the cycle of sonnets on which he would soon embark – may be surmised from the fact that the fellow-actors who collected his plays after his death, and published the First Folio in 1623, chose to dedicate the volume to him. It is possible that Pembroke's Men began life as an offshoot of the Queen's Men, given their irregular employment and the frequent dispersals caused by outbreaks of plague. There was, for sure, a special bond between the freelance dramatist, also an actor in Burbage's company, and the young nobleman who now paid their wages; such records as we have suggest that his plays were performed more often by Pembroke's Men than by any other company. But the Master of the Revels was more concerned with maintaining public decency than enforcing the rudimentary laws of copyright. Shakespeare's plays, like all plays, did the rounds.

The *Henry VI* plays must have crept into various repertoires over the previous couple of years, starting with *The First Part of the Contention betwixt the two famous Houses of York and Lancaster*, soon followed by *The True Tragedy of Richard, Duke of York*. For centuries the *Contention* and the *True Tragedy* (published separately in 1594–95) were believed to be the work of other unknown writers, refined and merged by Shakespeare into the second and third parts of his *Henry VI* trilogy – to which, supposedly, he then wrote Part 1 (not published in his lifetime) as a curtain-raiser. A later school of thought argued that they were in fact corrupt texts – bad quartos

– of Shakespearean originals. Against the convictions of many of today's university men, who still maintain (on stylistic grounds) that Part 1 was written last, as a crowd-pleasing 'prequel' to the two unexpected hits of an unknown playwright, there seems little reason to believe that Shakespeare did not in fact write the three plays in the chronological order in which we have received them, as printed in the First Folio. The three parts of *Henry VI* would then logically, and perhaps immediately, be followed by *The Tragedy of King Richard III.*

Given the scale and range of his eventual output, it seems wholly in character that Shakespeare chose to begin his work as a playwright with an ambitious tetralogy covering fifty years of comparatively recent British history – a theatrical feat never previously attempted, in a style which, while still rudimentary, was quite unlike anything that had gone before. By assigning character and motives, thoughts and feelings to historical figures still fresh in the national mind, and by holding them (rather than divine will) responsible for the consequences of their own actions, Shakespeare joined Marlowe in breaking free of the plodding, one-dimensional archetypes of the mediaeval tradition. Cycles of Miracle and Mystery plays, respectively dramatising the lives of saints and enacting stories from the Bible, had long been presented at large towns such as York, Wakefield, Chester and Coventry – only twenty miles from Stratford – and in turn bred the Morality plays, little more than sermons dressed up in dramatic form, featuring characters like Vice (or 'Ambidexter') and the Devil.

If Marlowe's *Dr Faustus* preserved this tradition, Shakespeare later showed his awareness of it in Hamlet's dealings with the players who arrive at Elsinore, begging them not to overact. King Herod was always a major character in these biblical plays, required to rant his way through such episodes as the Slaughter of the Innocents, as Shakespeare recalled when he had a Stanislavsky-like Hamlet deplore those players who 'tear a passion to tatters, to very rags, to split the ears of the groundlings'. Ham acting, to Hamlet, 'out-Herods Herod'. Shakespeare's childhood outings to these primitive dramas, which held the English stage for almost three centuries before going out of style with the Reformation, were also recalled by the canny clown Feste in *Twelfth Night*:

> Like to the old Vice . . .
> Who with dagger of lath,
> In his rage and his wrath,
>   Cries Aha! to the devil . . .

By the time he wrote that parody, more than a decade later, Shakespeare had long since achieved his ambition of breaking free of such restraints, and creating a new form of drama, vividly human, thrillingly alive. He began on the grand scale, with a rewriting of recent English history designed not as an accurate chronicle of events, not by any means, but as a dramatic exploration of humankind under pressure.

The historical King Henry VI (1421–71) was a pale shadow of his heroic, belligerent father, Henry V, to whom Shakespeare would return in due course. A child when he succeeded to the throne, Henry remained as impotent in adulthood in the face of the disputes among the rival noblemen jockeying for position in the absence of his supreme authority. In Shakespeare's scheme of things, reworking the 1587 edition of Holinshed's *Chronicles* and numerous lesser sources, the King remains a mere spectator in his own sad history, powerless to prevent the loss of France, the fall of Gloucester, the rise of York, the disintegration of his kingdom into virtual anarchy – even, eventually, his own death. In Part 3, symbolically, he is even powerless to speak, twice demanding his say and twice being denied it. This, to an Elizabethan audience, was the ultimate heresy against the divinity that still did hedge a king.

The cycle traces the long, slow decline of England after the death of its warrior-king, Henry V, as the collapse of his French conquests and the erosion of royal power leads inexorably to the dynastic squabbles that result in civil war. From the outset, with Henry's noblemen already arguing about the succession, Shakespeare has in mind an exploration of cause and effect on a vast, panoramic scale. As Exeter soon foresees:

> No simple man that sees
> This jarring discord of nobility,
> This shouldering of each other in the court,
> This factious bandying of their favourites,
> But that it doth presage some ill event.

''Tis much,' he continues, 'when sceptres are in children's hands
. . .' To Shakespeare, Henry VI's reign was a vacuum in which to
explore the onset of chaos and disorder. These would remain abiding
themes, still to the fore in his most mature tragedies, as would the
humanity with which he endowed the unfortunate monarch, who
grows gradually more eloquent as his fortunes decline. By Part 3,
at the height of the Battle of Towton, Henry withdraws from the
fighting to indulge in pastoral meditation:

> O God! methinks it were a happy life
> To be no better than a homely swain.
> To sit upon a hill, as I do now;
> To carve out dials quaintly, point by point,
> Thereby to see the minutes how they run:
> How many makes the hour full complete,
> How many hours brings about the day,
> How many days will finish up the year,
> How many years a mortal man may live . . .
> Gives not the hawthorn bush a sweeter shade
> To shepherds looking on their silly sheep
> Than doth a rich embroider'd canopy
> To kings that fear their subjects' treachery?

The unseen king then overhears the lamentations of a son who has
unwittingly killed his father, and a father who has killed his son.
The later Shakespeare would have had him respond with lyrical
fellow-feeling equal to such extreme events; the young poet merely
hands him another bout of self-pity as the prelude to his demise.
Likewise, the playwright so ahead of his time in the strength of
the parts he would soon write for women – though not even, at
the time, played by women – would surely not have allowed his
portrayal of Joan of Arc to pander to the English vogue for vilifying
the French.

The brash self-confidence of youth is apparent throughout the
cycle, with its vast epic sweep, its huge cast of characters, its preference
for pageantry and action over agonised introspection, and above all
its high, sententious style, in which the many and various voices are
barely differentiated. There are honourable exceptions, such as the

idiomatic prose of the Jack Cade sequence, and the emotional power of Young Clifford's verse on discovering the corpse of his father, both in Part 2. And there are thematic portents of the greater Shakespeare to come: the collapse of civic order, for instance, mirrored in that of families at war with themselves, brother plotting to kill brother, humanity reduced to the amoral anarchy of animals and the elements.

Part 3 also sees the emergence of a character quite distinct from the rest, a 'heap of wrath, a foul indigested lump' for whom Shakespeare clearly had further plans. 'Why, I can smile, and murther whiles I smile,' he says,

> And cry 'Content' to that which grieves my heart,
> And wet my cheeks with artificial tears,
> And frame my face to all occasions.
> I'll drown more sailors than the mermaid shall,
> I'll slay more gazers than the basilisk,
> I'll play the orator as well as Nestor,
> Deceive more slyly than Ulysses could,
> And, like a Sinon, take another Troy.
> I can add colours to the chameleon,
> Change shapes with Proteus for advantages,
> And set the murtherous Machiavel to school.
> Can I do this, and cannot get a crown?
> Tut, were it farther off, I'll pluck it down.

Our first sight of Richard, Duke of Gloucester seems to transport the poet into a new dimension, as if he were already writing his next play, the logical conclusion of the tetralogy. *Richard III* picks up where *3 Henry VI* left off, with Gloucester plotting at the dead king's funeral. In his celebrated opening speech – 'Now is the winter of our discontent / Made glorious summer by this son of York' – lie the seeds of the great soliloquies to come. Richard's wry explanation of his decision to play the villain is more of an extended aside than a soliloquy; but it carries the early hallmarks of the self-knowledge (or lack of it, leading to self-questioning) which would wring from Shakespeare some of his supreme moments. Richard's bitter eloquence in analysing his own villainy anticipates

Iago's much more interesting failure to do so, and Macbeth's paranoid ambivalence.

For his portrait of a monarch already demonised in the popular imagination, Shakespeare dug beyond his Holinshed and other *Henry VI* sources to Polydore Vergil's *Historia Anglica* and Sir Thomas More's *History of King Richard the Third*. 'Little of stature, ill-featured of limbs, crook-backed, his left shoulder much higher than his right,' wrote More, Richard was 'malicious, wrathful, envious, and, from afore his birth, ever froward.' From previous plays perpetuating this disputed historical portrait, notably Thomas Legge's Latin *Ricardus Tertius* (1579) and the anonymous *True Tragedy of Richard III*, Shakespeare derived the theatrical device of centring historical events, however loosely and inaccurately, around one supremely powerful character – if at the expense of much moral ambiguity. This in itself has proved enough to win *Richard III* a lasting place in the repertoire while the *Henry VI* trilogy is so unjustly neglected, rarely staged except in the form of highly edited, action-packed panoramas such as the Royal Shakespeare Company's *The Wars of the Roses* (1963) or *The Plantagenets* (1989–90).

It is, of course, the character of Richard himself, the first of Shakespeare's many engaging villains – whose delight in his own diabolical cunning audiences can only share – which has won so lasting a place for an otherwise still formulaic work, steeped in the Senecan revenge tradition, ringing with its antiphonal woes. Again, the female characters are woefully inadequate, merely passive and strident; only a supreme actress can lend the slightest credibility to Richard's successful wooing of Lady Anne – merely a foil, like so many other central characters, to feed the protagonist good lines. *Richard III* remains in many ways a rough-edged, patently early work, its flashes of brilliance only intermittent amid its pervasive melodrama; but it represents a quantum leap from the occasional longueurs of the history cycle.

If Ned Alleyn had made Shakespeare's first big part his own, coining it for himself and Henslowe as Henry VI, it was Richard Burbage (and thus Pembroke's Men) who cornered the sequel, as we know from a rare, if uncorroborated, Shakespeare anecdote. On 13 March 1601

a barrister of the Middle Temple named John Manningham entered
the following note in his diary:

> Upon a time when Burbage played Richard III, there was a
> citizen grew so far in liking with him, that before she went
> from the play she appointed him to come that night unto her
> by the name of Richard the Third. Shakespeare, overhearing
> their conversation, went before, was entertained and at his
> game ere Burbage came. Then, message being brought that
> Richard III was at the door, Shakespeare caused return to
> be made that William the Conqueror was before Richard
> the Third.

This, for Shakespeare biographers, is one of those unverifiable
vignettes too good to discard on the grounds of merely dubious
provenance. It conjures up the roistering Bard of the popular,
wishful-thinking imagination, the Bard who would later suffer at
least one dose of the clap, living the hell-raising London life of his
most earthy, engaging characters, with his wife and children at a safe
distance in Stratford – the irrepressible, fun-loving Bard who, sooner
or later, had to turn his hand to comedy.

At the end of 1589 the poet Edmund Spenser, who spent most
of his life in Ireland, returned to his native London for an audience
with the Queen. He also took the chance to entrust to the printer
the first three books of his majestic epic *The Faerie Queene*, evidently
admired by Shakespeare, who pays it due tribute in *Love's Labour's
Lost*. Now, within a year of his visit, the other great poet of the
age appears to have repaid the compliment. In *The Teares of the
Muses*, registered in December 1590, Spenser bemoaned the current
neglect of comedy on the London stage – with two honourable
exceptions. One was a player who had recently died – clearly
a reference to Dick Tarleton – while the other was a writer, a
'gentle Spirit',

> from whose pen
> Large streams of honey and sweet nectar flow,
> Scorning the boldness of such base-born men,
> Which dare their follies forth so rashly throw . . .

If Spenser's 'our pleasant Willy' was Shakespeare, constantly referred to by other contemporaries as 'gentle' and 'honey-tongued', then he may also have been the plausible, if pseudonymous object of further compliments from Spenser in *Colin Clout's Come Home Again*, written in about 1591, published in 1595:

> And there though last not least is Aetion,
> A gentler shepherd may no where be found:
> Whose Muse full of high thoughts' invention,
> Doth like himself heroically sound.

This 'Aetion' is often identified as Shakespeare's fellow Warwickshire poet, Michael Drayton; but there is surely little doubt which of the two writers' names, like their works, has the more 'heroic' ring.

If Spenser had seen a Shakespeare comedy before 1590, which one? On purely stylistic grounds – where purists fear to tread for such crude purposes as mere dating – the prime suspect would be *The Two Gentlemen of Verona*, the least sophisticated of all Shakespeare's comedies, believed to have been performed by the early 1590s. Its stagecraft is uniquely primitive, with few scenes accommodating more than two or three speaking roles, while its dénouement is notoriously inept. Few audiences of any age have been able to stomach the abrupt generosity of one Gentleman, Valentine, in forgiving the amorous treachery of the other, Proteus, by relinquishing his own true love as a supreme gesture of friendship. Again, a woman is being treated as a mere chattel, with no say in her own destiny. And there is no sense at all of place; we might as well be in Bankside as Verona, for all the topographical colours this eventual master of the Italian palette brings to his canvas. He would soon make amends in *Romeo and Juliet*, where the swords of young aristocrats flash in the sun with rather more localised resonance.

In a play about the respective claims of love and friendship, moreover, the most steadfast (and touching) relationship in the entire piece is that between Launce, the rough-hewn prototype of all Shakespearean clowns, and his mangy dog Crab – who all too often, all too easily, steals the show. As recently as 1986, perhaps with a dash of opportunism, the Oxford editors boldly adjudged *The Two Gentlemen of Verona* to be Shakespeare's first play, placing it even before the *Henry VI* cycle, again on stylistic grounds; its dramatic structure being 'comparatively unambitious', and its construction betraying 'an uncertainty of technique suggestive of inexperience', the play could be seen as 'a dramatic laboratory in which Shakespeare first experimented with conventions of romantic comedy which he would later treat with a more subtle complexity'.

The Arden editor claims the same privilege for *The Taming of the Shrew*, while others make a case for *The Comedy of Errors* as Shakespeare's first play. But both show signs of much more experienced stagecraft, and lie naturally with *Love's Labour's Lost* in the great comic burst ahead, after a poetic interlude, in 1593–94. First, he had to produce his own version of the Senecan revenge tragedy so much in vogue at the time – to fulfil his experimentation, in this first full flowering of his youthful talent, with all three of the genres – history, comedy, tragedy – that would shape his entire career and constitute the formal sub-divisions of his posthumously collected works.

Towards the end of his *Henry VI* trilogy, Shakespeare stages the murder of York standing on a molehill with a crown of paper on his head. The famous scene builds to a crescendo of violence so intense that 'horror turns to pity'. The same might be said of *Titus Andronicus*, recorded as 'new' in Henslowe's log when staged at the Rose by Sussex's Men on 20 January 1594. But 'new' need not be taken to mean newly written; if not merely an abbreviation for 'Newington Butts', the south London site of one of his theatres, it could signify newly licensed, or else a revision by the author or simply a new production. When *Titus* was published later that year, the title page asserts that this 'Most Lamentable Roman Tragedy' had been performed by 'the Right Honourable the Earl of Derby, Earl of Pembroke, and Earl of Sussex their Servants'. This latest performance by Sussex's Men at the Rose, therefore, was but the latest in a long line of a popular play dating back several years.

Ben Jonson would suggest as much a quarter of a century later: 'He that will swear *Jeronimo* or *Andronicus* are the best plays yet, shall pass unexcepted at, here, as a man whose judgement shows it is constant, and hath stood still, these five and twenty, or thirty years.' The sour verdict of the Scrivener, in his Induction to *Bartholomew Fair* in 1614, suggests that Jonson is as uncertain about the dating of Shakespeare's early plays as four subsequent centuries of scholars. But *Jeronimo* was an alternative title for Kyd's *Spanish Tragedy*, written at some point between 1585 and 1589; so, even allowing for a rounding-off of dates, Jonson's evidence attests that both Kyd's play and Shakespeare's *Titus Andronicus* were written before 1590.

Did Shakespeare intend his own Grand Guignol version of the revenge tradition as a homage to Kyd and Marlowe, or a grotesque parody? Amid other horrors, two brothers rape Titus' daughter Lavinia on the corpse of her husband, whom they have murdered, then cut out her tongue and sever her hands to prevent her revealing their names. When she traces them in the earth, with a stick clasped between her stumps, Titus kills the brothers, grinds their bones to flour, and cooks them in a pie which he serves to their mother. Only two of the play's central characters survive its dénouement, after which one sentences the other to be buried waist-deep and starved to death.

Titus has always been notoriously hard going for both cast and audiences; if not laughed off the stage, it requires extra paramedics to cope with the number of fainting spectators. 'It's just like a video nasty, isn't it?' suggested one twentieth-century player to the actress playing Lavinia in a BBC television production in the mid-1980s, when there was anguished public debate about the availability of violent films on video. 'It is very, very frightening,' she agreed. 'But somehow we've found . . . that the characters through their suffering grow closer. Titus has committed the most appalling deeds, and it isn't until he's maimed and his daughter's maimed that he learns anything about love.'

To understand *Titus Andronicus* thus, as the editor of the 1995 Arden edition puts it, is 'at once to perceive its proximity to *King Lear*, and to apprehend the difference between a slasher movie and a tragedy'. Tastes change, as Jonathan Bate observes. 'In its willingness to confront violence, often in ways that are simultaneously shocking and playful, our culture resembles that of the Elizabethans . . . Audiences may still be disturbed by the play's representations of bloody revenge, dismemberment, miscegenation, rape and cannibalism, but theatregoers who are also moviegoers will be very familiar with this kind of material.'

At the time, to Shakespeare and Henslowe, *Titus Andronicus* was probably written with the box-office in mind. If so, it proved a huge success; the play was very popular in Shakespeare's lifetime, appearing in three editions between 1594 and 1611. Drawing on Ovid, Seneca (especially his *Thyestes*, in which his sons are served him for dinner by Atreus) and various accounts of Roman history, the novice tragedian makes the endearing mistakes of youth: there was neither panther-hunting nor human sacrifice in ancient Rome, nor indeed the use of holy water at weddings. The play's verse is often lumpen, the structure episodic and the action surreal; but *Titus Andronicus* remains, at worst, the least of Shakespeare's achievements in a new genre he was to make his own, of lasting value as an interim milestone between the revenge tradition and *Hamlet*.

So by 1592 Shakespeare had written at least five, perhaps seven plays – more, if you accept the passionate arguments of Eric Sams, who has made a strong case for the admission to the canon of a play called *Edmund Ironside*. The Stratford man seems more likely to have had a collaborative hand in *Edward III*, also championed by Sams and others, at least some of which is now accepted into the canon by the editors of several of the standard editions of the *Collected Works*.

There is evidence beyond two topical references to the Spanish Armada that Edward III was written and performed as early as 1589, though not published (at the time, anonymously) until 1596. After a hamfisted opening scene, barely worthy of the schoolboy Shakespeare, the first two acts comprise a prolonged and elegant sequence in which the King permits an illicit attempt to seduce the Countess of Salisbury to distract him from urgent military matters in Scotland and France. Thus is established the theme of vows, oaths and their sanctity which sustains the action through three more uneven acts set on the battlefields of France. Tennyson has not been alone in considering the 'Countess of Salisbury section' impressive enough to be the work of Shakespeare, not least because it contains a line familiar from his (perhaps contemporaneous) Sonnets: 'Lilies that fester smell far worse than weeds.' A 1768 edition proclaimed *Edward III* 'a play thought to be writ by Shakespeare'. Subsequent scholars have attributed parts variously to Marlowe, Drayton, Lodge, Peele and Greene. Such collaborations were commonplace at this early stage in the development of Elizabethan drama, leading to resentful charges of plagiarism when Shakespeare's solo virtuosity left his lesser rivals behind.

For now such arguments would be adjourned, as the summer of 1592 brought an outbreak of the plague so severe that London's theatres were summarily closed. To the Church, the theatres themselves were nothing less than the cause of the plague. In the brutal logic of one Puritan preacher at Paul's Cross: 'The cause of plague is sin, if you look to it well; and the cause of sin are plays: therefore the cause of plague are plays.' To the authorities, not unreasonably, any kind of public congregation, such as that attracted by the theatres, was undesirable; given the unsavoury lifestyle of many groundlings, 'infected with sores running on them', theatres were 'perilous for contagion'. As the death-toll grew alarmingly towards the end of 1592, the Privy Council stepped in to suspend 'all manner of concourse and public meetings of the people at plays, bear-baitings, bowlings and other like assemblies' within a seven-mile radius of London – apart, of course, from church services.

For the various troupes of players, deprived of their livelihood, the indefinite closure of London's theatres was disastrous. As most left the capital, forced to tour in *ad hoc* groups, Shakespeare decided he had better things to do. Plays, after all, were ephemeral effusions, rarely revived once the box-office failed, printed only by pirates exploiting the law's failure to protect what was laughably called copyright. Poetry was the vocation of the true writer, and his best hope of immortality. So it was to poetry that he turned his hand during this theatrical interregnum, while his fellows ground their weary, unhappy way around the provincial inn-yard circuit.

By the time the theatres reopened, just as he was enjoying the success of his first major narrative poem, Shakespeare would find his name as a playwright made by the deathbed insult of a tired, jealous rival, a worn-out, drunken wreck of a writer reaching the end of both his tether and his mortal span.

V

THE 'UPSTART CROW'

1592–1594

Capitalising an initial letter, second only to moving a comma as the nicest of niceties among textual emendations, could see 24-year-old Shakespeare on the road with the Queen's Men in 1588.

> I sick withal the help of bath desired
> And thither hied a sad, distempered guest . . .

What can this mean? An out-of-sorts actor-poet in need of a hot bath? Capitalise the 'B' of Bath in Sonnet 153, and you have a sick player – no doubt after some post-performance over-indulgence with his fellows at the local inn – seeking solace in the waters of the West Country spa, already renowned for their medicinal properties. The Queen's Men made a documented visit to Bath in 1588. Was the hungover actor a new recruit, enjoying one of his first forays out of London? Or was he already a three-year veteran of the theatrical circuit?

> Alas, 'tis true I have gone here and there
> And made myself a motley to the view . . .

The bitter-sweet confession in Sonnet 110 has been taken to suggest that Shakespeare joined the Queen's Men earlier than 1587 – that he had gone to London as early as 1585, straight after his wedding to Anne Hathaway, fleeing the wrath of Sir Thomas Lucy over both his deer-poaching and his religion. The 'rude' Stratford boy was poor enough, it seems, to have 'sold cheap what is most dear'; in the next, again early-seeming Sonnet (111), he confirms that Fortune 'did not better for my life provide / Than public means . . .' (i.e., 'subsistence through pleasing the public') '. . . which public manners breeds'.

It has recently been argued that Shakespeare is 'far more likely to have gone to Stratford in 1587 as a Queen's Man than to have joined them there'. His rapid rise within the company 'might well have already put him in a position to propose Stratford as a staging-post, and one where he could surely count on a warm welcome and indeed a favourable fee authorised by his alderman father'. Eric Sams further suggests, rather charmingly, that the broken bench repaired for 16d resulted from overcrowding and payment *pro rata* as the town 'turned out in force to see its native son's success'. This extreme example of the 'early start' school of thought, suggesting that Shakespeare had been at work in London since 1585, relies in part on four words towards the end of a dense, ill-tempered pamphlet published in 1592, which would long since have been forgotten but for another, much more momentous phrase.

In *A Groatsworth of Witte, boughte with a million of Repentance*, an actor at work in the London theatre 'for seven years space' came in for thunderous abuse from the satirist Robert Greene, who accused him *inter alia* of being in love with the sound of his own voice, which had 'terribly thundered' from the stage. The object of Greene's wrath remains unidentified. Could it have been the same actor-turned-writer whom he nicknames 'Shake-scene' earlier in the same document, thus bequeathing posterity its first surviving mention of Shakespeare's presence in London as a playwright?

Of all young Shakespeare's contemporaries in literary London, none was more jealous of his early precocity (or so alert, perhaps, to his natural talent) than Greene, the most bohemian of the university-educated writers. The author of five plays, as well as numerous poems and pamphlets, he was only some four years older than the new, 'unschooled' arrival on the theatrical scene. Even if he had, as he himself implies, been among those to collaborate with Shakespeare on early versions of plays the Stratford man later reworked – with so much more box-office success than the originals they surpassed – that was scant cause for the crude charge of plagiarism, penned with a savage bitterness on his penurious deathbed, which has earned Greene his sour footnote in literary history.

In September 1592, left behind by his actor friends when the plague again drove them out of town, Greene lay dying of the pox (i.e., syphilis) in squalid poverty. In his early thirties, separated from his long-suffering wife Dorothea, he shared his filthy, rat-ridden London hovel with a distraught, nagging mistress, the sister of a disreputable acolyte named Ball, nicknamed 'Cutting' Ball. She had recently borne him an unhappy child to feed, even less happily named Fortunato.

Greene's terminal plight may well have re-entered Shakespeare's mind some six years later, when so vividly evoking the death of Falstaff. His taste for ale and Rhenish was eating up his liver, consuming the few crumbs he could earn by churning out pamphlets on the crime wave then sweeping London. Was it terminal desperation, or a belated fit of piety, which led Greene to abandon his satires for sensational disclosures? All we know for sure is that he was determined to settle some scores before he died.

Greene's last days saw him obsessed with the absent players – those greedy, script-hungry parasites who fastened on his fellow playwrights, gullible scholars all, and bled them dry for all-too-paltry reward. There they were now, far from the horrors of the plague-ridden streets of London, growing fat on provincial profits due to the literary hands that fed them. 'Trust them not,' Greene warned his fellow playwrights – primarily Nashe, Peele and Marlowe. One in particular, who had the nerve to show pretensions as a writer, he singled out for sarcastic denunciation:

> There is an upstart crow, beautified with our feathers, that with his 'Tiger's heart wrapt in a player's hide' supposes he is well able to bombast out a blank verse as the best of you; and being an absolute *Johannes factotum*, is in his own conceit the only Shake-scene in a country.

'Oh that I might entreat your rare wits to be employed in more profitable courses,' the dying writer begged his friends, 'and let those apes imitate your past excellence, and never more acquaint them with your admired inventions.'

The 'upstart crow' was, of course, Shakespeare. His 'tiger's heart wrapt in a player's hide' was a sneering echo of a celebrated line in *The True Tragedy*, alias *3 Henry VI*; after the Battle of Wakefield, the exultant Queen Margaret is denounced by the captured and condemned Duke of York, as she taunts him with a handkerchief dipped in the blood of his slaughtered son: 'O tiger's heart wrapp'd in a woman's hide!'

The awkward word 'beautified' – as in Greene's taunt 'beautified with our feathers' – may have been a deliberate echo of the young Shakespeare's lumpen use of it in *The Two Gentleman of Verona*, whose First Outlaw hails his colleague as 'beautified / With goodly shape'. Shakespeare would eventually take a stylish revenge in *Hamlet*, having Polonius mutter of the prince's love-letter to 'the celestial and my soul's idol, the beautified' Ophelia, 'That's an ill phrase, a vile phrase, "beautified" is a vile phrase.'

At the time the young *arriviste* appears to have contented himself with a complaint to the deceased's printer, Henry Chettle, provoking a prompt and fawning apology that December. Apparently sensing trouble, the publisher of random papers culled from the dead Greene's desk, William Wright, had gone to the unusual lengths of distancing himself from the resulting publication, passing the buck to Chettle when recording it in the Register at Stationers Hall on 20 September 1592 'upon the peril of Henrye Chettle'. Now, after complaints from 'divers of worship', Chettle felt obliged to grovel.

> About three months since died M. Robert Greene, leaving many papers in sundry booksellers' hands, among other his *Groatsworth of Wit*, in which a letter written to divers play-makers, is offensively by one or two of them taken; and because on the dead they cannot be avenged, they wilfully forge in their conceits a living author: and after tossing it to and fro, no remedy, but it must light on me. How I have all the time of my conversing in printing hindered the bitter inveighing against scholars, it hath been very well known; and how in that I dealt I can sufficiently prove. With neither of them that take offence

was I acquainted, and with one of them I care not if I never be: the other, whom at the time I did not so much spare, as wish I had, for that as I have moderated the heat of living writers, and might have used my own discretion (especially in such a case) the author being dead, that I did not, I am as sorry, as if the original fault had been my fault, because myself have seen his demeanour no less civil than he excellent in the quality he professes: besides, divers of worship have reported, his uprightness of dealing, which argues his honesty, and his facetious grace in writing, that approves his art.

Chettle was not so bothered about Greene's aspersions on Marlowe. He did not care, he said, if he never met the man; nor would he, for within six months Marlowe was to meet a premature death (in a violent manner apparently predicted with uncanny prescience by Greene: 'Little knowest thou how in the end thou shalt be visited'). On 30 May 1593, before he had even reached his thirtieth birthday, the immensely gifted playwright who had so influenced Shakespeare was fatally stabbed in the right eye in a Deptford tavern during a brawl which was said to have started over the bill. Killed by his own twelve-penny dagger, Marlowe would be mourned by his friend and admirer in a dark reference in *As You Like It* to 'a great reckoning in a little room'; Shakespeare, it seems, suspected the secret truth that Marlowe had been assassinated as a result of his espionage activities in the Elizabethan secret service.

Whatever Chettle's views on Marlowe, he was clearly rattled by the offence he had caused Shakespeare, on whose behalf people in high places had clearly interceded to powerful effect; having gone to the trouble of making this poet's acquaintance, he now found him as 'upright' and 'honest' a man as he was 'excellent' and 'graceful' a writer.

It may safely be assumed that these 'divers of worship', who had so put the wind up the reckless publisher, included Henry Wriothesley, 3rd Earl of Southampton, who had decided to become Shakespeare's patron. No wonder Greene, Nashe and the rest were quite so exercised about the 'upstart crow'. Just when they were all in need of money, he had wormed his way into the lucrative affections of the man best placed to offer it – the man whose patronage they had all been seeking. Greene and Nashe would both offer dedications to Southampton, but it was Shakespeare with whom the young earl had begun to develop a relationship, both professional and personal, of striking intensity.

At the age of twenty-eight, after at least five years in London, Shakespeare was clearly well established as an actor and playwright, with at least five plays to his name. In the autumn of 1592, as the plague appeared to ebb, his fellow players returned to the capital, where on 22 October Ned Alleyn married Henslowe's stepdaughter, Joan Woodward, thus earning himself a lucrative share in the freehold of the Rose. Much good did it do him that Christmas, when Henslowe again tried in vain to fill the theatre with the seasonal offering *Muly Mulocco*. But January 1593 saw a steady increase in takings with performances of Kyd's *The Spanish Tragedy*, Marlowe's *The Jew of Malta*, the late Greene's *Friar Bacon and Friar Bungay*, the anonymous *The Jealous Comedy* and Shakespeare's *Titus Andronicus* and *Henry VI* cycle.

But the cold winter had bought merely a temporary reprieve from the plague, which saw the theatres closed down again on 2 February – Candlemas Day, the eighth anniversary of the christening of Shakespeare's twin children. They were to remain closed throughout most of 1593, as the disease claimed more than 11,000 lives – at its height, a thousand a week. After a brief winter reopening, they were closed again in February 1594, reopened in April, then again shut down that summer. This proved the longest closure yet, threatening the fragile stability of most troupes, which gradually disintegrated under the pressures of provincial touring. When the plague finally abated, most had to start again from scratch.

Apart from periodic visits to his wife and children in Stratford, presumably for such occasions as the twins' birthday, Shakespeare stayed in London. With the theatres indefinitely closed, he bade his thespian colleagues an open-ended farewell as they headed off to the provinces, while he remained behind with the express intention of making his name as a poet. By doing so, of course, he ran the considerable risk that the plague might cut short a distinctly promising career; having survived it in infancy, however, he was still young enough to be capable of believing that he led a charmed life. Besides, returning to Stratford to ride out the crisis in London and write poems amid the distractions of a noisy, hard-pressed household was not an attractive option. With no theatrical income, he had to cast around for a patron. And now, to the malicious envy of the likes of Greene and Nashe, the country boy seemed to have found one.

Did it help, perhaps, that the handsome young Earl of Southampton – still only nineteen, nine years younger than Shakespeare – also came from a staunchly Catholic family, distantly related to that of the poet's mother? If the family connection were not reason enough for nobleman and poet to meet, they might well have known each other from one of the playhouses, a regular haunt of members of the Inns of Court, where Southampton had been sent after graduating from Cambridge at the age of sixteen. Or they may have been introduced by John Florio, the immigrant Italian scholar who also frequented the theatres while compiling his Anglo-Italian dictionary, *A World of Words* (first published in 1598). Florio was at the time Southampton's secretary, apparently giving the lie to frequent suggestions that Shakespeare himself held this post. But the Italian word-lover and the Warwickshire word-spinner were undoubtedly acquainted; the Italian proverb quoted by Holofernes in *Love's Labour's Lost* suggests that the character is in part an affectionate caricature of the Italian scholar who introduced Shakespeare, with such spectacular effect, to the works of Montaigne.

However they came to meet, Southampton and Shakespeare would swiftly have discovered dangerous matters of mutual concern to discuss in discreet corners. Back in Stratford, William's father was still flouting the religious laws; twice that year, in March and September, John Shakespeare's name appeared among lists of recusants who 'refused obstinately' to attend church 'for fear of process from debt'. At court, meanwhile, the elegant and erudite Southampton may have been a favourite of the Queen, but he was forging political and religious alliances which would eventually land him in trouble.

Southampton's father, a Catholic zealot whose own beliefs had seen him sent to the Tower, had died in 1581, leaving his eight-year-old son and heir a royal ward, entrusted to the guardianship of William

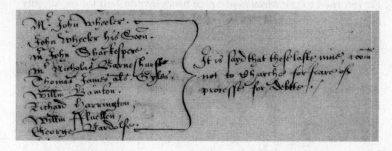

*Certificate by the commissioners for Warwickshire showing
John Shakespeare failing to attend church 'for feare of processe for debtte',
25 September 1592.*

Cecil, Lord Burghley, Lord High Treasurer of England. Over the
previous two years, since coming to London from Cambridge, Southampton had come under pressure from both Burghley and his mother
to marry, with a view to ensuring the succession to his title. Now
his grandfather, too, weighed in – another peer of the realm, Lord
Montacute (these days spelt Montague) of Beaulieu. As he entered
Southampton's circle, Shakespeare composed a cycle of seventeen
Sonnets urging a handsome young man to marry, primarily for the
sake of reproducing his own physical charms. The theme is stressed
from the opening lines of the very first poem:

> From fairest creatures we desire increase,
> That thereby beauty's rose might never die,
> But as the riper should by time decease,
> His tender heir might bear his memory . . .

This seems to suggest that the cash-strapped poet was initially in the
pay of Southampton's mother, enlisting his verse to help pressure her
reluctant son to reproduce. Or was he enjoying a private joke with his
narcissistic new patron? Although they brought a bold new dimension
to the current vogue for love-sonnets, most recently exemplified by
Sir Philip Sidney's much tamer cycle, *Astrophel and Stella*, which
appeared posthumously in 1591, Shakespeare's sonnets were never
intended for publication. But his next poem, about a beautiful young
man resisting the advances of an importunate woman, certainly was.

He returned to the *Metamorphoses* of his beloved Ovid for the subject matter of his first long venture into narrative poetry, prefacing it with an extravagant bow to the man on whose travails it was clearly a stylish *jeu d'esprit*.

'To the Right Honourable Henrie Wriothesley, Earl of Southampton and Baron of Titchfield', reads the dedication on the title-page of *Venus and Adonis*, entered in the Stationers Register on 18 April 1593:

> Right Honourable, I know not how I shall offend in dedicating my unpolished lines to your Lordship, nor how the world will censure me for choosing so strong a prop to support so weak a burden. Only if your Honour seem but pleased, I account myself highly praised, and vow to take advantage of all idle hours, till I have honoured you with some graver labour. But if the first heir of my invention prove deformed, I shall be sorry it had so noble a godfather, and never after ear so barren a land, for fear it will yield me still so bad a harvest. I leave it to your honourable survey, and your Honour to your heart's content, which I wish may always answer your own wish, and the world's hopeful expectation.
>
> > Your Honour's in all duty,
> > William Shakespeare

In this context, 'the first heir of my invention' means the first poem he deemed worthy of publication, or his first published work, not necessarily the first he had written. The volume was printed by Richard Field, Shakespeare's friend and contemporary from Stratford, who had had the good sense to marry the widow of his French master, Thomas Vautrollier, thus inheriting the business. As their professional partnership developed, rumour would have it that Shakespeare himself performed Field's 'office 'twixt his sheets' – no doubt while his old friend was on a trip home to Stratford, cheerfully bearing Shakespeare's greetings to his own family. As yet, however, it seems to have been purely a professional relationship, and a very successful one: *Venus and Adonis* was to enjoy nine reprints in his lifetime – the Elizabethan equivalent of a bestseller – and six more within twenty years of his death.

In the Induction to *The Taming of the Shrew*, written at much

VENVS
AND ADONIS

Vilia miretur vulgus: mihi flauus Apollo
Pocula Castalia plena ministret aqua.

LONDON

Imprinted by Richard Field, and are to be sold at
the signe of the white Greyhound in
Paules Church-yard.

1593.

*The title page of Shakespeare's first published work, the narrative
poem* Venus and Adonis *(1593).*

the same time, Christopher Sly's servants make devious attempts to convince him he is a lord:

> Dost thou love pictures? We will fetch thee straight
> Adonis painted by a running brook,
> And Cytherea all in sedges hid,
> Which seem to move and wanton with her breath,
> Even as the waving sedges play with wind.

In other words, mythological poems with a dash of eroticism would be sure to appeal to the Italianate tastes of the cultivated aristocracy of the day. The six-line stanza employed by Shakespeare in *Venus and Adonis*, drawing primarily on Book X of Ovid's *Metamorphoses*, had recently been used by Thomas Lodge in a poem published in 1589 entitled *Scilla's Metamorphosis*, which Lodge himself declared 'very fit for young courtiers to peruse and coy dames to remember'. Shakespeare is likely to have known Lodge's poem, and Book III of Spenser's *Faerie Queene*, both of which contain references to the myth of Venus and Adonis. It is also evident that he knew and much admired Marlowe's treatment of a similar theme, *Hero and Leander*.

But the young Shakespeare's Adonis seems less the insouciant narcissist of Ovidian myth, playing hard to get out of heedless self-love, than the naïve, unworldly Warwickshire lad the poet himself to some extent still was – more expert in the ways of horses, hares and birds than sultry temptresses pursuing him through hedgerows. In giving such extended direct speech to Venus, he was expanding the conventions of the genre as well as continuing to harp on the reproduction theme of the first seventeen Sonnets. But for all its immaturity, *Venus and Adonis* shows a natural fluency and vivid imagination which foreshadow, as Coleridge noted, such future ventures into similar territory as *A Midsummer Night's Dream*.

If Shakespeare's debut in print was too 'cold' for Hazlitt's taste, two centuries later, it was too hot for some of his contemporaries. Even by 1601, when he was rewriting *Hamlet* for the stage, a character in one of the anonymous Parnassus Plays, *The Return from Parnassus, Part 2*, satirises Shakespeare's early poetic style:

> Fair Venus, queen of beauty and of love,
> Thy red doth stain the blushing of the morn
> Thy snowy neck shameth the milk-white dove

and contends that the Stratford grammar-school boy might match up to his university-educated contemporaries,

> Could but a graver subject him content,
> Without love's foolish, lazy languishment.

The poem's covert references to Roman Catholicism would have pleased Southampton as much as Adonis' indifference to Venus' advances. The next batch of Sonnets, 18–39, probably written at much the same time, reverse the young earl's dilemma with even more eloquent expressions of unrequited love, presumably on behalf of an actual or imaginary suitor. The first, 'Shall I compare thee to a summer's day?', is but the best-known of a transcendent sequence moving on from the 'need-to-breed' theme to some of the most exquisite love lyrics ever written, often introspective about the power of love to inspire verse.

Although still addressed to the 'fair youth', presumably Southampton, these Sonnets should not be taken – as they so often are – to suggest that Shakespeare himself was homosexual. If these private poems are, to some extent, unavoidably about himself – 'with this key,' wrote Wordsworth, 'Shakespeare unlocked his heart' – Sonnet 20 makes the poet's heterosexuality brutally, if reluctantly, clear. With a pun on 'prick' – one of many such references to male and female genitalia throughout the cycle, nothing untoward for an Elizabethan sonneteer – the poet specifically laments the fact that the penis of his effeminate young 'master-mistress' is of no use to him:

> ... And for a woman wert thou first created,
> Till Nature as she wrought thee fell a-doting,
> And by one addition me of thee defeated,
> By adding one thing to my purpose nothing:
> > But since she prick'd thee out for women's pleasure,
> > Mine be thy love, and thy love's use their treasure.

Shakespeare would explore homosexuality elsewhere, as in *The*

Merchant of Venice, where the love of the merchant Antonio for his friend Bassanio is threatened by the wealthy Portia's quest for a husband. Elizabethan 'love' between men anyway functioned at several removes from Plato; figures as lusty as Falstaff or as macho as Coriolanus use the word 'lover' to denote a male friend. But any such ambiguity soon disappears from the Sonnets, where by 40–42 the poet appears to fear that the male object of his admiration has stolen his own female lover. In 78–86 he suspects that his place in the young man's affections has been usurped by another, superior poet – the so-called 'rival poet' of interminable scholarly speculation, perhaps Marlowe, more likely Chapman.

Did Shakespeare fear the loss of Southampton's patronage to his university-educated rival, the only contemporary for whose work he had much respect? If so, the problem appears to have been solved within the year, on the publication of his second long narrative poem. If Shakespeare's first dedication to Southampton had been arch and self-abasing, suggesting a dutiful distance between nobleman and poet, his second implies that they had become rather more intimate:

> The love I dedicate to Your Lordship is without end; whereof this pamphlet, without beginning, is but a superfluous moiety. The warrant I have of your honourable disposition, not the worth of my untutored lines, makes it assured of acceptance. What I have done is yours; what I have to do is yours; being part in all I have, devoted yours. Were my worth greater, my duty would show greater; meantime, as it is, it is bound to your Lordship, to whom I wish long life still lengthened with all happiness.
>
> > Your Lordship's in all duty,
> > William Shakespeare

Entered in the Stationers Register on 9 May 1594, thirteen months after *Venus and Adonis*, The *'Ravyshment' of Lucrece* amounts to the 'graver labour' Shakespeare had promised Southampton. Again printed by Richard Field – but this time for a different publisher, John Harrison, to whom he now also consigned the earlier poem – the quarto bears only the word 'Lucrece' on its title-page, while the running-heads have changed 'Ravyshment' to Rape. As with *Venus and Adonis*, Shakespeare himself seems to have corrected the proofs and taken an interest in every stage of production – a care, it is worth remembering, which he never lavished upon any of his plays.

Even to Shakespeare's contemporaries, *Lucrece* was a huge advance on *Venus and Adonis*. "The younger sort takes much delight in Shakespeare's *Venus and Adonis*,' noted Gabriel Harvey some ten years later, 'but his *Lucrece*, and his *Hamlet, Prince of Denmark* have it in them to please the wiser sort'. The story of Tarquin forcing himself upon a noble matron amounted to yet another allegorical twist on the sexual and marital pressures prevailing in the Southampton household. But this time Shakespeare displays considerably more self-confidence, with an impressive experiment in a much more ambitious genre.

For *Lucrece*'s 1,855 lines (as compared with *Venus and Adonis*' 1,194) he chose to adopt the seven-line rhyme-royal (or 'Troilus') stanza recently used by Samuel Daniel in his poem 'The Complaint of Rosamond' (1592), the fashionable style of the moment for tragic themes such as this lament. Drawing now on Ovid's *Fasti*, as well as Livy's history of Rome, he broke with convention by opening dramatically in the midst of the narrative, preceding it with a prose Argument to set forth the context. Then he returned to convention with a lengthy and finely detailed digression on the siege of Troy, with a focus on Hecuba anticipating her reappearance in *Hamlet*. But this darker, deeper work than *Venus and Adonis* otherwise carries the mature Shakespeare trademark of bold originality, more highly-wrought than its predecessor, reaching beyond the rhetorical extravagance characteristic of Kyd and Marlowe (and reminiscent of the female characters in *Richard III*) to a new and more vivid imagery, exploring such themes as honour, conscience and the nature of evil. As fine a sustained narrative poem as it is, *Lucrece* is the product of an essentially dramatic imagination.

While he was writing *The Rape of Lucrece*, as the plague raged through the streets of London, Shakespeare was probably living in the comfortable *cordon sanitaire* of Southampton House in Holborn, the earl's London home (if not at his country seat at Titchfield, Hampshire). Over these two plague-ridden years he was at work on two, perhaps three more comedies for the stage as well as continuing to pour out sonnets for himself, his patron and their intimate circle.

The last twenty-eight, 127–154, are addressed to a woman, a dark-skinned woman, whose identity has tantalised four centuries of scholars. 'Whoever she was, she enchanted the poet with her beauty and fiery passion, then tormented him with her infidelity,' as one scholar has racily put it. 'But great passion makes for great poetry. He wouldn't have been Shakespeare if he'd stayed quietly at home with Anne Hathaway. In the bed department, she was second best.'

Shakespeare would surely have been amused by the passion aroused among habitually passionless scholars by the identity of his 'Dark Lady'. This same current authority, Jonathan Bate, has recently argued the claims of John Florio's wife, forename unknown, sister of the poet Samuel Daniel. 'You *must* believe in Mrs Florio,' he pleads (paraphrasing Oscar Wilde). 'I almost do myself . . .' To be 'accounted most fair', according to Florio himself, a woman must have 'black eyes, black brows, black hairs'. But we have no idea what Mrs Florio looked like, any more than we do Emilia Lanier, the 'definitive . . . unanswerable' solution of the late A. L. Rowse, self-styled 'leading authority on the age in which Shakespeare lived and wrote', who swatted dissent aside as 'complete rubbish' from 'inferior minds'.

Emilia Lanier, *née* Bassano, was the daughter and wife of Italian musicians at the Queen's court, mistress of her Lord Chamberlain, and memorably described by the astrologer Simon Forman as an 'incuba' – echoing the poet's 'female evil' who

> Tempteth my better angel from my side,
> And would corrupt my saint to be a devil.

In 1610, the year after the Sonnets were eventually published, Emilia appears to have countered with her own poem, *Salve Deus Rex Judaeorum*, prefaced by some stinging remarks about men who defame women: 'Evil-disposed men who – forgetting that they were born of women, nourished of women, and that, if it were not by the means of women, they would be quite extinguished out of the world and a final end of them all – do like vipers deface the wombs wherein they were bred.'

There may seem more than a hint of racism in the assumption that a 'dark lady' must be of continental origin or connections; yet, as Bate himself observes, in Elizabethan love literature 'fairness and darkness have a great deal more to do with social status than with actual hair and eye colour'. So should we be looking further down the social scale? Other suspects have included Lucy Negro, notorious, dark-skinned Clerkenwell prostitute – not to be confused with Lucy Morgan, once one of the Queen's ladies-in-waiting, later a brothel-keeper.

But textual hints appear to support Rowse's insistence that the Dark Lady was 'a well known person . . . of superior social standing to Shakespeare'. This would enhance the claims of Penelope Rich, born Lady Penelope Devereux, sister of the Earl of Essex, and the original 'Stella' of Sidney's own sonnet cycle, *Astrophel and Stella*. Or Mary ('Mall') Fitton, maid of honour to the Queen, impregnated by the Earl of Pembroke, and lusted after by her father's lecherous friend Sir William Knollys, Controller of the Queen's Household, whom the poet supposedly caricatured as Malvolio (as in 'I want Mall').

In the end, as so often, posterity is left groping around in the shadows of Shakespeare, who has left us another enigma as elusive as allusive, to the point where all attempts to solve it can only wind up demeaning the rare poetry from which it springs. Perhaps it is best, with Anthony Burgess, to leave the Dark Lady 'anonymous, even composite', an immortal icon of 'some of the commonest experiences known to men – obsession with a woman's body, revulsion, pain in desertion, resignation at another's treachery', not to mention 'the irresistible lure of the primal darkness that resides in all women, whether white or black'.

Better, even, to think of the Dark Lady in Shakespeare's own fictional terms – as that prototype of Shakespeare's many assertive women, Rosaline in *Love's Labour's Lost*, the 'whitely wanton with a velvet brow', with dark 'pitchballs' for eyes, who has much the same plans for Berowne as had the Dark Lady for the poet of the Sonnets:

> How I would make him fawn, and beg, and seek,
> And wait the season, and observe the times,
> And spend his prodigal wit in bootless rimes . . .

In which case we must also cast Southampton as the King of Navarre, affecting to elevate scholarship over sex, and Shakespeare himself as the eloquent, skirt-chasing Berowne. For the French court setting read Southampton's equally cultured, if playful household, where the study (and production) of literature was constantly interrupted by amorous intrigues. In Rosaline's description of Berowne we can hear Shakespeare savouring an in-joke about himself, the in-house poet, as seen through his own eyes for the amusement of others:

> A merrier man,
> Within the limit of becoming mirth,
> I never spent an hour's talk withal.
> His eye begets occasion for his wit,
> For every object that the one doth catch
> The other turns to a mirth-moving jest,
> Which his fair tongue, conceit's expositor,
> Delivers in such apt and gracious words
> That aged ears play truant at his tales
> And younger hearings are quite ravished,
> So sweet and voluble is his discourse.

Again, what more eloquent description of Shakespeare himself could we have than 'begotten between thought and mirth, a child-god with grave lips and laughing eyes'? Yet this is the poet Swinburne, three hundred years later, also speaking of Berowne.

If this suave, sweet-talking gallant, duly attendant upon a nobleman, is indeed a playful self-portrait, he certainly savours the chance of revenge upon his Dark Lady. 'If thou marry,' Rosaline is told, 'hang me by the neck if horns that year miscarry.' Amid a fusillade of sonnets, Berowne himself bluntly proclaims her 'one that will do the deed / Though Argus were her eunuch and her guard'.

In Sonnet 130, his mistress's eyes are 'nothing like the sun'. In *Love's Labour's Lost*, women's eyes are

> the books, the arts, the academes
> That show, contain and nourish all the world.

But a woman's third eye – the one beyond the pitchballs, that will 'do the deed' – is her vagina. No wonder Dr Johnson thought the play full of 'passages mean, childish and vulgar', some of which 'ought not to be exhibited . . . to a maiden queen', as indeed they eventually were (if in revised form) at Christmas 1597, according to the First Quarto – distinctive, on its publication the following year, as one of the first to name Shakespeare as the author.

If it was originally written at the same time as the Sonnets, and equally full of in-jokes and *double entendres* about the goings-on in Southampton's circle, can it be any coincidence that *Love's Labour's Lost* is the first of only three plays for which Shakespeare plucked the plot, if not from thin air, from no other primary source? The refined literary style and elaborate wordplay of his most heavily-rhymed play amount almost to a homage to Sidney, with distant echoes of Lyly; and its 'open' ending (the longest scene in all Shakespeare) recalls Chaucer's *The Parliament of Fowles*. But the setting and framework sprang – as with his last solo work, *The Tempest* – from a contemporary event, in this case a diplomatic mission to Aquitaine during the recent French civil war, which ended in 1593 with the King of Navarre becoming King Henri IV of France. The names of Berowne and his fellow attendant lords, Dumaine and Longaville, echo those of commanders on opposite sides of the war, the Ducs de Biron, De Mayenn and De Longueville.

Shakespeare gave a different name to his King of Navarre, perhaps because Henri would have become an unsympathetic figure to English audiences – if not to the poet and his patron – upon the King's conversion to Roman Catholicism in July 1593. This covert show of recusant defiance, if such it be, is mirrored in a second sub-text satirising the current antics of those other poets and playwrights who had given him such a mean-spirited reception in London. *Love's Labour's Lost* is also Shakespeare's relatively good-humoured revenge on the 'University Wits', satirising the so-called 'School of Night' with which most of them were then involved.

'O paradox!' exclaims the King (alias Southampton) to Berowne. 'Black is the badge of hell, / The hue of dungeons and the school of night' – a direct (if textually disputed) reference to the secret philosophical society headed by Sir Walter Raleigh, under the patronage of the Earls of Northumberland and Derby, whose supporters included such writers as Marlowe, Chapman and Matthew Roydon as well as eminent European mathematicians, astronomers and other intellectuals including Southampton's sometime secretary Florio. In their scientific atheism, first importing Copernicanism to England, they were opposed by a group led by the Earl of Essex and his follower Southampton, whose adherents included such writers as Nashe and, it would seem, Shakespeare. His involvement, such as it was, amounted less to any philosophical posturing than an eye for satire and, of course, to the main chance.

Southampton was his paymaster. Some gentle ribbing of high-minded, disputatious men also gave him the chance to defend the honour of some well-born ladies close to his patron's heart. In the French princess and her ladies-in-waiting, Shakespeare was gallantly defending the Earl of Essex's sisters – the Ladies Penelope (whom we have already met) and Dorothy Devereux, Countess of Northumberland – against the imputation of the 'School of Night' that female beauty was of no account, a trivial distraction from loftier preoccupations. In this scenario, the *dramatis personae* of *Love's Labour's Lost* become an even more elaborate cypher, with Florio as the pedantic Holofernes and Antonio Perez, a Spanish ally of Essex, as Don Armado. In yet another interpretation, involving yet another academic dispute of the hour, the braggart Armado is a caricature of the scholar Gabriel Harvey, then involved in a public disagreement with Nashe, who becomes Moth – addressed in the play as Juvenal, just as he was by Greene in *Groatsworth*, and thus punning on green as the 'best' of complexions.

The salon sophistication of *Love's Labour's Lost* makes it feel like the beating heart of a corpus of comedies germinating throughout Shakespeare's sojourn with Southampton, written as light relief from the technical complexities of the Sonnets and narrative poems. It is tempting to see his (or his patron's) exasperation with the opposite sex reflected in Petruchio's with Katharina in *The Taming of the Shrew* – even to cite Petruchio's eventual triumph over adversity as evidence that *The Shrew* is the mysteriously missing *Love's Labour's Won*, a title listed among Shakespeare's comedies by his contemporary Francis Meres in 1598 but conspicuous by its absence from the First Folio. Meres does not mention *The Shrew*, whose genesis is further complicated by the existence of a distinctly inferior play called *The Taming of a Shrew*, which saw print in 1594 'as it was sundry times acted by the Right Honourable the Earl of Pembroke his servants';

if a 'memorial reconstruction', for it is too weak to be a pirated text or corrupt quarto of any Shakespearean original, this was the work of actors with very bad memories indeed.

Onstage, in recent years, some of these early comedies have fared less well in their own right – antique, mothballed specimens accorded merely ex-officio reverence – than as pirated libretti for twentieth-century musicals. As *The Comedy of Errors* spawned Rogers and Hart's *The Boys from Syracuse*, so *The Taming of the Shrew* inspired Cole Porter's *Kiss Me Kate*. But even that now seems a quaint period-piece, unacceptable to millennial sensibilities. Shakespeare's play can be performed as a pre-feminist slice of male chauvinist propaganda, or a subtler Elizabethan take on the battle of the sexes; but it is undeniable that women are again demeaned, indeed man-handled, to the point where *The Shrew* has become a difficult work to stage successfully at the turn of the twenty-first century. It is not only feminist critics who have trouble forgiving Shakespeare his political incorrectness, let alone agreeing with one (female) editor that the play has 'come honestly by' its enduring popularity in the theatre: 'Attitudes and turns of phrase that seem archaic, or even brutal, on the printed page, have a way of becoming entirely acceptable as soon as Katharina and Petruchio are actually speaking.'

Twin masters with twin servants belong to an Italian *commedia dell'arte* tradition which flourished in the seventeenth century but stretched back to long before – just as the termagant or shrewish wife had been a staple constituent of stage comedy since Plautus and Terence, via Chaucer to the Mystery Plays, where the nagging Mrs Noah was always causing trouble by refusing to abandon her fellow gossips to board the Ark even as the Flood threatened to overwhelm the earth. Although, as always, a significant advance on its originals, using an age-old theme for a more profound exploration of the respective rights and needs of the sexes, *The Shrew* is closer to farce than the later, mature Shakespeare comedies, as indeed is *The Comedy of Errors*. Both already display masterly stagecraft, a vivid sense of theatre, and a lightness of comic touch; but both seem the product of a less sophisticated, perhaps less battle-scarred mind than *Love's Labour's Lost*. Because of the haze surrounding the dates of their composition – all that can be said with any confidence is that all three had been written by 1594 – each has rivalled the *Henry*

VI trilogy, through the centuries, as candidates for the distinction of being Shakespeare's first solo work for the stage.

The early eighteenth century did not warm to *Love's Labour's Lost*. 'Since it is one of the worst of Shakespeare's plays, nay I think I may say the very worst, I cannot but think it is his first,' wrote the dull-witted Charles Gildon in 1710; more than two centuries later, in 1947, fellow critics such as T. W. Baldwin were still arguing that *Love's Labour's Lost* is Shakespeare's first play. More likely, it was the first to be performed (if not the first to be written) after the reopening of the theatres in 1594. We know that it was staged at court on 26 and 27 December 1594, followed on 28 December by *The Comedy of Errors*.

The Taming of the Shrew was Shakespeare's first play, according to its Arden editor, Brian Morris, on the less than convincing grounds that 'no other play in the canon refers so specifically and extensively to the county of his birth. It may well be that . . . Shakespeare was making dramatic capital out of personal nostalgia, recalling a countryside he had quite recently left.' The Induction's Christopher Sly is a Warwickshire man, to be sure, and there is some home-grown charm in his references to Wilmcote and Burton Heath, but the eponymous play-within-the-play is far more sophisticated than anything in *The Two Gentlemen of Verona*, which seems to issue from a quite different, less experienced actor-writer.

The Oxford editors concur to the extent of placing *The Taming of the Shrew* second in their version of the canon, after *The Two Gentlemen*, but still before *Henry VI*. Arden's Morris goes on to identify points of contact between *The Shrew* and *The Comedy of Errors*, which have 'many features in common'. Others cite overt references to the Spanish Armada to argue that the latter was Shakespeare's first comedy, written soon after the great English naval victory of 1588. In Act III Scene ii, Dromio of Syracuse plays a word-game with his (real) master about his twin's betrothed, Nell the kitchenmaid, who is 'spherical, like a globe; I could find out countries in her'. Spain, for instance, had sent 'whole armadoes of carracks' (galleons) as 'ballast' to the cargo of rubies, carbuncles and sapphires embellishing her nose. As if to prove the play more or less contemporaneous with *Love's Labour's Lost*, the recent French civil war reappears when Dromio is asked:

Where France?
In her forehead, armed and reverted, making war against
    her heir.

Did Shakespeare attend the public execution in October 1588 in
Finsbury Fields of William Hartley, a seminary priest? Some have
surmised as much from an apparent reference in the final act of *The
Comedy of Errors* to the scene of that execution – the precinct of the
dissolved Holywell Priory in Shoreditch, which was set in a 'vale'
between the Curtain and the Theatre:

                    the Duke himself in person
Comes this way to the melancholy vale,
The place of death and sorry execution
Behind the ditches of the abbey here.

The first recorded performance of *The Comedy of Errors* – at 1,777
lines the shortest of all Shakespeare's plays, and yet one of the busiest
– was at Gray's Inn on 28 December 1594. But its many stylistic links
with the narrative poems suggest that it must again have been written
during Shakespeare's retreat from the plague in the Southampton
household – less as a satire on domestic events, like its contemporary
comedies, than a dazzling display of what the house poet could do
with his Roman sources. Drawing on two plays of Plautus, *Menaechmi*
and *Amphitruo*, Shakespeare made life difficult for himself by adding a
second set of twins, and involving a wife rather than a courtesan in
apparent infidelity.

Beneath its Keystone Cops surface, for all the dexterity of its
plotting, *The Comedy of Errors* again sees Shakespeare exploring themes
which would haunt his later work, from witchcraft and sorcery to
the breakdown of social order, and the search for self complicated by
awareness of parallel selves. His resolution of this particular conflict,
with identity surprises too neat (or too absurd) for some tastes, has
been seen as offering more than merely a 'deliverance from moral bondage', specifically 'the re-establishment of responsibility among individuals
in a society in the light of a test undergone, or a penance endured'.

Even at this early stage of his dramatic career, Shakespeare was also developing the notion that, to carry conviction, happy endings must be won from 'a serious confrontation with mortality, violence, and time'. As the twentieth century has seen other disciplines hijack Shakespeare studies for their own ends, American psychoanalysis has even divined in *The Comedy of Errors* the poet's expression of 'an unconscious desire for incest with his mother'.

Be this as it may, the 'Dark Lady' seems to have been but one of several shrewish London women who put Shakespeare through spasms of sexual jealousy so agonising as to wring from him, a decade and more later, graphic portrayals of the 'green-eyed monster' (in each case unwarranted) in *Othello* and *The Winter's Tale*. From the strength of feeling he also devoted to another, closely allied sexual topic, it seems equally likely that during these years away from his wife and children in Stratford the thirty-year-old poet was rewarded for his adventures in London with a bout or two of the clap (gonorrhoea). He was lucky, perhaps, not to contract the pox (syphilis), like Greene, Peele and his godson, Davenant.

> Consumptions sow
> In hollow bones of man, strike their sharp shins,
> And mar men's spurring. Crack the lawyer's voice,
> That he may never more false title plead,
> Nor sound his quillets shrilly. Hoar the flamen,
> That scolds against the quality of flesh
> And not believes himself. Down with the nose,
> Down with it flat; take the bridge quite away
> Of him that, his particular to foresee,
> Smells from the general weal. Make curl'd-pate ruffians bald,
> And let the unscarr'd braggarts of the war
> Derive some pain from you. Plague all,
> That your activity may defeat and quell
> The source of all erection.

Anthony Burgess was not the first to discern, with some fellow-feeling, that this passage from *Timon of Athens* amounts to 'a fair description of some of the symptoms of syphilis'. Lear, too, invokes womankind as 'the source of degradation and disease':

The fitchew nor the soiled horse goes to't
With a more riotous appetite.
Down from the waist they are centaurs,
Though women all above;
But to the girdle do the gods inherit,
Beneath is all the fiends'.

The authentic rage in these outbursts, in so far as it may be attributed to the playwright rather than his characters, still lay some ten or more years ahead. So was Shakespeare still suffering bouts of the clap in his mid-forties, fifteen years after his arrival in London? Did he live a promiscuous life there throughout his two decades and more away from Anne, as seems to be the admission of Sonnet 152: 'in act thy bed-vow broke'? If so, did sex become to him merely 'the expense of spirit in a waste of shame'? There would seem to be some such subtext to Sonnet 129, expressing an early version of his exasperation with the perils concomitant upon sexual pleasure:

All this the world well knows, yet none knows well
To shun the heav'n that leads men to this hell.

At much the same time this was written, in 1594, amid all the sexual antics of the Southampton household, Shakespeare was portrayed as a poet with the clap in yet another anonymous satire at his expense, *Willobie his Avisa*, or *The True Picture of a Modest Maid, and of a Chaste and Constant Wife*, entered in Stationers Register on 3 September. The protagonist Willobie, or 'H.W.', has

. . . a familiar friend W.S. who not long before had tried the courtesy of the like passion, and was now newly recovered of the like infection . . . and in viewing afar off the course of this loving comedy, he determined to see whether it would sort to a happier end for this new actor, than it did for the old player.

In 1598, a few years after the bulk of them were written, Francis Meres would refer in print to Shakespeare's 'sugared sonnets among his private friends'. By then the actor-playwright would have another eight or so dramas to his name – maintaining his career average, over more than two decades, of one and a half to two plays a year. By the following year, 1599, a couple of his Sonnets (138 and 144) would find their way into print, without his prior knowledge or approval, in an anthology entitled *The Passionate Pilgrim*. Not until 1609 would they all be published – again, apparently, without his involvement or consent – by an enterprising printer named Thomas Thorpe, whose ornate dedication to 'Mr W.H.' has bequeathed the Shakespeare industry one of its most celebrated (and quite unnecessary) mysteries (*see* pp. 265–9). For now, as he intended, they were circulated privately in Southampton's circle and beyond – perhaps further, indeed, than Shakespeare would have wished, as the Sonnets returned to haunt the poet and his patron in most unwelcome guise.

The verses prefacing *Willobie his Avisa* include the first printed reference to Shakespeare as a poet (rather than a playwright):

> Though Collatine have dearly bought,
> To high renown, a lasting life,
> And found, that most in vain have sought,
> To have a fair, and constant wife,
>> Yet Tarquin plucked his glistering grape
>> And Shakespeare paints poor Lucrece' rape.

The 'University Wits' were at it again, lambasting the upstart country yokel for daring to pitch his tent on their turf, transplanting the central themes of the Sonnets to their satire while taking passing digs at other works from *Titus Andronicus* to *Venus and Adonis*. But this time his patron was also co-opted into the joke, which he would certainly not have appreciated.

The gist of *Willobie*'s 3,100 plodding iambic pentameters is that a character called H.W. enlists the help of his friend W.S. in seducing an innkeeper's daughter to whom he has taken a passionate fancy. The poem's tongue-in-cheek introduction, though apparently attributed to an unknown Oxford man named Hadrian Dorrell, ascribes the text to 'my very good friend and chamber fellow M. Henry Willobie, a young man, and scholar of very good hope' who 'departed voluntarily to her Majesty's service'. Tireless research has identified a Henry Willobie who was a young scholar at Oxford in 1594, and whose brother's wife's sister was married to the Oxford graduate and Stratford resident Thomas Russell, a friend of Shakespeare's and indeed the overseer and a beneficiary of his will. *Willobie* would go through several further editions in Shakespeare's lifetime – more than one, as it happens, coinciding with pirate publications (or republications, even posthumously) of the Sonnets. Its eponymous protagonist 'H.W.' has been variously identified as the Earls of Essex and Leicester, or a composite of both, given the vicissitudes of their standing with the Queen. Now as at the time, however, it seems perfectly obvious that he could be none other than Henry Wriothesley, Earl of Southampton.

The virtuous Avisa rejects H.W.'s advances in a series of epistles signed either 'Alwaies' or 'Alway the same'. Elizabeth I's personal motto was *semper eadem*. Southampton was also having his difficulties at court; Elizabeth was losing patience with his openly Roman sympathies. This kind of scurrilous, sleazy publicity would have proved not just embarrassing, but dangerous. With the *Willobie* poet (or poets) also indulging in some innuendo about bisexuality, it must suddenly have become a source of acute discomfort to Southampton that his employee W.S., a mere actor-playwright, had so publicly become so close a friend.

Southampton was already living dangerously, by hitching his star to that of the reckless Essex, and underestimating Elizabeth's self-imposed mission as defender of the faith invented by her father. By suggesting that W.S. 'not long before had tried the courtesy of the like passion', the poem also seems to imply that Shakespeare himself was risking displeasure at court, where he would now be known as a regular player, by failing to conceal his own or his patron's papist sympathies. H.W. is referred to not just as 'Henrico' or 'Harry' in the poem, but 'Italo-Hispanienses', drawing attention to his Roman sympathies and the uncomfortable fact that they allied him with that most hated of England's current adversaries, Spain.

To make matters worse, *Willobie* could further be seen as a sustained satire on Southampton's illicit pursuit of the Queen's maid of honour, Elizabeth Vernon, while continuing to reject Lady Elizabeth de Vere, the potential bride for whom his guardian, Lord Burghley, had won royal approval. So Elizabeth would have been far from amused by the suggestion that the earl had, in the course of all this misbehaviour, contracted a venereal disease. Just as 'W.S.' was 'newly recovered of the like infection', according to *Willobie*, so his friend H.W. was 'suddenly infected with the contagion'. There are references to 'the secrecy of his disease', which renders its victim 'weak and feeble'. With the Sonnets doing the rounds in London literary circles, these look like mischievous allusions to a line in 144 – 'till my bad angel fire my good one out' – long taken to mean, in the words of a recent edition, 'until my friend catches a venereal infection from my mistress'.

If both Shakespeare and Southampton had both paid so dearly for their sexual pleasure, who was the guilty female party? Enter, again, the Dark Lady of the Sonnets, variously identified by scholars through the ages as any or all of the above. Whatever the true identity of this Elizabethan *femme fatale*, she appears not just to have put Shakespeare through the miseries of the clap, but to have lost him his patron. Between them, by the look of it, *Willobie* and the Dark Lady proved too much for Southampton, who chose this moment to break off professional – if not yet personal – relations with Shakespeare.

But this poet, like any force of nature, had a lifelong talent for making his own luck. Just as he would have been wondering where next to turn for money, the plague at last abated sufficiently for the theatres to reopen.

VI

THE LORD CHAMBERLAIN'S MAN

1594–1596

As he parted company with one patron, so another returned from the past to his rescue, albeit inadvertently. It was during Shakespeare's time in the service of Southampton that his Lancashire employers of so long ago, the recusant Hesketh family, took an even bolder stand against the heirless Virgin Queen, with disastrous consequences for them but a happier ending for Shakespeare.

The playwright had maintained his Lancashire connections through his professional dealings with the players of the Earl of Derby, otherwise known as Lord Strange's Servants. What began life as a private troupe for occasional in-house entertainments had become one of the handful of leading London-based companies, mirroring Shakespeare's progress from hired hand to leading player, by the time it was inherited by Derby's heir Ferdinando, Lord Strange, on his father's death in September 1593. But now, barely six months after inheriting his father's title, Ferdinando himself was dead at the age of only thirty-five.

Conspiracy theorists continue to doubt the modern view that the new earl died of natural causes on 16 April 1594, preferring to suspect foul play following his betrayal of Richard Hesketh, the recusant son of Lancashire executed for his role in the papist plot to make Derby king. Whatever the truth, Derby's (or Strange's) players were already in some disarray at the time of their patron's death, thanks to the prolonged closure of the London theatres. Back in business, they now regrouped under the patronage of Henry Carey, first Baron Hunsdon, Lord Chamberlain to the Queen, and Her Majesty's closest intimate. With Richard Burbage at its helm, along with his friends Will Shakespeare and Will Kemp, the new troupe proudly took the name of the Lord Chamberlain's Men.

On 8 October 1594 Hunsdon formally requested the Lord Mayor of London to permit his 'new' company of players to return to the stage after their long absence, with a series of performances at the Cross Key inn in Gracious Street. Just as *Willobie* and the Dark Lady saw him estranged from Southampton – if only, as it transpired, briefly – a no doubt relieved Shakespeare found himself back in gainful employment, required to abandon his immortal longings in the shape of narrative poetry to return to the production of a steady stream of new plays. Old enemies were swift to fill the breach, with Nashe opportunistically dedicating *The Unfortunate Traveller* to Southampton: 'A dear lover and cherisher you are, as well as the lovers of poets, as of poets themselves . . .'

An old man with less than two years left to live, Hunsdon had been busy during the closure of the theatres, endearing himself to the travelling players by intervening on their behalf with regional bureaucracies, and (according to gossip emanating from the none-too-reliable Simon Forman) fathering a child by Emilia Bassano. Henslowe's diary records that Hunsdon's company had briefly performed that June at Newington Butts; now, over Christmas, they played twice at court. The accounts of the Treasurer of the Queen's Chamber dated 15 March 1595 cite William Shakespeare as joint payee, with Richard Burbage and William Kempe ('servants to the Lord Chamberlain') for performances before the Queen at her palace at Greenwich on 26 and 27 December 1594. The following night saw them perform *The Comedy of Errors* for the Christmas 'law-revels' at Gray's Inn – an evening of such 'disordered tumult and crowd', by one account, that 'it was ever afterwards called "The Night of Errors"'.

Shakespeare had now joined the theatrical company with which he would remain, throughout its changing guises, for the rest of his acting and writing life. Just as his income from Southampton dried up, it was the actor-playwright's good fortune that Burbage co-opted him and Kemp on to the management team of what soon became the pre-eminent stage troupe of the day, eventually to pass under royal patronage. The house dramatist and bit-part actor was also shrewd enough to become a shareholder in the Lord Chamberlain's Men.

Account of payment by the Treasurer of the Chamber to William Kemp[e], William Shakespeare and Richard Burbage for performing plays.

How did he afford it? There were rumours of a thousand-pound loan from Southampton, perhaps by way of a pay-off – the equivalent of half a million pounds today, an amount so huge as to seem unlikely to some, the product of the fertile imagination of Shakespeare's godson Sir William Davenant, for all Falstaff's intriguing admission in *2 Henry IV*: 'Master Shallow, I owe you a thousand pound.' As actor, *ad hoc* director, shareholder and above all 'ordinary poet' of the company, thirty-year-old William Shakespeare was already, in the words of one twentieth-century authority, 'the most complete man of the theatre of his time'. Few in any age, observes another, have served the stage so variously: 'not Racine or Ibsen or Shaw; only Molière, besides Shakespeare, among playwrights of world stature'. Not all metropolitan men of such stature remain mindful of the obligations of friendship; for the second marriage in 1594 of a Stratford friend, the schoolmaster Alexander Aspinall, he appears to have sewn his autograph into a 'posy' penned to accompany the groom's gift to his bride of a pair of gloves – perhaps from the Shakespeare glove emporium – just as this is 'perhaps the most trivial verse ever ascribed to a great poet':

The gift is small,
The will is all:
Alexander Aspinall.

Newly installed in lodgings in St Helen's, Bishopsgate, as close to the stews of Clerkenwell as the theatres of Shoreditch, Shakespeare would now have less time (and, perhaps, energy) to expend his spirit in a waste of shame. As his reconstituted colleagues gratefully staged the plays he had written during their exile from London, with the clown Kemp relishing the role of Costard in *Love's Labour's Lost*, the prolific house dramatist was already required to get to work on more.

Soon he would exorcise the demons of the clap with a tragically chaste love story, *Romeo and Juliet*. But first there was a non-fictional marriage to celebrate, which called for a stylish *pièce d'occasion*. Shakespeare may well have begun work on *A Midsummer Night's Dream* while still a member of Southampton's household. As resident poet, he would have been required to come up with an entertainment to mark the marriage of the earl's mother, the dowager countess Mary, to the Treasurer of the Queen's Chamber, Sir Thomas Heneage, on 2 May 1594.

> No doubt they rose up early to observe
> The rite of May

observes Theseus, Duke of Athens, in a courteous nod to the wedding-date, though the bride may not have been quite so flattered by his reference in the play's opening speech to

> a dowager,
> Long withering out a young man's revenue.

Much scholarly energy has been wasted in argument over any number of aristocratic weddings for which the play could have been written, dating between 1590 and 1600, when these and other Southampton references are so clear to behold. Had the noble earl occasionally complained to Shakespeare about his mother's longevity, postponing his inheritance of his birthright? As a financial beneficiary of both, the poet would have taken as close an interest as he did in those maternal pressures on the young earl to marry – already explored in the Sonnets and *Love's Labour's Lost*, now reflected in the chaotic pairings of *A Midsummer Night's Dream*, all caused (as in *Romeo and Juliet*) by a parent's attempt to foist an unwelcome match on an offspring in love elsewhere.

The unusually high number of female parts in the play, no doubt stretching the abilities of the available boy actors, may have constituted some gentle ribbing by the poet of his patron. If they had fallen out over the Dark Lady, or indeed any other female of the night, the rift between them was – as subsequent events would prove – short-lived, and more professional than personal, allowing Shakespeare to gratify his noble friend with some risqué jokes at his unwitting mother's expense.

By the mid-seventeenth century, when Samuel Pepys called it 'the silliest stuff that ever I heard . . . the most insipid, ridiculous play that ever I saw in my life', *A Midsummer Night's Dream* had been bastardised by Restoration sensibilities into a mere libretto for Purcell's opera, *The Fairy Queen*. As twentieth-century directors still hijack it to show off the extent of their own lurid imaginations, the play has always suffered from its apparently surface-thin veneer as a matter of mere 'gossamer and moonshine', a 'charming trifle to be eked out theatrically by as much music and spectacle as possible'. But amid the play's masque-like atmospherics – its fantastical confusions, its stock, one-dimensional characters, its witty relish of the supernatural – lurks a highly sexed allegory of marriage, as the priggish Theseus and Hippolyta turn into their racier subconscious selves, Oberon and Titania, en route to a truer, happier union. Their adventures also offer some of the poet's most beautiful flights of fancy, not least his haunting depiction of the poetic imagination, as good a job description as any poet ever offered his patron:

> The poet's eye, in a fine frenzy rolling,
> Doth glance from heaven to earth, from earth to heaven,
> And as imagination bodies forth
> The form of things unknown, the poet's pen
> Turns them to shapes, and gives to aery nothing
> A local habitation and a name.

Given the state of play between Shakespeare and Southampton by the time of the play's performance, this emerges more as the kind of reference the poet might hope his patron would give prospective future employers. In which vein he prefaced it, in the gently

self-mocking manner of Berowne, by permitting the presiding Duke
some wry satire:

> The lunatic, the lover and the poet
> Are of imagination all compact . . .

Another private joke? If Shakespeare meant Southampton to see himself in Theseus, these were topical themes close to both their hearts,
merging all the interrelated causes of their reluctant estrangement.
Shakespeare may have left the Southampton household by the time
the play was performed, but there are clues between the lines that their
personal relations remained intact. In more than merely its allusive
playfulness, *A Midsummer Night's Dream* has other umbilical links with
Love's Labour's Lost, also written as a private entertainment for the
Southampton household. Both plays are too dense in texture, too rich
in literary allusions, to have been written for the groundlings. As *jeux
d'esprit* for cultivated audiences on celebratory occasions, these are the
only two of Shakespeare's plays before *The Tempest* without a specific
primary source – beyond, in this case, the palpable influence of Ovid's
Metamorphoses (source of Pyramus and Thisbe) and the borrowing of
names and other details from Chaucer, North's Plutarch and Apuleius'
The Golden Ass, the apparent and obvious source, available in a 1566
translation by William Adlington, of Bottom's transformation.

Few of Shakespeare's other works so clearly demonstrate the pro-
digious breadth of his reading. The character of Puck, or Robin
Goodfellow, is derived from a then recent work by Reginald Scot,
The Discoverie of Witchcraft (1584), while rising above its mockery of
the supernatural as mere superstition. There are passing references to
Spenser's *Shepheardes Calendar* (1579), Bartholomew Young's translation
of Jorge de Monetmayor's *Diana Enamorada* (already used in *The Two
Gentlemen of Verona*), two recent romances in *Euphues* (1578) and *Euphues
and His England* (1580), debts to playwrights from Seneca to Lyly.

As always with Shakespeare, close comparison of the text and its
sources show his pillaging to be the prelude to layer upon layer of
miraculous enlargement, as often mundane details are reworked into
far more subtle, ingenious effects in a far grander scheme. Far from
being the plagiarism so crudely alleged by the envious Greene, this is
the hallmark of the genius drily noted by T. S. Eliot: 'Immature poets
imitate; mature poets steal . . .'

> Bad poets deface what they take, and good poets make it into
> something better, or at least something different. The good
> poet welds his theft into a whole of feeling which is unique,
> utterly different from that from which it is torn ... A good
> poet will usually borrow from authors remote in time, or alien
> in language, or diverse in interest. Chaucer borrowed from
> Seneca; Shakespeare and Webster from Montaigne ...

One measure of the gulf between Shakespeare and his sources is that some of the wilfully clumsy lines given to Bottom as Pyramus, in the burlesque of the play-within-the-play, were written as straightforward speeches in such obscure originals as Preston's *Cambises* (1561) and *Appius and Virginia* (1564). As Bottom-turned-Pyramus, Burbage would have relished the chance to parody Ned Alleyn's acting style, all swagger and bombast, with no hint or subtlety or humour – a mode of performance and indeed writing which Shakespeare and the Lord Chamberlain's Men were swiftly consigning to a bygone age.

From a complex celebration of marriage in the abstract to a brutally realistic portrayal of young love thwarted: *Romeo and Juliet*, Shakespeare's first new work for the Lord Chamberlain's Men to stage in the reopened theatres, his most candid nod yet to the box-office, and nothing less than the first romantic tragedy ever to be written. Tracing its lineage back through all the great love pairings of literature, from Ovid's Pyramus and Thisbe to Chaucer's Troilus and Criseyde, the play may again have bowed to Southampton in portraying the disastrous consequences of misplaced parental pressure in the matter of marriage; and it was again Southampton's circle which provided the context the poet needed to make his reworking of an age-old theme peculiarly Shakespearean.

The poet's last months in the earl's employ saw the climax of a dispute between friends and neighbours of Southampton's, the Danvers and the Longs, which dated as far back as the Wars of the Roses. Like all such feuds, it ebbed and flowed in intensity, reaching an especially violent climax early in 1594. The brothers Sir Charles and Sir Henry Danvers, friends and coevals of Southampton, were the sons of Sir John Danvers, a wealthy magistrate who held sway near the earl's country seat at Titchfield, Hampshire. The touch-paper was lit when Sir John committed one of Sir Walter Long's servants to jail for robbery, and Sir Walter intervened to rescue his employee from his old enemy's sentence. At the next assizes Danvers had Long himself committed to the Fleet jail, adding insult to injury by jailing another of his servants for murder while he was incarcerated, and so powerless to intervene. Upon his release Long and his brother Henry incited their staff to provoke disputes and brawls with their counterparts in the Danvers household. Soon one of Danvers's staff had been killed and another seriously wounded.

Henry Long meanwhile wrote a series of insulting letters to Danvers's son Charles, calling him all sorts of abusive names and threatening to 'whip his bare arse with a rod' (or words to that effect). That did it. Sir Charles and his brother rounded up some followers and surprised the Long brothers as they dined at the inn at nearby Cosham; Charles Danvers hit Henry Long twice with a truncheon, at which Long drew his sword and struck Danvers a grievous blow. Then Danvers' brother Sir Henry drew his pistol and fired at Henry Long, who fell dead. The Danvers brothers beat a hasty retreat and sought refuge with their friend Southampton – who, although in the midst of his twenty-first birthday celebrations, managed to help them evade arrest by arranging their flight to France.

So Shakespeare had vivid, first-hand experience of such mindless vendettas, prone to fatal consequences, as that symbolised by the Italian families of Montecchi and Capelletti (names to be found in Dante's *Purgatorio*), recently retold in Corte's history of Verona, published in 1594, and perhaps lent him by Florio. Unabashed about setting a second play in Verona, this time his first tragedy to be placed in his own century, Shakespeare may also have read a novelised account by Masucio Salernitano, published in 1576, itself a reworking of a 1530 version by Luigi da Porta, in which the feud between their families wreaks the doom of the young lovers Romeo and Giulietta.

He was already familiar with Arthur Brooke's 1562 poem 'The Tragicall Historye of Romeus and Iuilet', an English amalgam of two centuries of European folkloric tradition, on which he had drawn for *The Two Gentlemen of Verona*. In a prefatory Address to the Reader, the dull, moralistic Brooke stressed the role of fate in the downfall of his lovers; and it is this same Senecan element of chance in Shakespeare's adaptation, depriving his star-crossed lovers of responsibility for their own doom, which makes this poignant fable a mere staging-post en route to the greater tragedies. Again he drew on ancient traditions; a sleeping potion as a method of avoiding an unwelcome marriage dates back, for instance, as far as Xenophon's *Ephesiaca* in the fourth century AD. But by focusing so intently on a single source, as he was to do with a number of his mature plays, both comedies and tragedies, Shakespeare displays his readiness to transform a conventional morality by finding but a 'limited' place in his play for 'what had struck the author of his source as being the whole moral bearing of the story'.

In *A Midsummer Night's Dream* he had recently warned that passionate young love can lead as easily to tragedy as to comedy. 'So quick bright things come to confusion' he has Lysander tell Hermia at the very outset; although the play's three love stories all have happy endings, the fates of Pyramus and Thisbe echo those of Romeo and Juliet – perhaps written simultaneously, as Mercutio's virtuoso Queen Mab speech would seem to suggest. Now, in the Prologue to his 'most excellent and lamentable tragedy', Shakespeare follows Aristotelian conventions in giving the Chorus a sonnet specifically spelling out the doom awaiting the protagonists. So there is only one possible end to the subsequent 'two hours' traffic of our stage', as if wild and reckless young love were inevitably doomed. We cannot, of course, know to what extent Shakespeare was drawing on personal experience; but the beautiful simplicity with which the lovers speak at their moments of uncomplicated happiness, as opposed to the ornate rhetorical flourishes which fuel so much else in the play, irresistibly raises the notion – as if there had, after all, been an Anne Whateley or some such true love lost to his obligations to Anne Hathaway.

Romeo and Juliet has been deemed an even earlier work on the evidence of the Nurse's reference in Act I to an earthquake – 'and since that time it is eleven years'. Scholars citing the English earthquake of 1580 have thus placed the play as early as 1591, in defiance of all stylistic evidence; one might as logically cite the Verona earthquake of 1570, which would have Shakespeare writing this masterpiece of stagecraft by the age of seventeen. Mercifully, there was another English earthquake in 1584, placing the play at about its generally accepted date, 1595 – if, that is, we feel obliged to take the Nurse literally. Again, one can almost hear

Shakespeare's ghost cackling at the literal-mindedness of scholars – and, yes, biographers – clutching at the few straws he mischievously cast their way.

The first performances of *Romeo and Juliet* – which would have given Shakespeare the satisfaction (perhaps in the tiny role of the apothecary?), of seeing the groundlings moved to emotions far beyond anything ever before known in the theatre – came hard on the heels of another, more localised triumph.

A Midsummer Night's Dream would have carried even more resonance when revived by the Lord Chamberlain's Men, at the Queen's command, at another aristocratic wedding some seven months after that of Southampton's mother. On 26 January 1595 the Earl of Derby married Lady Elizabeth de Vere, the bride rejected by Southampton, to the dismay of his guardian, Lord Burghley, who had fined the recalcitrant earl the astonishing sum of £5,000. One can only hope that Burghley repaid his ward in full upon his granddaughter's marriage to an equally eligible nobleman.

To Shakespeare, who was privy to all this, it must have seemed that Her Majesty's Lord High Treasurer had been evaluating Lady Elizabeth's frustrated affections as if they were merely 'precious metal'. Coinciding as it did with a notorious scandal at court, resulting in a trial and execution which had all London agog, the episode emboldened him to venture into uncharted territory, writing Burbage his most powerful part yet as he followed one fable with another – a parable exploring his lifelong ambivalence about money, with especial reference to the usury which had so haunted his stricken father.

It was supposedly their practice of usury – lending money for interest, forbidden to Christians under canon if not secular law – which had caused Edward I to expel all Jewish residents from English soil in 1290. Three hundred years later, the ban was still technically in force; but a thin line of a few hundred Jews were to be found living in Elizabethan London, tolerated on the assumption that they disguised their religion, and kept any moneylending well out of sight of the law. By professing Christianity, some even managed to achieve acceptance in the highest circles, notably a Portuguese-born Jewish doctor named Roderigo Lopez, who rose to become physician to the Earl of Leicester, and then to the Queen herself.

Once a useful spy for Sir Francis Walsingham's secret service, Lopez was dangerously slow to transfer his loyalties to the Earl of Essex after Walsingham's death in 1590. On a trumped-up accusation of political intrigue, supposedly on behalf of a pretender to the Portuguese throne then exiled in London, Essex accused the Queen's doctor of trying to poison her. There were scant grounds for the charge, based on evidence invented by Essex and supposedly extracted by torture, but Lopez was tried for treason in February 1594 and executed at Tyburn on 7 June – castrated, hung, cut down while still alive, disembowelled and quartered in front of a baying crowd that might just have included an inquisitive (if appalled) Shakespeare, whose friend and former patron, Southampton, was one of Essex's most devoted followers.

Hitherto dormant in Elizabethan England, anti-Jewish sentiment was inflamed by the Lopez case, largely at Essex's orchestration. It was in the ambitious earl's interests to lend notoriety to the scandal he had sponsored, to which end he encouraged revivals of Marlowe's *The Jew of Malta* (1589), performed on no fewer than fifteen occasions during the period of the Jewish doctor's trial and execution. Sensing a box-office opportunity, Shakespeare too soon set about writing a 'play of the hour', *The Merchant of Venice*, in which there even appears to be a direct reference to the Lopez case as Gratiano harangues Shylock:

> Thy currish spirit
> Govern'd a wolf, who hang'd for human slaughter,
> Even from the gallows did his fell soul fleet,
> And whilst thou layest in thy unhallowed dam,
> Infus'd itself in thee . . .

As if a punning translation of his name were not enough, the word 'Wolf' is capitalized (significantly, unless it was a compositor's error) in the quarto. Drawing on Marlowe's *The Jew of Malta*, and the fourteenth-century Italian story *Il Pecorone* (The Simpleton), Shakespeare's scheme also incorporated two folk tales of ancient provenance. The legend of a brutal creditor who tries in vain to extract a pound of flesh in payment of a debt, widespread in Europe by the early Middle Ages, came originally from the East, specifically India and Persia; that of a lover who wins his lady by solving the riddle of a choice of caskets, quite as universal before its use by Boccacio and Gower in the fourteenth century, was available to Shakespeare via the mediaeval *Gesta Romanorum*, translated into English in 1577.

The first story of the fourth day in Ser Giovanni's prose collection *Il Pecorone*, written late in the fourteenth century and printed in Milan in 1558, concerns a loan from a Jew to a Venetian merchant named Ansaldo, for his 'godson' Giannetto to seek his fortune overseas. The terms of their bond stipulate that the Jew can extract a pound of the merchant's flesh, from whatever part of the body he may choose, if the debt be not repaid by the due date. Unknown to Ansaldo, Giannetto sets off to woo the 'Lady of Belmonte'; not succeeding until his third attempt, he forgets all about the bond, and rushes back to Venice to find the Jew demanding his forfeit. Unknown to her husband, the lady follows him to Venice disguised as a male lawyer; she argues that the bond does not allow the Jew to shed one drop of the merchant's blood, nor exact more or less than precisely a pound of flesh. When the Jew tears up his bond, the lawyer refuses payment, but asks for the ring given to Giannetto by his new wife. On Giannetto's return to Belmont with Ansaldo, his wife is angry that he has lost the ring, accusing him of giving it to a Venetian mistress. Only after furious argument is all finally revealed, allowing the story an uncomplicatedly happy ending.

There is no record of any English translation of *Il Pecorone* available to Shakespeare, though there may of course have been one, since lost; but he would have known another recent play deriving from it, *The Jew*, also now lost, but described in 1579 by Stephen Gosson as treating of 'the greediness of worldly choosers, and bloody minds of usurers'. For all his copious borrowing of plot from *Il Pecorone* and its derivatives – the Jew, the pound of flesh, the caskets, the ring, the name of Belmont – Shakespeare's treatment of the tale is again a profound advance on his sources, contrasting Bassanio's protracted wooing of Portia with that of Nerissa by Gratiano and Jessica by Lorenzo.

If Shakespeare's primary debt was to *The Jew of Malta*, it is a typical advance to differentiate his Shylock so utterly from Marlowe's Barabas – a caricature of a ruthless Machiavel, whose indiscriminate slaughter for no more than financial gain takes in an entire nunnery. Where Marlowe merely reflected stereotypical Elizabethan attitudes to Jews, seen in the popular imagination almost as 'mythical beasts: strange, evil beings who had once crucified Christ and might be expected to persevere in anti-Christian activities', Shakespeare painted a more profound portrait of racism and religious prejudices reeking of contemporary resonance for every subsequent era, not least our own.

Partly through centuries of sensitivity to charges of anti-Semitism, partly because the role is one of those Shakespearean wonders which has offered such opportunities to actors down the centuries, the character of Shylock himself has since loomed too large in responses to *The Merchant of Venice*. He appears, after all, in only five of the play's twenty scenes, speaking only 360 lines of verse or prose sentences. It is almost as if Shakespeare wrote the part of Shylock too well, more powerfully than even he himself realised, creating nor merely a show-stealing part for an actor, but what has been called the first of Shakespeare's 'internalised' hero-villains, in contrast with such 'externalised' forerunners as Aaron the Moor and Richard III.

In so far as *The Merchant of Venice* is a comedy – in the designated Shakespearean sense of the word, dealing with romance, marriages and idealised worlds elsewhere, in this case Belmont – it really revolves around the eponymous merchant, Antonio, whose affection for his 'bosom lover' Bassanio is evident (if not explicit) in his sense of melancholy at the play's opening: 'In sooth, I know not why I am so sad . . .' By proceeding to fret about the fortunes of his argosy, the fulcrum of the Shylock sub-plot, Antonio discreetly avoids revealing the true source of his gloom: Bassanio's romantic pursuit of a woman, Portia, fabled for her wealth and beauty. The merchant's resignation about death, when faced with it in the shape of Shylock's bond, flows from the loss of his Bassanio to this same woman – the very one, as it happens, who saves his life disguised as a man. And the eventual safe return of Antonio's argosy, in a numinous last act notorious for its trite tying-up of loose ends, only reinforces the fact that Shakespeare never intended Shylock to be the lodestar of the play. He does not appear in this last act; and we miss him, as the playwright artfully rounds off his theme of three contrasting marriages – with the eponymous merchant's wealth restored to him, as unexpectedly as his life, by way of consolation for his resigned surrender of Bassanio to Portia.

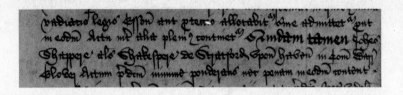

Exchequer information and proceedings against John Shakespeare for usury, 1570.

There is no doubt that Shakespeare's father, and probably the poet himself, developed a sideline as a money-lender, despite stern Tudor laws. Among documents only recently discovered are Exchequer transactions adding to John Shakespeare's track-record in usury, officially deemed 'a vice most odious and detestable'. In 1570 John 'Shappere alias Shakespeare' of 'Stratford upon Haven' was fined forty shillings for charging £20 interest on an £80 loan to one John Musshem of Walton D'Eiville. Shakespeare's father had been reported to the authorities by one of their most persistent informants, James Langrake of Whittlebury, Northamptonshire, who would name him again, more than once, for illegal transactions in wool. Whatever angst these public accusations and court proceedings caused Shakespeare's father seems to have made a lasting impression on his schoolboy son. For all his own practice of arranging loans, a distaste for the phenomenon of money, and all the trouble it can engender, would haunt much of his subsequent work, reaching a crescendo in *Timon of Athens*.

The summer of 1595 saw food riots on the streets of London. Eggs flew and butter smeared the pavements in protest at sudden price increases. A poor harvest had coincided with an outbreak of cattle disease, and the market traders were quick to capitalise. Martial law was proclaimed, rioters summarily executed on Tower Hill, and the theatres – potential hotbeds of seditious assembly – closed down for two months.

There are those who think the capitalist in Shakespeare saw him seize the moment, like many Londoners with sufficient funds, to cash in on the misfortune of others by buying grain cheap and selling it dear. Whatever his feelings about the evils wrought by money, the poet was never averse to accumulating it. This time the metaphors could wait – a dozen years, as it transpired, before surfacing as the fable of the belly told a restive crowd in Coriolanus' Rome. For now, there were other political developments to occupy his mind, challenge his powers of survival in smart society, and of course feed his work.

Since the Lopez affair, Essex had been out of favour at court. Shakespeare himself may have found much to deplore in his and Southampton's glee at the Portuguese Jew's unjust downfall; more important, to the career prospects of these noblemen, Elizabeth herself had been unamused by their hounding of her 'little ape'. In vain had even the monarch, reluctant to believe the evidence against Lopez, attempted to intervene in the legal process; now her only solace was to shun Essex, once her conspicuous favourite. The royal heart hardened all the more when Elizabeth saw his name as the dedicatee of a book whose title was calculated to fill her with foreboding: *A Conference About the Next Succession to the Crown of England*. As a second Spanish armada gathered, at a time when her leading admirals Drake and Hawkins were far distant on a voyage from which they would not return, the Catholic enemy appeared ready to take advantage of the Queen's continuing failure to name an heir. In truth she already had the Protestant King James VI of Scotland in mind, and was embarked on a long correspondence to test his mettle; but she kept her own counsel in the matter, lest Catholic assassins took it into their own impetuous hands.

Was it Shakespeare himself who chose this moment to return to historical drama, specifically a 'prequel' to his *Henry VI–Richard III* cycle, showing the origins of the primal curse on the House of Bolingbroke: the deposition and murder of Richard II by his cousin, Henry IV? Or was it at the suggestion of his friend Southampton, on a hint from Essex, that he decided to tackle the touchy theme of a nation labouring under weak leadership, so weak as to justify the intervention of a heroic usurper? There were lessons still for the Tudors to learn from the origins of the Wars of the Roses, and Shakespeare set out to dramatise them in his portrayal of Richard II. The deposition scene itself, tactfully omitted when the play was published two years later, and again when it was twice republished during Elizabeth's lifetime, would predictably return to cause trouble to all concerned. In the meantime, Shakespeare went to some pains to distance his subject-matter from too much topical relevance.

The historical Richard II, son of the Black Prince and last of the Angevins, was a weak, unjust and extravagant ruler. He was only fourteen when the Peasants' Revolt was put down with great severity, but it was his later attempt to abandon parliamentary government which proved his rapid undoing. Drawing on Holinshed's *Chronicles* (first published in 1577, revised and enlarged in 1587) and John Foxe's *Book of Martyrs* (1563), Shakespeare lent the King an introspective moral ambiguity which flattered him, rendering him quite distinct from the flamboyance of his hunchbacked successor, last of the Lancastrian line.

In intensely lyrical verse, Shakespeare embodies the old order in the nostalgic patriotism of John of Gaunt, whose imperious warnings the King ignores, and whose properties he confiscates after his death, inflaming his exiled son Henry Bolingbroke to return to England in search of justice. As the balance of power shifts, so do the audience's sympathies, with Richard eloquently lamenting the loss of his throne, and achieving a degree of self-knowledge in a fine soliloquy before his murder in jail at the hands of Piers Exton. Richard dies insisting, significantly to Shakespeare's audience, that he was still the rightful monarch:

> Not all the water in the rough, rude sea
> Can wash the balm off from an anointed king . . .

Henry denies reponsibility for Richard's death, but takes himself off on a guilt-ridden pilgrimage to the Holy Land, sowing the seeds of the Wars of the Roses with an inevitability echoing the scale and power of Aeschylus' *Oresteia*.

In Richard's ornate wordplay, sudden mood-swings and regal tantrums, Shakespeare created another virtuoso role for Burbage. In John of Gaunt's famous deathbed speech – 'This precious stone set in a silver sea . . . This blessed plot, this earth, this realm, this England' – he gave the groundlings the jingoistic morale boost they craved at a time of apparent danger from Spain. Rarely does it seem clearer that these were far from being the poet's own sentiments; qualified, anyway, by his lament for a lost England, fallen on hard times, Gaunt's patriotic zeal prepares the way for the dramatist's cynicism when he came to chronicle subsequent events. As the Lord Chamberlain's Men staged four performances for the Queen at the end of 1595, the *Henry IV–V* trilogy was already taking shape in Shakespeare's mind.

First, he would reach further back in English history, and indeed his own stage career, to hand his colleagues more topical box-office fare by reworking one of the hardy annuals of the Queen's Men, *The Troublesome Reign of King John*. With Calais fallen to the papist Spaniards, France exulting in the discomfiture of the English, and a fleet despatched to Cadiz under the joint command of a rehabilitated Essex and the Lord Admiral, Lord Charles Howard, the punters were in a mood to hear the French roundly scorned and the Pope put in his place. The relish with which he demeans the papal emissary, Cardinal Pandulph, suggests that Shakespeare was by now abandoning the last vestiges of any religious belief, orthodox or otherwise; in the condemnation of organised religion implicit in *King John*, a greater work of poetry than of drama, can be traced the beginnings of the poet's increasingly nihilistic progress through *Troilus and Cressida* to the great tragedies.

But they still lay ten years off. And that summer of *King John*, that hot August of 1596, Shakespeare of the waning faith had reason enough finally to forswear his Catholic God and rail against the cruelly arbitrary injustices of human life.

VII

'MY ABSENT CHILD'

1596–1599

If ever, throughout Shakespeare's twenty-five years in London, we can assume that he returned home to Stratford on a specific date, it would have been 11 August 1596 – to bury his son Hamnet, dead at the age of eleven.

We do not know what killed the poet's only male child – dead from 'fever or blood-poisoning or a fall from a tree or the bite of a mad dog'? – but we can begin to measure the impact on his father from the mourning strains which suddenly infuse a leaden historical drama with some of his most affecting verse. Laments Queen Constance, believing her own young son Arthur to have died:

> Grief fills the room up of my absent child,
> Lies in his bed, walks up and down with me,
> Puts on his pretty looks, repeats his words,
> Remembers me of all his gracious parts,
> Stuffs out his vacant garments with his form.

'I have heard you say,' she continues, 'That we shall see and know our friends in heaven: If that be true, I shall see my boy again.'

Shakespeare was only thirty-two, but his wife Anne was already forty, past the age to consider bearing him more children. Beyond the personal grief which now becomes a recurring strain in his work, through *Hamlet* to *The Winter's Tale*, Shakespeare had been robbed of a direct line of descent. That he cared about this seems evident from the fact that he had only recently reapplied, perhaps to please his father as much as to gratify his own *amour propre*, for the coat of arms denied John Shakespeare back in 1569. William's brothers Gilbert, Richard and Edmund were now thirty, twenty-two and sixteen respectively; but all four of them would be dead, with no surviving male issue, within fifteen years of their father. There was now no Fleance to stretch the Shakespeare line to the crack of doom. Now it would die just twenty years later with its most famous son.

Hamnet Shakespeare buried, 11 August 1596.

That personal grief outweighed any such dynastic ambitions is evident from the sudden change which overcomes Shakespeare's work-in-progress. Earlier that summer, he had been filling *King John* with the patriotic strains still ringing in his head from *Richard II*, echoing the national mood:

> Come the three corners of the world in arms
> And we shall shock them. Nought shall make us rue,
> If England to itself do rest but true.

Now enters a more personal note, lifting his history to quite another poetic plane, floating on a cloud of personal grief:

> I'll go with thee
> And find th' inheritance of this poor child,
> His little kingdom of a forced grave.

''Tis strange that death should sing,' says the play's Prince Henry, articulating the poet's own sense of the change incongruously overtaking his moralistic history lesson. It was as if, in the ensuing lines, the dead Hamnet was now playing cygnet to his father's grieving swan.

> 'Tis strange that death should sing.
> I am the cygnet to this pale faint swan
> Who chants a doleful hymn to his own death,
> And from the organ-pipe of frailty sings
> His soul and body to their lasting rest.

A fatalistic mood redolent of Greek tragedy, still lingering from his work on the Plantagenets, begins to suffuse the play, pre-echoing the bleak and bloody nihilism of *Macbeth*:

> There is no sure foundation set on blood,
> No certain life achiev'd by others' death.

Like *Richard II*, *King John* is written entirely in verse. But Shakespeare deviates even further from the historical facts – entirely omitting, for instance, the signing of Magna Carta – by rendering John all but a spectator in his own drama. A far more central role is given to Richard Cœur-de-lion's illegitimate son, Philip Falconbridge, the Bastard, precursor of such dark Shakespearean figures as Jaques and Thersites, Edmund, Apemantus and Caliban.

It is the Bastard's famous speech on 'commodity' which points up the play's central irony; best qualified to be king, but disbarred by the accident of his birth, he can divine the futility of the usurper John's attempt to secure his throne with a dynastic marriage between his niece and the French dauphin. As a bid to staunch vain bloodshed, it could only lead to more. At the emotional heart of the play is John's nephew, Prince Arthur, whose stronger claim to the throne renders him the poignant victim of plot and counter-plot, and the poet's lyrical template for his own lost son.

But it is again the Bastard who has the timely last word, as John's murder reunites his nobles in allegiance to his son Henry III, drawing a moral to bring the audience back to its own times:

> This England never did, nor never shall,

Lie at the proud foot of a conqueror
But when it first did help to wound itself.

As befits a born poet, Shakespeare would grieve for his son throughout his remaining work. The shade of young Hamnet would stalk his father's lines for many a play to come. At the time, ironically, this worst year of Shakespeare's life coincided with a sudden upswing in his worldly fortunes; as his wealth increased to the point where he could consider buying a substantial property, the College of Arms deigned to grant his family the coat of arms denied his father nearly thirty years earlier. Despite the irony that he had no son to continue the line, William Shakespeare could now command the respect due a gentleman quite as much as his proud father John. The formal grant of arms on 20 October 1596 spelt out the details of the new family crest:

> Gold, on a Bend sables, a spear of the first steeled argent. And for his crest or cognizance a falcon his wings displayed argent standing on a wreath of his colors; supporting a spear gold steeled as aforesaid set upon a helmet with mantels and tassels as hath been accustomed and doth more plainly appear depicted on this margent: Signifying hereby and by the authority of my office aforesaid ratifying that it shall be lawful for the said John Shakespeare, gentleman, and for his children, issues and posterity (at all times and places convenient) to bear and make demonstration of the same blazon or achievement on their shields, targets, escutcheons, coats of arms, pennons, guidons, seals, rings, edifices, buildings, utensils, liveries, tombs or monuments or otherwise for all warlike facts or civil use or exercises, according to the Law of Arms, and customs that to gentlemen belongeth without let or interruption of any other person or persons for use or bearing the same.

The Shakespeare family's somewhat half-hearted new motto seemed almost to acknowledge its surprise at the success of this second application: *Non Sanz Droict,* 'not without right' (later satirised by Ben Jonson as 'not without mustard'). Amid the heraldic pomp,

the crest touchingly united the Shakespeare bearings with those of
the Arden family, athwart a divided shield, in a symbolic closeness the
poet had already used in Helena's bond with Hermia in *A Midsummer
Night's Dream*:

> Like to a double cherry, seeming parted,
> But yet an union in partition,
> Two lovely berries moulded on one stem:
> So, with two seeming bodies but one heart,
> Two of the first, like coats in heraldry,
> Due but to one and crowned with one crest.

With his father approaching seventy, a great age for the day,
Shakespeare touchingly sought to exorcise John's fall from civic
grace by more than merely a grant of arms and the status of
gentleman. Now his loyal son, deprived of his own, saw to it
that the Shakespeares could be regarded as Stratford's ex-officio
first family, owners of the finest residence in town – a fit setting,
in due course, for his own retirement.

Since the mid-1590s Shakespeare had been a householder in London,
in the St Helen's parish of Bishopsgate ward, as we know from the
inclusion of his name among seventy-three property tax defaulters listed
by the Exchequer Office in November 1597 and October 1598. As
family dramas saw him journeying to and from Stratford with unusual
frequency, he also took a fancy to the idea of buying New Place, the
biggest house in Stratford, built in the 1490s by that same Clopton who
had become Lord Mayor of London, giving his name to the bridge
across the Avon where all journeys to the capital commenced.

New Place was sold to the newly genteel actor-playwright by
William Underhill, son of a prosperous lawyer-landowner who had

*Indenture by the London tax commissioners showing William
Shakespeare as a defaulter, 1 October 1598.*

restored the property from the state of 'great ruine and decay' in which he himself had purchased it thirty years earlier. With its sixty-foot frontage, ten rooms, two gardens, two orchards and two barns, this 'grete house' was a bargain at £60 – too much so, perhaps, in the view of Underhill's son, who poisoned his father two months later, for which he was duly hanged in Warwick.

It is tempting to suggest that drama seemed to follow Shakespeare around. But he was more concerned with the interminable complexities of the transaction, conducted under the bizarre property laws of the day. Although the purchase legally dated from May 1597, the records of Stratford's Chapel Street ward show the opportunist Shakespeare already storing corn and malt in the barns of New Place three months earlier, in February. The poet's family, in other words, was already in possession, if not in occupation. But the perverse laws of conveyance then required the purchaser to sue the vendor for wrongfully denying him possession; the compensation negotiated was, in effect, the purchase price – technically known as 'the foot of the fine', or the third (and lowest) section of the indenture (or contract), torn off as proof of authenticity. Within a few years, Shakespeare would have Hamlet mock these legal absurdities, when moved by the skull before Yorick's to speculate:

> This fellow might be in's time a great buyer of land, with his statutes, his recognizances, his fines, his double vouchers, his recoveries. Is this the fine of his fines and the recovery of his recoveries, to have his fine pate full of fine dirt? Will his vouchers vouch him no more of his purchases, and double ones too, than the length and breadth of a pair of indentures? The very conveyances of his lands will scarcely lie in this box; and must th' inheritor himself have no more, ha?

Leaving Anne and his daughters at last installed in a home of their own – and a handsome one at that, just around the corner from his parents in Henley Street – Shakespeare returned to London to find the backdrop of his professional life fast changing. The Queen had appointed a new Lord Chamberlain – another Lord Hunsdon, happily enough, son of the late patron of Shakespeare's troupe of players – while the fortunes of his other friend and former patron,

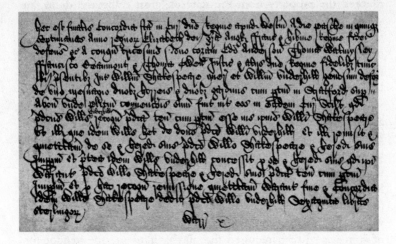

*Foot of Fine recording Shakespeare's purchase of New Place, Stratford,
in 1597.*

Southampton, were fluctuating dangerously with those of the Earl
of Essex.

The previous August, the same month as Hamnet Shakespeare's
death, Essex had returned in triumph from the fall of Cadiz –
heartening revenge, to public opinion, for the loss of Calais. But
Southampton was not, for once, at the ambitious earl's side as he
rode in triumph through the streets of London. The Queen had upset
him by keeping him back from the expedition, suspicious about his
flirtation with her lady-in-waiting, Elizabeth Vernon. Before long,
she would be proved right when Elizabeth became pregnant by
Southampton. Like his poet-friend, the earl did the honourable
thing by Mistress Vernon, marrying her in a secret ceremony in
Paris. On their return, the Queen signalled her extreme displeasure
by clapping them both in jail.

Shakespeare had his own distractions during this difficult period,
with the arrival on the theatrical scene of a rival talent in the shape
of Ben Jonson, eight years his junior, yet far more gifted than any
literary opposition he had yet encountered. Like Shakespeare, Jonson
had not enjoyed the benefits of a university education; thanks to the
kindness of a friend of his father, who died before he was born,
he had received a good enough classical grounding at Westminster

School to feel able to question Shakespeare's. But his stepfather then apprenticed him in his own trade, bricklaying, which Jonson escaped only by enlisting to fight in the Low Countries. On his return he became a lowly actor, playing Kyd's Hieronimo for second-rate touring companies, before joining Pembroke's Men as a writer.

Shunning Shakespeare's penchant for ambitious historical epics, sprawling over time and space, Jonson largely limited his horizons to the traditional unities of time and place, specialising in satirical characters based on the various 'humours' – blood, phlegm, choler, bile – then believed to be the varying constituents of human personality. Not for Jonson the pre-Freudian insights into the human soul which characterised Shakespeare's work; his was a narrower vision of human nature, expressed in broad, full-frontal satire, fearlessly braving the wrath of the authorities. In 1597, while Shakespeare worked on his protracted history cycle, Jonson teamed up with his old rival Nashe to produce a satire entitled *The Isle of Dogs*, which the City fathers considered slanderous and seditious. The Lord Mayor himself was sufficiently exercised to order not just the closure but the demolition of the playhouses, specifically naming the Theatre and the Curtain. Nashe fled town, but Jonson was thrown in jail, where he languished all summer, sustained by £4 advanced by Henslowe for signing on with the Admiral's Men. Whatever enforced company he encountered in the Marshalsea, Jonson had more to fear from his fellow-actors, who blamed him bitterly for endangering all their livelihoods.

By the autumn, with Shakespeare back in the capital, civic wrath had cooled. Not merely had no steps been taken to demolish the theatres; by early October they were reopened, and Jonson released. Before long, no doubt over many an ale-stained evening, he and Shakespeare had become friends. On the one hand, Jonson was an unlikely convert to Catholicism (until 1610, when he drank off the entire Communion chalice to mark his return to the Anglican church); on the other he had killed a man, for which his thumb was branded with a T for Tyburn. But what was that, in these unruly times, to Shakespeare? Besides, it had been in a fair fight over a theatrical disagreement; and here was a rival whose work the Stratford man could admire, for it was Shakespeare who brought

Jonson over to the Lord Chamberlain's company. The following year they gave the first performances of Jonson's *Every Man in His Humour*, with Shakespeare himself in the role of the elder Kno'well; when Jonson published his *Collected Works* in 1616, the year of Shakespeare's death, he accorded his friend pride of place among the 'principal comedians' in the cast list on the title page.

It was typical of Shakespeare's 'humanity and good nature', in Rowe's words, that he lent a helping hand to a rival then 'altogether unknown to the world'. After the *Isle of Dogs* fiasco, with Alleyn and Henslowe muttering about disloyalty and betrayal, Jonson was pushing his luck by offering his next satire to London's leading troupe of players.

> The persons into whose hands it was put, after having turn'd it carelessly and superciliously over, were just upon returning it to him with an ill-natured answer, that it would be of no service to their company, when Shakespeare luckily cast his eye upon it, and found something so well in it as to engage him first to read it through, and afterwards to recommend Mr Jonson and his writings to the public.

Ever after, Rowe continues, the two writers were 'professed friends, though I don't know whether the other ever made him an equal return of gentleness and sincerity'. Longer hindsight knows better. Shakespeare and Jonson show every sign of having remained firm friends until Shakespeare's death, after which Jonson did him due credit in a series of verse tributes, notably that adorning the frontispiece to the First Folio of the collected plays, published in 1623.

In *Richard II*, chronologically the first part of the mightiest history cycle ever written for the stage, Shakespeare had gone to some pains – often distorting the historical facts in Holinshed and lesser sources such as Daniel's *Civil Wars* – to reassert the prevailing belief that the English monarch was chosen by God. He or she was not on the throne by virtue of talent, prestige or prowess, but as 'God's substitute, His deputy anointed in His right'. As Elizabeth continued to resist increasing demands to name an heir, and therefore to face potential threats from Catholic usurpers, the playwright's obsession with comparatively recent English history was understandable. Amid the uneasy peace of the late 1590s, it seemed timely to reassert the received wisdom that usurpers would come to no good, even if fate took a few generations to catch up with them.

It had taken him three plays to cover the long, tortuous reign of Henry VI, one to capture the short, brutish one of Richard III. All this time, it seems, he had longed to square the circle by returning to the roots of all that evil, prefacing a two-part panorama of the usurper Henry Bolingbroke with his seizure of Richard II's throne, and following it with the short but glorious reign of his blameless son Henry V. Even on the eve of Agincourt, however, he has the great warrior-king acknowledge the retribution inevitably awaiting his father's offence sixteen years earlier in deposing – and then assassinating – a divinely-chosen monarch:

> Not today, O Lord!
> O not today, think not upon the fault
> My father made in compassing the crown!

Henry's prayers would be answered, and the price of his father's sins not extracted at Agincourt, nor indeed during the seven further years of his reign. But the closing Chorus does not shrink from a reminder that Henry died young, and his son's protector

> lost France and made his England bleed;
> Which oft our stage hath shown . . .

Shakespeare had already chronicled England's subsequent decline into civil war, the logical consequence of Henry Bolingbroke's original sin in 1399. Not until Richard III's death at Bosworth would Henry's crime finally be expiated, and the natural order restored.

With the completion of this mighty cycle – eight plays covering five reigns from 1377 to 1485 – Shakespeare sought to demonstrate the consequences of interfering with the divine order not merely as they affected the principal players, but also the hapless subjects whose lives are disrupted, often ended by decades of disorder and civil strife. Never more than in the two parts of *Henry IV* did he so vividly depict the suffering of the common man as the pawn of warring power-brokers. If Henry himself can never, like Macbeth, live to enjoy the throne he played so foully for – 'Uneasy lies the head that wears a crown' – so his offence affects the rest of the nation, which pays an equally heavy price.

As the plays oscillate between the court and its subjects, from the field to the inn, Shakespeare's humour breaks through for the first time in his history plays. In the process he created one of his most-loved roles, second only to Hamlet among characters in whom his readers see reflections of themselves. Sir John Falstaff was originally called Sir John Oldcastle, a name he revived from a play dating back to his days with the Queen's Men, *The Famous Victories of Henry V*. But recent history contained a real Sir John Oldcastle, a Lollard martyr hanged and burned in St Giles's Fields in 1417, during Henry V's reign, for denouncing the Pope as the Antichrist. This Oldcastle was also Lord Cobham, a title still worn with pride by his lineal descendant William Brooke, a Privy Councillor and Lord Chamberlain from August 1596 until his death on 5 March 1597.

It looks rather as if the papist Shakespeare deliberately caricatured the Protestant martyr Oldcastle as a roistering, cowardly, ale-quaffing rogue. There would also have been some topical satisfaction in such a joke: Brooke's son and heir Henry, a brother-in-law of Sir Robert Cecil and intimate of Sir Walter Raleigh, was an enemy of the Essex–Southampton circle who still retained Shakespeare's affectionate sympathy. It does seem unlikely that the poet simply underestimated the trouble his careless choice of name would cause, as is the pervading modern view. The powerful Lord Cobham lodged protests in high places, including the office of the Master of the Revels. Whatever threats were made – frustratingly, again, we have no specifics – Shakespeare felt obliged to change the name to that of the cowardly character already glimpsed in the first scene of his *1 Henry VI*:

> Here had the conquest fully been seal'd up,
> If Sir John Falstaff had not play'd the coward.

He, being in the vanguard plac'd behind,
With purpose to relieve and follow them,
Cowardly fled, not having struck one stroke.
Hence grew the general wrack and massacre ...

For the same reason, we must assume, he changed the names of the renegade knight's associates Harvey and Russell to Peto and Bardolph. But traces of Oldcastle still remain. In only the second scene of Part 1, the first time we meet Falstaff, Hal affectionately calls him 'my old lad of the castle'. Early in Part 2, a speech-prefix survives as '*Old*' rather than '*Fal*'. For safety's sake, 'our humble author' appended an epilogue (trailing *Henry V*) with a specific disavowal: 'Falstaff shall die of a sweat ... for Oldcastle died [a] martyr, and this is not the man.'

The inquest on this mysterious episode, still unresolved today, remained heated for half a century. The wily Henslowe tried to capitalise on his rivals' discomfiture by commissioning a play extolling Oldcastle's virtues; Michael Drayton, Shakespeare's fellow Warwickshireman, teamed up with the poets Anthony Munday, Robert Wilson and Richard Hathway to crash out the sourly-titled *The True and Honourable History of the life of Sir John Oldcastle, the good Lord Cobham*. To little effect. As soon as 1604 a Jesuit named Robert Persons, writing under the pseudonym of Nicholas Dolman, was chronicling Sir John Oldcastle as 'a ruffian-knight as all England knoweth, and commonly brought in by comedians on their stages'. In 1611 the historian John Speed retorted that Persons/Dolman 'hath made Oldcastle a ruffian, a robber and a rebel, and his authority, taken from the stage-players, is more befitting the pen of his slanderous report, than the credit of the judicious, being only grounded from the papist and the poet, of like conscience for lies, the one ever feigning, the other ever falsifying the truth'. By 1655 the church historian Thomas Fuller was summing up:

Stage-poets have themselves been very bold with, and others very merry at, the memory of Sir John Oldcastle, whom they have fancied a boon companion, a jovial roister, and yet a coward to boot, contrary to the credit of all chronicles, owning him a martial man of merit. The best is, Sir John

> Falstaff hath relieved the memory of Sir John Oldcastle, and
> of late is substituted buffoon in his place, but it matters as little
> what petulant poets, as what malicious papists have written
> against him.

So Shakespeare was a 'petulant' poet, and a 'papist' one, to demean
the memory of this Protestant martyr. But the episode became
celebrated enough for the name of Oldcastle, despite his substitution
of Falstaff, to stick. Seven years later, in his posthumously published
Worthies of England, Fuller was still muttering: 'Now as I am glad that
Sir John Oldcastle is put out, so I am sorry that Sir John Falstaff is put
in.' So, evidently, are the editors of the current Oxford edition, who
have deleted the name of Falstaff and restored the name of Oldcastle
to their text of the two parts of *Henry IV*, arguing merely that 'there
is reason to believe that even after 1596 the name "Oldcastle" was
sometimes used on the stage'.

Elizabeth I must have been aware of the controversy; indeed,
according to Rowe, it was the Queen herself who 'was pleas'd
to command' Shakespeare to 'alter' the name. Nonetheless, she
was sufficiently enamoured of the character of the indomitable old
knight to commission a sequel. Elizabeth was 'so well pleased with
the admirable character of Falstaff', according to a tradition begun
in 1705 by Charles Gildon, the minor writer satirised by Pope in
The Dunciad, 'that she commanded [Shakespeare] to continue it for
one play more, and to show him in love'. We have the word of
the serious-minded and responsible playwright John Dennis that *The
Merry Wives of Windsor* was written in ten days, two weeks at most,
which suggests that Shakespeare was none too pleased to be royally
diverted from his second historical tetralogy.

Nor did he make, by his standards, much effort. His least funny
comedy was indeed a rush job, as much to pay tribute to his
company's patron as to gratify the Queen's desire to see 'Falstaff
in love' (which, in fact, we *don't* see). Elizabeth, ever fonder of
Hunsdon, had now made him a Knight of the Order of the Garter,
whose annual feast was held in the Whitehall Palace on St George's
Day, 23 April 1597. Both monarch and Lord Chamberlain would
have been delighted by Shakespeare's courteous references to the
Garter knights – their stalls in the chapel at Windsor, their crests,

even their motto, *Honi soit qui mal y pense* – at the end of his little entertainment, repeated that summer to mark Hunsdon's formal installation at Windsor. Once again, Shakespeare seems to have pleased his monarch. The title page of the 1602 quarto specifies that *The Merry Wives* had oft been acted 'before Her Majesty'.

But the expansive character of Falstaff was demeaned by mere pantomime lechery. Without his brilliant wit, his sparkling repartee, his literary allusions, he was a pale shadow of the multi-faceted obstacle Shakespeare had deliberately placed in Hal's path to his father's throne. If Falstaff's creator had any doubts about killing him off before proceeding to *Henry V*, and the climax of his mighty history cycle, *Merry Wives* must have staunched them. To burnish his portrait of prodigal-son-turned-glorious-king, and to gratify the groundlings' vision of *Henry V*, Falstaff had to go.

The second part of *King Henry IV* may be less Sir John's play than the first, climaxing in his crushing rejection by the new king – 'I know thee not, old man' – but he is absent altogether from *Henry V*. The character had served his purpose. Yet even as the playwright moves on to less complex themes, vindicating the new Henry's rejection of his past, he diverts to pay him due homage with a noble death, in touching reported speech from his would-have-been wife, Mistress Quickly.

If the Queen was sitting up to Shakespeare, so was the theatre-going public. The second quartos of *Richard II* and *Richard III*, both published in 1598, marked the first time his name appeared on the title page as the author of any of his works, which had by now been appearing in print – in wholly random fashion, without his involvement or consent – for four years.

Titus Andronicus and *The First Part of the Contention betwixt the two famous houses of York and Lancaster* had appeared anonymously as long before as 1594, entered in the Stationers Register on 6 February and 12 March respectively. The same year saw the appearance of *The Taming of a Shrew* (a very different play from *The Taming of the Shrew*, never published in his lifetime). *The True Tragedy of Richard, Duke of York* (the 'bad quarto' of *3 Henry VI*) followed in 1595, with versions of *Romeo and Juliet*, *Richard II* and *Richard III* surfacing in 1597. So popular did they prove that the two Richards were swiftly reissued, now bearing the author's name, followed within another year by a 'newly corrected, augmented and annotated' (but still very flawed) version of *Romeo and Juliet*.

So by 1598 at least eight of Shakespeare's plays had appeared in print (nine if you count *A Shrew*). That he had written more we know from another of that year's publications, *Palladis Tamia*, or *Wit's Treasury*, by Francis Meres, that tireless chronicler of the literary and theatrical scene. Sub-titled *The Second Part of Wit's Commonwealth*, Meres's huge catalogue of literary witticisms, running to seven hundred octavo pages, showers praise on Shakespeare for 'mightily' enriching the English language, investing it in 'rare ornaments and resplendent habiliments'. In the process, he bequeathed the Shakespeare industry an invaluable (if partial) list of the plays he had written by 1598:

> As Plautus and Seneca are accounted the best for comedy and tragedy among the Latins, so Shakespeare among the English is the most excellent in both kinds for the stage. For comedy, witness his Gentlemen of Verona, his Errors, his Love Labour's Lost, his Love Labour's Won, his Midsummer Night's Dream, and his Merchant of Venice; for tragedy, his Richard the 2., Richard the 3., Henry the 4., King John, Titus Andronicus and his Romeo and Juliet.

Gratified, no doubt, to be hailed as a 'mellifluous and honey-tongued' poet of 'fine filed' phrases, 'the most passionate among us to bewail and bemoan the perplexities of love', Shakespeare was nevertheless unable to resist a wry smile at his champion's pedantry. If he knew Meres – a fellow countryman much his own age, who seems to boast of himself being one of the 'private friends' privy to those 'sugared sonnets' – he would soon offer, by way of thanks, a gentle parody of his prose style in Polonius' welcome to Hamlet's player-friends:

> The best actors in the world, either for tragedy, comedy, history, pastoral, pastorical-comical, historical-pastoral, tragical-historical, tragical-comical-historical-pastoral, scene individable or poem unlimited. Seneca cannot be too heavy, nor Plautus

too light. For the law of writ and the liberty, these are the
only men.

Meres, like Polonius, was smarter than he seemed – the first, in
print, to sense Shakespeare's true greatness, not hesitating to elevate
this actor-writer above his contemporaries, hoisting him on to a par
with the immortals. But success and fame, then as now, come at
a price. Neighbours will always be neighbours. With this sudden
renown following hard upon the heels of his *nouveau riche* purchase
of New Place, it is scant surprise that the only surviving item of
correspondence addressed to Shakespeare is a begging letter, written
at this time by a Stratford friend visiting London.

'You shall friend me much in helping me out of all the debts I
owe in London,' wrote Richard Quiney from the Bell inn in Carter
Lane, near St Paul's, on 25 October 1598, asking his 'loving good
friend and countryman Mr Wm. Shackespere' for a loan of £30.

*Richard Quiney's letter to Shakespeare asking for a loan of £30,
20 October 1598. The paper on which it was written was folded and
sealed and the address written on the back.*

Quiney was privy to his brother Adrian's hint to another mutual friend, Abraham Sturley, that Shakespeare might be 'willing to disburse some money' on land, property or other investments. According to his brother, Sturley told Quiney, 'our countryman Mr Shaksper . . . thinketh it a very fit pattern to move him to deal in the matter of our tithes'.

But there is no evidence that Shakespeare invested any money with Sturley, nor that he advanced Quiney that £30. The letter remained unsent; it was found among Quiney's papers after his death four years later. By then he was bailiff of Stratford again, mortally wounded while intervening in a drunken brawl involving some unsavoury associates of Shakespeare's brother Gilbert; in 1598 he was a city elder in London on Stratford business, petitioning the Privy Council for larger subventions to a town hard-hit by bad weather and two ruinous fires. It seems curious that he tried to sting Shakespeare on his own behalf, rather than Stratford's. Why was the letter not sent? Did Quiney think better of it? Or did he call on Shakespeare later that day at his lodgings, thinking a personal plea might prove more effective? Some biographers have assumed the poet generous (or crafty) enough to have made the loan, perhaps charging interest; others, citing Shakespeare's tight-fistedness, assert with equal confidence that Quiney returned home empty-handed. We have no way of knowing.

But one long-term worry may have made Shakespeare more than usually reluctant to part with cash just now, may indeed have had him feeling less prosperous than all other outward signs suggest. Throughout these last two years the Lord Chamberlain's Men had maintained their status as London's leading players against the dispiriting backdrop of an intractable legal crisis which threatened their very future. On 13 April 1597 James Burbage's twenty-one-year lease on the Theatre, the company's home since its foundation, had expired. For months he had been trying to negotiate a new lease with his absentee landlord, the recalcitrant Giles Alleyn, who was driving a very hard bargain. Burbage grew as desperate as his in-house players. He agreed to a vastly increased rent, from £14 to £24, and was even in the process of conceding Alleyn's eventual right to take possession of the building itself. Under the existing agreement Burbage owned the structure, Alleyn the land on which it stood.

Now Alleyn inserted a clause asserting his right, after only five more years' tenancy, to convert the Theatre 'to some better use'. Burbage's patience snapped.

Urgently he cast around for an alternative site, which he found in the disused refectory of the dissolved Blackfriars monastery, on the north bank of the Thames. Already it had been used by Lyly for genteel performances by his company of boy actors; but he too had fallen out with his landlord, leaving the run-down structure as the occasional venue for exhibitions of fencing. As part of a former monastery, though within the city walls, the building came under the aegis of the Crown, not the Lord Mayor and Council of London – a useful bonus which saw Burbage pledge the huge sum of £600 for the purchase of the structure, plus several hundred more for its conversion into a playhouse.

Just when the future again looked bright – with the intriguing promise for Shakespeare of writing plays for a wholly-covered, indoor playhouse – the well-heeled residents of Blackfriars thwarted Burbage, with a successful protest to the Privy Council at the prospect of all the low life a playhouse would attract into their fashionable back yard. In the midst of it all, in January 1597, bowed down by months of pressure and anxiety, James Burbage dropped dead.

Robbed of their impresario, whose sons Richard and Cuthbert desperately reopened negotiations with Alleyn, the Lord Chamberlain's Men struggled on for eighteen months – through the expiry of the lease in April, through the temporary closure of the theatres during the *Isle of Dogs* furore, and into the next autumn, by which time the unscrupulous landlord knew he had them at his mercy. The company's only other available venue, the Curtain, was too run-down to offer the players a secure long-term future. With Richard Burbage playing the charmer, and poor Cuthbert quite miscast as the hard-headed businessman, the landlord slyly held out hope, while again making impossible demands – all of which Cuthbert felt obliged to concede, until Alleyn refused to accept the Burbage brothers as their own financial guarantors. Now he threatened to 'pull down' the Theatre, and 'to convert the wood and timber thereof to some better use'. In the meantime he retreated to his country seat, leaving his defeated tenants to lick their wounds.

But something in the phrasing of this terrible threat, beyond the snide implications of the words 'some better use', gave the Burbages and their colleagues a wonderfully bright idea.

They may not have been able to hold on to the site of the Theatre, but at least they still owned the structure. On 28 December 1598 a conspiratorial group led by the Burbage brothers – and including, we can but hope, Shakespeare – convened in Shoreditch at dusk, with only the hours of darkness to carry out an ingenious plan. The widow Burbage is said to have 'looked on approvingly' as her sons supervised the dismantling of their late father's beloved Theatre.

The brothers' new financial partner William Smith was there, too, to see a team of a dozen workmen led by their chief carpenter, Peter Street, tenderly take the building down, plank by plank. The Burbages had found a new site across the river, in St Saviour's Parish, near the Rose. Thither, under cover of darkness, they proceeded to ferry the mortal remains of the Theatre – to reconstruct it over the next six months as a new playhouse, the finest yet built, to be called the Globe.

VIII

THE GLOBE

1599–1603

On 21 September 1599, 'after dinner, about two o'clock', a Swiss tourist named Thomas Platter

> went with my party across the water; in the straw-thatched house we saw the tragedy of the first Emperor Julius Caesar, very pleasantly performed, with approximately fifteen characters; at the end of the play they danced together admirably and exceedingly gracefully, according to their custom, two in each group dressed in men's and two in women's apparel.

The building of the Globe had taken the Burbages' carpenters all spring. But the theatre had opened several months before Platter's visit in September, probably as early as June. It is described as 'newly built' ('*de novo edificata*') on 16 May, in an inventory of the effects of the late Sir Thomas Brend, whose son Nicholas leased the site to William Shakespeare and others, by then already in occupation ('*in occupacione Willielmi Shakespeare et aliorum*'). In St Saviour's parish, on semi-cultivated land provocatively close to Henslowe's Rose, Shakespeare and the Burbages had overseen the swift rebirth of the Theatre's poor, bare planks as the most lavish, best-equipped playhouse in town, with a capacity of 2,500 to 3,000. Long-suffering

Henslowe, his Rose by then in a sad state of disrepair, decided that his only option was to play his rivals at their own game. Decamping in the direction whence they came, recrossing the river back to Shoreditch, he would soon steal their carpentry team to build a rectangular attempt to improve on the Globe called the Fortune.

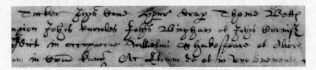

Post-mortem of Thomas Brend, showing Shakespeare and others occupying the Globe Playhouse.

Giles Alleyn, meanwhile, was predictably furious at the fiendish trick played on him by the Burbage brothers and their cronies. How it must have galled him that the Lord Chamberlain's Men remained respectable enough to play twice before the Queen at court over the Christmas holiday of 1599–1600 (as indeed they had the previous Christmas, and would the following year). Alleyn sued for £800 in damages, specifying £700 for the super-structure and 40s for 'trampling of the grass'. But the Burbages had good cause to be grateful for their late father's prescience. Anticipating trouble from Alleyn, who now charged that he had not spent the £200 maintenance required by their lease, the late James had kept meticulous records of all work done, including 'before-and-after' drawings by expert craftsmen. Alleyn's case collapsed. Dismissing his suit, the Court of Requests ordered him to refrain from further harassment of the Burbages.

But Alleyn was not a man to give up easily. Three years later, the indignation of the thwarted landlord is still most gratifying to hear, as he splutters with rage in his deposition for yet another lawsuit. On that dark December night in 1598, railed Alleyn, the Burbage brothers and their henchmen

> did riotously assemble themselves together and then and there armed themselves with divers and many unlawful and offensive weapons, as namely, swords, daggers, bills, axes and such like, and so armed did then repair unto the said Theatre. And then and there, armed as aforesaid, in very riotous, outrageous, and

forcible manner, and contrary to the laws of your Highness's realm, attempted to pull down the said Theatre, whereupon divers of your subjects, servants and farmers, then going about in peaceable manner to procure them to desist from that their unlawful enterprise, they, the said riotous persons aforesaid, notwithstanding procured then therein with great violence, not only then and there forcibly and riotously resisting your subjects, servants and farmers, but also then and there pulling, breaking and throwing down the said Theatre in very outrageous, violent and riotous sort, to the great disturbance and terrifying not only on your subjects, said servants and farmers, but of divers others of your Majesty's loving subjects there near inhabiting.

Again, Alleyn's case was dismissed. By now the Globe was doing booming business, and the Burbages' reputations riding almost as high as Shakespeare's – gloriously embarked on his most productive period, for the theatre which would play host to his greatest triumphs.

As well as being house playwright, and bit-part actor, he was a shareholder in the Globe, as testified by records of the Court of Requests. Under a legal contract signed on 21 February 1599 Shakespeare owned a tenth of the Globe, as did his fellow actors John Heminges, Will Kemp, Augustine Phillips and Thomas Pope. Larger shares were held by landlord Brend and the Burbage brothers. Trustees included wealthy merchants named William Leveson and Thomas Savage – the latter of Rufford, Lancashire, that same village where the young Shakespeare had served in the Hesketh household.

At much the same time, as befits a man whose life revolved around the theatre, Shakespeare moved his residence across the river. By 1599 he was living in Southwark, in the Liberty of the Clink, answerable to the Surrey authorities for the property taxes he was always slow to pay. It has become the tradition to see the actor-manager-writer, by now earning some £200 a year from the theatre, as tight-fisted. The belief that he was primarily concerned with accruing wealth, less so with a place among the literary immortals, dates from as early as 1737, thanks to Alexander Pope's taunt in *The First Epistle of the Second Book of Horace*:

> Shakespeare, (whom you and ev'ry Play-house bill
> Style the divine, the matchless, what you will)
> For gain, not glory, wing'd his roving flight,
> And grew immortal in his own despight.

But 'habits of business', as a Victorian biographer observed, 'are not incompatible with the possession of the highest genius'. Like most writers through the ages, Shakespeare was more likely impatient and inefficient about paperwork than a wilful tax-dodger. Writing two masterpieces a year, combing sources for inspiration while acting in the afternoons, does tend to clutter a desk.

The play most likely to have opened the Globe in the summer of 1599 is *Henry V*, whose opening Chorus contains an inaugural-sounding reference to 'this wooden O', within whose walls spectators are asked to lend their imaginations to 'piece out our imperfections with your thoughts'.

Shakespeare had finished the play in a hurry amid rumours that the Master of the Revels would soon be prohibiting all re-enactment of English history on the stage. The Church was up in arms. A Cambridge lawyer named Hayward had published an ill-timed work on Henry Bolingbroke's deposition of Richard II, brazenly dedicated to the Earl of Essex. The Archbishop of Canterbury saw to it that the dedication was removed and the book – all 1,500 copies of it, along with others including, as it happened, the dread *Willobie his Avisa* – publicly burnt. Still on uncertain terms with his monarch, Essex was despatched at the end of March to quell the rebellious Irish. So belligerent was the public mood that Shakespeare felt confident enough, for all the royal reservations about Essex, to make a direct reference to him in the Chorus to Act V of *Henry V*:

> Were now the general of our gracious Empress,
> As in good time he may from Ireland coming,
> Bringing rebellion broached on his sword,
> How many would the peaceful city quit
> To welcome him!

Essex, as it transpired, would return in disgrace that September, just a week after Thomas Platter's visit to *Julius Caesar*. So, for once, we can be very precise about dates, only to boggle again at Shakespeare's fecundity. He must have completed *Henry V* between March 1599 and the Globe's opening that summer, when all English hearts would have been rooting for the huge forces rallied against the Irish. And he must obviously have written *Julius Caesar*, turning to the safer historical themes of ancient Rome, by the time of Platter's visit to the Globe that September. In between, his appetite for comedy perhaps whetted by the Queen's whim to see Falstaff in love, he completed two entertainments to which he gave the throwaway titles of *Much Ado About Nothing* and *As You Like It*.

For the setting of *Much Ado* he turned again to the landscape where he seems, in the right mood, to have felt so at home: Italy, specifically Sicily. Not that it matters. The intrigues between followers of Don Pedro, Prince of Aragon, his bastard half-brother Don John, and Leonato, Governor of Messina, might as well have happened anywhere. But the groundlings liked hot Mediterranean blood in their tales of passion, whether comic or tragic.

The device of discrediting a bride on the eve of her marriage by falsely persuading the groom of her infidelity was his own variation on an age-old theme which existed in many guises. Shakespeare's primary debt was to two Italian versions, in verse and prose: Ariosto's *Orlando Furioso* (1516, translated into English verse by Sir John Harington in 1591), and Matteo Bandello's *Novelle* (1554, adapted into French by François de Belleforest in 1569). English versions also existed in verse and prose, in Spenser's *The Faerie Queene* (Book 2, canto 4, published in 1590) and George Whetstone's *The Rock of Regard* (1576). There was already another stage version in Anthony Munday's *Fedele and Fortunion* (1583), an adaptation of Luigi Pasqualigo's *Il Fedele* (1579).

But the play's distinctive sub-plot is entirely Shakespeare's creation: the romantic warfare, mostly in prose, of Beatrice and Benedick, a genteel update of Katharina and Petruchio, their sophistication counter-pointing the naïvety of Hero and Claudio. The need for broader comedy also saw him introduce a memorably English character into the Italian landscape: Constable Dogberry, a parody of all those country law officers whose number had once included his father.

Shakespeare also wrote Dogberry as the requisite part for Will

Kemp, resident company comedian since the death of Dick Tarleton ten years earlier. Now Kemp, too, quit the scene, if for rather different reasons. First, to make money, he would thrill the groundlings by morris-dancing, complete with cap and bells, all the way from London to Norwich. An Elizabethan forerunner of the sponsored walk (except that all proceeds went to the walker), the stunt was planned as a prelude to provincial exile as a writer. Charity, to Kemp, began at home. So Shakespeare's stake in the Globe increased to one-eighth as Kemp sold his shareholding in disgust at the direction the theatre was taking. Soon the veteran comic would make his views public in *Kemp's Nine Daies Wonder*, a satire ridiculing the preening pretensions of writers like 'my notable Shakerags' and predicting their imminent demise. All this high-falutin' Italianate stuff, with its ornate classical references, wasn't a patch on the good old days of the Mystery plays, with their scope for the vaudeville-style slapstick at which he excelled, along with the delights of the ad-lib and laughing at your own jokes.

Shakespeare's relief is almost audible as Kemp's departure enables him to dispense with low comedy for its own sake. Now he could move on to deeper, darker comic creatures, the Fool in *King Lear* being an interim climax en route to Thersites, Autolycus and Caliban. With his next tragedy already germinating, he would signal as much with his homage to the memory of Tarleton as Yorick, and a pointed rebuke to the camp Kemp in Hamlet's closing words to the players:

> Let those that play your clowns speak no more than is set down
> for them; for there be of them that will themselves laugh to set
> on some quantity of barren spectators to laugh too, though in
> the mean time some necessary question of the play be then to be
> consider'd. That's villainous, and shows a most pitiful ambition
> in the fool that uses it.

In Kemp's replacement, Robert Armin, himself also a writer, Shakespeare was blessed with the perfect vehicle for the subtler strain of humour inaugurated by Touchstone and Feste, stepping-stones to Lear's Fool. *As You Like It*'s clown is as wise as he is witty, to the point of pedantry, as in the set-piece 'degrees of the lie' speech (craftily placed to give Rosalind time to change out of her boy's disguise).

Touchstone was given surface wit enough to keep the groundlings happy, hidden amid classical allusion sufficiently erudite to bring a knowing smile to the face of the better sort of theatregoer. While wooing the dim-witted Audrey, for instance, he says:

> I am here with thee and thy goats as the most capricious poet,
>   honest Ovid, was among the Goths.

'O knowledge ill-inhabited,' comments the unseen Jaques, 'worse than Jove in a thatched house!' Audrey's blank reponse to such learning would have been echoed by the groundlings, who might enjoy the pun on 'goats' and 'Goths' without sharing the appreciation in the upper tiers of that on 'capricious' (both 'goat-like' and 'horny'), let alone the irony that Ovid – with whom Meres had recently compared Shakespeare – spent his exile among the Goths, or barbarians.

Shakespeare openly acknowledges his relish in this new, more complex vein of humour by having Jaques describe Touchstone as 'a material fool' – a fool as full of wise saws and modern instances as the melancholy misanthrope himself, whose very name was a pun on the Jonsonian humour he embodied: Ajax, a curmudgeon infused with too much black bile. For Jaques's own immortal set-piece, another tribute to the theatre and its players, Shakespeare unabashedly used the Globe's own motto, '*Totus mundus agit histrionem*', which translates almost literally as 'All the world's a stage . . .'

> And all the men and women merely players;
> They have their exits and their entrances,
> And one man in his time plays many parts,
> His acts being seven ages . . .

Thespian in-jokes still abounded. From *A Midsummer Night's Dream* to *Much Ado* – in which Benedick tells Don Pedro that Claudio is in love with 'Hero, Leonato's short daughter' – it is an elementary deduction that the leading boy-actors of the Lord Chamberlain's Men at this time were respectively tall and fair, short and dark. In *As You Like It*, Shakespeare gives Oliver identikit portraits of the supposed brother and sister he must seek out:

> The boy is fair,
> Of female favour, and bestows himself
> Like a ripe sister; the woman low
> And browner than her brother.

Still harping on the 'Dark Lady'? The whole play is riddled with theatrical self-reference, as if the entire company was still as excited about its new theatre as it was glad to see the back of its past, in the shape of the tediously self-obsessed Kemp. More than most of Shakespeare's plays, *As You Like It* can have a charm in performance which it lacks on the page. The playwright's own particular relish is clearly in the parts of Jaques and Touchstone, his own unique additions to his habitual reliance on a particular primary source, in this instance Thomas Lodge's romance *Rosalynde*, published in 1590.

In the spirit of a production where backstage morale seems to have been running high, the playwright himself took on the tiny role of old Adam, the loyal retainer with the seasoned wisdom of every ancient servant throughout fiction. No doubt he took equal pleasure in honouring his mother – and recalling his happy childhood – by naming his own pastoral Utopia, where men 'fleet the time carelessly, as they did in the golden world', the Forest of Arden.

In Adam's touching generosity to his young master – words first spoken on the stage by Shakespeare himself – we can hear in the (St Matthew-inspired) coupling of the words 'providence' and 'sparrow' a pre-echo of the mighty drama taking shape in his mind:

> I have five hundred crowns,
> The thrifty hire I sav'd under your father,
> Which I did store to be my foster-nurse
> When service should in my old limbs lie lame,
> And unregarded age in corners thrown.
> Take that, and He that doth the ravens feed,
> Yea, providently caters for the sparrow,
> Be comfort to my age. Here is the gold . . .

Comedy with one hand, history with the other; it was all by way of momentous preparation for the masterwork already long in the making. At Shakespeare's best, the two are invariably interlinked. In *Henry V*, amid the sombre progress of the 'madcap' prince to the 'mirror of all Christian kings', he comes up with the original joke about the Englishman, the Irishman, the Welshman and the Scotsman (in the respective shapes of Gower, MacMorris, Fluellen and Jamy). For all Falstaff's departure from the scene, while remaining a poignant offstage presence, the world he represented – the world of the groundlings – lives on in the ample shapes of his cronies Pistol, Bardolph and Mistress Quickly, now joined by Nym, who looks irresistibly like a parody of Ben Jonson. The sarcastic emphasis on the word 'humour' is only too clear when Nym tells Pistol: 'I have an humour to knock you indifferently well . . . I would prick your guts a little, in good terms, as I may, and that's the humour of it.' Pistol's reply, riddled with a hammy swagger worthy of Ned Alleyn, equally clearly speaks for Shakespeare:

> O braggart vile, and damned furious wight!
> The grave doth gape, and doting death is near.
> Therefore exhale.

Be it such bar-room badinage, or riskier political references, current events are never far away. As *Henry V* sees Shakespeare move on from the 'civil broils' of the previous histories to an England united in war against France, so it mirrors the campaign against Ireland which would come to grief even while the play still held the stage. At the time of its composition, the patriotic sentiments of *Henry V* were good box-office; through the centuries, alas, it has continued to serve as an unhappy vehicle for jingoistic sentiment, wheeled out at times of crisis to boost national morale (as when Churchill persuaded Laurence Olivier to film it during the Second World War). The device of prefacing each act with a Chorus lends the play an epic quality, while wryly offering the likes of Jonson a mock apology for the alleged inadequacies of the 'wooden O' in the representation of mighty events, transcending the theatrical traditions of time, space and mere humours.

Likewise, the civic unease bubbling beneath *Julius Caesar* reflected the nervous London summer of 1599, when talk of imminent Spanish invasion saw the gates of the capital locked and chains drawn across the streets against all comers. In this context, when unruly weather and hints of the supernatural portend disruption of the natural order, the Soothsayer takes on the broody millennial significance of a neo-Nostradamus. Shakespeare is as concerned with the consequences as with the causes of the assassination of Caesar, who is dead before the play is half over; he builds Mark Antony's pivotal speech – 'Friends, Romans, countrymen, lend me your ears' – on the merest of hints in Sir Thomas North's translation of the Greek historian Plutarch's *Lives*, published in 1579.

In the central character of Brutus, 'the noblest Roman of them all', it is tempting to see Shakespeare still speaking up for the embattled Essex, whose undisguised ambition was now beginning to prove his downfall. Far from trouncing the Irish leader, Tyrone, he had concluded a truce with him; Essex returned from Ireland with a name for creating more knights among his followers than corpses amid the enemy. There were rumours that he had advised Tyrone of an imminent shift of power in England – of mutual advantage, perhaps, to them both. Intent on succeeding Elizabeth, the earl rashly confronted the Queen in her bedchamber, still mud-stained from his journey. No man had ever before been permitted to see the Virgin Queen in her nightgown, with her hair down, *sans* make-up. Within a matter of hours, unsurprisingly, Essex had been placed under arrest. The real surprise was that his charmed if wayward life had lasted so long.

Whatever the state of his relations with Southampton, and whatever his residual feelings about Essex, Shakespeare was clearly absorbed by this dramatic turn of events. As he meditated upon the guilty conscience of the assassin, a theme to which he would return more than once, he was also intrigued by the notion of the overthrow of an absolute ruler for noble motives. In his arguments with his *quondam* alter ego, Brutus is a purer precursor of Macbeth; in the dignity with which he handles his dispute with Cassius, on the eve of both their deaths at Philippi, he has won plaudits since Shakespeare's own time, when the sympathetic response of the audience was first noticed by his family friend Leonard Digges:

THE LIVES

OF THE NOBLE GRE-
CIANS AND ROMANES, COMPARED

together by that graue learned Philosopher and Historiogra-
pher, Plutarke of Chæronea:

Translated out of Greeke into French by IAMES AMYOT, Abbot of Bellozane,
Bishop of Auxerre, one of the Kings priuy counsel, and great Amner
of Fraunce, and out of French into Englishe, by

Thomas North.

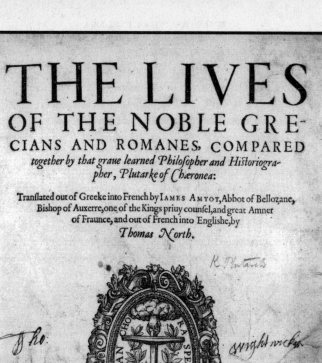

Imprinted at London by Thomas Vautroullier
and Iohn VVight.
1579.

The title page of Sir Thomas North's English translation of Plutarch
(1579), Shakespeare's main source for his Roman plays.

> So have I seen, when Caesar would appear,
> And on the stage at half-sword parley were
> Brutus and Cassius; O, how the audience
> Were ravished, with what wonder they went thence,
> When some new day they would not brook a line
> Of tedious though well-laboured Catiline.

Digges's last line is a timely dig at Jonson, whose *Every Man Out of His Humour* was staged by the Lord Chamberlain's Men in the same season as *Julius Caesar* – without Shakespeare, this time, in the cast. Legend has it that he changed a line of *Julius Caesar* at Jonson's suggestion; what was originally 'Caesar did never wrong but with just cause' (III, i, 48), as he dismisses Metellus Cimber's pleas on behalf of his banished brother, became

> Know, Caesar doth not wrong; nor without cause
> Will he be satisfied.

In his *Timber: Or Discoveries Made Upon Men and Matter*, a collection of jottings published three years after his death in 1637, Jonson followed his famous tribute to Shakespeare – 'I loved the man, and do honour his memory (on this side idolatry) as much as any' – with some qualifications, citing this line:

> Many times he fell into those things could not escape laughter:
> As when he said in the person of Caesar, one speaking to him:
> *Caesar, thou dost me wrong.* He replied: *Caesar did never wrong,*
> *but with just cause* and such like, which were ridiculous.

Jonson, who may well have acted in *Julius Caesar*, is still harping on the line ten years after Shakespeare's death in the Induction to *The Staple of News* (1626), when the Prologue says to Expectation: 'Cry you mercy, you never did me wrong, but with just cause.' He had by now made the line familiar enough for audiences to laugh with him at his 'ridiculous' rival.

Shakespeare's original version, presumably, read something like:

> *Caes.* . . . I spurn thee like a cur out of my way.
> *Met.* Caesar, thou dost me wrong.
> *Caes.* Know, Caesar doth not wrong but with just cause. Nor
> without cause will he be satisfied.

So the Folio version appears to justify Jonson's claim that Shakespeare changed the line at his suggestion – one of many instances giving the lie to the hoary old misconception that Shakespeare never revised his work, itself based on the excited boast of the editors of the First Folio to 'the Great Variety of Readers' that 'his mind and hand went together; and what he thought, he uttered with that easiness that we have scarce received from him a blot in his papers'. Even if their real meaning was that Shakespeare usually presented his players with 'clean' scripts in his own hand, Jonson could not resist jesting that the 'Swan of Avon' might have done better to have blotted a few more lines: 'Would he had blotted a thousand.' Resented by the King's Men for a 'malevolent speech' criticising their 'friend' Shakespeare, Jonson later felt obliged to defend his own 'candour':

> [Shakespeare] had an excellent fantasy, brave notions and gentle
> expressions: wherein he flowed with that facility that sometimes
> it was necessary he be stopped. *Sufflaminandus erat*, as Augustus
> said of Haterius. His wit was in his own power; would the rule
> of it had been so, too.

In his own *Sejanus* (1603), Jonson would soon attempt to show his rival how a Roman play should be written; in due course, Shakespeare would reply by making even better use of Plutarch's life of Mark Antony. Jonson's *Catiline* did not follow until 1611, by when Shakespeare was saying his farewells to the stage in *The Tempest*. In that autumn of 1599, their rivalry seems to have grown somewhat prickly. The management of the Globe, which of course included Shakespeare, considered *Every Man Out of His Humour* long-winded and preachy, demanding cuts. Jonson stalked out in a huff, taking his work back to the Lord Admiral's Men, down the road at the Rose.

Theatrical fashion seemed briefly to have been going Jonson's way, which may be another reason why Shakespeare now chose to spend longer than he ever had before on a play quite different in scale, texture and aspiration from anything he had previously attempted. It may also have been around this time that the two rival playwrights sat in a Bankside inn, or the Mermaid tavern in Bread Street, arguing over their craft, perhaps even their respectives fates with posterity, winding up with a drunken exchange of mutual epitaphs. One, however dubious, survives.

> Here lies Ben Jonson
> That was once one

began Jonson, handing the paper across the table to Shakespeare. 'Presently', no doubt after sucking on his quill for a moment, the Stratford man added:

> Who while he lived was a slow thing,
> And now, being dead, is no thing.

If this piece of doggerel is genuine, the joke is surely more genial than it sounds. *In vino veritas*, to be sure, but all contemporary judgements on Shakespeare (including Jonson's own) make him out a courteous, civil, mild-mannered man – not given, like Jonson, to inciting arguments or provoking brawls. Besides, there was really no professional contest between them. Shakespeare was by now famous enough for his name to be taken in vain, as the unscrupulous publisher William Jaggard proved by publishing five of his Sonnets (including three from *Love's Labour's Lost*, which had already appeared in print), plus sundry other poetic scraps of dubious provenance, under the title *The Passionate Pilgrim*. Some have barely more merit than the supposed Jonson 'epitaph', though many scholars including the Oxford editors look with favour on the lyric known by its opening line: 'Whenas thine eye hath chose the dame . . .'

That Shakespeare was displeased about the publication we know from his fellow playwright Thomas Heywood, nine of whose poems were added by Jaggard in a shameless reprint in 1612, still bearing Shakespeare's name on the title page. Heywood lodged a prompt protest at the 'manifest injury done me in that work'. Two long poems from his *Troia Britannica* were among those included in this 'lesser' volume 'under the name of another, which may put the world in opinion I might steal them from him'.

> But as I must acknowledge my lines not worthy his patronage, under whom he hath published them, so the author I know much offended with M. Jaggard (that altogether unknown to him) presumed to make so bold with his name.

The 'much offended' Shakespeare must also have lodged a protest with Jaggard in 1612, with much the same effect as he had chided Chettle twenty years earlier, for the printer hastily replaced the title page with a new one, omitting the poet's name. There is no evidence of his having taking any such action in 1599, when he assuredly had higher priorities than chasing piratical printers.

That autumn saw the Earl of Essex embark upon his last, suicidal adventure. Hauled before the Court of the Star Chamber on 29 November, he was kept under house arrest pending trial for 'maladministration' in Ireland. By February, to the anxiety of other courtiers, the Queen had taken pity upon her former favourite, and agreed to a Privy Council trial behind closed doors rather than a public examination in the Star Chamber. Come the hearing, on 5 June 1600, Essex threw himself on Her Majesty's mercy, pleading: 'The tears in my heart have quenched all the sparks of pride in me . . . God is witness how faithfully I dedicate the rest of my life to your majesty, without admitting any other worldly cares.'

For all the ferocious forensic skills of the Attorney General, Sir Edward Coke, who set out a lethal case against Essex, the Queen was in emollient mood. The earl had been gravely ill in the nine months since his arrest; he had behaved with a penitent dignity admired by a restive public; so it was agreed that he should for the time being remain confined to his palatial house on the Strand, pending Her Majesty's pleasure.

Elizabeth was wondering whether Essex might still be of use to her, and contemplating his release – to the horror of her most senior advisers, Cecil and Raleigh, who were naturally fearful that he might worm his way back into the Queen's affections, and resume his former influence over her. They were also wary of the strength of feeling among his many followers. 'How dangerous is it that this man goes loose!' says Claudius of Hamlet, just as Cecil and Raleigh were saying of Essex to the Queen, while complimenting her on staying her hand:

> Yet must not we put the strong law on him.
> He's lov'd of the distracted multitude,
> Who like not in their judgement but their eyes,
> And where 'tis so, th' offender's scourge is weigh'd,
> But never the offence. To bear all smooth and even,
> This sudden sending him away must seem
> Deliberate pause. Diseases desperate grown
> By desperate appliance are reliev'd,
> Or not at all.

On 26 August Elizabeth had Essex freed. In Ireland Lord Mountjoy was succeeding where he had failed, a public humiliation which the Queen seemed to consider punishment enough. But she hurt Essex's pride by banning him from court, and his wallet by depriving him of his monopoly of the import of sweet wines. In passionate letters, steeped in contrition, the desperate earl pleaded his case on both fronts. Her nerve steeled by the watchful Cecil, Raleigh and Francis Bacon, Elizabeth turned a deaf ear, threatening Essex with financial ruin by reverting his wine monopoly to the Crown. Essex House now became a focus of dissent, as every discarded courtier and passed-over military man (precursors of Iago) rallied to his cause, urging him to take action before he was ruined.

On 6 February 1601 a group of Essex partisans, led by Sir Gelly Meyrick, came to the Globe with a request that the Lord Chamberlain's Men mount a performance of *Richard II* – complete with deposition scene – the following afternoon. In vain did the company protest that the play was past its prime, that it would scarcely fill the theatre. Did they realise the political significance, and thus the potential dangers, of what they were being asked to do? If so, as seems likely, they were careful to hide behind purely theatrical excuses. *Richard II* was 'so old and out of use', in Augustine Phillips's sworn testimony, as later reported by Bacon, 'that they should have small or no company at it'. But the conspirators offered to underwrite the performance, to the tune of forty shillings beyond their 'ordinary' fee and box-office takings. Who were mere players to refuse such a lucrative commission from insistent eminences of high birth?

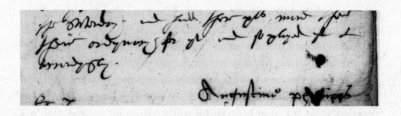

Examination of Augustine Phillips concerning the performance of Richard II *before Essex's rebellion, 18 February 1601.*

The following day, a Saturday, *Richard II* was duly played before a mix of restive groundlings and disenchanted aristocrats. Word of the special performance had spread around the city, where people were not slow to grasp its significance. Though not himself present, Essex was wilfully reminding the citizenry of a vivid precedent for the overthrow, and indeed assassination, of a capriciously favourite-prone monarch by a rejected nobleman – a terrible deed, to be sure, but a desperate act of *realpolitik* which had eventually bred a golden age.

The significance of that Saturday matinée did not escape Elizabeth, whose spies were everywhere. 'I am Richard II, know ye not that?' she declared. 'He that will forget God, will also forget his benefactors; this tragedy was played forty times in open streets and houses.' That same evening Essex was summoned to appear before the Privy Council; but he declined to leave the safety of his house, pleading that there was a plot to kill him, while in truth laying plans to seize the capital. The next morning, Sunday, saw a high-powered delegation including the Chief Justice, the Lord Keeper, the Earl of Worcester and Sir William Knollys descend on Essex House in the name of the Queen, to issue a stern warning against any potential act of treason. Confronted by an angry crowd, baying for their blood, the four notables found themselves taken hostage while Essex led two hundred troops in a mounted assault on the city.

But he found Ludgate locked against him, and the capital in no mood to rally to his cause. As a herald proclaimed him a traitor, some of his supporters fled; reinforcements promised from within the city did not materialise. Realising his cause was lost, Essex found his escape-route blocked by armed forces. There was a scuffle in which one of the Queen's men was killed, and one of his own taken prisoner, while Essex fought his way home via the river – only to find his hostages freed and his headquarters besieged. That evening, as the Lord Admiral threatened to blow up Essex House, the would-be usurper decided he had no option but to give himself up.

Receiving the news while dining alone, the Queen appeared unmoved. Next day she said simply: 'A senseless ingrate has at last revealed what has long been in his mind.' Brought to trial within a week, an insouciant Essex wore black – like the Danish prince then in the making – and quoted Shakespeare. 'I am indifferent how I speed,' he told the court. 'I owe God a death.'

Says Prince Hal to Falstaff in *1 Henry IV*: 'Why, thou owest God a death' – to which Falstaff, left alone on the battlefield, replies with his great 'catechism':

> 'Tis not due yet. I would be loath to pay him before his day.
> What need I be so forward with him that calls not on me? Well,
> 'tis no matter; honour pricks me on. Yea, but how if honour
> prick me off when I come on? How then? Can honour set to
> a leg? No. Or an arm? No. Or take away the grief of a wound?
> No. Honour hath no skill in surgery, then? No. What is honour?
> A word. What is in that word 'honour'? What is that 'honour'?
> Air. A trim reckoning! Who hath it? He that died o' Wednesday.
> Doth he feel it? No. Doth he hear it? No. 'Tis insensible then?
> Yea, to the dead. But will it not live with the living? No. Why?
> Detraction will not suffer it. Therefore I'll none of it. Honour
> is a mere scutcheon. And so ends my catechism.

The finest hour of Feeble, the 'woman's tailor' recruited by Falstaff in *2 Henry IV*, likewise comes with the words:

> By my troth, I care not. A man can die but once. We owe God
> a death. I'll ne'er bear a base mind. An't be my destiny, so; an't
> be not, so. No man's too good to serve's prince. And let it go
> which way it will, he that dies this year is quit for the next.

But Essex's day, unlike Falstaff's, had come. Like Feeble, he faced it with cool, fatalistic indifference, telling the court which condemned him to death: 'I think it fitting that my poor quarters, which have done Her Majesty true service in divers parts of the world, should now at the last be disposed of and sacrificed at Her Majesty's pleasure.' On the day of his execution, 25 February (Ash Wednesday), he confided to Cecil: 'I must confess to you that I am the greatest, the most vilest, and the most unthankful traitor that ever has been in the land.' Granted his last wish – a private execution within the Tower, lest the acclaim of a baying mob corrupt him at the last – the 34-year-old earl reportedly thanked God that he was 'thus spewed out of the realm'.

The manner of Essex's death still lingered in Shakespeare's mind five years later, when he had Malcolm report to his royal father of the execution of the Thane of Cawdor:

> .I have spoke
> With one that saw him die, who did report
> That very frankly he confess'd his treasons,
> Implor'd your highness' pardon, and set forth
> A deep repentance. Nothing in his life
> Became him like the leaving it. He died
> As one that had been studied in his death,
> To throw away the dearest thing he ow'd
> As 'twere a careless trifle.

He might also have had Elizabeth in mind, lamenting the betrayal of a former favourite among her courtiers, when he gave King Duncan the poignant reply:

> There's no art
> To find the mind's construction in the face:
> He was a gentleman on whom I built
> An absolute trust.

On the evening before the execution of Essex, Shrove Tuesday, the Lord Chamberlain's Men were commanded to distract Her Majesty with a play. There is no record of the piece chosen, whether by the

Queen or the players themselves, though it seems unlikely to have been *Richard II*. Shakespeare and his fellows must have been feeling nervous for their future, uncertain how compromised they were at court by their role in precipitating the attempted coup – performing 'that inflammatory tragedy at that inflammatory time' for 'forty pieces of silver'.

So the royal command would have been mightily reassuring. No doubt a few well-chosen words from their patron, Hunsdon, explaining the impossible position in which they had been placed, would have reassured the monarch of her favourite troupe's essential loyalty. Besides, they were merely actors, gulled by the likes of Meyrick, who had since confronted the hangman at Tyburn 'with a most undaunted resolution'. He it was, in the words of the Crown prosecutor, Francis Bacon, who had pressurised the unwitting players, 'so earnest was he to satisfy his eyes with the sight of that tragedy which he thought soon after his lord should bring from the stage to the state, but that God turned it upon their heads'.

The life of Shakespeare's friend Southampton, tried and condemned with Essex, was saved only by the intervention of his powerful and persuasive mother, the Dowager Countess. Moved by her pleas that her son was a biddable innocent, whose only fault was to have fallen into bad company, Cecil used his influence to have the earl's sentence commuted to indefinite imprisonment. Southampton was left languishing in the Tower. If there was something of Essex in Hamlet, there was something of Southampton in his loyal friend Horatio. But there was also something of Essex in Laertes, the courtier-turned-renegade who mounts his own reckless challenge against the throne.

Of all Shakespeare's plays, the vast, sprawling showpiece he had been writing all this time – noting and processing current events, while mobilising every stylistic weapon in his formidable armoury – defies such impertinent, of-the-moment footnoting. Yes, the theatrical world was in some turmoil, with so-called 'wars' being fought on two fronts; and, yes, Shakespeare makes reference to them in Hamlet's discursive meditations on actors and acting. But only for dating purposes need we note Hamlet's grilling of Rosencrantz about the 'little eyases', the 'eyrie' of child-actors who irritated the established troupes by mounting a successful season of revenge tragedies at the Blackfriars in 1600–1. Amid 'much throwing about of brains', Hamlet is told, the effects had been felt even by 'Hercules and his load' – the Globe itself, that is, whose logo depicted Hercules bearing the world on his shoulders (as, in his way, does Hamlet). There is even a reference to the Lord Chamberlain's Men's brush with authority over that risky matinée of *Richard II*; when Hamlet asks why the approaching players are on the road – 'How chances it they travel?' – he is told that 'their inhibition comes by the means of the late innovation', i.e., Essex's uprising that February.

Already a stylistic war raged among the playwrights, a 'War of the Theatres', or *poetomachia*, in which Jonson, John Marston and Thomas Dekker vied to outdo each other with florid displays of dramatised learning in a series of seven *ad hominem* satires from 1599 to 1602, performed by the boys' companies. Now the actors were back on hard times, Hamlet is told, not 'followed' as once they were, because of a bunch of schoolchildren – through whom an opportunistic Jonson meanwhile waged war on Shakespeare by giving them plays such as *Cynthia's Revels*. 'Giants fought giants', as it has been put, 'and dwarves fought both'. As with every last scrap thrown his way, Hamlet turns the news into another source of wonder at the wicked ways of a world turned upside-down:

> It is not very strange; for mine uncle is King of Denmark, and those that would make mouths at him while my father lived give twenty, forty, fifty, an hundred ducats apiece for his picture in little. 'Sblood, there is something in this more than natural, if philosophy could find it out.

With his plays performed at court in preference to Jonson's, Shakespeare could afford to rise above the *poetomachia*, while meanwhile deciding to turn necessity to definitive advantage. Revenge tragedies were suddenly all the rage, and not just in the box-office predominance of the Paul's Boys at the Blackfriars. The tradition begun by Aeschylus and Seneca was undergoing a revival sparked by Kyd's *Spanish Tragedy* and Shakespeare's own *Titus Andronicus*.

Now John Marston was enjoying a huge success with *Antonio's Revenge*, soon to be followed by Cyril Tourneur's *The Revenger's Tragedy* and John Webster's *The Duchess of Malfi*. So Shakespeare would write the most ambitious revenge tragedy of them all, turning to his advantage the perennial problem of plot construction: given the catalytic murder in the first act, and the requisite revenge-killing in the last, what do you do in the intervening three? Take the form head-on, he decided, and create a philosopher-revenger who spends those three acts and more crippled by moral doubts and mortal fears.

He had a ready model to rework in that crude revenge tragedy, now known as the ur-*Hamlet*, in which he had perhaps had a hand when first he came to London. This in turn had made use of the French poet De Belleforest's recent updating of a tale dating back to the thirteenth century, when the Danish historian Saxo-Grammaticus recounted the history of 'mad' Prince Amleth, son and heir of the King of Jutland, whose father was murdered by his brother King Fengo. The spectacular new version conceived by Shakespeare in 1600–1 comes down to us in three different versions, the cause of much textual agony among scholars, actors and directors: a corrupt quarto volume, piratically published in 1603; a second, significantly different quarto edition, which appeared the following year; and yet another, supposedly definitive version in the posthumous First Folio of 1623. The so-called 'full-length' *Hamlet*s of current theatrical vogue restore memorable chunks of the second quarto, such as the soliloquy 'How all occasions do inform against me . . .', which are mysteriously missing from the First Folio.

Coming at roughly the half-way point of his output, *Hamlet* marks a sea-change in Shakespeare's view of himself and his abilities. Everything he had written suddenly seems like preparation for this moment, as he reaches higher and wider than ever before, going out of his way to show off every aspect of his consummate art, dazzling his audience with flights of fancy and psycho-analytical wisdom whose mysteries will never be fully fathomed. This dizzying display of poetry and philosophy, wit and insight, finds its central focus in one man, one very mortal man, perhaps the most complex creation in literary history, in whom every subsequent generation has found multiple reflections of itself.

Not merely is *Hamlet* Shakespeare's longest play, and technically his most ambitious. As it lurches from comedy to tragedy, high art to low, violence to stillness, love to hatred, confusion to redemption, it tells the story of Everyman as never before or since, distilling as much individual and collective experience as can be contained in one frail, confused man of action, a poet-philosopher confronting all our own everyday problems while trying to solve one none of us will ever have to face.

In extended comparison of current events with those of English and Roman history, Shakespeare had developed a profound interest in the influence of evil on noble minds. He was yet to take it further, much further; for now it sufficed to place the weight of the world on Hamlet's shoulders as he tries to find a place for duty, responsibility, love, hate, sense of self in the lamentable scheme of things. In giving vent to his feelings of inadequacy he found himself, and all of us.

Hamlet is the launch-pad for a quite different, more profound and multi-layered Shakespeare from the merely talented and versatile dramatist we have known so far. Henceforth he will demonstrate the eternal frailties of humankind, by telling the stories of mighty men in terms of their mortal failings. It is as if the Stratford man suddenly lost patience with the petty squabbling around him – the snobbish disputes between university-educated playwrights and their peers, the eternal woes of the actor-managers and impresarios, the shifting tensions between the Queen and her courtiers – and lifted the art of drama on to an entirely new and far higher plane. *Hamlet* is the unilateral declaration of independence which marks the birth of the Jacobean Shakespeare, the author of *Othello* and *Macbeth*, *Lear* and those last plays in which tragic events breed built-in redemption.

In barely ten years he had already raised English drama from crude comedy, lumbering history and murderous melodrama to a level of intelligence, honesty, wit and humanity unmatched in any other era, before or since. Four hundred years later, at the end of the twentieth century, *Hamlet* speaks as vividly as it ever has to each succeeding generation, all of whom see almost too much of themselves in its 'mirror, held, as 'twere, up to nature'. Given the convenience of a millennial anniversary, it has also been voted the 'masterwork' of the last thousand years, surpassing Michelangelo's Sistine Chapel, Beethoven's ninth symphony, the King James Bible, the Taj Mahal.

At the time, this play was one of the crowning achievements of Elizabethan England, a golden age almost spent, the legacy of whose pre-eminently civilised monarch already included 'Byrd's anthems, the Royal Exchange, the circumnavigation by the *Golden Hind*, the Virginian settlement, the *Laws of Ecclesiastical Polity*, the joint stock companies, the defeat of Spain'.

Denmark was also a country suddenly – and unusually – on people's lips. Since the death of Essex, the perennial question of the Virgin Queen's heir had focused more than ever around the Scottish king, James, whose wife was a Danish princess, and a Catholic, named Anne. Beyond such localised perspectives, Shakespeare seems to have been in nostalgic mood while writing what he must have known was his masterpiece. In Yorick, he was paying a private homage to the ghost of Dick Tarleton, resident comedian of the Queen's Men, whom he might fondly remember as having borne him on his back (if only metaphorically) a thousand times. In his choice of setting for the death of Ophelia, who is reputed to have gone over a cliff in the ur-*Hamlet*, he was remembering a willow aslant a brook in the Stratford of his childhood, where a girl named Katharine – surname Hamlett – drowned in 1579. Gertrude's strikingly lavish description of the scene, a veritable almanac of blossoming Warwickshire flowers, perhaps atones for the starkness of the verdict on Katharine Hamlett of a Stratford inquest jury: *per infortunium*, accidental death. In Shakespeare's mind, the discussion of Christian burial rites begun by the gravedigger might almost refer as much to poor Katharine's death as to Ophelia's – the one was allowed, unlike the other, to be buried in consecrated ground – and all those bones and skulls again take us back to that scary charnel-house of the churchyard where the poet played as a child.

The memory of his own son Hamnet meanwhile lends the play's parallel father–son relationships an especially poignant charge. Some recent biographers feel free, for obvious reasons, to modernise the spelling of Hamnet's name to Hamlet. But there is no need for such perilous short cuts; to immortalise the son's memory in the title of his father's single most substantial achievement, we need only note that the name 'Hamnet', in the Warwickshire dialect of the day, would have emerged from his parents' mouths as 'Hamblet', which in moments of heat or speed, and eventually everyday parlance, simplifies readily enough to 'Hamlet'. They were, in effect, the same name.

In the Ghost of Hamlet's Father, Shakespeare meanwhile seems to be paying tribute to his own, now a shadow of his former self, on the very threshold of that bourn from which no traveller returns. The young prince's agonised exchanges with his father's spirit, replete with covert Romanist references, are among the most moving moments in a play sustained at an unsparingly high pitch of emotional intensity. The Ghost of Hamlet's Father was, indeed, the part Shakespeare himself played in the original production by the Lord Chamberlain's Men, if Rowe is again to be believed:

> His Name is printed, as the Custom was in those Times, amongst those of the other Players, before some old Plays, but without any particular Account of what sort of Parts he us'd to play; and tho' I have inquir'd, I could never meet with any further Account of him this way, than that the top of his Performance was the Ghost in his own Hamlet.

Burbage, of course, played Hamlet, as he had Brutus in *Julius Caesar*. The same actor who had played Caesar, probably Heminges, was now Polonius, as is clear amid all the in-house jokes. In his university days, the old courtier tells Hamlet, he had been 'accounted a good actor'.

Hamlet: And what did you enact?
Polonius: I did enact Julius Caesar. I was killed i' th' Capitol. Brutus killed me.
Hamlet: It was a brute part of him to kill so capital a calf there.

Unlike Polonius, Shakespeare makes no claims for himself as a player; even as a playwright, the only characters in the canon he names after himself are a lazy schoolboy in *Merry Wives* and a country bumpkin in *As You Like It*, both already behind him. A century later, an unknown theatregoer would bluntly report that Shakespeare was 'a much better poet than player'. If the Ghost in *Hamlet* was 'the top of his performance', what could be a more touching tribute to the septuagenarian patriarch still holding court in Henley Street?

Sigmund Freud, of course, took all this much further. In Freud's famous reading of the play, Hamlet's inability to take revenge on the man who killed his father, and then took his father's place in his mother's bed, is explained in the repressed instincts of his own childhood; the paralysed prince's hatred for his uncle is overtaken by self-hatred – evidence, to Freud, of Shakespeare's own 'Oedipus complex' in the wake of his father's death. Alas for Freud, the record shows that, during the writing of *Hamlet*, the poet's father was still very much alive. Not until 8 September 1601 did Shakespeare return to Stratford again, to bury him in the churchyard of Holy Trinity.

John Shakespeare had lived into his seventies, a mighty age for the time, but we know little of his fortunes beyond his middle years. Most of his friends had long since quit the scene, by now as fond a memory as his own prominence as a civic leader; but we can be sure that in later life the retired glover enjoyed a certain dignity around town as a local eminence, relishing the reflected glory of a son making a name for himself in the capital, new owner of the biggest house in town.

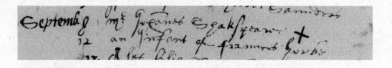

Record of John Shakespeare's burial, 8 September 1601.

In the summer of 1601 Richard Quiney, son of Adrian, rode to London to plead Stratford's case in a dispute over the appointment of the market toll-gatherer, which the lord of the manor, Sir Edward Greville, was trying to wrest from the borough. Among the civic dignitaries who had lent their names to the petition in Quiney's saddlebag was 'Jhon Sackesper'. After all his early business difficulties, which had seen him sell off Greenhill Street, Shakespeare's father died prosperous enough to have maintained the double-fronted house in Henley Street, which now passed via his will to his oldest son William. Four years since his purchase of New Place, the poet-playwright was suddenly something of a property tycoon.

It appears that his mother Mary, who would outlive her husband by seven years, moved in with her daughter-in-law Anne and her grand-daughters (now eighteen and sixteen) at New Place, pending her son's permanent return from London. Another room was rented out against that day, earning a handy income to sustain the Stratford Shakespeares, perhaps even saving the new paterfamilias from having to send cash home from the capital.

Now head of the family, William seems to have been no different from most sons in regarding his father's death as a singular reminder of his own mortality. It was perhaps at this moment, plunged into a predictable bout of melancholy, that he felt confirmed in discarding any vestigial religious belief. The fatalism of *Hamlet*, so appealing to the existential angst of four centuries of adolescents, now curdles to the bleak nihilism of *Troilus and Cressida*, the darkest, most pessimistic play he ever wrote. Shakespeare took the ancient legend of the war-separated lovers, which he had known in Chaucer's version since his schooldays, and turned it into more than a mere indictment of inconstancy, or just another fable of man's inhumanity to man. In this work more than any other, a broad array of characters – most of them worldly leaders – fail to live up to their own ideals. They are all talk and no action, until eventually goaded by the basest of motives, a far remove from the ideals they claim to represent. Few have many redeeming features. The only character in the entire play who remains true to himself throughout, and consistently speaks the most sense, is the cynical, vagabond clown Thersites – another great part for Robert Armin.

Of all Shakespeare's plays, *Troilus and Cressida* has been uniquely adopted by the twentieth century, apparently the first since Shakespeare's day to find sombre echoes of itself in his cerebral vision of a world collapsed by war. Ignored by actors and managers until the turn of this last century, the play has enjoyed a rebirth since the Second World War, as central a member of the core repertoire as any of its better-known siblings. That it defies classification, wandering between the comedy, tragedy and 'problem play' sections of different editions of Shakespeare, is due as much to its own apartness within the canon as to the confusion surrounding its early publishing history.

The editors of the First Folio evidently moved the play, amid copyright and pagination problems, from among the tragedies to an ambiguous position in no-man's-land between the histories and tragedies. But greater mystery surrounds a quarto edition of 1609, six years after it was first entered in the Stationers Register, when permission was granted to one James Roberts to print 'when he hath got sufficient authority for it, the book of Troilus and Cressida, as it is acted by my Lord Chamberlain's Men'. Shakespeare (if he was even involved) appears to have refused any such authority, for the Roberts edition never appeared. The 1609 version of the play was the first in print, with a title page making the strange claim that this was a 'new' play, 'never staled with the stage, never clapper-clawed with the palms of the vulgar, and yet passing full of the palm comical . . .'

> Take this for a warning, and at the peril of your pleasure's loss, and judgements, refuse not, nor like this the less, for not being sullied with the smoky breath of the multitude; but thank fortune for the scape it hath made amongst you, since by the grand possessors' wills I believe you should have prayed for them rather than been prayed.

The pirates making these mendacious protestations, Richard Bonian and Henry Walley, substituted them – after printing had begun – for a title page which had originally announced *Troilus and Cressida* as 'acted by the King's Majesty's servants at the Globe'. This would have been consistent with its first registration in 1603, a couple of years after it was first written and played. So why did Bonian and Walley claim it as a 'new' work, hitherto unperformed? In their economy with the truth, they were even brazen enough to steal a distinctive phrase from the play, in which Thersites derides the warring armies as 'clapper-clawing' one another. Sharp practice would be nothing unexpected from such copyright sharks; but they may have been able to claim justification by adding a prologue and epilogue post-dating the original production. The suggestion is that the play flopped at the Globe; too sophisticated for the groundlings, it was not sophisticated enough for the Inns of Court, so Shakespeare felt obliged to top and tail it with sardonic quasi-apologies to a smart private audience. If so, it would have been the only time in his career that he made any such misjudgement, belying his unfailing sense of both his actors and his audience, and his uncanny ability 'to please the most diverse tastes with the same play'.

Even so, the indications are that *Troilus and Cressida* did less well at the Globe than in private performances for well-educated lawyers and courtiers. In this vein, while *Hamlet* continued to pack them in, Shakespeare kept his Chaucer at his elbow (and his Bible still in mind) for a personal homage to *The Parlement of Fowles* in his next published work, untitled but traditionally known as 'The Phoenix and Turtle'. A sixty-seven-line elegy in trochaic tetrameter, it was appended with other 'commendatory' poems by Jonson, Marston and Chapman to *Love's Martyr, or Rosalin's Complaint* by Robert Chester, subtitled as 'allegorically shadowing the truth of love, in the constant fate of the phoenix and turtle'. Chester's own poem was dedicated to his patron, Sir John Salisbury, with whom Shakespeare had no known connection (although Salisbury's first wife had been a Stanley, illegitimate child of an Earl of Derby). So either he was playing second fiddle to lesser talents for financial reasons, a nonce-poet responding to an offer too lucrative to refuse, or his work had yet again been pirated. But this seems unlikely in view of his poem's direct connection with the anthology's title, and the sympathy of its subject-matter with his then mood, forsaking the comfort-blanket of orthodox religion for a more metaphysical dialectic.

The eighteen stanzas of 'The Phoenix and Turtle', dense but elegant, amount to a celebration of idealised love, as a congregation of birds convene to mourn the mythical flame-survivor and the turtle-dove, conventionally a symbol of chaste fidelity. A difficult poem, but 'knowingly so', this rare *pièce d'occasion* sees Shakespeare exploring 'the transcendence of Reason by Love'. Although less immediate than the Sonnets, this lyric may well have echoed some recent personal adventure; now thirty-seven years old, parted from his wife for most of each year, Shakespeare would still have been enjoying an active social life in London.

After the Herculean effort of *Hamlet*, moreover, his productivity rate had slowed appreciably. Another *annus mirabilis* lay just ahead, but the first years of the new century see his output halve, albeit briefly, to just one play a year. Uniquely, in this mid-period of his career, he also deigned to stoop to collaboration. He had shared writing credits with others at the start of his career, and would relax into partnership again at the end; at the height of his powers, for the most part, he left teamwork to others, notably Dekker, Middleton and Webster, even Jonson (who joined hands with Chapman and Martson on *Eastward Ho!*). But now, as Elizabeth's glorious reign drew inexorably towards its close, Shakespeare was persuaded to undertake some rescue work on a piece which, because of its delicate subject-matter, had fallen foul of the censor.

Sir Edmund Tilney, Master of the Revels, had demanded extensive cuts and alterations to Anthony Munday's play about Sir Thomas More. In the case of the man who had so famously crossed the Queen's beloved father, royal sensitivities were very much at stake. Dekker became involved, as did Heywood, picking their way tactfully around the question of the (unspecified) 'articles' to which More declined to subscribe; no fewer than five different hands have made additions to the original manuscript, still to be seen in the British Library, complete with Tilney's complaints. Among them, by general consent, is that of Shakespeare.

Hand D, in folios 8 and 9, is the only example of his handwriting we possess, beyond the five or six authentic signatures. Intriguingly, Hand D also spells 'silence' as 'scilens' – the same eccentric spelling as occurs six times in the speech-prefixes for Justice Silence in the quarto of *2 Henry IV*.

With their paymasters away on tour, and the Admiral's Men waiting for Henslowe to complete work on his new playhouse, it was only natural that his rival playwrights should turn in desperation to the colleague who was also a stakeholder in the Lord Chamberlain's Men. He was now an independent writer of means with no need to collaborate for mere pecuniary gain. But the conscience of the Catholic martyr was a subject with an obvious appeal to Shakespeare, even if his own faith had lapsed. The consciences of noble minds prepared to pay the supreme price was a theme which had preoccupied him since *Julius Caesar*, and would sustain him through *Macbeth* and beyond.

The pivotal scene he was required to write, amounting to 147 lines of verse and prose, depicts More at his most eloquent, attempting as Sheriff of London to calm the rebellious apprentices protesting against foreign residents on the 'ill' May Day of 1517. Even his skills, however, could not win round the Revels Office; the play remained unperformed in the Queen's lifetime, and indeed his. Not until the twentieth century, in fact, has any theatre company been enterprising (or rash) enough to attempt to stage what survives of this unsatisfactory text. At the time, of course, Shakespeare was not one to let his work go to waste. The pleas of Sir Thomas More to the

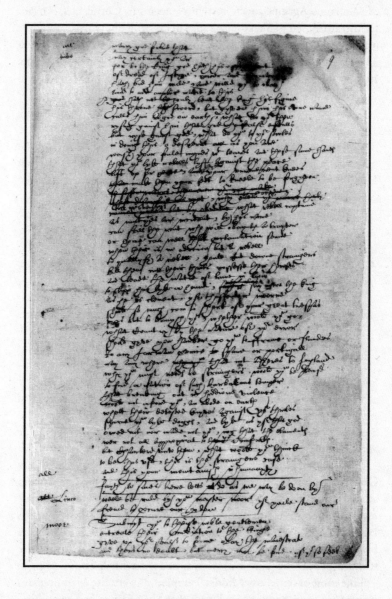

'Ill May-Day': Addition IIc to Sir Thomas More, *the only surviving example of Shakespeare's handwriting apart from six signatures.*

London apprentices in Hand D would find distinct echoes in those of Menenius Agrippa to the restive plebeians in Coriolanus' Rome.

Also attributed to Shakespeare, not in his hand but worth quotation in full as a unique curiosity, is the so-called Addition III to *Sir Thomas More*, a soliloquy in which the new Lord Chancellor contemplates his appointment:

> It is in heaven that I am thus and thus,
> And that which we profanely term our fortunes
> Is the provision of the power above,
> Fitted and shaped just to that strength of nature
> Which we are born withal. Good God, good God,
> That I from such an humble bench of birth
> Should step as 'twere up to my country's head
> And give the law out there; ay, in my father's life
> To take prerogative and tithe of knees
> From elder kinsmen, and him bind by my place
> To give the smooth and dexter way to me
> That owe it him by nature! Sure these things,
> Not physicked by respect, might turn our blood
> To much corruption. But More, the more thou hast
> Either of honour, office, wealth and calling,
> Which might accite thee to embrace and hug them,
> The more do thou e'en serpents' natures think them:
> Fear their gay skins, with thought of their sharp stings,
> And let this be thy maxim: to be great
> Is, when the thread of hazard is once spun,
> A bottom great wound up, greatly undone.

On 2 February 1602, Candlemas Day, the law student John Manningham attended a feast at the Middle Temple, followed by an entertainment from the Lord Chamberlain's Men. 'We had a play called Twelfth Night or what you will,' Manningham recorded in his diary. 'Much like the Comedy of Errors . . . a good practice in it to make the steward believe his lady widow was in love with him . . .'

Like most of his fellow Middle Templars, the erudite Manningham needed no source notes to tell him that Shakespeare had again borrowed elements of his plot from Plautus, specifically the *Menaechmi*.

Like audiences ever since, he particularly enjoyed the come-uppance of the preening steward Malvolio,

> by counterfeiting a letter as from his lady in general terms, telling him what she liked best in him, and prescribing his gesture in smiling, his apparel etc, and then when he came to practice, making him believe they took him to be mad etc.

On 6 January the previous year, Twelfth Night 1601, Elizabeth I had commanded the Lord Chamberlain's Men to stage a play at her Whitehall palace to mark the state visit of Don Virginio Orsino, Duke of Bracciano, a small province of western Italy. Did Shakespeare take the name of the Queen's VIP guest in vain, by making him the lovesick Duke of Illyria? Did he call the play *Twelfth Night* (or, *What You Will*) because no other title suggested itself? All three of his mid-period comedies have throwaway titles. The name of the piece performed that night was not entered in the court record; but the Duke wrote home to his wife that he was fêted with 'a mixed comedy with pieces of music and dances'.

A strong case has been argued, for obvious reasons, that this was the first night of *Twelfth Night*; but the play seems more likely to date from later that year, with its title and the Duke's name suggested by the festivities at court that January. *Twelfth Night*, after all, signals the end of the reign of the Lord of Misrule, whose spirit of mischief informs the play, with its quirky reversals of fortune disrupting the natural order in Olivia's household. Like many of Shakespeare's comedies, especially when commanded for private performance, *Twelfth Night* lends itself especially to an airing on public holidays, when celebratory loss of inhibition can release otherwise inaccessible truths.

> If music be the food of love, play on
> Give me excess of it; that surfeiting,
> The appetite may sicken, and so die.

The play's famous opening lines, spoken by Orsino, Duke of Illyria, may also constitute a private (and somewhat risqué) expression of sympathy from Shakespeare to his friend Southampton, still languishing in the Tower, for whom he had expressed such similar sentiments in the opening to Sonnet 8: 'Music to hear, why hear'st thou music sadly?'

Numerous sources were available for the notion of a girl disguised as a boy falling in love with her master, in this case Barnabe Riche's prose narrative *The Tale of Apolonius and Silla* (in his *Farewell to Militarie Profession*, 1581), itself but the latest reworking – via De Belleforest and Bandello – of an anonymous Italian play, *Gl'Ingannati* (The Deceived), published in 1537. Malvolio was a caricature of the unpopular, po-faced Controller of the Queen's Household, Sir William Knollys, who lusted after her maid of honour Mary ('Mall') Fitton. As he makes an unwonted effort to smile, and his face is creased into 'more lines than is in the new map with the augmentation of the Indies', the character also gives us the play's *terminus a quo*, as just such a map had been published in 1599.

Though popular in Shakespeare's lifetime, *Twelfth Night* somehow seems to have escaped publication, first appearing in print in the First Folio of 1623. As it took its place in the Globe's popular repertoire, Shakespeare's stakeholding was beginning to pay dividends. On 1 May 1602 he paid the considerable sum of £320 to William Combe and his nephew John for one hundred and seven acres of arable land in 'old' Stratford, farming country to the north of the town. He did not trouble to return home for the transaction, delegating his brother Gilbert to represent him at the formal handover of the four 'yardlands'. Six months later, that October, he also purchased a cottage on the south side of Chapel Lane, across the road from New Place, apparently as the home for a gardener.

When it came to property and other investments, Shakespeare was never fussy about those with whom he did business. These Combes were not the most popular family in Stratford; by lending money at the high rate of 10 per cent – known as 'ten in the hundred' – old William's nephew John soon became the wealthiest man in town, and one of the least liked. In Shakespeare's retirement, shortly before his death, the poet's peace of mind would be threatened by Combe's intent to 'enclose' the land in which he had bought an interest.

Legend has it that, drinking with mutual friends one day, Combe told Shakespeare 'in a laughing manner' that he supposed he would eventually write his epitaph; so, in case he predeceased the poet, he would like to hear it now. 'Immediately', so the story goes, Shakespeare replied:

> Ten in the Hundred lies here ingrav'd,
> 'Tis a Hundred to Ten, his Soul is not sav'd:
> If any Man ask, Who lies in this Tomb?
> Oh! ho! quoth the Devil, 'tis my John-a-Combe.

'The sharpness of the satire,' according to Rowe, 'stung the man so severely that he never forgave it.'

This is but one of several random epitaphs attributed to Shakespeare, another of which concerns another Combe. 'Everybody knows Shakespeare's epitaph for John-a-Combe,' according to the jottings of a mid-eighteenth-century Leicestershire parson, Francis Peck, offering another he subsequently wrote for his brother Tom, known as 'Thin-Beard':

> Thin in beard, and thick in purse;
> Never man beloved worse:
> He went to th'grave with many a curse:
> The Devil and He had both one nurse.

Different versions abound in different traditions, lending these stinging verses a less than reliable, word-of-mouth provenance. And the record shows that Shakespeare did not fall out with the Combes. Far from it. Not merely did he continue to do business with them; upon the death of John Combe (who had indeed predeceased him), the poet found that he had been left £5 in his will, so he himself bequeathed his sword – no insignificant keepsake – to John's nephew Thomas.

At the end of 1602, a humdrum writing year by his standards, it is intriguing that Shakespeare's mind was as much on his Stratford

Shakespeare named in John Combe's will, proved 10 November 1615.

landholdings as on his work. As both poet and dramatist, he seems to have become becalmed. It is almost as if he required some new impetus, perhaps from the exterior world beyond his own, to renew his creative energies and drive him forward to a new phase of work, a new level of achievement. Very much a creature of his times, as well as eternally above them, he found just such a stimulus in the momentous events of early 1603 – long-awaited, but no less for that an upheaval of state.

On 2 February 1603 the Lord Chamberlain's Men performed a play before their Queen for what proved to be the last time. Six weeks later, on 24 March, after a forty-five-year reign which still stands among the most glorious in English history, Elizabeth I finally breathed her last.

IX

THE KING'S MAN

1603–1606

*E**xeunt* the Tudors; enter the Stuarts. Not until she was on her deathbed did Elizabeth finally deign to name her heir, whispering to attendant Privy Councillors that she could not possibly be succeeded by anyone but a king – 'and who should that be but our cousin of Scotland?' Horsemen rushed the news to Edinburgh, whence King James VI of Scotland and I of England embarked on a triumphal progress south.

Two years younger than Shakespeare, James was a cultivated but unlikeable, self-indulgent man, fond of his pleasures, not least food and wine – which he preferred served to him on bended knee, preferably by the barons who vied to entertain him in splendour on his stately six-week journey to London. En route the new King dispensed justice as liberally as honours, creating no fewer than three hundred new knights while straining to appear even-handed with offenders against the law. In Newark, on 21 April, he magnanimously freed all the prisoners in the castle while ordering the immediate execution, without trial, of a cutpurse caught red-handed in the crowd struggling for a glimpse of him.

Such extremes of justice and mercy gave Shakespeare ideas, as did James's reluctance to put his royal personage on show to the common people. When he arrived in the capital on 7 May, the new King chose to free select prisoners from the Tower (including the Earl of Southampton), but did not relish the acclaim of the mob pressing to see his parade. 'God's wounds,' he protested, 'I will pull down my breeches and they shall also see my arse!' Or, to put it another way:

> I love the people,
> But do not like to stage me to their eyes;
> Though it do well, I do not relish well
> Their loud applause and *aves* vehement;
> Nor do I think the man of safe discretion
> That does affect it

Already James was offering Shakespeare material for the new play his company could perform before him the following Christmas.

Warrant for the Letters Payment appointing Shakespeare and his companions to be the King's Players, 1603; enrolment of the same Letters Patent, also 1603.

Within ten days of arriving in London, although besieged by other claims for his attention, the new King took the Lord Chamberlain's troupe under his own royal patronage. Shakespeare was now one of the King's Men. He is named in the Letters Patent prepared on James's instructions by Keeper of the Privy Seal, the newly ennobled Lord Cecil, and issued under the Great Seal of England on 17 May 1603. The royal warrant licenses and authorizes these our servants Lawrence Fletcher, William Shakespeare, Richard Burbage, Augustyne Phillips, John Heminges, Henrie Condell, William Sly, Robert Armyn, Richard Cowly, and the rest of their associates, freely to use and exercise the art and faculty of playing comedies, tragedies, histories, interludes, morals, pastorals, stage plays, and such others like as they have already studied or hereafter shall use or study, as well for the recreation of our loving subjects as for our solace and pleasure when we shall think good to see them during our pleasure . . .

If this opening carries echoes of Polonius' litany of 'tragical-comical-historical-pastoral', what follows amounts to a royal command to treat the actors according to their deserts – or, God's bodykins, much better. Whether they were performing at 'their usual house called the Globe', or in any city, university town or borough of the realm, all justices, mayors, other officers and loving subjects were instructed 'to allow them such former courtesies as hath been given to men of their place and quality, and also what further favour you shall show to these our servants for our sake'.

By taking them under his royal wing, James had officially confirmed the standing of the Lord Chamberlain's Men as the leading theatrical company in the land. The royal patronage bestowed on London's other main companies was distinctly less grand, the Admiral's troupe and the Earl of Worcester's becoming merely Prince Henry's and Queen Anne's Men. As one of the King's Men, Shakespeare was now an ex-officio Groom of the Bedchamber, a member of the royal household entitled to four and a half yards of scarlet cloth for his livery, to be worn at the coronation. In the 'issue of cloth' accounts kept by the Master of the Great Wardrobe, Sir George Home, Shakespeare's name heads the list of lucky recipients. No doubt to his relief, as a writer who had spent much of his working life puncturing the pomposity of courtiers, the royal parade was cancelled when London again found itself in the grip of the plague. The public was barred from attending James's coronation, and the festivities radically curtailed. So the King's Men were spared the embarrassment of dressing in borrowed robes, a gaggle of reluctant bit-players on the fringe of another man's show.

Shakespeare's name heads the list of players in the accounts of the Master of the Great Wardrobe for the issue of red cloth to the King's Men.

But James was to prove a valuable patron to Shakespeare and his fellows. In the thirteen years between the King's accession and the poet's death, the King's Men would play at court no fewer than 187 times – an average of thirteen royal command performances a year, compared with three during Elizabeth's reign. He paid twice as much, what's more, reckoning his post-prandial entertainment a legitimate drain on the Privy Purse. For the King's Men, this meant gainful employment even when the theatres were closed by the plague – as, for instance, that August, when they were paid £21 12s to entertain the new Spanish ambassador, Don Juan Fernandez de Velasco, at Somerset House (which, with a peace treaty with England's old foe in the offing, the King had placed at his disposal).

As the upper crust evacuated London for the duration, which turned out to be almost a year, the King repaired to Wilton House, near Salisbury, as a guest of the Countess of Pembroke. In the autumn of 1603 his players were summoned to perform *As You Like It* there, for which they were paid the munificent sum of £30. 'We have the man Shakespeare with us,' the Countess wrote to her son William, who had his own troupe of players, the Earl of Pembroke's Men.

But a royal command is a royal command. For the new Earl of Pembroke, who had succeeded to the title only two years earlier, this was also his chance to consolidate his standing at court. Out of favour with the old Queen since his seduction of Mary Fitton, he divined from James's generosity to Southampton and others that the new monarch was content to wipe slates clean. So Pembroke hied him to Wilton, where he seems to have renewed his acquaintance with Shakespeare. This, after the poet's death, was the man to whom Heminges and Condell would co-dedicate the First Folio of his collected works. His name being William Herbert, he is the man some identify as the 'Mr W.H.' to whom the Sonnets are mysteriously inscribed; some go so far as to consider him the 'fair youth' to whom many are addressed. Both notions, alas, are merely fanciful.

But Pembroke's mother, the Dowager Countess, was indisputably the sister of the late Sir Philip Sidney, herself cultured enough to have edited his Sonnet sequence *Astrophel and Stella* after his death at the

Battle of Zutphen. Here at Wilton she had worked with Sidney on his prose romance *Arcadia*. Now forty-two, still renowned as a beauty to be reckoned with, a hostess of elegant, learned house parties, she loved the theatre enough to have tried her own hand as a playwright. During this sojourn, it has been suggested, she might have showed the man Shakespeare her own modest effort *Antonius*, adapted from the *Marc-Antoine* of the 'somewhat insipid' French Senecan Robert Garnier. Did he praise it dutifully, while really thinking what an opportunity had been missed, and making a mental note to return in due course to North's Plutarch?

Whether or not she gave Shakespeare the idea for a play about Antony and Cleopatra, the formidable Countess certainly inspired a distinctive figure at the heart of his work-in-progress. Or so George Bernard Shaw believed, whatever admirers of Juliet or Portia, Rosalind or Cleopatra may think of Shaw's claim that the Countess of Rousillon in *All's Well That Ends Well* is 'the most charming of all his women, young or old'. Her son Bertram spurns an arranged marriage, just like the Countess of Pembroke's own son, not to mention that other nobleman who weaves in and out of Shakespeare's life, the Earl of Southampton. For another comedy with a throwaway name, so elegant as to have been written more for private than public performance, he was again treating of matters uncomfortably close to home.

Drawing on the tale of Giletta of Narbona in Boccaccio's *Decameron*, probably via William Painter's recent version in his *Palace of Pleasure* (1566–67, revised 1575), Shakespeare added to the traditional folk-loric mix the distinctive characters of the Countess, the lord Lafew, the clown Lavatch and Parolles, the 'man of words' who is as much the darker new breed of Shakespearean nihilist as the braggart warrior dating back to Roman comedy. 'Simply the thing I am,' he concludes grimly, 'shall make me live.' The poet's sympathies seem to lie with poor Helena, the humble doctor's daughter who falls in love with the heedless Bertram; he inverts the central values of his source by making the older characters morally and socially flexible, the young much more conscious of class and respectability. The age-old 'bed trick' with which Helena eventually entraps her nobleman, a bolder variant of that in *The Comedy of Errors*, seems as crude as it will just when re-used in his next play – another so-called comedy with dark overtones, landing its central characters with dilemmas more painful than amusing. The apparently happy endings are, in both cases, only tentatively so. Along the tortuous route by which these couples have arrived at their unions, we suspect, lie the seeds of further trouble ahead. Hence the ironic note in the title of *All's Well That Ends Well*, to which he might well have appended a question mark.

The deserted wife who overcomes impossible odds to regain her husband is as ancient a motif, dating back to the Greek myths, as the corrupt ruler who perverts justice to gratify his lust. In *Measure for Measure*, Shakespeare's mood grows even darker, weaving religious language and imagery into a work obsessed with sex, hypocrisy and death. The very title comes from the New Testament, specifically St Matthew's account of Christ's Sermon on the Mount, which he would have read in the Geneva translation: 'Judge not, that ye be not judged. For with what judgment ye judge, ye shall be judged: and with what measure ye mete, it shall be measured unto you again.'

As it moves between Angelo's inner sanctum, a prison and a brothel, this remains one of the most cerebral of all Shakespeare's works, while also one of the most sexually charged. Chaste and virtuous to the point of priggishness, Isabella is about to enter a convent when her brother Claudio is cruelly condemned to death for impregnating his bride-to-be; Angelo's insistence on her sexual favours in return for her brother's life is played out on a plane high above Shakespeare's immediate source: the tale of Juriste, Epitia and her brother Vico in a dramatisation of his own novella by the Italian poet Giovanni Batista Cinthio, who would also provide the inspiration for Shakespeare's next, equally sex-obsessed work.

Cinthio's drama *Epita*, published in 1583, was itself based on a true story which had recently intrigued writers all over Europe. An Italian judge had extorted sex from the wife of a condemned murderer, then executed him anyway, only to be betrayed by the widow, forced to marry her and then himself executed. The story had most recently been reworked in England by Thomas Lupton in *Too Good to be True* (1581). As he developed ideas from both works, Shakespeare seems to have known his Cinthio in the Italian, though it was available in an English version by another writer haunted by the story, George Whetstone, whose *Promos and Cassandra* (1578) and *A Mirror for Magistrates* (1584) offered further nuances. The character of Mariana was Shakespeare's own distinctive invention, to rub salt in Angelo's wounds, enabling him to re-use the 'bed trick' of his last play, *All's Well*, to even more effect. It enables Isabella to retain her virtue, even forgive Angelo, without having to marry him. But the Duke's sudden whim to marry her himself, at the end of a notoriously protracted final scene, remains as unconvincing as any authorial afterthought – almost as if something deep in Shakespeare was already reaching towards the themes of redemption which would crown his final works.

Two other sources are of more than merely scholastic interest: *The Time Triumphant*, reputedly by Shakespeare's fellow-player Robert Armin, offered detail of King James's arrival in London; it was published in 1604, a year after the King's own *Basilicon Doron*, unique in British history as a bestseller by a king on kingship. Among other contemporary references, Lucio's mention of peace talks refer to the negotiations with Spain which resulted in a peace treaty that August, while Mistress Overdone's talk of 'the war . . . the sweat . . . the gallows' appear to concern the prior war with Spain, the plague gripping London while Shakespeare was writing the play, and the execution of co-conspirators of Sir Walter Raleigh – all major events of 1604. The theatres reopened that April, after a closure of all but a year; but the first recorded performance of *Measure for Measure* was that before the King eight months later, on 26 December. Another chamber-piece more suited to private than public performance, its failure to appear in print before the First Folio suggests that it did not fare well at the box office.

In the year from November 1604 to 31 October 1605, according to the accounts of the Master of the Revels, Shakespeare and the King's Men performed at court at least eleven times – ten different plays, including seven by Shakespeare, mostly hardy annuals from *The Comedy of Errors* and *Love's Labour's Lost* to *The Merry Wives of Windsor*. The one play James specifically asked to see twice was *The Merchant of Venice*. In *Measure for Measure*, Shakespeare was again taking risks: gratifying the King's interest in justice and mercy while chronicling his own disenchantment with both.

As a comedy, his twelfth, it seems to end a line of dramatic inquiry he had been pursuing throughout the fifteen or so years of his writing career, refining it to the point where the twentieth century has trouble calling this a comedy, preferring to label it a 'problem' play. Its bleak mood, savage humour and 'predominant harshness of tone' – a comedy which takes place almost entirely in darkness, shadows or dingy interiors – suggests Shakespeare felt he had mined this vein to its very core, to what he considered a natural conclusion. The problems posed by the final scene further suggest that, immersed in Cinthio, he was already brooding about *Othello*.

Measure for Measure was the last comedy Shakespeare would write. The great tragedies immediately ahead were already taking shape in his mind.

'Let's kill all the lawyers,' he had written as early as *2 Henry VI*. As he worked on this last statement on the law and its administrators, steeped in disillusion with both, Shakespeare was venting a personal as well as philosophical rage. The law's failure to protect a writer's copyright continued to plague him, as the appearance of a 'bad' quarto of *Hamlet* in 1603 (which records, *en passant*, that it had already been performed 'in the two universities of Oxford and Cambridge') now moved his company – not the playwright himself – to supervise the publication of a revised, more accurate text, thus sparing posterity the laughable 1603 'memorial reconstruction' of the most famous speech in all literature.

> *Ham.* To be, or not to be, I there's the point,
> To Die, to sleepe, is that all? I all:
> No, to sleepe, to dreame, I mary there it goes,
> For in that dreame of death, when wee awake,
> And borne before an euerlasting Iudge,
> From whence no passenger euer retur'nd,
> The vndiscouered country, at whose sight
> The happy smile, and the accursed damn'd.
> But for this, the ioyfull hope of this,
> Whol'd beare the scornes and flattery of the world,
> Scorned by the right rich, the rich curssed of the poore?

'To be or not to be' as misremembered by unscrupulous actors assisting the 'pirate' publisher of the 1603 'bad' quarto of Hamlet.

Legal niceties meanwhile continued to dog his business dealings back in Stratford. That spring he felt obliged to sue his neighbour

Philip Rogers, an apothecary, for payment of a paltry debt barely exceeding £2; having sold Rogers twenty bushels of malt, and then lent him two shillings, Shakespeare had received only six shillings in repayment. He demanded ten shillings damages on top of the 35s 10d due. There is no record how the court ruled, or that he ever received his due; but this would not be the last time he chose to pursue debtors.

At the same time, ironically, he was living in London amid domestic complexities which would return to torment him in the shape of a protracted lawsuit – not, for once, as plaintiff or defendant, this time as a character witness.

During the plague year of 1604 Shakespeare was lodging in Silver Street, Cripplegate, with a family named Mountjoy. He had probably known them some years, as he had given their Huguenot name to the French herald in *Henry V*, written as he and the Globe had crossed the river in 1599. Probably he met them through his friend Richard Field, the printer from Stratford, who lived over his own shop in nearby Wood Street, and whose French wife Jacqueline would have worshipped alongside Mary Mountjoy at London's French church. Why and when Shakespeare moved back across the river, to this north-west corner of the city walls, we do not know; the plague may well have been cause enough, and it may be no coincidence that his colleagues and friends John Heminges and Henry Condell lived nearby, in the next-door parish of St Mary's, Aldermanbury.

Silver Street was the centre of the lucrative wig industry, once patronised by the late Queen herself; from Ben Jonson we know the delicious details that 'her teeth were made in Blackfriars, both her eyebrows in the Strand, and her hair in Silver Street'. Shakespeare's landlord, Christopher Mountjoy, was a prosperous maker of 'tires', or expensively jewelled adornments for the headgear of well-to-do ladies. In 1604, while Shakespeare lived under their roof, the Mountjoys' daughter – Mary, like her mother – was being courted by one of her father's apprentices, Stephen Belott. The Mountjoys approved of the match, but Belott was holding out for a larger dowry, so Shakespeare was asked to intervene. According to one of the serving maids, Joan Johnson, Mountjoy 'did send and persuade one Mr Shakespeare that lay in the house to persuade the plaintiff to the same marriage'. The poet succeeded in negotiating a financial settlement to the satisfaction of both parties – £60 on the celebration of the nuptials and £200 on Mountjoy's death, according to Belott – and the couple were married on 19 November at the parish church of St Olave.

That might have been the end of the matter – and no more than a tantalising glimpse of Shakespeare playing reluctant Pandarus – had not both parties reneged on the deal. Instead of staying on in Silver Street as expected, presumably to inherit the family business, Belott took Mary off to start up a rival emporium, hiring an apprentice of his own; so the enraged Mountjoy handed over a mere £10, throwing in some sticks of old furniture and a random assortment of cast-off chattels from worn blankets to a small pair of scissors. In vain did Mountjoy's wife plead with him to treat their daughter better; but the elder Mary's death less than two years later, in 1606, effected a temporary *rapprochement*. The Belotts moved back in to look after her widowed father, and did indeed become his partners in the business. All too soon the partners fell out again; Belott flounced out, taking his wife with him; the elderly Mountjoy was left alone to drown his sorrows in a life of increasing debauchery. By 1612, when Shakespeare was back in Stratford, enjoying a supposedly peaceful retirement, rumours reached Belott that the embittered, ever more dissolute old man, who was anyway drinking away his inheritance, intended to cut him off without a penny.

So poor Shakespeare was summoned to London to give evidence in a court case attempting to establish the truth of the original marital settlement. By now it was all of eight years before, and his memory was hazy. While describing the apprentice Belott, in his deposition, as 'a very good and industrious servant' who 'did well and honestly behave himself', the poet recalled the sum due as £50, and had no recollection of the £200 supposedly promised on Mountjoy's death. In the matter of Belott v Mountjoy the Court of Requests adjourned for a month, asking Shakespeare to reappear for further examination; but the second time around he did not show up. It was all so long ago, and he'd had a lifetime of lawyers. The court eventually took a dim view of the conduct of both the irascible father and the erratic son-in-law, and split the difference by awarding Belott twenty nobles, or £6 13s 4d. There is no record that Mountjoy ever paid up.

This tawdry domestic drama, the stuff of a kith-and-kin farce if he had not long ago left such antics behind him, offers a touching vignette of Shakespeare as the amenable lodger – 'a man among men', as he has been described in this context – willing to lend a hand in sorting out another family's problems. But this glimpse ahead to the elderly playwright, losing his memory, irritated to be summoned up and down to London from the peace of his rural retirement, assumes a particular poignancy in 1604, when this sorry saga started. For the year of his fortieth birthday was certainly a watershed in his life, when a sudden change of dramatic gear suggests a sense of physical as well as mental foreboding.

It is now that Anthony Burgess begins to fret about Shakespeare's diet, wishing upon him less of the 'quick snack, then back to work' and more of 'the odd American-style salad'. Still acting as well as writing – the records show him onstage in Jonson's *Sejanus* in 1603 – the poet-actor-playwright was certainly driving himself as hard as ever. He was as prone as any Londoner to the effects of too much liquor – water was not yet drinkable, tea had not become the English way – and too many carbohydrates. But there is no need to take too anxious a cholesterol count. As Burgess himself suggests, Shakespeare sounds like less of a glutton than Jonson. Even Falstaff's over-eating was largely confined to high-protein capons, though Hal does tick him off over too much 'sugar-candy'; nourishing pippins and cheese are served in *The Merry Wives of Windsor*, root vegetables in Timon of Athens' cave; Macbeth seems to speak for a 'nothing to excess' regime on Shakespeare's part when he toasts his dinner guests:

Now good digestion wait on appetite,
And health on both.

If Shakespeare was developing problems, they were more spiritual than physical. As he turned forty, the world was too much with him. The exuberant gaiety of his early work is no more. His last plays to be called comedies are the work of a gravely reflective man, nostalgic for times past, not so much cynical as sceptical, more battle-hardened than world-weary, old before his time.

Forty was quite an age for the day, five years beyond the average life expectancy, especially for those choosing the lawless, polluted, disease-ridden life of the capital. Where his soul had been scarred by the death of his son, the demise of his father had merely aged him. The natural *joie de vivre* had gone, to return only fitfully in his writings, replaced by the more sombre, searching spirit of inquiry which would now produce his mature masterworks.

Whatever else was troubling him, Shakespeare next chose to address a subject unexplored in any of his previous twenty-six plays, but to which he would return, as if obsessively: sexual jealousy. Whether reading or watching *Othello* and *The Winter's Tale*, or indeed lingering over the Sonnets, it is hard to resist the conclusion that the poet capable of evoking the 'green-eyed monster' in such violent language must have experienced its unique horrors himself.

Othello and Desdemona make 'the beast with two backs'; her father, Brabantio, is told that an 'old black ram' is 'tupping your white ewe'; Leontes thinks he sees his wife and best friend 'paddling palms and pinching fingers', then turns to tell the audience:

> There have been,
> Or I am much deceiv'd, cuckolds ere now,
> And many a man there is, even at this present,
> Now, while I speak this, holds his wife by th' arm,
> That little thinks she has been sluiced in 's absence,
> And his pond fished by his next neighbour, by
> Sir Smile, his neighbour.

It is impossible to believe that the man who wrote these lines, who fastened on that word 'sluiced' and the image of 'Sir Smile, his neighbour', had not himself experienced the full anguish of sexual jealousy. Nor can we think for a moment that it was caused by his long-distance wife Anne, with some observers (including James Joyce's Stephen Dedalus) who have gone so far as to suggest that Shakespeare's brother Richard had done the poet's office betwixt his sheets. The Dark Lady was as good for sexual jealousy as for the clap – more so, perhaps, than other London women of easy virtue with whom Shakespeare might have expended his spirit in a waste of shame. But who might have caused him such powerful emotions at this particular time, feeding the frenzy behind Othello's 'goats and monkeys'? Who, for one, but the indirect cause of his future legal woes, Mary Mountjoy senior?

Cuckoldry at court tends to survive the vagaries of time, living on in diaries and letters to shiver the reputations of those involved; further down the social scale, it takes some freak event for guilty secrets to survive four hundred years and more. Unfortunately for Mary Mountjoy, she chose to consult the physician-astrologer Simon Forman, an assiduous keeper of notebooks, on discovering that she was pregnant by a neighbour named Henry Wood, a mercer and trader in cloths around the corner in Swan Alley. 'Mary Mountjoy alained' (or 'concealed'), reads Forman's cryptic note of her visit – preserved in the Bodleian Library, Oxford, along with his jottings on Richard Burbage's wife Winifred, and indeed Philip Henslowe, whom he treated in February 1597 for 'tingling and itching in his head' and 'much melancholy'.

Just as well, for Mary Mountjoy's pregnancy proved to be a false alarm. So her marriage survived to see the younger Mary marry the apprentice, with all that followed. Was Mary senior flighty enough to seduce her lodger – himself not averse, as we shall see, to taking advantage of his landladies – and then to torment him with her attentions to Wood or indeed her husband? Had she and Shakespeare secretly been lovers for five years or more before he moved in, the name of Mountjoy in *Henry V* being his coded thanks for her flirtatious help with the play's adventures in French? Or did Christopher Mountjoy pour out to his long-suffering lodger the agonies of knowing his wife was in love elsewhere?

These are passing thoughts, no more, for Shakespeare himself surely knew enough of the pangs of jealousy before moving in with the Mountjoys; the later Sonnets are full of the agonies which would now shudder so terribly through *Othello*. He had also been a player at court four years earlier during a prolonged visit by the Moorish ambassador of the King of Barbary, an exotic figure who attracted much attention; he and his Muslim retinue, being 'strange in their ways', were naturally described as 'Barbarians'. A portrait of the ambassador painted during his visit, and inscribed '*Legatus regis barbariae in Angliam*', settles the age-old debate about the precise ethnic background Shakespeare intended to convey by the word Moor. 'Is it too fanciful,' asks one of the play's most recent

The Moorish ambassador to Queen Elizabeth's court, 1600–1, while
Shakespeare was writing Othello.

(and perceptive) editors, 'to suppose that this very face haunted Shakespeare's imagination and inspired the writing of his tragedy?'

'No nation in the world is so subject unto jealousy, for they will rather lose their lives than put up any disgrace in the behalf of their women,' wrote John Leo, a Barbary-bred Moor, of his 'very proud and high-minded, and wonderfully addicted unto wrath' fellow-countrymen. 'Their wits are but mean, and they are so credulous that they will believe matters impossible which are told them.' Shakespeare undoubtedly consulted John Pory's English translation of Leo's *A Geographical History of Africa*, published in 1600 during the Moorish embassy to London. Leo himself speaks of women who wear gowns 'curiously embroidered', just like that fateful handkerchief. Pory's summary of Leo's 'great travels' mirrors Othello's vivid account of his own adventures, as does Philemon Holland's 1601 translation of Pliny's *Natural History of the World*, which mentions 'the medicinal gum of the Arabian trees, mines of sulphur, a state made of chrysolite, mandragora and coloquintida', not to mention the Pontic Sea, the Anthropophagi, and 'men whose heads / Do grow beneath their shoulders'.

For the power structure of Venice – then renowned in England for the loose morals of its courtesans – Shakespeare consulted Sir Lewis Lewkenor's *The Commonwealth and Government of Venice*, largely a translation of the Latin text of Cardinal Contrarini, published in 1599. But his main source was again Cinthio, specifically a short story from his collection entitled *Hecatommithi*, published in Italy in 1565. We do not know of an English translation available to Shakespeare, though versions existed in French and Spanish. Again, he makes countless significant advances on the original story; to judge how far he rose above his source this time, we need only note that Cinthio's Iago teamed up with Othello to kill Desdemona, beating her to death with a stocking filled with sand, then pulling down the ceiling in an attempt to make her murder look like an accident.

Again, Cinthio appears to have based his own tale on a true recent episode. In 1565 the story circulated Europe of an Italian diplomat in France drawn home by false reports, spread by his enemies, of his wife's infidelity; having confronted her with the accusations, he accepted her denials, but strangled her anyway – apologising as he did so – in the name of his honour. Shakespeare plays with time, with class, nobility, credulity, domesticity, with the concepts of knowledge and honesty. In Othello he creates the first example of a 'noble' black man, however fallible, in Western literature. At a time when Cecil was hearing protests about the number of blackamoors 'infiltrating' English society, it was (to say the least) bold of Shakespeare to make a noble non-savage the most sympathetic of all his tragic heroes – as enlightened on racial prejudice, as pioneeringly anti-bigotry, as he had been in *The Merchant of Venice*.

In Iago he fashions the most diabolical of all his images of evil incarnate, made all the more chilling for the fact that, unlike Richard III and Aaron, he does not kill anyone – except by proxy. The ensign's supposed motives for poisoning his master's mind against his bride – that he had been passed over for the lieutenantship, that Othello had seduced his own wife – are so inadequate (the latter stretching even his own belief) as to take on the eeriest notes of bewildered, almost apologetic self-justification. Coleridge's famous verdict, 'the motive-hunting of motiveless malignity', has never been bettered.

In the absence of any supernatural element (as in *Hamlet* and *Macbeth*), or extreme psychological disturbance (as in *Lear*), *Othello* remains the most intimate, the most direct of Shakespeare's four great tragedies. It is as a private, not as a public man that its protagonist is undone, causing passing political embarrassment to the state to which he has done some service, but no great disruption of the natural order. This play is more 'insistently time-bound' than the others, 'concerned with the here and now rather than with the eternal verities'. As such, lacking the metaphysical complexities of *Hamlet* or *Lear*, it can often have a more direct impact on audiences. When one of the great nineteenth-century Othellos, William Macready, took Iago by the throat, a gentlemen in the audience could bear it all no longer, and famously cried out: 'Choke the devil! Choke him!'

Jealousy and envy: to Elizabethan audiences, familiar with their humours, Othello and Iago were complementary characters, opposite sides of the same coin. If there was much of Shakespeare himself in such of his characters as Hamlet and Lear, he seems to be aware of two sides to his own personality in *Othello*'s complementary central figures. As indeed did Ben Jonson – unable to conceal his reservations, perhaps unwittingly, while trying to pay Shakespeare a posthumous compliment. Says Iago of Othello:

> The Moor is of a free and open nature,
> That thinks men honest that but seem to be so.

Says Jonson of Shakespeare: 'He was indeed honest, and of an open mind and free nature.'

Was the King offended by *Othello* when it was performed before him on 1 November 1604? We have no reason to suppose so. But that Machiavellian villain's name, of course, means James – in Spanish, moreover, the language of England's old enemy, while the names of all the play's other Venetians are appropriately Italian. Refusing to believe that Shakespeare could be so 'tactless', some scholars have used this reason to look for others to move the play earlier, to make it an Elizabethan rather than a Jacobean work – coming straight after *Hamlet*, before the old Queen's death, before peace was made with Spain.

'Echoes' of *Othello* have been spotted in that 'bad' quarto of *Hamlet*, published in 1603, suggesting synchronicity, or even that *Othello* might have pre-dated it. 'To my unfolding lend your prosperous ear', says Desdemona to the Duke of Venice, mirroring Q1 *Hamlet*'s 'to my unfolding / Lend thy listening ear'. The adjective 'Olympus-high' appears in both texts. 'Look on the tragic loading of this bed', Lodovico's words to Iago at the end of *Othello*, supposedly find an 'echo' in Q1 *Hamlet*'s 'Look upon this tragic spectacle'. But echoes have to have a source. Might not the lines in Q1 *Hamlet*, which Shakespeare might have been revising for republication while writing *Othello*, be the original rather than the echo?

The unusual name Montano, which occurs only in *Othello*, appears unexpectedly in Q1 *Hamlet* in lieu of Reynaldo, as if Shakespeare were making an 'unconscious substitution' because the same actor played both parts. On similar grounds the Arden editor links *Othello* to *Twelfth Night*, which follows hard upon *Hamlet*, casting Orsino as Othello, Sir Toby Belch as Iago, Viola as Desdemona, Maria as Emilia, Sir Andrew Aguecheek as Roderigo, Sebastian as Cassio and Malvolio as Brabantio – unless, of course, Burbage insisted on playing Malvolio as well as Othello, in which case Orsino becomes Cassio and Sebastian is downgraded to Montano. This is an entertaining little game, playable with most of Shakespeare's plays, written for a repertory company of actors changed only by age, death, the occasional Kemp-style flouncing-out and the breaking of boy-actors' voices. But this, too, cuts both ways. Did Burbage find Othello fitter training for Malvolio than the other way around? It is hard to see why *Othello* need be wrenched from its logical context after *Measure for Measure*, on that darkening curve via two helpings of Cinthio towards the ultimate bleakness of *Lear*.

One might as well point out, with several twentieth-century editors, that *King Lear* contains distinct 'echoes' of *Measure for Measure*. Beyond the use in both plays of phrases like 'furred gown', 'unaccommodated'/'accommodations' and distinctive deployments of words like 'warped' and 'evasion', they contain parallel themes in the abdication of responsibility by a ruler, and a running debate on justice and authority, permeated with religious language and imagery. The phrase 'Keep me in patience' occurs in both plays. The Duke's words of Isabella, 'Her madness hath the oddest frame of sense', echoes the 'method' spotted by Polonius in Hamlet's 'madness' and pre-echoes the 'reason in madness' observed by Edgar in *Lear*. All this means is that Shakespeare was not above recycling good phrases as he returned, *en passant*, to recurring themes. It tells us nothing about the order in which the plays were written.

Richard Burbage would certainly have considered the role of Othello a more suitable warm-up for Lear than Malvolio. Laurence Olivier, who had played all the Burbage roles before finally tackling Othello at the age of fifty-six, had a theory about this 'monstrous burden' of a part: 'I think Shakespeare and Burbage got drunk together one night and Burbage said, "I can play anything you write, anything at all". And Shakespeare said, "Right, I'll fix you, boy!" And then he wrote *Othello*.' If Olivier had been playing the chronology game, he might have capped his joke by adding the two 'monstrous burdens' for any actor which Shakespeare wrote next.

Were they also monstrous burdens for James I to watch, seeing reflections of himself – 'the play's the thing' – like Claudius in *Hamlet*? If *Othello* took liberties with his name, *King Lear* mocked his love of flattery and the Scottish play to follow held uneasy, home-based echoes of a recent attempt on his life. No, James was too self-admiring to take offence at nuances in *Othello* and *Lear*, too cultured a theatre-lover to derive anything but sheer pleasure from his very own acting troupe's prolific and erudite playwright. Shakespeare's great burst of self-confidence may have driven him perilously close to the royal bone, suggesting that kings need to be told harsh truths by their licensed retainers, and stripped of their creature comforts to appreciate that they are, in the end, as much of a 'poor, bare, fork'd animal' as their humblest subject. He may even, as has recently been argued, have been covertly trying to 'discredit the values of absolute monarchy, thereby paving the way for the English revolution'.

But the play's most interesting exterior references are to himself. If Shakespeare is playing the Fool to James's Lear, he is even more playing the real-life father tragically deprived of his beloved son, and pouring all his paternal love, sharpened by years of guilty absenteeism, into his daughters. Only twice more, in *Coriolanus* and *The Winter's Tale*, would Shakespeare give his protagonists an even remotely significant son, in each case still children, as if young Hamnets frozen in time. The emphasis from *Lear* onwards is otherwise exclusively, almost obsessively, on daughters. Her purity intensified by her evil sisters, Goneril and Regan, Cordelia is the forerunner of Marina, Imogen, Perdita and Miranda. Shakespeare's mind was on his daughters, Susanna and Judith, now twenty-two and twenty, and far the most eligible young women in Stratford.

With their dowries in mind, perhaps, he now set about enlarging his Warwickshire property portfolio, this time with a huge purchase. On 24 July 1605 he spent no less than £440 on 'tithes of corn, grain, blade and hay' in the town itself, old Stratford, Welcombe and Bishopston. New Place had cost less than a seventh as much. Shakespeare had bided his time before acting on that advice seven years before from Abraham Sturley, on a hint from Adrian Quiney, that tithes might be a good investment. In the deeds of purchase from Ralph Hubaud of Ipsley, a former county sheriff, we catch tantalising glimpses of Shakespeare's true and trusty Stratford friends. Again a witness, as he had been three years earlier to the poet's last land purchase, was Anthony Nash of Welcombe, to whom Shakespeare would entrust the collection of his rents, and whose son would marry the poet's granddaughter; another was the lawyer handling the transaction, Francis Collins. Both would be remembered in Shakespeare's will, which Collins himself oversaw.

In London, Shakespeare himself was now remembered in the will of another longstanding friend, Augustine Phillips, fellow actor and co-founder of the Lord Chamberlain's Men a decade and more earlier. His name heads the list of bequests in Phillips's will upon his death in the spring of 1605. 'Item. I give and bequeath to my fellow William Shakespeare a thirty shilling piece in gold.' From a man with a widow and four daughters to look out for, it was a substantial bequest, a measure of the depth of the bond between them. Of their fellow actors, only Henry Condell received as much.

By 1605, four years after his father's death, Shakespeare had rebuilt his family's fortunes. The residence in Henley Street now known as The Birthplace; the handsome spread flourishing around New Place, complete with full-time gardener; extensive landholdings within the town and all around it: this was an estate more than substantial enough to ensure his family's future. At the age of forty-one, he need never work again. So this is the moment when we can reflect, with as much relief as satisfaction, that Pope got it wrong. Shakespeare did not write plays only for the money. There was plenty more he wanted to say.

Shakespeare was also at the height of his fame. London publishers felt free to attach his name to any old play in the hope of boosting sales. In 1595 and 1602 they had merely attached the initials W.S. to apocryphal works such as *Locrine* and *Thomas Lord Cromwell*; now, in 1605, the full name of William Shakespeare was brazenly appended to another play he did not write, *The London Prodigal*, as it would be again in 1608 to another called *A Yorkshire Tragedy*. Far from writing one of these routine, bums-on-seats comedies of manners or tear-jerking bodice-rippers, Shakespeare was at the time completing the most intricate, profound and perplexing work even he would ever lay before an audience.

Since the previous year, 1604, King James's central political priority had been a sustained campaign to persuade the English Parliament to endorse a formal union with Scotland. In speech after speech he made repeated reference to the troubles brought upon early Britain by its divisions. Shakespeare, insofar as he was a political animal, seems to have been pro-union; the central theme of James's speeches certainly chimed with the sustained motif in his own work of the disruption of the natural order brought about by division and disunion. In seeking a source for a play which might please the King, while taking his own ideas further, he looked beyond Holinshed and Geoffrey of Monmouth to an old warhorse from his early repertory days with which he had long been familiar, and in which he may well himself have acted.

That May, probably by no coincidence, also saw publication of *The True Chronicle History of King Leir,* performed at the Rose by the Queen's and Sussex's Men as long before as 1594, when it was also entered in the Stationers Register but apparently not printed. The authorship of *The True Chronicle* is unknown; cases have been made for Peele, William Rankins and the true author of *Locrine.* Its publication used to be taken by scholars as a *terminus a quo* for the date of Shakespeare's play, on the grounds that he drew upon it; more likely, it was published in an attempt to capitalise on the box-office success of his new version. Shakespeare was familiar enough with the *True Chronicle* to know what he wanted to make use of, and what to discard.

The Leir of the *True Chronicle* has a daughter named Cordelia who has vowed not to marry a king except for love; the play begins with Leir devising a cunning plan 'to try which of my daughters loves me best', assuming that Cordelia's protestations will corner her into accepting a royal husband of his choice. But his plan is betrayed by the wicked Skalliger to Cordelia's sisters Gonorill and Ragan, who promise to marry whomever their father chooses, while Cordelia refuses to be drawn into flattery. Leir does not banish her, but divides his kingdom between her sisters. Visiting Brittayne in disguise, to check out reports of the beauty of Leir's daughters, the Gallian king woos and weds Cordelia, who still cannot be persuaded by her father's loyal friend Perillus to claim her due share of her father's kingdom. While lamenting Leir's stupidity, Perillus vows to stay loyal to him. Mistreated by his other daughters, who even plot to kill him, Leir accepts an invitation to visit Gallia, where he meets the king and Cordelia disguised as countryfolk, and is reconciled

with his daughter. Gallia invades Brittayne on Leir's behalf, defeats
the forces of his other daughters' husbands, Cornwall and Cambria,
and restores the king to his throne – on which, it would appear,
he reigns happily ever after.

So neither Leir nor Cordelia dies. Although Perillus is the
protoype of Kent – and perhaps the role Shakespeare himself had
played – there is no equivalent of Gloucester or his sons (whom
he took in part from Sidney's *Arcadia*). Leir is not portrayed as a
particularly old man, nor an especially foolish one. He does not
lose his wits. There is no storm; there is no Fool. The magpie
Shakespeare, as was his wont, plundered detail from a few other
handy sources: Samuel Harsnett's *Declaration of Egregious Popish
Impostures* (published in March 1603), William Strachey's sonnet
on Jonson's play *Sejanus* (August 1605), perhaps a pamphlet entitled
*Strange fearful & true newes which happened at Carlstadt, in the Kingdome
of Croatia* (February 1606). But *King Lear* otherwise represents one of
the most extreme stretches of his dramatic and poetic imagination.
'Never,' as C. J. Sisson noted, 'did Shakespeare take a more deliberate
or more striking decision than to reject version after version of the
story,' and reshape it as he did.

A former Lord Mayor of London, Sir William Allen, had recently
in his dotage divided his estates between his three married daughters,
and arranged to stay with each of them in turn. The story went that
they resented the cost of their father's upkeep, and his rudeness to
their servants; raining curses on their heads, he died alone and in
misery. This tale doing the rounds may have prompted some detail
in Shakespeare's first scene, so much more compact than that of
the *True Chronicle*; but one might as well make specific claims for
his reading of Florio's translation of Montaigne, whose spirit clearly
permeates the play. Or wonder what Edmund Shakespeare had done
to merit the hijacking of his name for one of his brother's cruellest
and most unscrupulous villains. Wherever else scholars may delve
in wide-eyed attempts to pin the butterfly of Shakespeare's genius,
the fact remains that Gloucester's suffering, Edmund's malignity,
Edgar's role-playing, the loose morals of Goneril and Regan and
the Fool's devastating commentary are nowhere to be found in
any previous version of this story. Nor, one might add, is poetry
so raw, so suited to its bleak subject-matter that to the poet and

critic A. Alvarez it is 'as though Shakespeare were dispensing with the blossom, leaves and even the branches of language, and was using the roots themselves'.

As with so many of his most ambitious works, it defies belief that Shakespeare effortlessly knocked off *King Lear* in a few months, six on his then average, with accordingly little prior thought, meditation or background reading, let alone blood, sweat and tears. The writing of this of all his plays must have stretched over a long period, from the second half of 1604 well into the following year, perhaps into 1606. Whole books have been written about the dating of *King Lear*, and indeed the complex variations between the first quarto (published in 1608, often known after its publisher's sign as the 'Pied Bull' quarto), a second quarto (not published until 1619) and the First Folio (1623). So significant are the differences – with the Folio text giving more than a hundred lines not found in the quartos, and lacking nearly three hundred that are (including a whole scene, Act IV Scene iii, forcing the renumbering of those following it) – that the Oxford editors felt obliged to print both the quarto and Folio versions of *Lear* in their 1986 *Collected Works* and its companion *Original Spelling Edition*.

For our present purposes, it is necessary only to note that Shakespeare must have begun work long before 17 September 1605, when southern England witnessed an eclipse of the moon, followed on 2 October by an eclipse of the sun. So Gloucester's prophetic words in Act I to his bastard son Edmund – 'These late eclipses in the sun and moon portend no good to us' – must either have been written in anticipation of these events, in light of previous eclipses, or inserted afterwards, perhaps even after the play's first performance, to capitalise on current events. Shakespeare, in other words, was flexible, ready to improvise. Contrary to four centuries of received wisdom, based on the bardolatrous 'nary a blot' evidence of the editors of the First Folio, he was constantly revising his work. Hence the understandable confusions between the published versions of this and many other plays.

It is also amusing to note that Cordelia's death by hanging seems to have been forced unwittingly upon Shakespeare by Spenser's need for a rhyme in *The Faerie Queene*, whence he lifted the form of her name:

M. William Shak-speare:

HIS
True Chronicle Historie of the life and death of King L E A R and his three Daughters.

With the vnfortunate life of Edgar, *sonne* and heire to the Earle of Gloster, and his sullen and assumed humor of T O M of Bedlam:

As it was played before the Kings Maiestie at Whitehall vpon S. Stephans *night in Christmas Hollidayes.*

By his Maiesties seruants playing vsually at the Gloabe on the Bancke-side.

LONDON,
Printed for *Nathaniel Butter,* and are to be sold at his shop in *Pauls* Church-yard at the signe of the Pide Bull neere S^t. *Austins* Gate. 1608.

The title page of the 'Pied Bull' quarto of King Lear *(1608).*

And ouercommon kept in prison long,
Till wearie of that wretched life, her selfe she hong.

There is no other need for Cordelia to meet so strikingly violent an
end – as is also true of the Fool, of whom we have seen and heard
nothing since his last words, 'And I'll go to bed at noon', in Act III,
suggesting that Robert Armin had cause to plead with Shakespeare
for an early exit. He must have had pressing reasons, presumably
domestic, for the part is otherwise the richest Shakespeare wrote
for Armin, with Burbage in the title role also given more scope
than ever to show off his enormous range.

To A. C. Bradley, the influential early-twentieth-century analyst
of the tragedies, *King Lear* was 'Shakespeare's greatest achievement,
but . . . *not* his best play'. It was 'simply too huge for the stage';
otherwise, as 'the fullest revelation of Shakespeare's power', it
ranked alongside '*Prometheus Vinctus* and the *Divine Comedy*, even
with the greatest symphonies of Beethoven and the statues in the
Medici chapel'. Dr Johnson, too, expressed baffled distaste for
a play whose greatness was hardly in dispute. The seventeenth
century found its grim resolution unbearable, replacing it with
a happy ending. Tolstoy, often perverse on Shakespeare, actually
expressed a preference for the primitive *True Chronicle*, arguing
that its unknown author had made a better job of the opening
scene. The Romantics felt differently; to Shelley, *Lear* was 'the
most perfect specimen of dramatic poetry existing in the world';
and Hazlitt, for once, was speechless with admiration: 'We wish
we could pass this play over, and say nothing about it. All that
we can say must fall short of the subject, or even of what we
ourselves conceive of it.' *Lear* has fared better than ever on the
twentieth-century stage because, in Edmund's words, 'Men / Are
as the time is' – or, in Frank Kermode's, such moments as the trial
scene or Gloucester's attempted suicide seem 'absolutely modern' to
playgoers used to Beckett. 'From our particular vantage-point we
can perhaps see a *Lear* that Bradley, for all his power, could not
apprehend . . . *Lear* is, in part, a play about the end of the world,
and twentieth-century critics must owe something to the fact that
they know an "image of that horror".'

All Shakespeare's previous work came together in *King Lear* –

his most intense and passionate meditation – almost a series of symphonic variations – on love, mortality, kingship, ingratitude, faith, justice, truth, the family, the forces of darkness. *De nihilo nihilum, in nihilum nil posse reverti*, in a well-worn phrase dating back to Aristotle: nothing can come of nothing, nor can return to it. *King Lear* has been called Christian and anti-Christian, drawing on the books of Job and Revelation in its portrait of a man brought lower than any other in the canon – and a king, what's more, 'anointed flesh', with all hope of redemption brutally snatched away at the last. For all its apocalyptic scale, *Lear* is less about the divine order than man's suffering; for all its resonance about the human condition, it is about one reckless individual who had 'ever but slenderly known himself'. For all its unremitting bleakness, and the merciless blackout of its ending, it leaves behind a sense of affirmation.

By the time *King Lear* was performed before King James at his Whitehall palace on 26 December 1606, it must already have been playing at the Globe most of that year, as Shakespeare's next play – an even darker, if less universal tragedy – had received its first performances that summer. Whatever the playwright thought James might make of *Lear*, *Macbeth* was much more overtly addressed to the monarch: a Scottish play, distorting history to pay tribute to his ancestry while thinking the unthinkable, uneasily topical: a successful attempt at regicide.

Late the previous year, on 5 November 1605, a Catholic plot to kill the King was foiled when conspirators were caught in the act of attempting to blow up the Palace of Westminster while James was opening the new session of Parliament. The Gunpowder Plot, as it has become known to history – or the 'Powder Treason', as it was called at the time – might well have succeeded, were it not for a warning letter sent anonymously by one of the conspirators, Francis Tresham, to his Catholic brother-in-law, Lord Monteagle: 'I would advise you, as you tender your life, to devise some excuse to shift of your attendance at this Parliament . . . Retire yourself into your country, where you may expect the event in safety. For though there be no appearance of any stir, yet I say they shall receive a terrible blow this Parliament; and yet they shall not see who hurts them . . . The danger is past as soon as you have burned this letter.'

He didn't, of course. Monteagle took the letter straight to Cecil, who took it to the King. James lived in paranoid dread of assassination, the very fate which had befallen his own father, Lord Darnley. The Palace was immediately searched; and the guilty name which has passed beyond history into folklore is that of Guy Fawkes, the fearless soldier caught in the Westminster cellarage on the point of lighting the fuse to the twenty barrels of gunpowder he had smuggled in, on top of which he had piled inflammable faggots and iron bars to ensure maximum destruction. But the conspiracy's true leader, nowhere near the scene of the crime, was Robert Catesby of Warwickshire, son of that same Sir William Catesby known to Shakespeare's father, from whom he had perhaps obtained the Catholic Testament found hidden in the roof of Henley Street.

Catesby saw the bombing of Parliament as the spur for a Catholic uprising, emanating from the Midlands. He had convened a hunting party in Warwickshire that day, bringing together leading members of the Catholic gentry, hand-picked to help the conspirators seize power after the death of the King and many of his peers, both Protestant and Catholic. Once unmasked, Catesby was shot dead while resisting arrest in Staffordshire; Fawkes was so severely tortured that, after his trial in front of Sir Edward Coke the following February, he had to be helped up the steps to the scaffold to be hung, drawn and quartered.

Shakespeare's recusant Warwickshire connections were perilously close to returning to cause him trouble. Names far more obscure than that of the sometime William Shakeshafte were ruthlessly tortured out of the conspirators before they were put to death. It is another index of how well Shakespeare covered his tracks, to the eternal despair of his biographers, that he did not merely survive this dangerous episode, but felt emboldened to work it into his next play – performed before the King in August 1606, during a visit from his brother-in-law, the King of Denmark.

Macbeth was riddled with references to the 'Powder Treason', only too clear to contemporary audiences. Its running theme of 'equivo-cation' made topical play of the Jesuit doctrine by which a prisoner under interrogation might in good conscience disguise the truth to avoid incriminating himself. The last 'Powder Treason' conspirator to be tried, Father Henry Garnet, was the author of a learned treatise on equivocation; his execution in May 1606 was very fresh in the public mind. In the Porter's speech Shakespeare was making light – for public consumption, not least by the King – of a serious matter once close to his heart. Elsewhere in the play, he pays his most serious attention (as would James and his government) to the prevailing moral belief that equivocation was a surrender to the forces of evil, tantamount to an alliance with the devil. The Weird Sisters are temptresses dragging Macbeth, via his own equivocations, into just such a Faustian pact. But Shakespeare stresses that he makes it of his own free will – riddled with eloquent, equivocal doubts which render him, both before and after his crime, an unlikely Everyman.

That court performance of *Lear* came barely a year after the Gunpowder Plot. So James would have nodded sombrely when Gloucester spoke of 'those late eclipses in the sun and moon' – only weeks, to the audience, before that dastardly attempt on his life – as portending 'no good to us ... in cities, mutinies; in countries, discord; in palaces, treason'. Now, in *Macbeth*, the King would have noted with equal gravity the ingredients prepared by the Third Witch for her cauldron: along with 'root of hemlock digged i' th' dark' and 'liver of blaspheming Jew',

> Gall of goat, and slips of yew
> Sliver'd in the moon's eclipse,
> Nose of Turk, and Tartar's lips,
> Finger of birth-strangled babe
> Ditch-deliver'd by a drab.

James (like the 'rival poet' of Sonnet 86) believed in witchcraft. He took sorcery seriously enough to have written a treatise on the subject, *Daemonologie*, published in 1599. In August 1605, during a visit to Oxford, he had sat through an entertainment called *Tres Sybillae*, in which forerunners of Shakespeare's Three Witches loyally hailed his royal ancestry, then led a discussion of 'whether the imagination can produce real effects'.

Does Macbeth, for instance, really see the witches, the dagger, Banquo's ghost? Of course he does, even if others don't. James certainly believed so; as James VI of Scotland, the son of an assassin's victim, he had been deeply disturbed by the discovery of a waxen image of himself, made with murderous intent by his mother's third husband, according to its inscription: 'This is King James the Sixth, ordained to be consumed at the instance of a nobleman, Francis, Earl of Bothwell.' But James was duly reassured when a witch declared him '*un homme de Dieu*'; if he had the devil's own word that he was under God's protection, then it must indeed be true. So the King would have approved of the notion of Macbeth's entanglement with the Weird Sisters. Such figures, to him, were no mere fantasies; they represented, as in Shakespeare's play, a central facet of man's permanent struggle against the powers of evil.

Whatever his private feelings (which appear to leave room for doubt), James also affected to believe in the ancient tradition, dating back to Edward the Confessor, of the power of the 'King's touch' to cure scrofula and other diseases. It handily buttressed another aspect of monarchy he was at pains to re-emphasise – the 'Divine Right' of English kings, chosen and anointed by God, thus rendering any attempt on their lives blasphemy as well as treason. For all his distaste at mingling with *hoi polloi*, let alone touching their running sores, he had recently revived the practice of 'touching' the afflicted, earning himself another polite nod from Shakespeare via Malcolm, exiled at the London court:

> 'Tis called the evil—
> A most miraculous work in this good king,
> Which often since my here-remain in England
> I have seen him do. How he solicits heaven
> Himself best knows; but strangely visited people,
> All swoll'n and ulcerous, pitiful to the eye,
> The mere despair of surgery, he cures,
> Hanging a golden stamp about their necks,
> Put on with holy prayers; and 'tis spoken,
> To the succeeding royalty he leaves
> The healing benediction. With this strange virtue
> He hath a heavenly gift of prophecy,
> And sundry blessings hang about his throne
> That speak him full of grace.

The King liked his plays short, as the resident playwright of his own company would surely have known, even if James had not said as much publicly during that recent visit to Oxford. In the wake of his narrow escape, when the 'Powder Treason' might so easily have exposed his papist past, Shakespeare evidently felt it prudent to gratify as many royal whims as possible. Not content with laying on the flattery with a trowel, he wrote in *Macbeth* a Jacobean Scottish play only half as long as the 'full-length' Elizabethan *Hamlet* (and better played, as a result, without an interval, though few theatre managements muster the nerve to pass up their bar takings). As a result, textual scholars have fretted over apparent abridgements or lost scenes, such as the previous, more robust discussion between Macbeth and his wife implied by her words 'Nor time, nor place, / Did then adhere'. Was Cawdor, unknown to Macbeth, secretly in league with the King of Norway? Did Banquo unwittingly disturb Macbeth's sleep? How to explain the sudden appearance of the mysterious Third Murderer of Banquo? These are questions that can never be answered. If Shakespeare's ghost seems untroubled, given the place *Macbeth* still holds in the repertoire, his own contemporaries were concerned enough about the play's brevity to add material, notably the apocryphal Hecate scenes and two songs attributed to Middleton. Quite rightly, they are rarely performed.

But the central tribute paid by the wary King's man to his employer was a wholesale rewriting of history to boost the Stuart ego. In Shakespeare's primary source, Holinshed's *Chronicles*, Duncan is a young and weak king murdered at Inverness by a group of conspirators including both Macbeth and Banquo. Shakespeare takes the murder in his play from elsewhere in Holinshed, where Donwald is 'set on' by his wife to murder an earlier Scottish king, Duff, at his castle in Forres; ensuring his own alibi by sharing the watch on the battlements, Donwald has hirelings commit the deed, then rushes in to kill the king's guards, whom he has earlier plied with drink. Elsewhere in Holinshed, King Kenneth's sleep is disturbed by the ghostly voice of a nephew he has murdered.

The banquet scene and the appearance of Banquo's ghost are entirely Shakespeare's invention. Otherwise, he could console himself that his distortion of the historical facts achieved as much by way of dramatic effect as royal gratification. At the time of Duncan's death

the Scottish monarchy was an elective office; Shakespeare chooses
to ignore this by having Duncan nominate his son Malcolm as his
heir. He makes Duncan old and venerable to blacken Macbeth's
dark deed yet further, and conveniently ignores the fact that
the historical King Macbeth, a respected warrior given neither
to introspection nor remorse, in fact ruled very capably for ten
years. The real Macbeth's wife had also been previously married;
hence the understandable confusion aroused within the play by her
'I have given suck, and know / How tender 'tis to love the babe
that milks me', while Macduff later exclaims of Macbeth: 'He has
no children.'

Above all, Shakespeare transforms Banquo from a murderous
conspirator into an honourable martyr, engineering the escape of his
son Fleance, much to Macbeth's anguish, to father a line of monarchs
down to and including the very king sitting in the audience. James
frequently said in public speeches that he hoped the House of Stuart
would reign over Britain 'to the end of the world'; and the mirror
borne by the last monarch in Act IV's 'Show of Kings' – carried
in the King's Men's production, it has been suggested, by a figure
representing James's own mother, Mary, Queen of Scots – suggests
as much: that the Stuart line, recently traced back to Banquo in
Leslie's *De Origine Scotorum* (1578), would stretch from Fleance past
James 'to th' crack of doom'.

Amid the play's all-permeating darkness – more suited to post-
prandial, torchlit performance at court than daylight matinées at
the Globe – Macbeth's own mood grows increasingly dark, again
to the point of nihilism. The 'unmanning' of Macbeth, to the point
where he receives the news of his wife's death with such fatalistic
resignation, is measured in terms of increasingly guilty fear – itself
in turn measured by his lack of that 'season of all natures', sleep.

> Methought I heard a voice cry, 'Sleep no more!
> Macbeth does murder sleep'—the innocent sleep,
> Sleep that knits up the ravell'd sleave of care,
> The death of each day's life, sore labour's bath,
> Balm of hurt minds, great nature's second course,
> Chief nourisher in life's feast . . .
>   Still it cried 'Sleep no more' to all the house;

'Glamis hath murdered sleep, and therefore Cawdor
Shall sleep no more, Macbeth shall sleep no more.'

Nor does he. Lady Macbeth may walk in her sleep, but it is a blessing no longer available to her husband. 'I'll drain him dry as hay,' warned the First Witch,

Sleep shall neither night nor day
Hang upon his penthouse lid.
He shall live a man forbid.
Weary sennights nine times nine
Shall he dwindle, peak, and pine.

On what turns out to be his last night on earth Banquo could not sleep, although 'a heavy summons' lay like lead upon him. But Duncan is already in his grave: 'After life's fitful fever, he sleeps well.' To the Porter, sleep is one of the three things 'especially' provoked by drink, as demonstrated by Duncan's drunken guards, whose sleep is 'swinish'. Macbeth's only chance of sleep, once Birnam Wood is come to Dunsinane, is to avoid a man not of woman born:

That I may tell pale-hearted fear it lies,
And sleep in spite of thunder.

The theme of sleep, or lack of it, becomes obsessive. Is it entirely idle to wonder if Shakespeare himself was suffering sleepless nights while writing *Macbeth*? He had cause enough, as papist families of his long acquaintance went to the gallows in the wake of the 'Powder Treason'. He also had reason to believe that his friend Ben Jonson, now back at the Globe, had a hand in the unmasking of Catesby and the rest; there is evidence that Jonson played a covert role in the exposure of the conspirators. It is certainly no coincidence that Shakespeare gave such a central role in *King Lear*, and to a lesser extent *Macbeth*, to the discovery of treachery through letters.

Lack of sleep would fit with the symptoms of the nervous illness about to overwhelm him. Never in his adult life, as mightily productive as it had already been, had he poured so much of himself into four such ambitious and draining works. So hard upon the heels of *Hamlet*, these three great tragedies – *Othello*, *King Lear*, *Macbeth* – had followed in quick succession over some eighteen months. In the words of the late Tony Tanner, who completed his masterly series of introductions to the Everyman Shakespeare shortly before his recent, untimely death, the 'relatively short period' in which these four titanic works were written, one after the other, simply 'beggars belief'.

X

THE 'ANTIQUE ROMAN'

1606–1608

With Warwickshire at the heart of the Gunpowder Plot, it is a moot point whether Shakespeare would have been travelling up and down to Stratford any more than usual during 1605. The received wisdom, dating from the diarist John Aubrey, is that he made at least one protracted trip home each year, riding back and forth for shorter visits as warranted by business dealings or special family occasions.

Property transactions, as we have seen, he was largely content to leave to his brother Gilbert, friends and professional colleagues. But the creator of Cordelia was now taking understandable interest in the marital prospects of his own daughters. Already, we must assume, Susanna was being courted by the Stratford physician, Dr John Hall, whom she would soon marry; Judith, a rather more flighty creature, may well by now have become entangled with some suitors, gold-diggers included, as unsuitable as her own eventual husband. Alerted by regular letters from Anne, and mindful of the circumstances of their own marriage, the suddenly protective father would surely have wanted to cast an eye over any potential sons-in-law.

But 1605 was also one of the heaviest writing years of his life, and even the briefest trip home would have taken a valuable week out of his schedule. Our particular interest in the summer of that year, specifically May–June, as he travelled between the capital and his home town, lies in the local legend that he fathered an illegitimate child en route.

At the beginning of his professional career, Shakespeare would have taken four days to walk from Stratford to London, stopping overnight at Banbury, Oxford and Beaconsfield before proceeding down what is today the Uxbridge Road through Shepherd's Bush, on via Tyburn, dread scene of the gallows (now Marble Arch), past Westminster and Whitehall (seat of the government and court) to the city gate near Blackfriars. Even in later, more prosperous years, on horseback, he would always break his two-day ride at the same tavern in Oxford – then the Bull, later the Salutation, now the Crown, today hidden behind the inevitable McDonald's fast-food joint at No. 3 Cornmarket.

The landlord and his wife, John and Jeanette Davenant, were long-standing friends. During the 1590s they were London wine importers, based directly across the Thames from the Globe, where Shakespeare would first have met them. Like his friend John Donne, 'a great frequenter of plays', John Davenant was 'an admirer and lover of plays and play-makers, especially Shakespeare'. He and Jeanette lived in Maiden Lane (now Skinners Lane, EC4), near the parish church of St James Garlickhithe, as close to Shakespeare's own lodgings as to the wharf where their precious cargo was unloaded. From there they could see the flag being raised at the Globe, even hear the trumpets sound to herald the start of a performance.

From backstage, meanwhile, where he spent so many afternoons kicking his heels between exits and entrances, Shakespeare would have had a prime view of the galleons arriving from southern France with barrel upon barrel of the Davenant wine to which he was more than partial. 'There's a whole merchant's venture of Bordeaux stuff in him,' says Doll Tearsheet of Falstaff in *2 Henry IV*. 'You have not seen a hulk better stuffed in the hold.'

The Davenants came from an adventurous clan long prominent in the mercantile life of London. According to the Domesday Book, the De Avenants were among the ancient families who first came to England with William the Conqueror. Sir William's grandfather, John, a Merchant Taylor like his own, had taken part in the Muscovy

Company journeys to Russia and Persia chronicled in Hakluyt's *Voyages*. So when his son John wed Jeanette Sheppard in 1593, he was marrying beneath his social status; but the Sheppards, originally from County Durham, derived a certain sheen from a long tradition of service to royalty. As well as providing the royal perfumes, Jeanette's brothers Thomas and Richard Sheppard were, coincidentally enough, makers of the royal gloves: By Appointment. If the Sheppards had not already made the acquaintance of the glover's son Shakespeare at court, or in court circles, they would certainly have known the family with whom he was then living, the Mountjoys, suppliers of headgear to the Queen.

John Davenant himself supplied wine to the royal cellars. Near their home in Maiden Lane he and Jeanette also kept a wine-tavern dating back to the fourteenth century, when it had been owned by a member of the Chaucer family. But these London years, although prosperous, were not happy ones for the Davenants. Jeanette bore John six children, all of whom died in infancy. Like Shakespeare's other lady-friend of that period, Mary Mountjoy, she consulted the astrological and medical guru Simon Forman. 'She supposeth herself with child,' he noted in his casebook, 'but it is not so.'

In truth little more than a quack, Forman was something of a magus to his clientele. Whatever advice he gave Jeanette, clearly desperate to try for more children, she and her husband decided to leave the polluted capital and seek healthier climes upstream, moving their worldly goods by barge to Oxford in the new-start year of 1600. There, as if to prove a turn-of-the-seventeenth-century ecological point, Jeanette Davenant proceeded to bear John no fewer than seven more children, all of whom survived into adulthood, most to ripe old ages.

'A very beautiful woman,' says Aubrey, 'of a very good wit and of conversation extremely agreeable,' Jeanette was past thirty by the time she moved to Oxford, and a well-preserved thirty-seven when she bore her third child there, a second son, at the end of February 1606. That Shakespeare agreed to be William Davenant's godfather is a well-attested Oxford tradition; there is even a word-of-mouth account of the long-standing family friend holding the infant beside the font at his christening at the parish church of St Martin Carfax, just down the road from the Bull, on 3 March. The boy was presumably named after his parents' celebrated playwright friend. But was Shakespeare also his natural father?

So Sir William Davenant, poet laureate, playwright and impresario, himself liked to claim in later life, usually in his cups, wassailing with cronies like the writer Samuel Butler. 'When he was pleasant,' Aubrey continued, 'over a glass of wine with his most intimate friends, Sir William would sometimes say that it seemed to him that he writ with the very spirit that [did] Shakespeare, and was contented enough to be thought his Son . . .'

The author of significant works ranging from revenge tragedies (such as *Albovine*) to tragicomedies (*The Colonel* and *The Witts*), and volumes of lyric poetry (*Madagascar*) to epic verse (*Gondibert*), Davenant maintained a swaggering, man-about-town persona despite the unsightly loss of his nose to the mercury treatment then in common use for syphilis. 'He got a terrible clap of a black handsome wench that lay in Axe-yard,' wrote Aubrey (presumably meaning 'pox'), 'which cost him his nose.' It nearly cost him his life, too. After a long and painful recovery, a rueful Davenant vowed in future to 'take care, that Plenty swell not into vice':

> Lest by a fiery surfeit I be led
> Once more to grow devout in a strange bed.

So the talented Davenant was an engaging rogue, whose boast may have been no more than wishful thinking. But four centuries of detective work have failed to disprove it, only adding to the tantalising evidence. Certainly, Shakespeare stayed with Davenant's parents in Oxford as a close friend of the family, dating back to their London days, rather than as a paying guest. Wine-taverns, of which the city of Oxford was limited to three under the Wine Act of 1553, are all too easily confused in the modern mind with inns. Where an inn sold beers and ales, like today's pubs, with overnight accommodation available to travellers at a price, a tavern was more like a twentieth-century wine bar, retailing a range of wines without offering bedrooms. Across the road from the Bull was (and still is) an inn, the Golden Cross, with rooms for rent; anyone who stayed at the tavern, owned and leased to the Davenants by New

Io. Grenhill pinx.   W. Faithorne Sculp.

S. William Davenant K.

Sir William Davenant, his nose ravaged by syphilis, the poet and
playwright who was Shakespeare's godson and claimed to be his
'natural' son.

College, did so at the invitation of the host and hostess. Shakespeare, according to Aubrey, 'did commonly lie at this house in Oxon, where he was exceedingly respected'. It seems likely that, after 1600, the playwright broke all his journeys to and from Stratford with an overnight stay with the Davenants. He became so close to the family that William's older brother Robert, by then a respectable country parson, told Aubrey that Shakespeare had 'given him a hundred kisses' as a child.

Aubrey is often maligned, perhaps unfairly, as a less-than-reliable witness. But in this instance he was compiling a life of Sir William Davenant unusually long and detailed by his standards, for the use of his friend and mentor Anthony à Wood, the grave, 'splenetic and melancholy' Oxford scholar, in his own account of his eminent contemporaries, *Athenae Oxonienses*. It is significant that the austere and scholarly Wood, who once scorned Aubrey as 'magotie-headed', nevertheless used his notes on the Davenant family almost without alteration.

At the Bull, one of his own favourite Oxford watering-holes, Wood spent long hours testing Aubrey's evidence with Sir William's sister Jane, who ran the tavern from 1636, after their parents' deaths. John Davenant, who had risen to become Mayor of Oxford, Wood describes as 'a very grave and discreet citizen . . . of melancholic disposition, seldom or never seen to laugh'. When it comes to Jeanette, the meticulous Wood uses all but the same words as Aubrey, endorsing his description of her as 'very beautiful, of a good wit and conversation' – adding only, but significantly, 'in which she was imitated by none of her sons except this William'. In 1698, with heavy innuendo, Charles Gildon noted that Shakespeare often stayed at the Davenant tavern, 'whether for the beautiful mistress of the house, or the good wine, I shall not determine'. By 1709 the rumours about Davenant's parentage had been noted as 'an Oxford tradition' by a source as unimpeachable as a keeper of the Bodleian Library, Thomas Hearne, also a respected local antiquary. Shakespeare was Davenant's godfather and 'gave him his name', recorded Hearne, who could not resist adding parenthetically: 'In all probability he got him.'

Within decades, Alexander Pope would enjoy telling the story that the young Davenant, aged seven or eight, would 'fly' from school to greet Shakespeare whenever he heard of his arrival. On one such occasion,

> an old townsman, observing the boy running homeward almost out of breath, asked him whither he was posting in that heat and hurry. He answered, to see his god-father, Shakespeare. There's a good boy, said the other, but have a care that you don't take God's name in vain.

When Pope told this story at the Earl of Oxford's dinner table in the 1740s, one of those present asked him why he had not printed it in the preface to his edition of Shakespeare's works. 'There might be in the garden of mankind,' came the portentous reply, 'such plants as would seem to pride themselves more in a regular production of their own native fruits than in having the repute of bearing a richer kind of grafting.' Nonetheless, Pope continued to assert that the notion of Davenant being Shakespeare's son was 'common in town', and that Sir William himself 'seemed fond of having it taken for truth'. In 1749 the Drury Lane prompter, William Rufus Chetwood, reported that 'Sir William Davenant was, by many, supposed to be the natural son of Shakespeare'. Examining the portrait of Sir William in the front of the 1673 edition of his *Works*, Chetwood found that 'the features seem to resemble the open countenance of Shakespeare' while conceding that 'the want of a nose gives an odd cast to the face'.

Few others have been able to see the likeness. But Davenant certainly turned out to be a son – or perhaps merely a godson – in whom Shakespeare would have been well pleased. In 1656, forty years after the poet's death, the first attempt to revive drama since the Puritan prohibition was made by Sir William Davenant, who successfully petitioned King Charles II for the right of 'making fit' nine Shakespeare plays; he himself 'reformed' *Macbeth* and *The Tempest*, the latter in partnership with John Dryden, who praised Davenant as 'a man of quick and piercing imagination'. Dr Johnson did not approve: 'The effect produced by the conjunction of these two powerful minds was that to Shakespeare's monster Caliban is added a sister-monster Sycorax; and a woman who in the original play had never seen a man is in this brought acquainted with a man who had never seen a woman.'

The plays were, of course, ruined; Benedick and Beatrice were transferred from *Much Ado* to *Measure for Measure*, which was snappily retitled *The Law Against Lovers*. But at least Shakespeare was back on the stage. In 1660 he was regarded as 'just another of those rude Elizabethans'; even Dryden accused him of 'bombast, obscurity, incoherence'. Had it not been for Davenant's despoliations, in short, the plays of Shakespeare might never have been revived on the stage. 'We have to concede,' in the words of the poet and literary historian Ian Hamilton, 'that Shakespeare might have done worse than claim the imperfect attentions of the two most gifted poets of the day . . . Had [he] not been "refined", he might well have been ignored and this would, in some obvious and no doubt several hidden ways, have altered the literature that followed, the literature we now possess.'

A tireless and versatile man of letters, Ben Jonson's successor in 1638 as poet laureate, Davenant was one of those prominent writers not afraid of political risks. Knighted in 1643 by Charles I for running supplies across the English Channel, he was thrown in the Tower eleven years later for espousing the Stuart cause in its Parisian exile, carrying messages between the King and Queen, and attempting to help embattled American royalists. He languished in the Tower for two years, 'pretty certain that I shall be hanged next week'; it is said that 'Milton saved him from execution and that ten years later Davenant was able to return the favour'. By the time of his death in 1668, he had reinvented himself as a dramatist, theatre manager and producer, founding such celebrated London theatres as Covent Garden and Drury Lane. In the process, he also introduced female actors to the English stage.

Thanks to Davenant's boasting, combined with Aubrey's and Wood's eulogies, his mother meanwhile passed into Shakespeare folklore in all manner of guises – as a woman 'of very light report', according to Aubrey's interviewees, 'whereby she was called a whore'; as the illegitimate daughter of John Florio, in the florid imagination of the eighteenth-century art historian George Vertue (writing a century after her death in 1622, six years after Shakespeare's and two weeks before her husband's); as the 'Dark Lady' of the Sonnets, according to George Bernard Shaw and other treasure-hunters; and as the 'good-looking, laughing, buxom hostess of an inn between Stratford and London', according to Sir Walter Scott in his novel *Woodstock*.

'Out upon the hound!' splutters Scott's Colonel Everard on hearing of Davenant's claim to be Shakespeare's son. 'Would he purchase the reputation of descending from poet, or from prince, at the expense of his mother's good fame?' Adds the colonel, who clearly had a lot to learn about Davenant: 'His nose ought to be split!'

Recent Shakespeare biographers prefer to squabble over the decor of the inner sanctum of the tavern – the room in which Shakespeare may or may not have bedded Jeanette Davenant, with or without her husband's knowledge or connivance. The Bull was a four-storey building of twenty or more rooms, 'not a "two-storey" edifice as is stated in a documentary life of the poet', crows Park Honan, scoring a triumphant point against the magisterial (and recently deceased) Samuel Schoenbaum. Nor were the walls of the best bedroom 'decorated with an interlacing pattern of vines and flowers', as Schoenbaum would have it. 'In fact,' snorts Honan, 'a New College inventory of 1594 clearly shows that this and other rooms at the tavern were covered with wainscoting well before the Davenants arrived.'

Whatever the pattern on its quilt, did the bed in this room witness the fathering of another Shakespeare son to take the place of the lost Hamnet? Our poet did not mention Sir William Davenant in his will, but he had every reason not to. He would no more have told his wife about an illegitimate child by his regular Oxford hostess – only recently, by definition, revisited – than he would have regaled her with gory details, not least the clap, of his nocturnal adventures in London. Besides, the Davenant family was prosperous enough for William to be amply provided for. Shakespeare could, of course, have reached some discreet financial arrangement with Jeanette, against the day of his own death – which came, as it happened, when the future Sir William was only ten.

Davenant's most recent biographer, Mary Edmond, concludes that 'although in later life Sir William would not be averse to giving his intimate friends the impression that he was Shakespeare's son, it could mean no more than that he liked to regard himself as Shakespeare's literary heir'. Amid such commendable restraint, however, even she cannot resist mentioning that Sir William was the only one of the many Davenant children to have turned out to be a writer – a poet and playwright, just like Shakespeare, and indisputably devoted to his memory. To Ian Hamilton, 'There was, to be sure, something recognisably filial in Davenant's approach to Shakespeare's memory.'

Over the ensuing centuries, the beauty of Jeanette Davenant has continued to exercise a fascination over fusty Shakespeare scholars which they cannot, however reluctantly, quite bring themselves to relinquish. Shaw is not alone in naming Jeanette as his candidate for the 'Dark Lady' of the Sonnets, who seems to have caused Shakespeare such paroxysms of jealousy. Given the date of her son William's birth – and the possibility that he was the product of an extended liaison, more than merely a one-night stand – Jeanette may in fact have been a spur to the creation of Shakespeare's Desdemona, moving him to Othello-like agonies as he rode on to Stratford or London next morning, leaving her to return to her husband's bed.

Was William Davenant born some six weeks prematurely? If so, it is an enticing thought that he might have been conceived in August 1605, during that royal visit to Oxford, when James might well have included his house playwright in his retinue for a week of plays including. *Tres Sybillae* and, at Christ Church, *Vertumnus*, a Latin play during which the King fell asleep.

Nine months before William Davenant's birth, Shakespeare would have been finishing *Macbeth* – with his next work, as was his wont, already taking shape in his head. Cleopatra, according to Shakespeare's copy of North's Plutarch, was thirty-eight years old when her tempestuous fling with Mark Antony ended in her suicide – exactly the same age as Jeanette Davenant while Shakespeare was writing *Antony and Cleopatra*. Shakespeare himself was forty-three, some ten years younger than Antony. Was it pure coincidence, if he was bedding the wife of the Oxford tavern-keeper, that he now chose to conjure up – through the besotted eyes of an older man – the most alluring, highly-sexed woman ever to emerge even from his capacious and libidinous imagination, a woman for whom her lover would surrender 'half the bulk o' th' world', a woman whom age could not wither, 'nor custom stale her infinite variety'?

Hercules at the Crossroads: the hero forced to choose between the paths of Pleasure and Virtue might as well have been Shakespeare himself, reluctant to leave the pleasures of Oxford for the virtuous roads north or south. It is also, of course, Mark Antony, abandoning

his reponsibilities in Rome for a voluptuous dalliance in Egypt: 'I'
th' East my pleasure lies.' Just as Cleopatra is associated with Venus
throughout Shakespeare's next play, so is Antony with Hercules –
substituted for the Bacchus of his original, North's 1579 translation
of Plutarch, in the tiny but haunting scene where the Roman hero's
personal god finally abandons him:

> 'Tis the god Hercules, whom Antony lov'd,
> Now leaves him.

As *Julius Caesar* was informed by the external events of the moment,
so its sequel seems to derive its unique richness and vitality from
Shakespeare's own internal life at the time. In the wake of *Othello*,
Lear and *Macbeth* he was riding a mighty creative wave, intent on
only the broadest of horizons; if he was also enjoying a dangerous love
affair in Oxford, spiced with guilt about his domestic responsibilities,
the synchronicity moved him to some of his boldest, most bravura
writing.

The 'happy valiancy' (in Coleridge's phrase) with which the play
flits dizzily from place to place, often empires apart, causes none of
the traditional problems to this century of cinema; it may also mirror
Shakespeare's own, unwonted sense of dislocation if he were riding
up and down the Oxford road – sometimes without proceeding on
to Stratford – rather more often than usual. Certainly, he chose not to
take the time to alter the flow of events in North's Plutarch as much as
he usually refined his sources, skilfully compressing time while making
poetry from North's prose with at times startling fidelity. Compare
Enobarbus' famous encomium to Cleopatra:

> The barge she sat in, like a burnish'd throne,
> Burned on the water. The poop was beaten gold,
> Purple the sails, and so perfumed that
> The winds were love-sick with them; the oars were silver
> Which to the tune of flutes kept stroke. For her own person,
> It beggar'd all description: she did lie
> In her pavilion – cloth of gold, of tissue –
> O'er-picturing that Venus where we see
> The fancy outwork nature. On each side her

> Stood pretty dimpled boys, like smiling Cupids,
> With divers-color'd fans . . .

with the original at the poet's elbow:

> the poop whereof was gold, the sails of purple, and the oars of
> silver, which kept stroke in rowing after the sound of the music
> of flutes, hautboys, citherns, viols . . . And now for the person
> of herself, she was laid under a pavilion of cloth of gold of tissue,
> apparelled and attired like the goddess Venus commonly drawn
> in picture; and hard by her, on either hand of her, pretty fair
> boys apparelled as painters do set forth god Cupid, with little
> fans in their hands . . .

Antony and Cleopatra did not appear in print before the First Folio of 1623. It was entered in the Stationers Register by the printer Edward Blount on 20 May 1608, but perhaps merely as a 'blocking entry', a device to deter pirates, for it seems to have remained unpublished. Echoes of Shakespeare's play in Daniel's revised version of his own *Cleopatra* (originally published 1594, revised 1607) and Barnes's tragedy *The Devil's Charter*, acted by the King's Men in February 1607, strongly suggest that Shakespeare had written it by then – during 1606, in other words, as stylistic evidence would seem to confirm.

He had perhaps had it in mind to return to North's Plutarch since drawing on its 'Life of Marcus Antonius' for *Julius Caesar* seven years earlier. The action of *Antony and Cleopatra* opens in 40 BC, two years after the end of the earlier play, and covers (if imperceptibly) a period of ten years. Antony himself is distinctly older, though his rival Octavius remains, with dramatic licence, 'scarce-bearded'. These and other central characters are built largely on Plutarch's own shrewd foundations, but such distinctive figures as Antony's right-hand man, Enobarbus, and Cleopatra's handmaidens, Charmian and Iras, are Shakespeare's own creatures.

He would also have known versions of the story in Horace, Virgil, Spenser and Tasso, but Shakespeare makes this doomed coupling very much his own. There is a strong sense of predestination throughout the play, as if both these mighty public figures were playing out aspects of human frailty en route to an inevitable personal tragedy. Rarely did even he so powerfully intertwine the global and the domestic. 'Antony and Cleopatra seem to us larger than life,' as the Arden editor puts it, 'because the future of the world appears to depend on their relationship.'

The triumvirate formed in *Julius Caesar* is now disintegrating, not least because of Antony's infatuation – echoing Caesar's – with Egypt's exotic Queen. The mighty Roman who defended Caesar's memory against his assassins, then saw them off at Philippi, is now himself brought low by his own appetites, meeting a similar doom at Actium. Where Caesar was assassinated, Antony (like Cleopatra) commits a noble suicide to avoid further humiliation; whereas Caesar was brought low by his public aspirations, Antony's doom is wrought by his private priorities. It is a mirroring which echoes the contrasts in Shakespeare's own life and preoccupations as he wrote the respective plays.

Cleopatra herself is one of his boldest creations, an extravagant, capricious creature as capable of hopping through the public streets or having herself delivered to Caesar in a blanket as of challenging the might of Rome. Feminist critics have inevitably seized on her vanity, frivolity and selfish, quirky unpredictability as cruel caricatures of womankind; but the 'sublime self-transcendence' with which Cleopatra 'faces and embraces' death (in the words of the Oxford editors) is worthy of any male character in the canon, heroic or otherwise. To Burgess, indeed, she is reminiscent of Elizabeth I: 'Cleopatra's Nile could be the Thames of thirty years before.' Shakespeare's portrait of Cleopatra is, moreover, symptomatic of a 'fine excess' of language, dramatic action and individual conduct throughout the play, in contrast with the classical restraint of *Julius Caesar*. The style is deliberately hyperbolical, 'overflowing the measure' of the iambic pentameter. To its Riverside editor, *Antony and Cleopatra* is 'one of the most highly-wrought of all the tragedies . . . rightly considered to be among Shakespeare's supreme achievements'.

As Antony's will becomes 'lord of his reason', the epic scale of their mutual tragedy is exquisitely expressed by Cleopatra herself:

> O, wither'd is the garland of the war,
> The soldier's pole is fall'n! Young boys and girls

Are level now with men; the odds is gone,
And there is nothing left remarkable
Beneath the visiting moon.

The historical Mark Antony did not commit suicide on the same day as Cleopatra – nor so soon after his defeat at Actium as Shakespeare, for obvious dramatic reasons, suggests. In Plutarch's account, the disillusioned Antony 'forsook the city and company of his friends, and built himself a house in the sea by the Isle of Pharos . . . and dwelt there, as a man that banished himself from all men's company: saying that he would lead Timon's life, because he had the like wrong offered him, that was before offered unto Timon: and that for the unthankfulness of those he had done good unto, and whom he took to be his friends, he was angry with all men, and would trust no man'.

Rather than forfeit his compact, ineluctable ending to *Antony and Cleopatra*, Shakespeare chose to pick up on Plutarch's mention of Timon of Athens, and convert this episode into a play bearing his name. His longstanding interest in the dangerous properties of money, and the complexities of money-lending, returned to supply a motive – nowhere mentioned in Plutarch – for Timon's disenchantment with his fellow countrymen. Were the begging letters still arriving from Stratford? Had the borough applied to Shakespeare for financial assistance, having offered none to his father in his hour of need? For whatever reason, he was again besieged by thoughts of man's ingratitude – with money, this time, as its corrosive currency – and worked out his feelings in a polemic whose power is too often underestimated. There are notorious textual problems with *Timon*, leaving the version we have from the First Folio clearly in need of revision, but they are too easily deployed to devalue a work whose 'intensity' and 'directness of purpose' were clear enough to Hazlitt.

There is confusion about the value of the Athenian 'talent'. The Poet and the Painter take an age to arrive after Apemantus has announced their approach, and then appear to know what has been discussed in their absence. The text as we have it – never printed before the First Folio, in which it was moved with evident haste into the Tragedies, specifically to the slot originally intended for *Troilus and Cressida* – uses two contradictory epitaphs for Timon, both taken directly from Plutarch. All these are wrinkles which Shakespeare would certainly have ironed out for performance, let alone publication.

The play opens smoothly enough, with emblematic roles for the Poet and the Painter, their quests for patronage couched in words reminiscent of Shakespeare's own dedications to Southampton. Their reappearance at the end of the play is clearly emblematic of the diptych he had in mind, of Aristotelian clarity, if fate had bequeathed us the finished version. Such problems as there are, involving unpolished dialogue and loose ends of plot, accumulate towards the end. It has been suggested that Thomas Middleton may have tinkered with Shakespeare's text, with or without his consent; if so, it would have been the only example of collaboration at the height of Shakespeare's writing career. More likely, the piece was another written for private performance, perhaps to commission, and rarely performed at the Globe – leaving few participants to help Heminges and Condell resolve textual problems.

Middleton appears to have been the author of an earlier play about Timon, performed at the Inns of Court only five or six years earlier. But Shakespeare also draws on Plutarch's life of Alcibiades, Painter's *The Palace of Pleasure* and a Greek dialogue by Lucian, *Timon the Misanthrope*, dating from the second century AD. None of these sources sends Timon, as does Shakespeare, out into a Lear-like wilderness. But he follows Lucian's lead in having Timon turn misanthrope because of fair-weather friends who relish his largesse in prosperity, only to desert him in poverty. Like Lucian, he also rubs salt in all available wounds by having the self-exiled Timon strike gold and see the parasites reconvene to claim their slice of the action. 'Hate all,' says Shakespeare's Timon to his honest servant Flavius, to whom he gives most of the treasure, 'curse all; show charity to none.' The rest he gives to the unjustly banished Alcibiades, who re-enters Athens with a promise to 'use the olive with my sword'.

Where Othello loved 'not wisely but too well', Timon is free with his fortune 'unwisely, not ignobly'. In the remarkable character of Apemantus, that 'opposite to humanity', a true Cynic of a philosopher even more churlish than Thersites, the dramatist is at his boldest, creating a human yardstick for the sheer violence of the change in Timon, the reversal of his outlook on the world and his fellow-men. He it is who bludgeons Timon with a personal truth as telling as any from Lear's Fool: 'The middle of humanity thou never knewest, but the extremity of both ends.' If Timon himself is the only fully realised character, with many of the supporting cast merely two-dimensional archetypes and foils, this is clearly a text to which the poet intended to (and, for all we know, did) return. But it is none the less powerful for all its rough edges. This is Shakespeare at his most revealingly bitter, railing against womankind as mere purveyors of disease, ready to compare the betrayal of Timon with that of Christ by Judas (as in *Richard II*). The tenderness with which he sketches an honest man like Flavius only underlines the magnificence of the invective he hands the disillusioned Timon – an exceptionally long role, even by Shakespeare's standards, given a personal music quite as haunting as Othello's.

So felt is the fury Shakespeare gave Timon that it is tempting to look for external events which might have had the poet himself in misanthropic mode, railing at the world and all its works as his own life took unwelcome turns for the worse. But this is a period of which we know little, and can assume less, beyond his satisfaction in the marriage of his 24-year-old daughter Susanna to the estimable Stratford physician, Dr John Hall, on 5 June 1607.

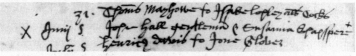

John Hall marries Susanna Shakespeare, 5 June 1607.

Was Shakespeare ready to 'turn his back on London', like Timon on Athens? Not yet. Late payments, both as debtor and creditor, continued to plague his creative peace of mind, but he was otherwise at his most ferociously productive. In an age of usury, whose capacity for evil had touched his own life – 'for loan oft loses both itself and friend' – Shakespeare perhaps saw himself offering his own Olympian brand of fashionably topical satire in *Timon*; for, as this new burst of Roman plays took to the stage between 1606 and 1608, Ben Jonson was giving the King's Men some of his most powerful, of-the-moment satires in *Volpone* and *The Alchemist*.

But Shakespeare had the Roman bit securely between his teeth. In Timon he had created an archetype of what have been called his 'minimized' heroes – those tragic figures with whom he does not seem to require his audience to sympathise or engage to any great degree of fellow-feeling. Now he would achieve the supreme example of this 'marginalized' man, the great-hearted public figure 'incapable of adjusting himself to society', in Coriolanus.

The first time we see Caius Martius, the arrogant military hero who would turn politician – yet, unlike his creator, so detests the common herd – he is telling them:

> He that trusts to you,
> Where he should find you lions, finds you hares;
> Where foxes, geese. You are no surer, no,
> Than is the coal of fire upon the ice,
> Or hailstone in the sun.

In January 1608, during the coldest winter London had known since 1565, fires were lit along the frozen Thames. The previous year had seen riots around the Midlands over rising food prices; ever fearful of mobs, especially unruly ones, James had issued a proclamation deploring the 'notorious' development that 'many of the meanest sort of our people have presumed lately to assemble themselves riotously in multitudes'. Shakespeare himself, still hoarding grain in those barns at New Place, kept one commercial eye on his own financial advantage while turning another blazing one on the incompetence of witless aristocrats-turned-politicians.

Snobs like Coriolanus, observed Wyndham Lewis, must have 'pullulated' in the courts of Elizabeth and James – overgrown schoolboys with 'crazed' notions of privilege and a 'demented' ideal of authority. That Shakespeare despised them is clear throughout his work. But where once, as in the history plays, he filled their mouths with pompous rhetoric, he is now intent upon their enlightenment, their alteration, perhaps even their salvation. Even he does not yet quite trust the people to take charge of their own destiny.

Noblesse oblige is not, to say the least, Coriolanus' strong suit. Man or beast (a recurrent question as much about the mob as its rulers), he is a definitively unMachiavellian prince. Properly modest about his achievements as a warrior – 'I had rather have one scratch my head i' th' sun . . . than idly sit / To hear my nothings monstered' – this crude, unseasoned patrician cannot muster the same decorum when required to go canvassing for votes among the plebs, to him 'scabs'. For all the 'sovereignty' of his nature, he 'commands' the peace

> Even with the same austerity and garb
> As he controll'd the war.

Banished for treason from the city he saved ('Alone I did it'), only to go over to its enemy, the military hero remains an unshaped mother's boy – stung to lethal rage by being called a 'boy', but still subservient to the formidable Volumnia, who must shoulder her share of the blame for her son's failure to see the rights and responsibilities attendant upon privilege. 'One on's father's moods,' she crows proudly when her grandson is seen tormenting a butterfly, then tearing it to shreds. 'Indeed, la, 'tis a noble child,' replies the child's mother, Valeria, feebly, as wary of her husband as his mother is exultant in him.

These vividly active and passive women, potent figures in a man's world, are Shakespeare's own elaboration on the sketches in Plutarch, whom again he mines selectively, poetising those chunks of North's translation that suit his needs while still cherry-picking, compressing, shifting emphases. With characteristic craft he enlarges the stalwart Menenius Agrippa, to whom he gives the central 'fable of the belly' – reflecting the diseased body politic, and derived in part from William Camden's *Remains of a Greater Work Concerning Britain* (1605). A paragon among patricians, doggedly loyal to Coriolanus but ultimately rejected by him, Menenius functions as an impartial commentator while counterpointing his protegé's inadequacies. Where Plutarch's Coriolanus is merely 'churlish and uncivil, and altogether unfit for any man's conversation', Shakespeare's is altogether more complex – a potentially great man, of undoubted integrity, undone by his brute incapacity for fellow-feeling. He has his share of great moments, as in 'I banish you!', when exiled from Rome; 'There is a world else-where.' But the self-same speech is unrepentantly, uncompromisingly anti-patrician:

You common cry of curs, whose breath I hate
As reek a' th' rotten fens, whose loves I prize
As the dead carcasses of unburied men
That do corrupt my air . . .

While writing *Coriolanus*, a supreme master of his craft long rid of any youthful insecurities, Shakespeare would have been feeling some nostalgia for his early years in London as an aspirant poet. In Volumnia, for sure, he was in part paying a discreet private homage to the late Queen. But the events he was now dramatising followed hard upon those he had addressed fifteen years earlier in *The Rape of Lucrece*. Fifth-century Rome was a very different place after the expulsion of the monarchy; now, with all the fellow-feeling his protagonist lacks, Shakespeare can expand the role of the Tribunes to shape the nearest he ever came to a statement of his own political views, in its way an essay on class and democracy, very much on the side of the common man, the fickle, wilful but 'poor, bare, fork'd' animal – as yet an unruly mob, as much in need of civic education as their aristocratic overlords.

As if for that purpose, he seems suddenly to create yet another new language, entirely his own: harsh, austere, driven, at times comic, at times angry, always in deadly earnest. With *Coriolanus*, as with *Lear*, we can almost hear Shakespeare inventing the English language as we have inherited it, driving each syllable forward from its crude, rough-edged origins to a range and eloquence we owe solely to him. (Shakespeare's vocabulary runs to more than twenty-one thousand words, as compared with Milton's eight thousand, or the three to four hundred of the average Stratford clod of the day, or indeed the three to four thousand of today's Oxbridge graduate.) Philosophically, meanwhile, he shows himself capable yet again of arguing an empirical case, this time a political one, in terms of the most profound humanity. T. S. Eliot has not been alone in calling *Coriolanus* Shakespeare's 'finest artistic achievement in tragedy'; George Bernard Shaw was making much the same point, in a typically perverse paradox, by calling it the best of his comedies.

As Shakespeare again weighs personal failings against national destiny, his inflexible hero at the last shows a tenderness which might, had it emerged earlier, have been the making of him; as it is, he does so knowing that it will prove dangerous to him, if not 'most mortal'. Redemption, of a kind, was already playing around the edges of the poet's mind. Soon it would take centre-stage.

Antony, Timon, Coriolanus: mighty, larger-than-life men, but all deeply flawed, to a sufficient extent to discourage the natural sympathy we have felt for such recent tragic heroes as Hamlet, Othello, Lear, Macbeth. Shakespeare has travelled far indeed since Titus, Romeo, Shylock and Falstaff. The portraits on the walls of his imagination are steadily growing, if not larger and deeper, ever closer to home. Of late he had taken to inhabiting his own plays more directly, more unsettlingly than ever. Soon the strain would inevitably tell.

But the unavoidable consequence of these outpourings, tightly controlled as they were, would coincide with an important new era in the life of the King's Men. As Shakespeare sought ways to transcend mere tragedy, to journey beyond it towards the redemption befitting a man now ageing fast, he was unexpectedly blessed with the very catalyst he needed for the next – and final – phase of his dramatic development: a new forum for his art, a new arena in which to parade the poetry of his ideas. A new theatre, in short – smaller, with room for only some 700 spectators paying higher prices, for all were seated. And protected from the elements. The Blackfriars theatre had a roof.

Writing for an indoor theatre, lit by candles, would wring from Shakespeare one last, great burst of creative innovation, the startling but logical culmination of all that had gone before. At the same time, it meant that the King's Men could more than double their business, running a winter season at the Blackfriars on top of their summer afternoons at the Globe. As a major shareholder, he would have played a significant part in the ambitious decision to take over the lease of the Blackfriars from Henry Evans, the Welsh scrivener-turned-impresario whose 'little eyases' had caused Hamlet and the King's Men such grief at the turn of the century.

Nine years later, after a prosperous decade courting the kind of controversy which did the box-office no harm, they had finally gone too far. Those local worthies who had not wanted the Lord Chamberlain's Men in their back yard were now only too happy to welcome the King's Men after a series of unwelcome alarums. The last straw was the royal displeasure occasioned by the boy-actors' 1608 production of *The Conspiracy and Tragedy of Charles, Duke of Byron*, by that same George Chapman who had collaborated with Jonson and Marston on *Eastward Ho!*. Its caricature of the King of France so outraged the French ambassador that King James himself felt obliged to close them down. So Evans – already the subject of lurid tales concerning his 'press-ganging' of reluctant children – was in no position to drive a hard bargain with the Burbages over his lease, which they secured for a mere £40 a year. It was shared between a seven-strong syndicate including Shakespeare.

The Blackfriars agreement was signed on 9 August 1608. Within a week one of the seven new joint-lessees (or 'housekeepers'), an actor named William Sly, dropped dead. Along with Heminges, Condell, the Burbage brothers and a mysterious investor named Thomas Evans, Shakespeare now owned one-sixth of the business. It had cost him £5 14s 4d; and it would eventually prove many times more lucrative than his share of the Globe, by now only one-twelfth. By 1636, twenty years after his death, Shakespeare's heirs would be receiving £90 a year from the Blackfriars as compared with £25 from the Globe.

As shrewd as ever with his money, one eye already fixed on his daughters' inheritance, Shakespeare did not warm to the Blackfriars for the pecuniary gain so much as the new dramatic opportunities it offered. As much as he owed the groundlings, for whose rudimentary tastes he had contentedly catered all these years, he could now bid them a fond farewell and concentrate solely on the more refined, profound level beneath all those 'two-tier' plays since *As You Like It*.

By accident or design, *Coriolanus* became an appropriate adieu, complete with cautionary warning, to the 1d playgoers who liked their humour broad, their heroes princely and their action bloody. Now he could charge 6d, and rein himself in to the sublime.

XI

BLACKFRIARS

1608–1611

Yet again a change of mood, another voice, a new set of preoccupations reflected in a new mode of drama – all but a fresh start for the veteran poet-playwright. In his mid-forties, after some thirty-two plays, Shakespeare's powers of invention were clearly as fresh as ever. But such shifts in creative direction tend to be dictated as much by internal as external events. Over the last four years he had put himself under tremendous strain; if his private life had remained adventurous, if indeed he had suffered the stress of an eventful extra-marital affair, he had also produced three of his mightiest tragedies, moving straight on to the two Roman plays generally held to be quite comparable achievements. Business activities and political events, with all the complexities of life at court, would also have taken their toll.

If *Timon* marked a tighter focus, perhaps showing signs of tiredness, *Pericles* would see Shakespeare entering a whole new world of the imagination, where the once dark powers of the supernatural become a shining force for good, wringing miraculous deliveries from apparent disasters, finding pots of philosophical gold at the end of distinctly dubious rainbows. From *Timon* to *Pericles* is a giant conceptual leap. Although the two plays appear to have been written in the same year, 1607–8, it is impossible not to believe that something happened in

between, something in Shakespeare's offstage life to change the tint
in his window on the world.

It was a period of domestic woes – and joys – both in Stratford
and in London. In the last week of 1607, his brother Edmund died
at the age of only twenty-seven. A jobbing actor of no particular
renown, the only member of the family to have followed William
into the theatre, Edmund was buried on New Year's Eve in the
church of St Mary Overy, Southwark (now Southwark Cathedral),
within a bell's toll of the Globe. Brothers Gilbert and Richard would
presumably have come down from Stratford to join William for the
occasion, the three older brothers representing their elderly mother
in mourning the youngest.

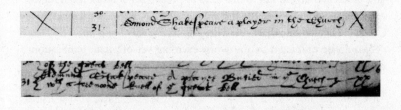

Edmund Shakespeare's burial certificate, 31 December 1607.

It seems that Edmund had only recently smiled in the direction of
his namesake in *King Lear* by fathering an illegitimate son of his own,
who died in infancy; the entry for 12 August 1607 in the register for the
church of St-Giles-without-Cripplegate reads: 'Edward, son of Edward
Shackspeere, player, base-born.' The clerk who wrote 'Edward' for
'Edmund' also wrote Joan for Joanna, Eleanor for Helen, Orton for
Horton, Morgan for Martin. 'Someone of means', as has rightly been
pointed out, must have paid for Edmund's curiously lavish funeral four
months later, which involved a 'rather large' burial fee on top of that for
'a forenoon knell of the great bell'. If this someone was his prosperous
brother, as surely it was, the 'forenoon' tolling of that bell would
indicate a midday funeral, enabling the bereaved and his fellow-actors
to return to the theatre in time for their afternoon performance.

The following February, as he approached his forty-fourth birthday,

Shakespeare meanwhile became a grandfather. Only eight months after marrying Dr John Hall, Susanna bore him a daughter, baptised with the name Elizabeth in Stratford on 21 February. Like father, like daughter; Susanna herself had been born six months after her parents' hasty ('o'erhasty'?) marriage. 'Witty above her sex', according to her epitaph, and 'wise to salvation', the feisty Susanna may have taken after her father in other ways, too. In May 1606 her name was listed among those who had broken the law by failing to receive the Sacrament the previous Easter. She did not turn up in court on the due date for her appearance, but the charge was eventually dismissed.

Whatever her feelings about two generations of offspring conceived out of wedlock, Mary Arden lived – just – to see the birth of her first great-grandchild. But on 9 September Shakespeare was back at Holy Trinity to bury his mother, dead at the age of sixty-eight. Amid all this unwonted activity he still found time to pursue his debtors, that August suing John Addenbrooke for the recovery of £6, plus 24s damages, in a Court of Record case that would drag on till the following June. By then he would be distracted by the worst example yet of pirate publication, while writing a play yet further sanctifying daughters.

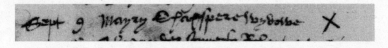

Record of Mary Arden Shakespeare's burial, 9 September 1608.

It was against this domestic background that Shakespeare changed course so radically between *Timon* and *Pericles* – one of the most undervalued (and so least performed) of his plays. We who admire him – struggling, like Jonson, to stay 'this side idolatry' – do our Bard a disservice by pretending that he never wrote a limp word, a clumsy line, a misjudged scene, a troublesome ending. Some of his plays – and we all have our personal lists – are less for us than others. *Pericles*, for many, is one such, with its pastiche Chorus (the poet Gower), the fantastical twists and turns of its elaborate plot, its abrupt jump in time, its surreal solutions to insoluble problems. Jonson himself sneered at *Pericles*, if only from jealousy of its popular success, as 'a mouldy tale'.

Was Shakespeare reworking an inadequate piece by another hand?

The first two acts, to be sure, seem less to be entirely his than the last three, when his voice gradually begins to ring through loud and clear. A novel by George Wilkins, *The Painful Adventures of Pericles, Prince of Tyre*, appeared in 1608; and it has been suggested that Shakespeare was given the task of polishing a crude dramatisation by Wilkins, merely tinkering with the first two acts before feeling moved to rewrite the rest wholesale. Some have also, if unconvincingly, discerned the hands of Thomas Heywood and John Day. No author was specified by the printer Edward Blount when he entered 'A booke called Pericles prynce of Tyre' in the Stationers Register on 20 May 1608 – again, it seems, as a 'blocking' device to ward off pirates, but this time an unsuccessful one, as Shakespeare's name appears on the title page of a bad quarto swiftly printed by Henry Gosson, a particularly corrupt text which went through several reprints. By 1623 Heminges and Condell were so unsure of the status of the text available to them as to omit *Pericles* from the First Folio.

But Wilkins's work seems more likely to have been a 'novelisation' of Shakespeare's; it proclaims itself to be 'the true History of the Play of Pericles, as it was lately presented by the worthy and ancient poet John Gower' – and as 'performed . . . by the King's Majesty's Players'. There seems no real need to go in search of some reason why Shakespeare should suddenly agree to resort to collaboration, or a demeaning rewrite, at this climactic stage of his career. He might, at most, have picked up the first two acts of a manuscript submitted to the King's Men by Wilkins or whoever, tinkering with them unenthusiastically until moved to make it wholly his own, swept away by the ideas of resurrection and redemption which turn *Pericles* into the gateway to his late romances.

He had, after all, had his say on the nature of kingship – the central theme of the first two acts, which set up a new version of the fifth-century tale of Apollonius of Tyre, drawing on Book VIII of Gower's *Confessio Amantis* (available in a 1554 edition) and Laurence Twine's prose romance *The Pattern of Painful Adventures . . . That Befell Unto Prince Apollonius* (1576, reprinted in 1607). But there are clues to Shakespeare's involvement from the start. The name of Apollonius sounds uncomfortably like Polonius; that of Pericles occurs in Sidney's *Arcadia*, on which he had drawn before – as indeed he had on Gower, for the framework of *The Comedy of Errors*.

And there are distinct enough echoes of his own recent work – the brothel with its Bawd and Boult, for instance, glancing back to *Measure for Measure* – and poetry worthy of those 'roots' of the language in *Lear*.

> The blind mole casts
> Copp'd hills towards heaven, to tell them the earth is throng'd
> By man's oppression, and the poor worm doth die for't.

There are foretastes, too, of the works to come. Just as the lost and refound Marina is Cordelia brought back from the dead, so Pericles' drowned and miraculously redelivered wife, Thaisa, anticipates Hermione in *The Winter's Tale*.

Shipwrecks, riddles, resurrections: Shakespeare is palpably excited to have found a brave new imaginary world to explore, new themes consonant with his altered mood, mellow, reflective, forgiving. In *Pericles* he can begin to see his route towards *The Tempest*, the natural end of the long intellectual road he had travelled. It marks the start of a clear course towards his farewell and retirement, laying the foundations of the great triptych which would draw all his work together towards a logical, contemplative, serene conclusion.

The evident alteration in Shakespeare, and the slow burn towards the exhilaration with which he rises to this last plateau, upon which his poetry reaches its most exalted, inexorably combine to signify some radical occurrence during 1608. The influential Victorian critic Edward Dowden found in the calmness and maturity of Shakespeare's last plays evidence of his emergence from 'the depths of despair'; the poet's final work proceeded from 'an elderly serenity, a marvellous rural detachment, a hard-won peace'. Similar thoughts beset the magisterial E. K. Chambers, fifty years later in the early 1920s, to the point where even this most sober of Bardographers felt moved to speculate that the poet had suffered 'a serious illness', perhaps even 'a nervous breakdown'.

Shaken by his own temerity in straying beyond acceptable academic limits, Chambers promptly lost his nerve, 'frankly' admitting that a breakdown was mere 'conjecture', and retreating behind the banal climbdown that 'it could have been merely the plague'. (*Merely?*) Since the King's Men had secured the lease of the Blackfriars theatre, ironically enough, London's playhouses had been closed down by yet another epidemic. Not until the autumn of 1609 were they in full-time business at the Blackfriars, with *Pericles* proving a box-office success and

Shakespeare at work on the next instalments in his radical new genre of indoor theatre. At the same time he was obliged to cope with the most irritating invasion to date of his literary and personal privacy.

During 1609, soon after Bonian and Walley had issued that mysterious edition of *Troilus and Cressida*, a printer named Thomas Thorpe published 154 of Shakespeare's Sonnets, which had been circulating privately since he first wrote them while in Southampton's household some ten years before. Also in the volume was a mannered, 329-line poem in seven-line 'rhyme royal' stanzas entitled 'A Lover's Complaint', which seems highly unlikely to be even the young Shakespeare's work; but the Sonnets certainly were. Unlike *Venus and Adonis* and *The Rape of Lucrece*, whose publication Shakespeare had personally overseen, the Sonnets were riddled with misprints, arranged in suspect order, and prefaced on the second leaf of the quarto by an ornate inscription which has since caused as much trouble as the riddle of the Sphinx:

TO.THE.ONLY.BEGETTER.OF.
THESE.ENSUING.SONNETS.
Mr W.H.ALL.HAPPINESS.
AND.THAT.ETERNITY.
PROMISED.
BY.
OUR.EVER–LIVING.POET.
WISHETH.
THE.WELL–WISHING.
ADVENTURER.IN.
SETTING.
FORTH.
T.T.

'More nonsense has been talked and written' on Shakespeare's Sonnets, wrote W. H. Auden, 'more intellectual and emotional energy expended in vain . . . than on any other literary work in the world'. Unfortunately, Auden himself promptly proceeded to add to that *sterquinarium* by arguing that the poems unequivocally show that his 'Top Bard' was homosexual, and so that he wrote them 'as one writes a diary, for himself alone, with no thought of a public'. The scholarly research devoted to the Sonnets over the years – or, as Auden sniffed, 'what passes today' for scholarly research – was 'an activity no different from that of reading somebody's private correspondence when he is out of the room, and it doesn't really make it morally any better if he is out of the room because he is in his grave'.

While Auden seems to me wrong about Shakespeare's bisexuality, and the notion that he wrote the Sonnets 'for himself alone', he is surely right about the amount of 'nonsense' they have inspired, and that the poet never intended them for publication. As recently as 1998, twenty-five years after Auden's protestations, one biographer has gone so far as to suggest that Shakespeare had been waiting for his mother's death before daring to publish the Sonnets – an opportunistic conjunction of dates which, while ignoring the fact that he had nothing to do with their publication, forgets that his mother was unable to read. (Nor was book-buying in Elizabethan and Jacobean England quite the same social-climbing activity it is today; Mary Shakespeare is unlikely to have accumulated a proud shelf-full of her son's output, pirated or otherwise, while waiting for him to send home his latest quarto to show off to her Stratford friends.)

At much the same time, *The Times* of London devoted most of a prominent news page to the claim of a retired British physicist, Dr John Rollett, to have cracked a fiendishly complex code in the dedication to the Sonnets – his elaborate cryptography laboriously leading to the remarkable discovery that Mr W.H. was none other than Henry Wriothesley, 3rd Earl of Southampton. Dr Rollett was not the first to reach this conclusion, nor to waste precious time and grey cells on the delusion that the 'only begetter' of the Sonnets, that mysterious Mr W.H., was therefore the same person as the 'fair youth' to whom they are addressed. The plain, inescapable fact, which could have saved whole forests from destruction is that, whatever the dedication may mean, and whatever the identity of its dedicatee, it was written and signed not by Shakespeare himself but by the piratical printer, Thomas Thorpe. Mr W.H. is not the 'fair youth', but the man who procured a set of the Sonnets and handed them over to Thorpe – who is now, dutifully if over-elaborately, thanking him.

Candidates for *this* Mr W.H., the unscrupulous rogue who slipped the Sonnets to a buccaneer printer – probably for a slice of the proceeds, and probably knowing full well that Shakespeare regarded them as private, to be circulated only among friends – have been almost as numerous as candidates for the Mr W.H. who never existed, the Mr W.H. wrongly identified as the 'fair youth' to whom they are addressed. Contenders for both roles have ranged from Henry Wriothesley (with his initials craftily reversed to avoid detection) to William Herbert, Earl of Pembroke, a respectable enough patron and admirer to be Heminges's and Condell's choice as the co-dedicatee of the First Folio; and Sir William Hervey, third husband of Southampton's mother. Hervey is the hot favourite to be Thorpe's supplier because, as soon as his wife died in 1608, he published a 'poetical testament' which she had deemed 'too intimate' to share with the public; the 'eternity promised by our ever-living poet' has been explained in terms of Harvey's remarriage, the following year, to a much younger wife, Cordelia Annesley. But why would any of these titled noblemen be addressed by a social inferior as plain 'Mr'?

Beyond these usual suspects, leading contenders have included the stationer William Hall, whose name leaps out from the dedication by removing the second point in 'Mr W.H.ALL'. Then there is William Hatcliffe, Prince of Purpoole (Lord of Misrule) at the Grays Inn Christmas revels of 1587–88. Great energy has been devoted to the unlikely hypothesis that this once golden youth, now an obscure Lincolnshire lawyer dogged by debt, travelled to London twenty years later to flog his set of the Sonnets to Thomas Thorpe. Just as valid is the engagingly dotty theory of the German scholar D. Barnstorff that Mr W.H. was none other than 'Master William Himself', a boon to those who believe the poet addressed his Sonnets to himself, but on a par with Professor Donald Foster's wishful thinking – pinning the rap, yet again, on the hard-working, long-suffering compositors – that 'Mr W.H.' is a misprint for 'Mr W.Sh.'. No, perhaps the most likely thief of the Sonnets – a distinctly non-literary figure into whose hands they could easily have fallen, and whose life was one long litany of debt litigation – was in fact much closer to home: Shakespeare's indigent brother-in-law, William Hathaway.

The wrong Mr W.H., the non-existent one with whom Shakespeare was supposedly in love, is worth lingering over as a figment of so many distinguished literary imaginations. Among the gems he has inspired is Oscar Wilde's short story 'The Portrait of Mr W.H.' published in July 1889. Its central thesis was developed from a letter in the *Atheneum* magazine of 30 August 1873, in which C. Elliot Browne revived a theory dating back to the eighteenth-century Chaucer scholar Thomas Tyrwhitt, and grudgingly endorsed by Malone, that the mystery had something to do with one William Hewes (or Hughes), a musician who may have moved in the same circles as Shakespeare.

Hewes was employed by the first Earl of Essex as his resident musician. The night before his death on 22 September 1576 (according to a contemporary account by his retainer, Edward Waterhouse), Essex summoned Hewes to play for him upon the virginal. 'Play my song, Will Hewes,' said Essex, 'and I will sing it myself.' And so he did, 'most joy-fully . . .' Wilde quotes the episode in his story, though citing a different source, and conceding that this William Hewes himself could not have been Mr W.H., as the poet was only twelve years old when Essex died. 'Perhaps Shakespeare's young friend was the son of the player on the virginals?' muses Wilde's anonymous narrator, deliberately entering the realms of fantasy, and setting up his theory that Mr W.H. was a boy-actor in Shakespeare's company by pointing out that 'the first English actress was the lovely Margaret Hews, whom Prince Rupert so loved'.

In 'The Portrait of Mr W.H.' – a miniature of the contemporaneous *The Picture of Dorian Gray* – the narrator is persuaded by his friend Erskine that the Sonnets are addressed to a boy-actor with whom Shakespeare was in love, but who betrayed him by leaving to join the troupe of a rival poet, probably Marlowe. Erskine himself has been convinced of the theory by an effeminate schoolfriend named Cyril Graham, who produced a portrait of William Hewes, leaning on the dedication page of the Sonnets, as definitive proof. When Erskine discovers that the portrait is forged, Graham commits suicide, a martyr to his poetic cause. Erskine himself loses faith in the theory, but arouses the curiosity of the narrator, who sets about proving it.

Wilde shows off his knowledge of Shakespeare, reading vivid new meanings into the Sonnets, in a long central passage which climaxes in a letter from the narrator to Erskine declaring himself, too, convinced that Mr W.H. was William Hewes – this boy-actor for whose very existence there is no historical evidence, but who seems to have passed into literary history as a misprint for the name of the dying Essex's physician, William Howes. As soon as the letter is sent, the narrator's own faith ebbs – 'perhaps the mere effort to convert anyone to a theory involves some form of renunciation of the power of credence' – while Erskine's is revived. The two men argue, as once

Erskine did with Graham, to the point where Erskine also commits suicide for the sake of the theory. Or so he says. When the horrified narrator arrives too late to save him, he finds that Erskine has in fact died of natural causes. His suicide – like the eponymous portrait of Mr W.H., which he leaves the narrator in his will – is a forgery.

A lifelong poseur always fascinated by fakery, and its particular use in proving unprovable theories, Wilde seems to have convinced even himself of the Hughes reading of Shakespeare's Sonnets, based on the puns in line 7 of Sonnet 20: 'A man in hue, all hues in his controlling . . .' How typically mischievous of Wilde (picking up on the original spelling of 'hews') to choose the same Sonnet which, in truth, unequivocally demonstrates Shakespeare's heterosexuality. The last line of the story has the narrator gazing at the portrait and concluding, 'I think that there is really a great deal to be said for the Willie Hughes theory of Shakespeare's Sonnets.'

Wilde later said to his friend Helena Sickert: 'You must believe in Willie Hughes. I almost do myself.' He seems even to have convinced his fellow Irishman James Joyce, whose Mr Best says in *Ulysses* (if inaccurately) that 'the most brilliant of all is that story of Wilde's, where he proves that the Sonnets were written by Willie Hughes, a man of all hues . . .' André Gide, too, described Wilde's theory as 'the only, not merely plausible, but possible interpretation of the Sonnets'. In our own time, Brigid Brophy has written of the 'social and psychological plausibility' of Wilde's Willie Hughes. But the fundamental doubts and ambiguities littering Wilde's version were, surely, quite deliberate; fretting that his conceits would not withstand scholarly scrutiny, he chose to couch it as fiction rather than fact, revelling in a pyrotechnic display of critical insight and expertise, dressed up as a homoerotic fantasy of tantalising subtlety. In 'The Portrait of Mr W.H.', in the words of his biographer Richard Ellman, Wilde 'dazzlingly offered a theory, withdrew it and half offered it again, in fiction that anticipates Borges'. The same goes for most such theories about Mr W.H., the 'fair youth' who never existed.

On 6 January 1610 King James presided over a sumptuous ceremony in Whitehall at which his son Henry, the fifteen-year-old heir to the throne, was installed as Prince of Wales. Who could know that he had less than three years to live? The Stuarts being a theatrical family, the

Prince himself played the leading role of Moeliades – an anagram of *miles a deo*, or 'soldier from God' – in a masque specially written for the occasion by Ben Jonson, and directed by Inigo Jones, master of the sumptuous visual effects which had become the masque's hallmark.

James loved a good masque almost as much as Shakespeare disdained them. The King lavished large amounts of money on these refined, post-prandial entertainments, in which allegorical contests between vice and virtue were invariably won by the latter. It was a chance for the ladies to shine, even show off their legs, as the stage prohibition on female actors did not apply to masques, invariably performed by amateurs in elaborate costumes – usually courtiers and other aristocrats – and often featuring live animals. So dependent were they on songs and dances as to anticipate the birth of opera; Monteverdi's *Orpheus*, first performed in 1607, would have been seen in England as a super-masque. The King himself was not above entering into the spirit of things by taking part; sometime he would play the role of a pagan god, with his wife as a classical queen – James's way of making a statement about his concept of monarchy.

Shakespeare's scorn for masques held firm despite his awareness of his royal paymaster's fondness for them. In *A Midsummer Night's Dream* he had made merry with an episode at Stirling Castle, when the ladies were frightened by a pride of lions introduced into a masque laid on for James, then King of Scotland only. 'Will not the ladies be afeard of the lion?' asks Snout during rehearsals for the mechanicals' masque. 'Masters,' replies Bottom, 'you ought to consider with yourselves: to bring in (God shield us!) a lion among ladies is a most dreadful thing; for there is not a more fearful wild-fowl than your lion living.' Bottom's solution is to have Snug

> name his name, and half his face must be seen through the lion's neck, and he himself must speak through, saying thus or to the same defect: 'Ladies', or 'Fair ladies, I would wish you' or 'I would request you' or 'I would entreat you not to fear, not to tremble. My life for yours. If you think I come hither as a lion, it were pity of my life. No, I am no such thing. I am a man, as other men are' – and there, indeed, let him name his name, and tell them plainly he is Snug the joiner.

Even at this early stage of his career, when it was far from clear that James would one day be his King, let alone his employer, Shakespeare is still making his distaste for the 'art' of the masque pretty clear. Even after James had become his royal patron, Shakespeare never stooped to writing in a genre he saw as ephemeral. He could have made more easy money that way – a one-act masque earned its writer as much as a five-act play – but he rested content to leave it to the university types, themselves still giving him a hard time, moved to scorn by jealousy of his success. This was an age in which 'every Scrivener's boy shall dip / Profaning quills into Thessalia's spring', according to an anonymous play of 1610, *Histriomastix, Or the Player whipt*, in which one character speaks of a knight who 'shakes his furious Speare'. To those who believe that the ur-*Hamlet* was Shakespeare's, this buttresses Nashe's gibe that it was written by 'a scrivener'.

Ben Jonson had jumped on the lucrative bandwagon as early as the King's progress south in 1603, when the royal party paused at Althorp, the Spencer estate in Northamptonshire, for an alfresco performance of his masque *Satyr*. 'The form was good for Ben,' wrote his admirer Anthony Burgess. 'It curbed two of his biggest faults – prolixity and preachiness.' Jonson kept on churning out one-act masques – for one-off performances – even after the ingenuity of Inigo Jones had turned them primarily into designer entertainments, inventing such wonders as the proscenium arch and the revolving stage to the point where the look of a masque became far more important than its content.

Jonson swallowed his pride to work with Jones on 'a royal exercise in negritude' called *The Masque of Blackness*. 'It was her Majesty's wish,' he later sighed, 'to have them blackamoors . . .' But even his patience eventually wore thin, not least because the post-prandial nature of the entertainments often saw the performers drunk and unruly. One of the most notorious examples occurred in July 1606, during the state visit of the Queen's brother, King Christian IV of Denmark, when the royal banquet laid on for James and his brother-in-law by Lord Salisbury at his Hertfordshire estate, Theobalds, was followed by the masque *Solomon and Sheba*. 'The entertainment went forward and most of the presenters went backward, or fell down, wine did so occupy their upper chambers,' according to one of those present, the wit Sir John Harrington. The women seem to have made particular spectacles of themselves.

> 'Hope' and 'Faith' were found vomiting in an ante-chamber; 'Victory' expired after trying in vain to present the King with a symbolic sword. 'Peace' forgot herself completely, laying about all and sundry with olive branches that formed part of her costume.

James himself was apparently 'unmoved by declining standards at court' as the notoriously Dionysiac ways of the Danes infected his own normally restrained courtiers. Christian himself would not have been too discomfited by events, as he 'collapsed early in the proceedings, a victim of too much drink and a coating of jellies, cakes, spices and sundry sweetmeats which had been poured over him when the girl playing Sheba, equally inebriated, had tumbled at his feet, dropping her sickly "gifts"'.

No doubt amused by reports of the evening, Shakespeare would have rested content with getting the ways of the Danish court right five years earlier in *Hamlet*:

> *Hamlet:*   The King doth wake tonight and takes his rouse,
> Keeps wassail, and the swagg'ring upspring reels,
> And as he drains his draughts of Rhenish down
> The kettle-drum and trumpet thus bray out
> The triumph of his pledge.
> *Horatio:*   Is it a custom?
> *Hamlet:*   Ay, marry is 't,
> And to my mind, though I am native here
> And to the manner born, it is a custom
> More honour'd in the breach than the observance.

There were no such disturbances when *Macbeth* was performed in honour of the King of Denmark during the same state visit the following month. Shakespeare was content to keep the masque in its place, as a brief cabaret in a much larger scheme of things. One of his few concessions to the Jacobean vogue for them was to make use in his next play of the latest technology, with such stage directions as

1. The 'Chandos' portrait.

2. Clopton Bridge, Stratford, in the eighteenth century.

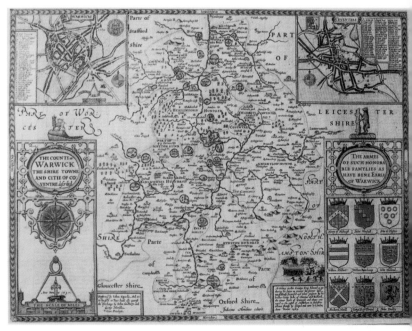

3. Map of Warwickshire by John Speed, 1610.

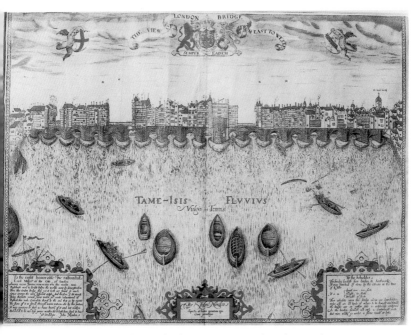

4. *The View of London Bridge from East to West*, by John Norden, 1597.

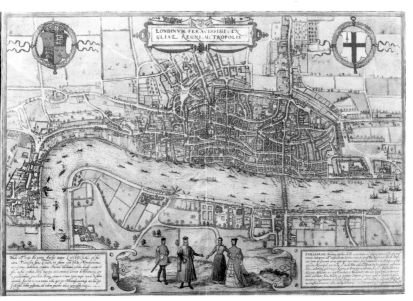

5. Map of London from the Braun and Hogenburg atlas, 1572.

6. Shakespeare's royal patrons: Queen Elizabeth I (the so-called 'Armada Portrait', by Marcus Geeraerts the Younger, 1588) and King James I (portrait attributed to John de Critz, *c.* 1605).

7. Henry Wriothesley, 3rd Earl of Southampton (1573–1624).

8. Shakespeare's friend Richard Burbage, the first man to play Richard III, Hamlet, King Lear, Othello and Macbeth.

9. *Twelfth Night* is performed in an inn yard, *c.* 1600.

10. Images of Shakespeare: portrait by Soest (*top left*); a Hilliard miniature of a man thought to be Shakespeare, from 1588 (*top right*); and a nineteenth-century German woodcut.

11. Shakespeare's bust and (*below*) his tombstone in Holy Trinity Church, Stratford-upon-Avon.

'Jupiter descends in thunder and lightning, sitting upon an eagle', then 'throws a thunderbolt', and to write a short masque into his last play, *The Tempest*. The Blackfriars, after all, was suited to the performance of a masque, if relegated to a ritual entertainment rounding off a richer evening. Masques would never have worked as well at the Globe.

With a more sophisticated audience, and no unruly groundlings to disrupt proceedings, Shakespeare could write much more intimate scenes for the indoor Blackfriars theatre than for the roofless play-houses. His relish in this new freedom is evident early in the new play on which he was working for the Blackfriars while James and his son made spectacles of themselves in court masques. In the second act of *Cymbeline*, the villainous Iachimo tiptoes around the sleeping Imogen's chamber, where he has been hiding in a trunk. By the light of a single taper, he notes down the room's contents: the paintings, the window, the bedclothes, the pictures on the arras. Then he leans over the sleeping girl herself, notes the mole on her left breast, the title of the book left open on her bedside table, removes her bracelet, is even tempted to kiss her:

> How bravely thou becom'st thy bed! Fresh lily,
> And whiter than the sheets! That I might touch,
> But kiss, one kiss! Rubies unparagon'd,
> How dearly they do 't! 'Tis her breathing that
> Perfumes the chamber thus. The flame o' th' taper
> Bows toward her, and would underpeep her lids,
> To see th' enclosèd lights, now canopied
> Under these windows, white and azure-lac'd
> With blue of heaven's own tinct.

The terrifying beauty of this scene had Simon Forman holding his breath when he saw *Cymbeline* in April 1611, six months before his death. 'Remember,' he recorded in his notebook, 'in the deepest of that night, she being asleep, he opened the chest and came forth of it, and viewed her in her bed, and the marks of her body; and took away her bracelet . . .' The scene would be just as effective, of course, during the play's seasonal transfer to the Globe (where Forman may, indeed, have seen it); the point is that, before the Blackfriars, Shakespeare might not have been minded to write it.

Cymbeline appears as the last of the tragedies in the First Folio, where it was first published, although it is really a tragicomedy, or romance. Heminges and Condell could not quite categorise Shakespeare's late plays, and appear to have thought that anything concerning an English king should be treated with due gravity – even though the play, via a somewhat tortuous route, ends happily. Its gods are Roman, but *Cymbeline* inhabits the same pre-Christian, semi-mythical England as *King Lear*; Shakespeare took his title and landscape from the legend of Kymbeline, or Cunobelinus, said to have reigned from 33 BC until shortly after the birth of Christ. For incidents and names he returns to Holinshed's *Chronicles*, and his *History of Scotland*, while mining an old play, *The Rare Triumphs of Love and Fortune* (1589) for the King's daughter, Imogen (or 'Innogen', as in innocence), and a sinister second queen who plots her husband's overthrow by her own malevolent and loutish son, Cloten. Imogen has married against her father's wishes; Cymbeline, almost as foolish as Lear, banishes her 'poor but worthy' husband, Posthumus Leonatus, whose wager on his wife's chastity Shakespeare adapts from an episode in Boccaccio's *Decameron*. He may himself have acted in another old work, *Sir Clyomon and Clamydes* (1599), from which he derives the gruesome scene in which Imogen mistakes Cloten's headless body for that of Posthumus.

> A father cruel and a stepdame false,
> A foolish suitor to a wedded lady
> That hath her husband banished . . .

The plot as summarised by Imogen before it is scarce begun, proceeding to move between ancient Britain, Renaissance Italy, classical Rome and the realms of Snow White, moved Samuel Johnson to lose patience with *Cymbeline*'s 'unresisting imbecility'. Where Hazlitt admired the final scene, in which 'the fate of every person in the drama is made to depend on the solution of a single circumstance', George Bernard Shaw took it upon himself to rewrite the entire last act, dismissing it as 'a tedious string of unsurprising dénouements sugared with insincere sentimentality after a ludicrous stage battle'. But this is no mere pantomime. The fact that all end happily except the Queen (who dies 'with horror, madly dying, like her life') springs from the essence of Shakespeare's new mood; as Imogen and her husband are reunited, and Cymbeline majestically submits to the defeated Romans, even Iachimo is pardoned. But all have come close to death to earn their redemption; as the complex plot proceeds towards its miraculous resolutions, Shakespeare's verse blossoms into some of his most sublime. To return to life as a *nonpareil* among Shakespeare's women, Imogen herself must apparently die as a boy, over whose supposed corpse is sung that most exquisite of all dirges – another memorial, perhaps, for poor, dead Hamnet:

> Fear no more the heat o' th' sun,
> Nor the furious winter's rages.
> Thou thy worldly task hast done,
> Home art gone and ta'en thy wages.
> Golden lads and girls all must,
> As chimney-sweepers, come to dust.

If the plot of *Cymbeline* relies on what Shaw called 'infantile joys', it is perhaps because Shakespeare at last seems to feel free, via some of his liveliest and most diverse imagery, to allow poetic effects precedence over the dramatic. The point seems proved by the fact that this of all his plays was the favourite of Tennyson, who thought Posthumus' exquisite tribute to Imogen 'among the tenderest lines in Shakespeare', and is reputed to have repeated it to his own wife on his deathbed:

> Hang there like fruit, my soul,
> Until the tree die.

'Then shall . . . Britain be fortunate, and flourish in peace and plenty.' If *Cymbeline* is a fantasy, 'an experimental exercise in virtuosity', it was a stepping-stone between Pericles and the two great romances to follow, steeped in a lifetime's reading, but bedded in Sidney's *Arcadia*.

Since Shakespeare had returned to it for *Lear*, and briefly for *Pericles*, Sidney's prose romance had perhaps given the exhausted, ailing playwright the vision he needed for this one last, great burst of creativity. An old work based upon it, *Mucedorus*, remained one of the most popular of Elizabethan plays not just for its comic element, but its 'utilization of good old reliable romantic motifs'. The text was clearly fresh in Shakespeare's mind as he and the King's Men performed *Mucedorus* before James I at Whitehall on Shrove Sunday 1610. Among the customary 'additions' on this occasion was some 'spectacular business', including the appearance of a live bear.

Marianne Moore wanted poets to be 'literalists of the imagination', presenting for inspection 'imaginary gardens with real toads in them'. There can be few more apt descriptions for the poetic landscape of Shakespeare's final romances, even before he anticipated her all too literally by presenting an imaginary seashore (if in a landlocked country) prowled by a real bear.

The most celebrated stage direction in theatrical history – 'Exit pursued by bear' – comes on the threshold from tragedy to redemption in his next play, carefully (for once) entitled *The Winter's Tale* – a phrase analagous since the mid-sixteenth-century with what was even then called an 'old wives' tale', thus readying his audience for a story of romantic improbability, to be marvelled at rather than taken at face value. George Peele's *Old Wives' Tale* (1595) had spoken of 'a winter's tale to drive away the time'; and Shakespeare himself had made mention in *Macbeth* of 'a woman's story at a winter's fire', much the same as the 'old tale' in *The Two Gentlemen of Verona*, 'which will have matter to rehearse, though credit be asleep and not an ear open'. Two separate characters in the last act of *The Winter's Tale* liken its events to those of 'an old tale', while it is the latest reincarnation of Hamnet, poor young Mamillius, who is made to remind us before he dies that 'a sad tale's best for winter'. Poignantly for the playwright – or by way, perhaps, of artful self-torture – the boy-actor playing Mamillius would later be resurrected as his lost-presumed-dead sister, Perdita.

Perdita is a young woman as idealised as Marina and Imogen, if not more so, in a direct line of ascent from Cordelia and beyond, distributing flowers with all the abandon of a happier Ophelia:

> Here's flow'rs for you:
> Hot lavender, mints, savory, marjoram,
> The marigold, that goes to bed wi' th' sun,

And with him rises, weeping. These are flow'rs
Of middle summer, and I think they are given
To men of middle age. Y' are very welcome.

Shakespeare's preoccupation with his daughters, amid his continued
mourning for his lost son, sees this latest paragon a true child of
nature, rejoicing in her natural surroundings, rejecting anything as
unnatural as cosmetics, flirting (despite her unknown royal birth)
with egalitarianism ('The self-same sun that shines upon his court
/ Hides not his visage from our cottage') and having her worst fears
confirmed when her lover's royal father angrily refuses to accept a
mere shepherdess as his daughter-in-law:

This dream of mine,
Being now awake, I'll queen it no inch further
But milk my ewes, and weep.

The Winter's Tale was not published before the First Folio, where
it appears as the last of the comedies. Simon Forman's diary tells
us that he saw it at the Globe on 15 May 1611. In November of
that year the account book of the Office of the Revels records a
performance at court by the King's Men of 'Ye Winters night Tayle'.
But the play had largely been written the previous year; the satyrs'
dance during the Whitsun sheep-shearing feast, in which three of
the twelve countrymen are said to have already 'danced before the
King', appears to be a reference to the satyrs' dance performed before
James on New Year's Day 1611 in Ben Jonson's *Masque of Oberon*.
That *The Winter's Tale* followed hard upon *Cymbeline* we know from
a slice of source material Shakespeare kept in reserve for Armin's use
as the comic rogue Autolycus, 'snapper-up of unconsidered trifles',
in terrifying the poor Clown:

He has a son, who shall be flayed alive; then 'nointed over
with honey, set on the head of a wasp's nest; then stand till
he be three quarters and a dram dead; then recover'd again
with aqua-vitae or some other hot infusion; then, raw as he
is (and in the hottest day prognostication proclaims), shall he
be set against a brick-wall, the sun looking with a southward

eye upon him, where he is to behold him with flies blown
to death.

A 'philosopher of roguery', like Falstaff, Autolycus was Shakespeare's
own brainchild, as were the pivotal characters of Leontes' steward
Antigonus and his formidable wife Paulina. Otherwise, he is indeed
dramatising an 'old tale', dating from 1588 – and an ironic choice,
too, in *Pandosto: The Triumph of Time* (later retitled *Dorsastus and
Fawnia*) by his old enemy Robert Greene. What better farewell
to the London stage – the first of several, as it transpired, no
doubt further irritating the 'University Wits' – than a seigneurial
improvement on the work of the man who had so scornfully greeted
his arrival in the capital?

The first three acts of *The Winter's Tale* correspond closely with
Greene's *Pandosto*, and its verse offspring in Francis Sabie's *The
Fisherman's Tale* and *Flora's Fortune* (1595). Driven by 'affection'
in the Ciceronian sense (i.e., 'a disposition of mutation happening to
body or mind: trouble of mind'), an irrationally jealous king wrongly
believes his wife guilty of infidelity with his boyhood friend, to the
point of rejecting his own newborn daughter in the belief that she is
their illegitimate child. But Shakespeare changes Greene's Pandosto
of Bohemia into Leontes of Sicilia, and his Egistus of Sicilia into
Polixenes of Bohemia, switching their kingdoms around as he seizes
a chance to rework the ancient myth of Proserpina – set, of course,
in Sicily – in the play's miraculous resolutions. The daughter of Ceres,
carried off by Pluto to become queen of Hades, is specifically invoked
by Perdita of Sicily, now of Bohemia, beset by problems even deeper
than she knows:

> O Proserpina!
> For the flow'rs now, that, frighted, thou let'st fall
> From Dis's waggon!

This Bohemia is really, of course, an English Arcadia, a revisited
Forest of Arden, where Shakespeare departs from his sources to
throw an extended party, a multi-layered pastoral celebration, a
prolonged carnival of flirtation and foolery stretching into the longest
single scene he ever wrote. Two years earlier he had played with
the King's Men in John Fletcher's *The Faithful Shepherdess*, which

had proved a box-office failure. According to a crestfallen Fletcher, the audience expected 'a play of country hired shepherds in gray cloaks, with curtailed dogs in strings' – low characters, in other words, like Shakespeare's shepherd, clown and Autolycus. 'Missing Whitsun-ales, cream, wassail and morris-dances,' continued Fletcher, the groundlings 'began to be angry'. So Shakespeare learnt from Fletcher's mistakes by writing a fable elevated enough to satisfy his upmarket audience, while enlivening it with country shepherds a-plenty, scope for dogs, and the Whitsun festival to end them all.

As he approaches the end of his writing career, there is in Perdita's words as its rustic queen not just a saucy reference to Fletcher's woes, but a dash of nostalgia for the tradition from which Shakespeare sprang, those cumbersome seasonal dramas of his youth:

> Methinks I play as I have seen them do
> In Whitsun pastorals.

'Thou met'st with things dying, I with things new-born': in the old shepherd's words to his son lies the hinge of the unprecedented transition from a three-act tragedy to hard-wrought redemption via carnival chaos. As in Greene, the abandoned baby is brought up a shepherdess, falls in love with her supposed father's son, only to be recognised as her real father's daughter; but there the similarities end. As in *Pericles*, a supposedly lost daughter and wife are restored to a royal husband who has endured a long ordeal in no expectation of its earning them back. But in *Pericles* the audience was in on the secret; the miraculous ending of *The Winter's Tale* is as much of a surprise to the groundlings as to Leontes. Robert Greene's falsely accused queen does, indeed, merely die. By bringing Hermione back to life, in a device none too surreal to devotees of the masque, Shakespeare completely recasts Greene's ending to suit his newly optimistic, almost demob-happy mood.

Retirement was already beckoning. As was the Warwickshire countryside, rarely celebrated with such lavish affection as in those flowers Proserpina is 'frighted' of letting fall from Dis's wagon:

>   . . . daffodils,
> That come before the swallow dares, and take
> The winds of March with beauty; violets, dim,
> But sweeter than the lids of Juno's eyes
> Or Cytherea's breath; pale primroses,
> That die unmarried, ere they can behold
> Bright Phoebus in his strength (a malady
> Most incident to maids); bold oxlips, and
> The crown imperial; lilies of all kinds
> (The flower-de-luce being one) . . .

If Shakespeare had never particularly missed his wife, he seems to indulge in some wishful thinking about the marriage he never had via the old shepherd's moist-eyed Whitsun memories of his own, and her gift for hospitality:

> This day she was both pantler, butler, cook,
> Both dame and servant; welcom'd all, serv'd all;
> Would sing her song and dance her turn; now here,
> At upper end o' th' table, now i' th' middle;
> On his shoulder, and his; her face o' fire
> With labour, and the thing she took to quench it
> She would to each one sip . . .

Was he offering Anne an oblique apology, trying in his long-distance way to atone for his own inadequacies as husband and father? These final plays, not least the final poetic testament he was now drafting, yearn not only for reconciliation but 'the survival into a new world of the children of those who had quarrelled'. Shakespeare was more than ready to leave London, even to quit writing, and return to his roots, to the bosom of the growing family he had so long neglected. If he was going to bid the stage farewell, however, he was intent on doing so with one final, philosophical, yet highly theatrical, flourish.

On 24 July 1609 (while Shakespeare was writing *Cymbeline*) a sudden storm at sea broke up a small fleet of ships belonging to the Virginia Company which had set sail from Plymouth on 2 June. All eventually managed to arrive at Jamestown the following month, with the sole exception of the flagship, the *Sea Adventure*, carrying the admiral, Sir George Somers, and the future governor of Virginia, Sir Thomas Gates. Both men, along with all hands, were assumed to have perished.

Nine months later, on 23 May 1610, to the astonishment of the colonists, two small craft arrived at Jamestown carrying the full complement of the *Sea Adventure*. Somers and his crew, it transpired, had run aground on the island of Bermuda – a dread name to mariners then as now, for modern legends about the perils of the 'Bermuda Triangle' seem to have grown directly from the island's reputation in Elizabethan times as 'the Isle of Devils', where dire practices including cannibalism awaited any travellers unfortunate enough to land there.

But the stalwarts of the Virginia Company had encountered no such dark mysteries. On the contrary, they reported, they found Bermuda and its climate delightful, rich in food and shelter, with enough wood to build the small pinnaces in which they eventually completed their voyage to the New World.

Their story provoked enormous interest, both in Virginia and back home in England. One of the crew, Sylvester Jourdan, wrote an account published in pamphlet form as *A Discovery of the Bermudas, Otherwise Called the Isle of Devils*. The Virginia Company soon replied with its own version entitled *The True Declaration of the Estate of the Colony in Virginia, with a confutation of such scandalous reports as have tended to the disgrace of so worthy an enterprise*. And a further report, by William Strachey of the *Sea Adventure*, circulated in the form of a letter; entitled *The True Reportory of the Wrack and Redemption of Sir Thomas Gates*, it was dated 15 July 1610 and eventually published in *Purchas His Pilgrims* in 1625.

It is known that Shakespeare read Strachey's account in its manuscript form, and probably both pamphlets, as he seems to acknowledge in *The Tempest* with Ariel's revelation that once, at midnight, Prospero sent him to fetch dew from the 'still-vex'd Bermoothes'. Given the framework for his final play, he had also studied (in John Florio's 1603 translation) Montaigne's essay 'On Cannibals' – which has nothing to do with cannibalism in its modern, carnivorous sense. The word 'cannibal' (of which Caliban is a virtual anagram) derives directly from 'Carib', the original term for a native American inhabitant of the

A
DISCOVERY
OF THE BARMV-
DAS, OTHERWISE
called the Ile of
DIVELS:

By Sir THOMAS GATES, Sir
GEORGE SOMMERS, and Cap-
tayne NEWPORT, with
diuers others.

Set forth for the loue of my Country, and also for the good of the
Plantation in Virginia.

SIL. IOVRDAN.

LONDON,
Printed by *Iohn Windet*, and are to be sold by *Roger Barnes*
in *S. Dunstanes* Church-yard in Fleet-streete, vn-
der the Diall. 1610.

*The title page of Sylvester Jourdan's account of the adventures of
the Virginia Company's crew after foundering off Bermuda, one of
Shakespeare's sources for The Tempest.*

lands colonised by European adventurers in the fifteenth and sixteenth centuries. Montaigne has nothing but praise for the unspoilt, primitive society recorded by the first visitors to the New World, seeing it as an ideal state superior to Plato's Republic:

> It is a nation, would I answer Plato, that hath no kind of traffic, no knowledge of letters, no intelligence of numbers, no name of magistrate, nor of politic superiority; no use of service, of riches, or of poverty; no contracts, no successions, no partitions, no occupation but idle; no respect of kindred but common, no apparel but natural, no manuring of lands, no use of wine, corn or metal.

Compare this (Florio's translation) with Gonzalo's description of the ideal commonwealth in the first scene of Act II of *The Tempest*:

> I'th'commonwealth I would, by contraries
> Execute all things; for no kind of traffic
> Would I admit; no name of magistrate;
> Letters should not be known; riches, poverty,
> And use of service, none; contract, succession,
> Bourn, bound of land, tilth, vineyard, none;
> No use of metal, corn, or wine, or oil;
> No occupation; all men idle, all;
> And women too, but innocent and pure:
> No sovereignty . . .

All the lesser sources for *The Tempest* show us, 'in their very dullness', to one twentieth-century editor, 'what it was that Shakespeare habitually did'. In Thomas's *History of Italy* (1549), for instance, one Prospero Adorno is mentioned as being Duke of Genoa for a brief period in 1460 before being deposed, only to return as ruler of Genoa, lieutenant of the Duke of Milan, in 1477. Suspected in Milan of conspiring with Ferdinando, King of Naples, Prospero was soon deposed again. By 1488 the Milanese had grown so weary of these plots and counter-plots as to resubmit themselves to Genoa, who appointed Antony Adorno as Governor. Shakespeare made use of this curious history for more than merely its entertainment value;

'passed through his fire', it took on renewed significance 'in terms of man, of nature and of human life'.

But Prospero and Stephano are also names of characters in Ben Jonson's *Every Man Out of His Humour*, in which Shakespeare himself had acted ('and which perhaps taught him the correct pronunciation of Stephano, which he got wrong in *The Merchant of Venice*'). However strongly they may now resonate through the canon, such names are mere ornaments to Shakespeare's choice of the romantic story as the mode in which to make his last poetic investigation into the human soul and human society, taking supernatural elements with all the seriousness becoming his royal patron. To Frank Kermode, he had 'deliberately' chosen the pastoral tragicomedy as the genre in which this enquiry could best be pursued. Shakespeare's thinking is 'Platonic, though never schematic'. The pastoral romance gave him the vehicle for 'a very complex comparison between the worlds of Art and Nature', while the tragicomic form enabled him to merge 'the whole story of apparent disaster, penitence, and forgiveness into one happy misfortune, controlled by divine Art'.

Above (and below) this surface, Shakespeare blends his own responses to Montaigne with the recent adventures of the Virginia Company's crew to create a fantasy island rooted in the Old World, placeless if distinctly Mediterranean, but part-peopled by the New. Thanks to another shipwreck, its indigenous 'New World' inhabitants have come under the natural command of the ousted Duke Prospero of Milan, whose 'art' (or what we would now call 'science') is pitched against the complex Elizabethan concept of 'nature' – a theme already explored in *King Lear* and *The Tempest*'s immediate predecessors, *Cymbeline* and *The Winter's Tale*.

Are 'natural' values, as symbolised by Caliban and Ariel – and, to Miranda's innocent eyes, by some of the arrivals from another shipwreck – inherently superior to those of the so-called civilised world? There is very little plot in *The Tempest*, less than in any of Shakespeare's previous thirty-five plays, and much ornate poetry, steeped in the metaphysical cadences of his great religious contemporaries. For what he clearly intends to be his swansong, in other words, unusually adopting the Aristotelian unities of time and place, Shakespeare embarks on nothing less than a philosophical discussion of the values which constitute civilisation.

There could be no more majestic or appropriate coda. To G. Wilson Knight, *The Tempest* 'repeats . . . in miniature, the separate themes of Shakespeare's greater plays . . . It distils the poetic essence of the whole Shakespearean universe'. To Kermode, too, *The Tempest* was 'a necessary development' which 'ends and transcends the great series of Shakespeare's plays'. The Arden editor is unsurprised, if dismayed, that the play has sent its would-be exegesists 'whoring after strange gods of allegory'. With Shakespeare's other late works, notably *Coriolanus* and *Timon of Athens*, *The Tempest* represents 'a maturity of conception, a control of the medium, both linguistic and dramatic, which we scarcely know how to begin to understand . . . In its uncompromising victory over the means to truth, its control over vision and expression, and its refusal to be seduced by any temptation to betray the principles of *architectonicé*, the last period represents the summit of Shakespeare's achievement.'

To what extent is Prospero an autobiographical character, looking back on a long and richly varied life, by way of giving his final word on a God-forsaken world before symbolically breaking his staff and drowning his book?

> Graves at my command
> Have wak'd their sleepers, op'd, and let 'em forth
> By my so potent art. But this rough magic
> I here abjure; and, when I have requir'd
> Some heavenly music – which even now I do –
> To work mine end upon their senses that
> This airy charm is for, I'll break my staff,
> Bury it certain fathoms in the earth,
> And deeper than did ever plummet sound
> I'll drown my book.

It was the minor Scottish poet Thomas Campbell who, in his 1838 edition of Shakespeare, first found in *The Tempest* an allegory of the poet's farewell to the stage, divining 'a sacredness as the last work of a mighty workman'. These oft-quoted lines certainly apply more to Shakespeare than to Prospero, as has recently been pointed out: 'The magus of *The Tempest* has waked no sleepers from the grave, as has the author of *Richard III* and *Hamlet*.' For this soliloquy, in truth, Shakespeare was again returning one last time to his beloved *Metamorphoses*, which he knew both in Ovid's Latin and Arthur Golding's translation (1565–67).

When writing Prospero's farewell to arms, Shakespeare was consciously writing his own. Later in the same scene, he promises to tell 'the story of my life',

> . . . and so to Naples . . .
> And thence retire me to my Milan, where
> Every third thought shall be my grave.

For Milan, with Burgess, 'read Stratford'.

The Tempest was first performed before the King in the Banqueting House at Whitehall on Hallowmas Night, 1 November, 1611. Shakespeare would have ridden down from Stratford for the occasion, enjoying an overnight stay en route in Oxford with the Davenants, dandling his five-year-old godson William on his knee. For by then he had retired to his rural roots. It was ten years before Andrew Marvell would be born, forty before he would hear 'Time's wingèd chariot hurrying near', but Shakespeare's own intimations of mortality can be equally clearly heard in his extended rendition – replete, even at so solemn a moment, with backstage in-jokes – of Montaigne's '*La vie est un songe . . . nous veillons dormants et veillant dormons*':

> Our revels now are ended. These our actors
> (As I foretold you) were all spirits, and
> Are melted into air, into thin air;
> And like the baseless fabric of this vision,
> The cloud-capp'd tow'rs, the gorgeous palaces,
> The solemn temples, the great globe itself,
> Yea, all which it inherit, shall dissolve,
> And like this insubstantial pageant faded
> Leave not a rack behind. We are such stuff
> As dreams are made on; and our little life
> Is rounded with a sleep.

XII

'A MERRY MEETING'

1611–1616

As one Greene dated Shakespeare's arrival in London, so another marks his return to Stratford-upon-Avon after twenty-five years without parallel in literary history. Since their daughter Susanna had married and moved out of New Place, the Shakespeares had taken in a lodger until such time as the paterfamilias decided to come home for good. According to a surviving document, Thomas Greene was the name of the town clerk who in 1610 made ready to move out and look for lodgings elsewehere.

Shakespeare seems to have postponed his planned return by at least twelve months; the previous September Greene had bought himself a house, against the expectation of moving out, only to find he could rent it out, 'the rather because I perceived I might stay another year at New Place'. But now, in his forty-seventh year, the master of New Place was finally in permanent residence. Or so it seemed.

If 'every third thought' was his grave, he was determined to make the most of the other two. According to local tradition, Shakespeare kept his own earthen half-pint mug at a local inn, 'out of which he was accustomed to take his draught of ale at a certain public house in the neighbourhood of Stratford every Saturday afternoon'. Our source for this engaging vignette is, for once, as respectable as a Treasury man, James West, who 'assured' George Steevens of this solemn truth in the 1770s, while he was co-editing his monumental edition with Dr Johnson.

Could Shakespeare really give up writing, just like that, to sit in his garden counting his money and watching his mulberry tree grow? Henry James is but the most eloquent of many who have refused to believe it. '*How* did the faculty so radiant,' protested James, 'there contrive . . . the arrest of its divine flight? By what inscrutable process was the extinguisher applied, kept in its place to the end? What became of the checked torrent, as a latent, bewildered presence and energy, in the life across which the dam was constructed? What other mills did it set itself turning, or what contiguous country did it – rather indeed did it *not*, in default of these – inevitably ravage?'

Burgess, too, is so incredulous as to ignore the clues left by the town clerk and have Shakespeare back in Stratford much earlier, trying to give up work but reluctantly nudged into new ideas for plays by sitting in his garden reading Chaucer and Gower, Montaigne and Boccaccio, even his old enemy (and lodger's namesake) Greene. But if Spenser's *Faerie Queene* was too 'tedious', and his copies of North's Plutarch and Holinshed's *Chronicles* 'worn out', why on earth would he have returned (as Burgess suggests) to the diet of his schooldays, Chaucer?

New Place sketched by George Vertue, 1737.

No, Shakespeare was surely still based in London when he wrote those 'final retrospective' plays for the Blackfriars, though the date of *The Tempest*'s first performance suggests that he might have taken this last work-in-progress home with him, to polish at his leisure as he tried to readjust to family life.

Anne was now fifty-four years old, their daughters in their mid-twenties – as, of course, would have been poor, dead Hamnet, the mention of whose very name seems still to have moved his tender-hearted father close to tears:

> Prithee no more, cease. Thou know'st
> He dies to me again when talked of.

At least, as he had demonstrated in Marina and Imogen, Perdita and Miranda, he could derive great comfort from his daughters. Susanna lived just around the corner from New Place, with her busy doctor husband and infant daughter; Judith was still at home with her parents, apparently unable to land as upstanding a husband, for she was now almost as old as her 'on the shelf' mother when so carelessly impregnated by her father – who would now have to learn to be a family man for the first time in nearly thirty years of marriage.

It was not a role in which he had ever been well cast. At first he busied himself with property and financial transactions, even allowed himself to be tempted into town business like his father before him. In 1611 'Mr Wm. Shackspere' is named by his kinsman and former lodger, the town clerk Thomas Greene, among subscribers cajoled into forking out 'towards the charge of prosecuting the bill in Parliament for the better repair of the highways and amending divers defects in the statutes already made'. As one who travelled the 'wretched' roads of England more than most – and would, despite himself, continue to do so – Shakespeare would consider this a cause close to his heart, although he had long since complained of the consequent inconvenience with all the indignation of a latter-day motorist calling the government's 'cones hotline':

> Why, this is like the mending of highways
> In summer, where the ways are fair enough.

There were, as always, debts to collect; on 5 October 1611, just as he would have been heading south for rehearsals of *The Tempest*, a vintner and Henley Street neighbour named Robert Johnson, landlord of the White Lion, died owing £20 for 'a lease of a barn that he holdeth of Mr Shaxper'. But, predictably enough, such diversions would soon prove too petty for so restless a soul, so mighty a mind. Before long he would be coaxed out of this rural tranquillity to collaborate on two more plays with his successor as 'ordinary poet' of the King's Men. Perhaps Henry James was right; perhaps this born writer, whose every waking moment yielded matter for conversion from eye or ear to scroll, found himself simply unable to lay down his quill. Various pieces of doggerel dubiously attributed to him might also date from this period. But first, according to an even ghostlier tradition, Shakespeare teamed up with his old rival Ben Jonson to polish up the Psalms as we now know them.

The theory goes like this. By 1610 a committee of learned clerical scholars had been at work for six years on a new translation of the Bible, commissioned (or 'authorized') by King James I to replace the Geneva Bible, whose marginal notes he found unacceptably anti-monarchist: 'very partial, untrue, seditious, and savoring too much of dangerous and traitorous conceits'. Under the chairmanship of the solicitor-general, Sir Francis Bacon, the work of these scholars was submitted for approval to bishops and theologians, then to the Privy Council and finally to the King himself, before its eventual publication in 1611 as the Authorised Version of the Holy Bible. But certain sections, in this instance the Psalms, were also farmed out to appropriate experts, in this instance poets, for a final coat of paint. Who more appropriate, in the case of the most poetic section of the entire work, than the two leading poet-playwrights of the day?

The riddle lies buried in Psalm 46 in the Authorised Version ('God is our refuge and strength: a very present help in trouble'). The forty-sixth word from the beginning happens to be 'shake' (as in verse 3: 'Though the waters thereof roar, and be troubled, though the mountains shake with the swelling thereof'). Set aside the word 'Selah' – not part of the text, but a standard Hebrew musical notation – and the forty-sixth word from the end turns out to be 'spear' (verse 9: 'He maketh wars to cease unto the end of the earth, he breaketh the bow and cutteth the spear in sunder, he burneth the chariot in the fire'). Why the obsession with the number 46? Those who believe that Bacon wrote Shakespeare, and cryptically claimed the credit for it in his translation of the 46th Psalm, point out that the committee under his command had forty-six members. Those who think it more likely that Shakespeare himself 'poetized' the Psalms, and was damned if he was going to let Bacon take the credit, make the rather more intriguing point that in 1610, when this work was done, Shakespeare was forty-six years of age.

He was undeniably a writer who liked wordplay and verbal games, as John Buchan pointed out at their London club to Rudyard Kipling, who proceeded to explore the notion in the last short story he wrote, 'Proofs of Holy Writ' (1932), substituting Isaiah for the Psalms. Sitting in the summer-house in the orchard at New Place one hot afternoon, both somewhat the worse for drink, Shakespeare and Jonson squabble over stylistic details in previous translations of two passages from the Prophets. Kipling even works in the real name of one of the leading clerics known to have served on the committee, an Oriental scholar, later Bishop of Gloucester; the passages have been submitted to Shakespeare for discreet improvement by 'the most learned divine', Miles Smith of 'Brazen Nose' College, Oxford, who 'heard I had some skill in words, and he'd condescend . . . to inquire o' me privily, when direct illumination lacked, for a tricking-out of his words or the turn of some figures'. After brushing up the English version for Smith, Shakespeare sets himself 'neatly and quickly to refolding and cording the package' and sliding it anonymously into the saddlebag of a horse-borne courier.

'Who will know we had a part in it?' Jonson asks him.

'God, maybe,' replies Shakespeare, 'if He ever lay ear to earth . . .'

Kipling's choice of title, echoing Iago's thoughts on purloining the fatal handkerchief, may offer a clue as to how seriously he took the whole idea:

> Trifles light as air
> Are to the jealous confirmations strong
> As proofs of holy writ.

But Burgess, too, is sorely tempted to believe the legend that

Shakespeare had a hand in the Authorised Version of the Bible, specifically Psalm 46: 'If this is mere chance, fancy must allow us to think that it is happy chance.' Whether or not he had occasion to polish the Psalms, and lodge an ironic little claim to fame with posterity in the process, Shakespeare otherwise had scant time for the leisurely retirement he might idly have envisaged. Relaxation does not, anyway, seem to have been in his nature. Even after the royal première of *The Tempest* in November 1611, his monarch was certainly not content to have heard the last of his favourite playwright, whose private life also remained fraught with incident.

On 3 February 1612 Shakespeare buried his brother Gilbert – dead, having never married ('*adolescens*'), at the age of forty-five. A year later, on 4 February 1613, his brother Richard followed, also unmarried, at the age of thirty-eight. As he entered his fiftieth year, the oldest of the Shakespeare brothers was now the only one left living, the only one to have taken a wife and bred children. Of all eight Shakespeare siblings, only William and his sister Joan, five years his junior (who would outlive him by thirty) now survived. For all his parents' longevity, Shakespeare's own generation was not faring well; after his own recent illness, it would hardly be surprising if – now more than ever – he felt a sense of living on borrowed time.

Between Gilbert's and Richard's deaths he allowed himself to be tempted back into writing for the King's Men. A royal command could scarcely be disobeyed, even by a respectably retired subject who had already done the state some service. But James's daughter, Elizabeth, was to be married on St Valentine's Day 1613 to Frederick, the Elector Palatine of the Rhine, a symbolic figure to European Protestants and claimant to the throne of Bohemia. A mere sixteen years old, like her husband-to-be, Elizabeth was the King's only surviving daughter. Major celebrations were planned – including, of course, a new play.

Shakespeare cannot have needed much persuading. Since he had left the London field clear for his rivals, he must have watched with mixed feelings as Ben Jonson advanced towards top billing, with lesser lights like John Webster, George Chapman, Cyril Tourneur and Thomas Heywood all vying with him for the mantle of Marlowe. Still churning out masques – not until 1630 would he have his terminal row with Inigo Jones – Jonson was producing his best dramatic work over the decade that had begun with *Volpone* in 1606 and included *The Alchemist* four years later. It was now, in 1612, that Webster's *The White Devil* was first performed; two years later he too would come up with his masterpiece, *The Duchess of Malfi*. Webster may also have had a hand in Tourneur's (or Middleton's?) *The Revenger's Tragedy*, first performed in 1607; the shadowy Tourneur's lesser-known work, *The Atheist's Tragedy*, had not been performed until 1611, though its distinct echoes of Shakespeare's *King Lear* suggest that it may have been written much earlier. The wayward Thomas Heywood had not managed to improve on his 1603 domestic tragedy *A Woman Killed With Kindness*. Chapman, too – once Henslowe's dramatist for the Admiral's Men, imprisoned with Jonson in 1605 for upsetting the King with their collaboration on *Eastward Ho!*, in trouble again when he outraged the French ambassador with his *Charles, Duke of Byron* – had never bettered his tragedy for the boys of Paul's, *Bussy D'Ambois* (1604). The poet Swinburne thought his *All Fools* (also 1604) 'one of the finest comedies in the English language', but Chapman remains best known for the translation of Homer which moved Keats to his famous sonnet.

Could Shakespeare rest content that all these considerable talents merely confirmed his own effortless pre-eminence? The genteel life of Stratford was already – and understandably – beginning to weary him, as the town's growing Puritan element chose to snub its most famous son by banning all dramatic performances in the borough. If anything was calculated to drive Shakespeare back to London amid a hail of curses, fleeing the embrace of his weeping wife and daughters in the process, whatever the state of the roads, that would do it.

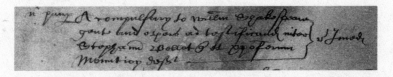

Shakespeare is summoned to testify in Stephen Belott v Christopher Mountjoy, *Court of Requests, 1612.*

As if to remind his rivals he was still around, he anyway had other reasons to remain a familiar figure on the London scene. In 1612 he rode south to give his evidence in that protracted litigation between his former landlords, the Mountjoys, and their son-in-law Stephen Belott. That same year also saw him complain to the printer William Jaggard about his new edition of *The Passionate Pilgrim*, first published in 1599 – but still containing five of Shakespeare's Sonnets, still with his name on the title page, and still without his knowledge or consent. Heywood, whose *Troia Britannica*, was similarly pirated for the same volume, seems to be trying to curry favour with Shakespeare by associating him with his own stern protest in an epistle to the printer appended to his *An Apology for Actors*. A chastened Jaggard, as we have seen, promptly reprinted the title page, omitting Shakespeare's name.

For all the detail of his love–hate relationship with Jonson, there is no record at all of Shakespeare's dealings with the other poet-playwrights of his day. But he evidently looked benignly on the work of Francis Beaumont and John Fletcher – twenty and fifteen years, respectively, his juniors – whose greater success as collaborators than as individuals perhaps posed no threat. Beaumont had written *The Woman Hater*, and possibly *The Knight of the Burning Pestle*, before his name was indissolubly linked with Fletcher's in commendatory verses prefixed by Jonson to *Volpone*. Since 1608–9 he had teamed up with Fletcher to produce, according to a bewildering array of disputatious scholars, anything from six or seven to as many as fifty-three plays, notably *Philaster* in 1610, followed by *A Maid's Tragedy* and *A King and No King* in 1611. The higher total seems unlikely, as Beaumont died in his early thirties in 1616, only six weeks before Shakespeare, having given up writing for the stage after his last collaboration with Fletcher, *The Scornful Lady*, upon his marriage in 1613.

Or was Beaumont terminally offended by his partner's defection to the enemy? In the first years of the new century the precocious young Fletcher had written several plays for the Queen's Revels, notably *The Woman's Prize* and *The Faithful Shepherdess*, before the wily Jonson sabotaged his solo reputation, too, by linking it so publicly with Beaumont's. Perhaps Jonson felt as threatened as Shakespeare felt magnanimous; the younger, impressionable Beaumont was much more of a Jonsonian, a conservative moralist hooked on his mentor's doctrine of 'humours', while the more mature Fletcher was the finer poet, with the broader brow and more vivid imagination. Long after he had left Beaumont behind, Fletcher enjoyed continued success with such comedies as *Monsieur Thomas* and *Wit Without Money*, and such tragedies as *Bonduca*.

Who asked whom we will never know – perhaps the King himself – but in 1612 Shakespeare saw fit to collaborate with Fletcher on at least one play, possibly two. The possible one is *Cardenio*, a lost work acted by the King's Men some time before 20 May 1613, and ascribed to Shakespeare and Fletcher forty years later. On 9 September 1653 the London publisher Humphrey Moseley entered in the Stationers Register a number of plays including '*The History of Cardennio*, by Mr Fletcher and Shakespeare'. Fletcher had outlived Shakespeare by only nine years, dying in his mid-forties in 1625; but contemporary documents support the tantalising suggestion that such a play did once, indeed, exist. Privy Council records show that on 20 May 1613 the sum of £20 was paid to John Heminges, leader of the King's Men, for the performance at court of six plays, one of which is listed as '*Cardenno*'. Six weeks later, on 9 July, Heminges was paid £6 13s 4d for his company's performance of *Cardenna* before the ambassador of the Duke of Savoy.

The text appears to have survived into the next century, adapted in 1728 by Lewis Theobald into a play called *Double Falsehood*, or the *Distrest Lovers* – 'revised and adapted', according to the playwright himself, from a play about Cardenio 'written originally by W. Shakespeare'. Theobald's play was a minor success at the Drury Lane theatre, given fourteen performances over the six months after its première on 13 December 1727 before enjoying revivals (and intermittent republications) between 1740–41, 1767, 1770 and as late as 1847. Soon after its last eighteenth-century revival, though it seems hard to believe, the 'original manuscript' of Shakespeare's play was reported by a London newspaper to be 'treasured up' in the Museum of Covent Garden Playhouse; in 1808 the entire theatre, including its library, was destroyed by fire.

Cardenio is a character in Part 1 of *Don Quixote*, masterwork of the Spaniard Miguel de Cervantes – born seventeen years before Shakespeare, though he was to die the very same day. An English translation was published, as it happens, in 1612, the year that Shakespeare and Fletcher agreed to get together to contemplate the King's commission in advance of his daughter's wedding. From Theobald's *Double Falsehood*, otherwise no more than 'an interesting curiosity', we can divine parallels with Shakespeare's late plays in the theme of a heroine who disguises herself as a boy to win back the lover who has wronged her, and the painful reconciliation of children with their parents. But even Theobald did not include the play in his own edition of Shakespeare (which slavishly followed the First Folio, also omitting *Pericles* and *The Two Noble Kinsmen*); and although he claimed to own 'several' manuscripts of Shakespeare's *Cardenio*, while noting that its style seemed more like Fletcher's, not one has managed to survive. If Theobald *really* possessed a manuscript of an unknown play by Shakespeare – or indeed, as he claimed, several copies – why on earth did he not publish it? His own version of events is not easy to accept at face value.

Shakespeare had pretty much covered such themes as there were in *Cardenio*, so could have got involved merely to oblige his old friend Burbage – after some tavern arm-twisting, no doubt – by lending a helping hand to the work of the apprentice admirer who had succeeded him as resident dramatist of the King's Men. The notion of another history play, to round off his cycle while gratifying James on his daughter's wedding day, would have carried rather more interest for him. The bride, moreover, was called Elizabeth; now that the long prohibition on English history plays had at last been relaxed, what more appropriate for young Elizabeth's wedding present than a piece celebrating her late, great namesake via her father – with due discretion, of course, by chronicling only the dramatic events leading up to her birth. Shakespeare's double tetralogy had ended with the accession of the first Tudor monarch. His successor, Henry VII, was a grey, unattractive figure, whose reign offered a dramatist little to sink his teeth into beyond the remarkably Shakespearean-sounding names of Lambert Simnel and Perkin Warbeck. But *his* son, Henry VIII – ah, there was a different matter. While the old Queen lived, her father was strictly off-limits to saucy scriveners; now that she was gone, and her successor but a distant blood relation, here was an opportunity indeed.

Shakespeare's final plays for the King's Men had all been written with the Blackfriars in mind; they were playable at the Globe, of course, but lacked the swaggering alfresco action which had proved such good box-office for so long. Burbage must have pleaded with his lifelong comrade-in-arms to think of their mutually beloved Globe, this time, as much as of Whitehall and the King. Either he felt he had to tread carefully, however, or the tired old playwright's heart wasn't really in it. *Le vrai* Shakespeare would have steeped himself in the unparalleled dramatic potential of that reign, from the neo-Falstaffian Bluff King Hal's cavalier treatment of all those wives to its grave religious consequences for Romanist families like the Shakespeares themselves.

What emerged instead was a pallid, pompous, prettified version of events from 1520 to 1533, from the Field of the Cloth of Gold to the christening of Princess Elizabeth. Drawing on the chronicles of Holinshed and Edward Hall, John Speed's recent *History of Great Britain* (1611) and John Foxe's *Book of Martyrs* (for the 'testing' of Cranmer in Act V) – and making hay, as it goes, with the true chronology of events – *Henry VIII* sees the scheming Cardinal Wolsey emerge as the villain of the piece, plotting the downfall of another Duke of Buckingham, only to lose his own head for his pains. Such is the abuse of power at the heart of the play, while Henry himself is merely seen abandoning Katharine of Aragon for the charms of young Anne Bullen, who finally bears him a daughter rather than the longed-for son and heir. *Henry VIII* is surely less Shakespeare's work than Fletcher's, especially the sickeningly fulsome tribute to Elizabeth and her successor – father of the bride, patron of the actors, progenitor of the play – with which it ends.

> This royal infant—heaven still move about her!
> Though in her cradle, yet now promises
> Upon this land a thousand thousand blessings
> Which time shall bring to ripeness. She shall be—
> But few now living can behold that goodness—
> A pattern to all princes living with her,
> And all that shall succeed . . . [*etc. etc.*]
>   . . . As when
> The bird of wonder dies, the maiden phoenix,
> Her ashes new create another heir
> As great in admiration as herself,
> So shall she leave her blessedness to one,
> When heaven shall call her from this cloud of darkness,
> Who from the sacred ashes of her honour

> Shall star-like rise as great in fame as she was,
> And so stand fix'd. Peace, plenty, love, truth, terror,
> That were the servants to this chosen infant,
> Shall then be his, and, like a vine, grow to him.
> Wherever the bright sun of heaven shall shine,
> His honour and the greatness of his name
> Shall be, and make new nations. He shall flourish,
> And like a mountain cedar reach his branches
> To all the plains about him. Our children's children
> Shall see this, and bless heaven.

Cranmer begins this encomium – made, he protests, on orders from heaven – with the warning: 'The words I utter / Let none think flattery, for they'll find 'em truth.' Was it Shakespeare, cringing with shame at this interminable guff (*pace* the fine image of the cedar), who at its end could not resist dissociating himself by having even Henry deem Cranmer a bit over the top – 'Thou speakest wonders' – thus launching him, with all the tedium of a neo-Polonius, into another burst of florid royal sycophancy. Let it never be doubted (as it often is) that the man from Stratford, however much he had to demean himself to earn his living from royalty, understood republican instincts. As early as *Julius Caesar*, Shakespeare gave Cassius the definitive statement of any true democrat's belief that no 'poor, bare, fork'd animal' should king it over another:

> I cannot tell what you and other men
> Think of this life; but for my single self,
> I had as lief not be, as live to be
> In awe of such a thing as I myself.

The envious Cassius famously proceeds to tell Brutus of the day he saved Caesar from drowning in the Tiber:

> . . . And this man
> Is now become a god, and Cassius is
> A wretched creature, and must bend his body
> If Caesar carelessly but nod on him . . .

and of once witnessing, in Spain, one of the great man's epileptic fits:

> ... Ye gods, it doth amaze me
> A man of such a feeble temper should
> So get the start of the majestic world
> And bear the palm alone.

Now he's getting personal. But the anti-imperial theme continues throughout Shakespeare's work, as we have seen only two years before in the guileless Perdita's natural reaction to the insufferably pompous presumptions of a king:

> The self-same sun that shines upon his court
> Hides not his visage from our cottage ...

Now at least one canny aristocrat watching *Henry VIII* at the Globe finally grasped the subversive truth of what Shakespeare had been up to all his working life. The play, wrote the diplomat Sir Henry Wotton to his nephew, Sir Edmund Bacon, 'represented some principal pieces of the reign of Henry VIII, which was set forth with many extraordinary circumstances of pomp and majesty ... sufficient in truth within a while to make greatness very familiar, if not ridiculous'. Poor Fletcher. Did he realise how wily old Shakespeare was using him? No doubt Burbage did.

Heminges and Condell believed there was enough of Shakespeare in *Henry VIII* to include it in the First Folio; although they entitle it *The Life of King Henry the 'Eight'*, in line with the titles of all the preceding history plays, the play was also known in Shakespeare's lifetime as *All Is True* (as the Oxford editors pedantically prefer, choosing to overrule Heminges and Condell). The master playwright's seasoned hand is most clearly seen in its first two, establishing scenes; the juxtaposition of Anne and Katharine in Scenes iii–iv of Act II; the exchanges between Henry and Wolsey in the first half of Act III, Scene ii (which thereafter deteriorates rapidly); and the first scene of Act V, with its touching exchange between Henry and Cranmer, and the news of Elizabeth's birth.

It was Tennyson who first divined Shakespeare's hand in these particular passages, attributing the rest to Fletcher – and perhaps others, with Jonson a prime suspect for the florid Prologue and Epilogue. The poet laureate's reading was conveyed, anonymously at first, in an 1850 article by James Spedding pleading with 'the individual consciousness of each reader' to concede that 'the effect of this play *as a whole*' is so 'weak and disappointing' as to be an 'inept' collaboration. Tennyson's analysis has since won broad acceptance, though some scholars have refused to believe that any hand other than Shakespeare's could have written such great set-pieces as Buckingham's speech before his execution (Act II, Scene i), Wolsey's farewell (III, ii) and Katharine of Aragon's death scene (IV, ii). But it takes a lifelong isolationist like G. Wilson Knight to see the work's progression 'from normality and order, through violent conflict to spiritualized music, and thence to concluding ritual' turn *Henry VIII* into 'the paradigm of Shakespeare's whole career and thus his culminating work'.

The play's empty emphasis on pomp and pageantry – one of the few theatrical reasons why it still enjoys occasional revivals – confirms that *Henry VIII* was one of no fewer than fourteen plays, six of them by Shakespeare, performed between the royal wedding on 14 February 1613 and the happy couple's departure for Germany two months later. To see his players revive *Much Ado About Nothing*, *Othello*, *The Winter's Tale* and *The Tempest* would have reminded the melancholy King of happier times. James's heir, that same young Henry who had played Jonson's 'soldier from God' on his installation as Prince of Wales two years earlier, had died the previous November, aged only eighteen; now his younger brother, Charles, was finding it hard to fulfil Henry's promise. Hence, perhaps, James's determination to marry off his favourite daughter in such extravagant style, lavishing no less than £6,000 on a mock sea battle on the Thames. The King's Men, by contrast, received a mere £93 6s 8d for their pains, on top of £50 for six other court performances that season (also believed by some to have been part of the wedding celebrations). In Westminster Abbey, at the marriage service itself – and so, presumably, at the subsequent theatricals – the 'drab and melancholy' appearance of the King, still mourning the loss of his beloved son, made a stark contrast with the bejewelled beauty of the bride.

Four months after its royal première, the lavish stage business of *Henry VIII* saw it pass into theatrical history for a quite different, if equally lamentable reason. A performance at the Globe on the afternoon of 29 June 1613 ended abruptly soon after Act I, Scene iv, line 49 – 'Look out there, some of ye', appropriately enough

– when a spark from the firing of a cannon to mark King Henry's arrival at Cardinal Wolsey's house (to take part, as it happens, in a masque, at which he would first fall for Anne Bullen) strayed into the theatre's thatched roof, starting a fire which saw the building razed to the ground within an hour. Mercifully, no one was hurt – 'nothing did perish but wood and straw, and a few forsaken cloaks' – although one man's breeches caught fire, 'that would perhaps have broiled him, if he had not by the benefit of a provident wit put it out with a bottled ale'.

The bar to the rescue again. This charming detail of this tragic disaster comes from the eyewitness account of that same titled toff, Sir Henry Wotton, once secretary to the Earl of Essex, who had deplored the play's mockery of aristocratic pretensions. No doubt he thought it divine retribution when

> certain chambers being shot off at his [Henry VIII's] entry, some
> of the paper, or other stuff, wherewith one of them was stopped,
> did light on the thatch, where being thought at first but an idle
> smoke, and their eyes more attentive to the show, it kindled
> inwardly, and ran round like a train, consuming within less than
> an hour the whole house to the very grounds.

Wotton – yes, that same witty Sir Henry, ambassador to Venice until the previous year, who had once defined a diplomat as 'an honest man sent to lie abroad for his country' – was not alone in finding it all a huge joke. As a contemporary ballad soon had it:

> No shower his rain did there down force
> In all that sunshine weather,
> To save that great renowned house;
> Nor thou, O ale-house, neither.
> Had it begun below, sans doubt,
> Their wives for fear had pissed it out.

Puritans like Wotton saw the hand of God in the 'sudden fearful burning' of Shakespeare's 'straw-thatched house' beside the Thames. To the players themselves, not to mention the shareholders – and, indeed, posterity – it was of course a catastrophe. Just as Prospero forecast, the great Globe itself had dissolved – and, with it, who knows what? How many manuscripts of Shakespeare's plays, accurate prompt copies of works we think we know, as well as others we never will? Not to mention costumes, properties and other worldlier goods representing months and years of work, the livelihoods of those with nothing to fall back on. 'See the world's ruins,' sympathised Ben Jonson.

And yet within a year, on 30 June 1614, one diary-keeping Londoner called on a friend, only to be told that she had 'gone to the Globe, to a play'. From the ashes of Shakespeare's original 'wooden O', like the phoenix in Cranmer's mercifully undelivered tribute to Elizabeth that terrible afternoon in 1613, arose 'another heir / As great in admiration as herself' – a new Globe, this one with a tiled roof. Who had paid for it? There were rumours that the King himself corralled his richer sycophants into coughing up, however reluctantly, to replace the noble building ravaged during that glutinous celebration of himself and his predecessor, even though neither of them (whatever Tom Stoppard would have us believe of Queen Elizabeth) had ever actually set foot in the place.

More likely, in an age not yet blessed (or cursed) by insurance companies, the costs would have been borne by the shareholders, required by the terms of their lease to underwrite the maintenance of the building. By one account, 'each sharer was at first assessed £50 or £60 towards the charges, but ended up having to pay much more'. At least one went broke in the process. Shakespeare, with one foot in Stratford, might well have seen this as the moment to cut his losses, sell off his stake in the business, and make a second attempt to spend more time with his family in rural retirement in Stratford, leaving London and the theatre behind him.

So did the 49-year-old poet, as has been seductively suggested, brood over the razing of the Globe 'while pruning the Great Garden of New Place', and decide that this was 'a good time to sell his share of the moiety in the company which he had served, to the best of his abilities, for nigh on two decades'?

No, he assuredly did not. He may have seized the moment to cash in his chips at the Globe, but not to ease his (already comfortably-off) retirement in the bosom of the family with whom he was always so ill at ease. Since earlier that year, while in London for the wedding of the King's daughter, and at least three months before the fire at the Globe, Shakespeare had been negotiating to buy the gate-house of the former Blackfriars monastery beside the Thames – little more than a hundred yards from the stage-door of the Blackfriars theatre.

Conveyance of the Blackfriars gate-house from Henry Walker to William Shakespeare, 10 March 1613.

His friend and colleague John Heminges, according to the title deed signed on 10 March 1613, was co-opted as trustee, along with William Johnson, landlord of the nearby Mermaid Tavern, and one of its habitués, John Jackson, a shipping magnate from Hull who enjoyed the company of actors. This Jackson was also married to the sister-in-law of Elias James, whose brewery lay at the foot of the street in which the gate-house stood, Puddle Dock Hill, and for whom Shakespeare supposedly wrote an epitaph:

> When God was pleas'd, (the world unwilling yet)
> Elias James to Nature paid his debt,
> And here reposeth: As he liv'd, he died,
> The saying strongly in him verified,
> Such life, such death: then a known truth to tell,
> He liv'd a godly life, and died as well.

Originally part of the huge Dominican priory at Blackfriars, the gate-house was described as a 'dwelling-house or tenement' built over a 'great gate' at the head of a street leading down to the river at Puddle Wharf, where wherries waited to taxi customers across the river to Bankside and the Globe. Adjacent was a parcel of land, entitling the new owner to 'free entry through the gate and yard' and thence to 'all and singular cellars, sollars [upper rooms and lofts], rooms, lights, easements, profits, commodities, and hereditaments whatsoever to the said dwelling house or tenement belonging, or in any wise appertaining'. For all this Shakespeare paid £140, including £80 up front in cash. The rest was subject to a complex deal, involving a temporary loan from Walker for the balance of £60, which has led some biographers to suggest that he purchased the gate-house purely as an investment, to rent out rather than living there himself.

But not for another three years, not until he made his will in 1616, is there any documentation suggesting that Shakespeare let the Blackfriars gate-house to a tenant. In April–May 1615, following the death of the elderly widow who owned the land to the west of his property, Shakespeare became involved in litigation with the Court of Chancery to assist her son and executor in handing over the 'letters patents and other deeds' relating to the 'messuages, tenements and premises' of what was by now quite a substantial property. His closest friend, Richard Burbage, lived and also owned property nearby. Close to their favourite tavern, let alone both theatres in which the King's Men plied their trade, the gate-house was the perfect London *pied-à-terre* for Shakespeare, if not his principal residence. That it claimed a special place in his heart, which was nothing to do with his wife and children, is clear from his trustees' interpretation of a clause in his will, which posthumously conveyed the entire property to two young men whose careers in London he hoped to encourage: John Greene of Clement's Inn and Matthew Morris of Stratford. The latter had close ties with Shakespeare's daughter Susanna; he named his own children Susanna and John, after Mrs Hall and her husband, and is also remembered (as 'my man' Morris) in the will of her father-in-law, William Hall.

No, for the next year at least, until failing health finally drove him back to his family for good, the Blackfriars gate-house was Shakespeare's home-from-home. His brief, half-hearted attempt at retirement to Stratford had made him realise how bored he would be in his native rural backwater, for all his fondness (tinged with guilt) for his daughters. London, for all its petty irritations, had long since replaced Warwickshire as his natural habitat. (When I recently remarked to the Shakespearean actor and scholar Peter O'Toole how surprising it was that none of his plays was set in London, O'Toole replied: '*All* his plays are set in London.' When I subsequently tried this out on Frank Kermode, then completing his own life's work on Shakespeare, he replied with a sympathetic smile: 'Well, of course, he's right.')

Besides, there was still money to be earned in the capital. Even at the end of his career and the height of his renown, Master Shakespeare of Stratford was not averse to the most menial of London tasks if well enough paid. In March 1613, while concluding the purchase of the Blackfriars gate-house, he accepted the substantial fee of forty-four shillings to devise the *impresa* – a motto to adorn the insignia, 'allegorical or mythological . . . painted on paper shields' – to be borne by Francis Manners, 6th Earl of Rutland, in a tournament on 24 March to mark the tenth anniversary of the King's accession. For this unusual assignment he would have relished a new dimension to his long partnership with Richard Burbage, almost as talented a painter as actor, who received the same handsome fee for 'painting and making' the earl's *impresa*. The laconic (and apparently ubiquitous) Sir Henry Wotton remained unimpressed, complaining after his day out at the 'tilt' that these *imprese* were 'so dark that their meaning is not yet to be understood, unless perchance that were their meaning, not to be understood'.

It may be convenient (not to say sentimental) for Shakespeare's biographers to retire him prematurely to Stratford, to 'prune his vines' or 'watch his mulberry tree grow', but it certainly wasn't for Shakespeare. Even Burgess yields to the temptation, dating the 'broken-hearted' playwright's withdrawal from June 1613, the month of the Globe fire, which marked no less than 'the end of his career'. Burgess's beloved 'Will' had 'put so much of himself into the life of the playhouse that its destruction was like the destruction of a faculty or limb. It was time go home in earnest.'

'He slunk past in life,' as Henry James put it. 'That was good enough for him, the contention appears to be. Why therefore should he not slink past in immortality?' Now Shakespeare again manages to slink past his more romantic biographers, by refusing to retreat poignantly to Stratford – no doubt to quaff ale from that earthen half-pint mug in his habitual corner of the local inn – and opting to hang around in London, to co-write one very last play. Henry James, the kindred spirit who refused to believe that this of all writers could fold his scroll, hang up his quill and go home to count his money, would be delighted.

Nor is there any call, this last time, for some scholars to quibble about stylistic evidence, while others protest that stylistic evidence is but a dubious basis for dating. We have an entry in the Stationers Register for 8 April 1634 and the title page of a subsequent quarto edition to assure us that *The Two Noble Kinsmen* was a 'Tragi-Comedy' by 'the memorable Worthies of their time, Mr John Fletcher, and Mr William Shakespeare, Gent[lemen]', which had oft been presented at the Blackfriars 'by the King's Majesty's servants with great applause'. Eighteen years after Shakespeare's death, moreover, and nine after Fletcher's, this particular quarto was at last published by a printer of probity, John Waterson, who had recently issued other plays belonging to the King's Men, and would have worked only from a reliable manuscript – made available to him by the players themselves, who would surely have verified the identities of its authors. If Shakespeare and his theatrical business partners had not been prepared to part with their exclusive rights on his plays during his lifetime, rating high finance above high art, his successors seem to have learned from Heminges and Condell a sense of their duty to posterity.

We also know from a 'scrap of paper' emanating from the King's Office of the Revels that *The Two Noble Kinsmen* was in the repertory of the King's Men by 1619, probably long before, but was only now being 'considered for performance at court'. The names of two actors which inadvertently 'slipped' into the text also suggest that there was a revival in the mid-1620s, confirming that a stable script would have been available to Heminges and Condell as they edited the First Folio. And yet, like *Pericles*, *The Two Noble Kinsmen* does not merit a place in their 'catalogue of the several Comedies, Histories and Tragedies' of the late William Shakespeare. Joint authorship cannot, in itself, have breached their criteria for inclusion; *Henry VIII*, after all, earns its due place at the end of the Histories. *Pace* copyright or typographical problems, the exclusion of *The Two Noble Kinsmen* seems to suggest that Shakespeare's fellow-players considered *Henry VIII* worthy of their late, esteemed colleague, but deemed this last vogue 'tragicomedy' to be rather more Fletcher's work than his. As if to confirm this, *The Two Noble Kinsmen* earns pride of place in the 1679 Second Folio of the *Collected Works* of Beaumont and Fletcher, which naturally included many such collaborations, and in most subsequent editions of their works, while fighting the while to gain a firm foothold in the Shakespeare canon.

Four centuries on, this remains an infinitely fluid field of scholarship in which pretty much anything can crop up. As recently as 1965, for instance, the American critic Paul Bertram mounted a passionate case that *The Two Noble Kinsmen* was Shakespeare's alone. Bertram was buttressed by as reassuring an ally as De Quincey, who hailed the first and last acts as 'perhaps the most superb work in the language and beyond all doubt from the loom of Shakespeare'. Others, before and since, have attributed the work in whole or in part to Fletcher's more familiar partner Beaumont, their contemporary Henry Massinger, and divers others. But the consensus – measured by the Oxford, Riverside, Arden and other standard modern editions, not to mention the title page of the First Folio – remains that *The Two Noble Kinsmen* was a second (and last) collaboration between Shakespeare and Fletcher.

So whose was the upper hand? The academic battlefield has been little redrawn since 1833, when it was first mapped out by the Scottish scholar William Spalding, who gave Fletcher the Prologue and Epilogue, plus the 'pretty' song which opens the first scene. Otherwise, Spalding carved the play up as follows:

Act I, i–Act II, i:	Shakespeare [? Act I, iv–v]
Act II, ii–vi:	Fletcher
Act III, i:	Shakespeare
Act III, ii–V, i, 33:	Fletcher [? Act IV, ii]
Act V, i, 34–173:	Shakespeare
Act V, ii:	Fletcher
Act V, iii–iv:	Shakespeare

One hundred and fifty years later, the editors of the 1986 Oxford edition could not but endorse Spalding's division of responsibility, on the basis of Shakespeare's distinctively 'rhetorical' and 'ritualistical' skills, plus 'emblematically spectacular episodes related to his other late plays'. Fletcher, meanwhile, is credited with the mere mechanics of the rivalry of the eponymous cousins, Palamon and Arcite – the closest of friends, all but indistinguishable, until both fall in love with the same woman, Emilia, sister-in-law of Theseus, Duke of Athens. Fletcher also handled the sub-plot – the only significant departure from their source – about the complications caused by the simultaneous, unrequited love for Palamon of a less suitable (if more passionate) woman, the Jailer's daughter, and the

entertainments devised by rude mechanical-style rustics for Duke
Theseus.

As was the way of such tragicomedies – all the rage during the first
years of the seventeenth century – the conflicting claims of innocence
and experience, lust and duty, love and friendship (with all of which
Shakespeare had dealt quite differently a quarter of a century earlier,
at the start of his career, in *The Two Gentlemen of Verona*) are finally
resolved by formal combat, with Emilia going to the winner and
death to the loser. But there is, of course, a tantalising twist: as the
loser, Palamon, prepares to pay the supreme price, Arcite suffers a
fatal fall while out riding. The dying victor commends Emilia to his
vanquished friend, and the Duke rounds things off with a meditation
on the fickleness of fate – a menacing presence from the very start of
the proceedings. As Arcite puts it at the outset:

> Let th' event,
> That never-erring arbitrator, tell us
> When we know all ourselves, and let us follow
> The becking of our chance.

Little more than a dramatisation of Chaucer's 'Knight's Tale', on
which Shakespeare had already drawn for the characters of Theseus
and Hippolyta in *A Midsummer Night's Dream*, *The Two Noble Kinsmen* can also be dated to 1613 from the morris dance led by the
Schoolmaster at the climax of its third act, into which Fletcher
writes characters from the second 'antimasque' in his erstwhile partner
Beaumont's *Masque of the Inner Temple and Gray's Inn*, played by
the King's Men for their royal patron on 20 February that year.
James enjoyed it so much that the dancers among Shakespeare's old
colleagues begged him to persuade Fletcher to build more dancing
into the piece on which they were both working at the time. Ben
Jonson adds to the unusually generous helping of hard contemporary
evidence the following year, 1614, by referring to a character named
Palamon in *Bartholomew Fair*.

Shakespeare, however minimal his contribution, was in familiar
territory. As in *Pericles* he had adapted the poet Gower, so in *The
Two Noble Kinsmen* he was jointly reworking Gower's contemporary
Chaucer, in a world quite as remote from Jacobean England – for

Thebes and Athens read Antioch, Tharsus, Mitylene and Ephesus – under the sway of supernatural forces as cruelly arbitrary. Emilia is quite as hapless an innocent as Marina, Imogen, Perdita and Miranda, equally subject to the whims of heartless forces beyond her control. If the play mirrors other familiar Shakespearean motifs, such as the agonies inflicted by Hamlet on Ophelia, it is because Fletcher was rarely averse, in this or any other of his works, to echoing his mentor's work in the guise of an *hommage*.

The subtle refinements of Chaucer's groundwork are, of course, invariably Shakespeare's rather than Fletcher's. Amid the textual gamesmanship which will no doubt fuel the Shakespeare industry for centuries yet, few have better summed up their respective poetic qualities than that canniest of Bardolaters, Charles Lamb:

> His [Fletcher's] ideas move slow; his versification, though sweet, is tedious; it stops every moment; he lays line upon line, making up one after the other, adding image to image so deliberately that we see where they join: Shakespeare mingles everything, he runs line into line, embarrasses sentences and metaphors; before one idea has burst its shell, another is hatched and clamorous for disclosure.

A great success, by all accounts, in the few years left to Shakespeare, and over the next few decades, *The Two Noble Kinsmen* has since fared less well. Revived by the ferociously loyal William Davenant in 1664, in a typically free adaptation entitled *The Rivals*, the play was rarely performed over the two centuries and more before it was boldly chosen to open the Royal Shakespeare Company's new Elizabethan-style auditorium in Stratford, the Swan, in 1986.

By his fiftieth birthday, in April 1614, Shakespeare finally *was* back in Stratford, his health gradually beginning to fail, his family rallying round. Now he found himself doubly fortunate in his son-in-law, John Hall, not only a good and loving husband to Susanna, but a sound and dutiful physician to his father-in-law. The retired – yes, finally, irrevocably, retired – playwright was scarcely a model patient, but nor had he yet sunk quite to the level he had himself satirised in his mid-thirties – that descent, at the dread stage six out of seven,

> Into the lean and slipper'd pantaloon,
> With spectacles on nose and pouch on side,
> His youthful hose, well sav'd, a world too wide
> For his shrunk shank, and his big, manly voice,
> Turning again toward childish treble, pipes
> And whistles in his sound.

Nor, mercifully, would he ever act in his own 'last scene of all / That ends this strange, eventful history':

> second childishness and mere oblivion,
> Sans teeth, sans eyes, sans taste, sans everything.

Shakespeare's glory days in the capital might finally be over – now, his private grief no doubt mitigated by the extra income, he could indeed rent the Blackfriars gate-house to the John Robinson documented in his will as his tenant – but he was still as determined as ever to enjoy himself. Few of those 'third thoughts' were preoccupying him yet. His lifelong friend, coeval and fellow Warwickshire poet-playwright, Michael Drayton – who had collaborated on dramas with Dekker, Webster, even Henry Chettle, but never with Shakespeare – often stayed with highly civilised mutual friends, Sir Henry and Lady (Anne) Rainsford, barely two miles across the Avon in the village of Clifford Chambers; Drayton would bring the latest gossip from London, as ready to trash rising reputations as he was to reminisce. Ben Jonson, with whom uncomplicated friendship appears to have blossomed from years of rivalry, now ready to play disciple to the man he recognised as his mentor, was eager to stay in touch, even pay the occasional visit to Stratford as he walked the length and breadth of the nation, in a vain attempt to lose weight. Shakespeare was godfather to one of Jonson's children; 'I'll e'en give him a dozen latten spoons,' he had written to Ben, 'and thou shalt translate them.' So Jonson, it seems, was already teasing Shakespeare about his 'small' Latin.

Jonson, too, had lost a son in childhood – a second Ben, dead of the plague in 1603 – and written a very moving poem, 'On My First Son':

> Farewell, thou child of my right hand, and joy;

My sin was too much hope of thee, loved boy,
Seven years thou wert lent to me, and I thee pay,
Exacted by thy fate, on the just day.
Oh, could I lose all father now. For why
Will man lament the state he should envy?
To have so soon 'scaped world's, and flesh's rage,
And, if no other misery, yet age?
Rest in soft peace, and, asked, say here doth lie
Ben Jonson his best piece of poetry;
For whose sake, henceforth, all his bows be such
As what he loves may never like too much.

These lines – and their author – could console Shakespeare whenever the ghost of Hamnet stalked his soul.

Perhaps retirement would not be so dull and dispiriting, after all. For another thing, Shakespeare could gratify his father's ghost by lording it over the locals, entertaining at New Place such notable visitors as the preacher invited to give the Whitsuntide sermon; the borough corporation even subsidised him to the tune of 20d for 'one quart of sack and one quart of claret wine' to keep his house-guest happy. That summer, on 9 July, New Place and his other properties were fortunate to escape a 'sudden and terrible fire' which swept through Stratford, the third in living memory. Boosted by a high wind, its force was 'so great . . . that it dispersed into so many places thereof whereby the whole town was in very great danger to have been utterly consumed'. More than fifty dwelling-houses were razed, along with stables and barns storing precious grain and hay.

There was a collection for the victims, to which we can only assume that Shakespeare contributed. But the patron saint of fellow-feeling was not averse to standing on his dignity when his own financial interests were at stake. That same summer of 1614 saw the start of a tumultuous local dispute which would not be finally resolved until after his death. It affected men of property, and it affected men of none – those who supported their families by working on the soil. The dispute over 'enclosure', in short, affected everyone, high and low, in ways which might be expected to have earned Shakespeare's sympathy. But he maintained a judicious public silence throughout, watchful for his own interests.

The purpose of enclosure was to consolidate the 'yardlands' – those parcels of land of which he had bought more than a hundred acres in 1602 – into larger units bounded by hedges or fences. Often this meant the conversion of arable land, like Shakespeare's, into pastures for grazing sheep, which yielded a smaller income per square acre than grain and hay, but produced a greater net profit as it was less labour-intensive. This was, in short, more efficient agriculture, as 'the communal tillage of open fields was not conducted on scientific lines, and obviously no one would spend capital on improving his scattered and unenclosed plots for the benefit of his neighbours'. But it reduced employment, as pasture-land required less maintenance than arable, and inflated the price of grain. So the interests of high and low, landowners and men of the soil alike, were directly affected by the plans of Arthur Mainwaring, steward to the Lord Chancellor, to enclose the common fields of Welcombe, just outside Stratford. Large stretches of it belonged to Shakespeare, whose name was placed by town clerk Greene at the head of the list he compiled that September of interested parties, or 'ancient freeholders in the fields of Old Stratford and Welcombe'.

Mainwaring's plans enjoyed the enthusiastic support of an aggressive young local landowner named William Combe, 28-year-old nephew of Thomas, the moneylender who had persuaded Shakespeare to pen his epitaph. The precedents were not encouraging; a previous attempt at enclosure had come to naught, despite the involvement of the lord of the manor, Sir Edward Greville. But Combe and Mainwaring pressed ahead confidently, to the mounting concern of Greene, who had himself recently invested £300 in 'tithe-interests' in the area. Suddenly Shakespeare's kinsman became leader of the anti-enclosure movement as well as supposedly neutral town clerk; in vain, however, did he pepper his celebrated cousin with memoranda on the subject. Publicly, Shakespeare remained aloof; privately, he was watching developments with cautious interest.

Even more privately, he was taking prudent measures against the enclosure of his land. The town council, swayed by Greene, had unanimously voted in September to oppose enclosure; and, two months later, given reason to fear that Mainwaring and Combe would proceed regardless, further voted to use 'all lawful means' to prevent them. Evidently, this did not reassure Shakespeare, who that October negotiated a private contract with Mainwaring's cousin and partner,

William Replingham of Market Harborough, guaranteeing himself
or his heirs financial compensation for any and all 'loss, detriment
and hindrance' to his annual income from his land 'by reason of any
enclosure or decay of tillage there'.

*The last page of the agreement between Shakespeare and William Replingham
concerning proposed enclosures at Welcombe, 28 October 1614.*

The previous month Shakespeare, for reasons we do not know but
are not hard to guess, had been in London. So, on corporation business,
was Greene, who took the chance to lobby Stratford's most famous son
on the dispute tearing the town asunder. On the 17th, notes Greene,
'my cousin Shakespeare coming yesterday to town, I went to see him
how he did'. When Greene moved the conversation to enclosure,
Shakespeare told him he had been 'assured' that Mainwaring and
Combe 'meant to enclose no further than to Gospel Bush, and so

up straight (leaving out part of the dingles to the field) to the gate in Clopton hedge, and take in Salisbury's piece, and that they mean in April to survey the land, and then to give satisfaction and not before'. Greene had heard much the same from Shakespeare's son-in-law, Dr John Hall.

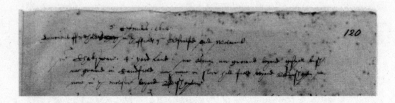

Thomas Greene's memorandum on visiting Shakespeare in London to discuss the enclosure crisis, 5 September 1614.

Both were misinformed, or had been misled. The survey scheduled for April took place as soon as December, when Combe and Mainwaring rejected the pleas of a six-man delegation from the council begging them to desist. Desperately Greene canvassed support from local notables, including Shakespeare, as Mainwaring pledged to start digging ditches and planting hedges as soon as a thaw permitted. Greene wrote to remind him of the devastation caused by the recent fires, adding menacingly that enclosure, 'by tending to the ruin of the borough, would bring on his head the curses of the 700 almsfolk living there'. Even this lurid plea – threat, almost – fell on deaf ears.

Later that December, when Combe's men duly started digging a ditch, and erecting hedge-mounds, they had reached a distance of at least fifty perches (some 300 metres) before the council decided to resort to *force majeure*, and sent out a team to fill them in again. A scuffle ensued, watched from horseback by a laughing Combe, who joked that they were 'good football players' as his men threw the council's to the ground. While denouncing the corporation as 'puritan knaves and underlings', Combe was privately worried enough to offer Greene a £10 bribe to call off his campaign. But the town clerk proved incorruptible, and the will of the majority finally prevailed over the greed of two unscrupulous landowners. The following day saw women and children from Stratford join their husbands and fathers in filling in the rest of Combe's ditch.

The enclosure dispute dragged on several more years. Once the council's legal power to forbid it was endorsed at Warwick Assizes the following March, Mainwaring and Replingham admitted defeat; but Combe still refused to give up. Over the next two years he systematically terrorised his tenants, buying up their land and property to the point where he owned the entire village of Welcombe, and was indeed its only resident (apart from his domestic staff). Even then, the majesty of the law prevented Combe from polishing off this seventeenth-century version of 'ethnic cleansing' by enclosing his own land; at the Lent Assizes of 1616 no less a figure than the Chief Justice of the King's Bench, Sir Edward Coke, told Combe to 'set his heart at rest; he should never enclose nor lay down his common arable land'. Publicly, Combe was forced to admit himself finally 'out of hope ever to enclose'; privately, he continued to lobby the council to change its mind. That summer he was still making rather more polite approaches to his 'very loving friends and neighbours', only to be told to get lost.

By then Shakespeare was dead. But the enclosure episode reveals a hitherto unseen side to the playwright of the people; while publicly supporting their aims, and no doubt genuinely sympathising in private, he was quietly hedging his bets by doing clandestine deals with the enemy. This side of the supposedly reactionary, self-interested Bard was cruelly traduced in a stage play called *Bingo*, written by the English playwright Edward Bond in 1973. 'The town wrote to him for help and he did nothing,' in Bond's own words. 'He may have doubted that the enclosers would succeed, but at best this means he sat at home with his guarantee while others made the resistance that was the only way to stop them.' Lear, he adds brutally, 'divided up his land at the beginning of the play, when he was arbitrary and unjust – not when he was shouting out his truths on the open common'. Bond drives home his point by having the local gentry invite Shakespeare to serve on the borough council, like his father before him. Wearily, he turns them down. After all those years as a 'rogue and vagabond' player, reluctantly subservient to the whims of hereditary paymasters, standing on his civic dignity was not something that came naturally to Shakespeare. With due respect to his late father, it never had. Gentleman, to John Shakespeare's son, was 'less a rank than a role', as Burgess puts it, with a typically brash afterthought of which Shakespeare would surely have approved: 'No artist of any stature can ever be wholly a gentleman.'

Susanna's husband, John Hall, was proving himself the very model of a Jacobean gentleman, though Judith's husband-to-be would prove quite the opposite. Dr Hall, who had come to Stratford via Cambridge in 1600, was one of the most dedicated and sought-after physicians in the region, working tirelessly day and night to apply his patent remedies to the ailments of both rich and poor, aristocrats and their servants. So respected did Hall become that the corporation tried to draft him in as an unelected burgess; so professionally popular was he that he felt obliged to decline their generous offer because of pressure of work. His eloquent case-books are full of innovative herbal remedies for all afflictions, major and minor, crammed with fascinating period detail on treatments for conditions from dropsy to scurvy, the itch to the pox, not hesitating to detail those applied to the ailments of all his patients, down to his own wife and daughter, even himself.

Like his father-in-law, Hall was an egalitarian with republican instincts; in 1626, ten years after Shakespeare's death, he declined King Charles I's offer of a knighthood, preferring to pay the £10 fine. His Puritan views and stern record as a churchwarden – more important, to Hall, than merely civic duties – may make the worthy doctor seem something of a prig. But he proved otherwise by standing by his wife in her potentially ruinous hour of most need.

In July 1613 Susanna Hall travelled to the consistory court at Worcester Cathedral to sue John Lane of Alveston Manor, two miles outside of Stratford, for slander. Five weeks earlier, by the terms of her indictment, Lane had 'reported' that Mrs Hall had 'the running of the reins and had been naught with Rafe Smith' – that she had contracted gonorrhoea, in other words, after committing adultery with Smith, a 35-year-old Stratford haberdasher, nephew to Hamnet Sadler and brother-in-law to town clerk Greene. Lane, her accuser, was a notorious wastrel, the scion of local gentry with a record for causing trouble, usually when drunk. Why he came up with this accusation against Susanna, well respected locally as the virtuous, churchgoing wife of the upstanding Stratford physician, has never become clear. He failed to appear in court to give evidence, and was excommunicated for his pains.

So Susanna's name was cleared; but she and her respectable husband had to endure years of knowing looks in a community as small and gossipy as Stratford. She predeceased her husband, who eventually died in 1635, at the age of sixty. The epitaph he placed on their joint tombstone in the chancel of Holy Trinity pointedly describes his wife as 'most faithful', *fidissima conjunx*, and we must take his marble inscription at its word. The agonies Shakespeare went through during his daughter's public discomfiture can only be left to our distressed imaginations. In *The Herbal Bed*, his elegant dramatisation of this murky episode, staged by the Royal Shakespeare Company in 1996, the playwright Peter Whelan sensibly (and most effectively) keeps Susanna's ailing father hovering, unseen, in the wings.

Susanna's sister Judith was less fortunate in her own eventual choice of a husband, Thomas Quiney, son of Shakespeare's importunate friend Richard, who had written that begging letter all of eighteen years before. A vintner by trade, young Quiney was twenty-six, and Judith thirty-one, when they married at Holy Trinity on 10 February 1616. Any uncomfortable memories that may have spoilt the day for the bride's mother, herself eight years older than her husband, were staunched by the dire dramas surrounding the event. The least of the newlyweds' woes was that, for their own reasons, they chose to break canon law by marrying in Lent without the requisite special licence, which resulted in their joint excommunication a month later.

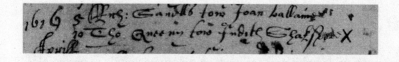

Thomas Quiney marries Judith Shakespeare, 10 February 1616.

But there was worse. Shortly before their wedding day, Judith had discovered that another local woman, Margaret Wheeler, was pregnant by her husband-to-be. Hence, perhaps, their own o'er-hasty progress to the altar. Within a month of their nuptials, Margaret Wheeler died in childbirth, and her infant with her. Both were buried, according to the parish register, on 15 March.

Quiney's was a crime far worse than the harmless fornication-before-marriage which had seen Claudio condemned to death in his father-in-law's sombre *Measure for Measure*. On 26 March, eleven days after his wedding, Judith's husband was summoned before the local vicar's ecclesiastical court, where he pleaded guilty to 'carnal copulation' (*fassus est se carnalem copulationem habuisse*) and was sentenced to perform public penance by wearing a white sheet in church, in front of the entire Stratford congregation, on three successive Sundays. Whether or not the influential Shakespeare intervened, to spare his daughter this dire humiliation as much as her husband, we have no way of knowing. But Quiney's sentence was mysteriously commuted, within days, to a meagre fine of five shillings, and a private display of penitence to another local vicar rather than an extended public ordeal. The newlyweds' blushes were spared; but their marriage was not, to say the least, off to the best of starts.

Quiney subsequently lived up to these dubious beginnings, thwarting his own attempts to achieve local respectability on the town council with a long track-record of drunken scrapes. He allowed his chums to drink illegally in his house; watered down the wine at his inn, the Cage; and eventually tried to cheat his wife by selling the family business behind her back. Shakespeare's surviving kinsmen, long after his death, intervened in time to protect his daughter's interests. But Judith had married a bad lot, and can be excused for suspecting some sort of divine retribution when all three of her children by Quiney died long before her. The first, christened Shakespeare Quiney a year after his grandfather's death, perished in infancy on 8 May 1617. Two more sons, Richard and Thomas, born over the following three years, both died within a month of each other in 1639, aged twenty-one and nineteen.

Susanna was literate, Judith was not. Shakespeare may have taken more pride in his more refined, worldly-wise, locally respected older daughter, but he knew that he had not been much of a father to either. His ghost would probably shrug with fatalistic resignation at the failure of both to keep his name alive. Susanna never had more than the one daughter, Elizabeth, who herself died childless (despite two marriages) in 1670, at the age of sixty-one. Nor did Judith ever have any more children; she died in 1662, at the remarkable age of seventy-seven, having outlived her older sister by thirteen years. Within a generation, the Shakespeare line was extinct. Never expecting his writings to outlive him, and knowing that his brothers had all failed to preserve the family name, John Shakespeare's son appeared to have wasted his time securing that proud family crest and motto.

It was surely at Judith's wedding reception that Shakespeare enjoyed the 'merry meeting' with his old friends Jonson and Drayton at which they 'drank too much', giving the Stratford man the fever from which he would never recover. Judith's twin brother, his son Hamnet, dead these twenty years, would obviously have been on his mind that day; further depressed by the dubious marriage his daughter was making, and the dire developments overshadowing the ceremony, perhaps this man of moderation in most things did for once permit himself to over-indulge.

Shakespeare had never been much of 'a company keeper', as Aubrey heard it from his friend Beeston's son. He 'wouldn't be debauched' – to the point of telling white lies; 'if invited', he would pretend that he was 'in pain'. On this occasion, however, he himself was the host; and his two fellow writers would surely have brightened up the dreary guest-list of Stratford worthies at his second daughter's wedding, typified by the local physician and cleric, John Ward, whose memoir is the only witness we have of the events leading up to Shakespeare's death:

> Shakespeare, Drayton and Ben Jonson, had a merry meeting, and it seems drank too much, for Shakespeare died of a fever there contracted.

Ward was an admirer of Shakespeare's work, and the source of several legends about his productivity and earnings; on his arrival in Stratford he had made a note to himself 'to peruse Shakespeare's plays, and be versed in them' so as not to be 'ignorant in the matter'. We would much rather have had the poet's son-in-law and personal physician, Dr Hall, as expert witness; but his earliest extant case-book, most frustratingly, dates from early the following year, leaving the imaginations of biographers all too free to run riot:

> Shakespeare ate too many pickled herrings and drank too much Rhenish whine . . . Will may have been weak already – from venereal disease, from a seasonal cold, from Bürger's arterial blockage . . . He may have drunk with abandon, encouraged by Ben, then sweated in a hot room, walked out hatless and cloakless to speed his guests on their way, pooh-poohed warnings of the danger of a chill April night . . . A quick attack of pneumonia which his son-in-law's emetics and electuaries would do nothing to relieve, was enough to affect his quietus.

Entertaining (and indeed plausible) though all this may be, the sole, stark documentary fact is that William Shakespeare died on 23 April 1616, supposedly his fifty-second birthday, of causes unknown.

Prudently, and perhaps with gloomy prescience, he had summoned his lawyer friend Francis Collins to take dictation of his last will and testament barely six months earlier, during the long, bleak days of the turn of the year which proved his last. The document was revised in March, to take account of Judith's wedding. Although it describes Shakespeare as 'in perfect health and memory', the signature validating the changes had grown much weaker in the two months since he had first signed the foot of each page. The wording is largely that of a standard legal document, between the lines of which peeps little of the character, let alone the literary style of the man now apportioning his considerable estate. Quite the reverse. 'In the name of God, Amen', it begins,

> I, William Shakespeare . . . do make and ordain this last will and testament in manner and form following. That is to say, first I commend my soul into the hands of God my creator, hoping and assuredly believing through the only merits of Jesus Christ my Saviour, to be made partaker of life everlasting; and my body to the earth whereof it is made.

This is lawyer Collins, not scrivener Shakespeare, obliging his client with the formulaic introduction which was then standard legal practice; it should not be used (as, of course, it has been) to conjure up a dramatic picture of a deathbed religious conversion. The old playwright was too tired to insist on theological niceties; his prime concern was that his estate be divided as he deemed fit.

To Judith – who, as the catalyst for revision, came first – he left his 'broad silver-gilt bowl' and £150, the money on unusual conditions which demonstrate his concern about her choice of husband-to-be. One hundred pounds his daughter would receive on marriage; but receipt of the remaining £50 required her to forgo her claim to the cottage in Chapel Lane, 'one copyhold tenement . . . being parcel or holden of the manor of Rowington'. Judith was to receive a further £150 'if she or any issue of her body be living at the end of three years next ensuing the day of the date of this my will'. (Should she

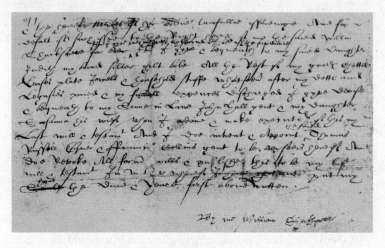

The last page of Shakespeare's will.

die childless within this period, £100 of the £150 was to go to his granddaughter, Elizabeth Hall, and the other £50 to his sister Joan Hart and her children.) His executors were to see that Judith enjoyed the interest earned by this second £150, but could not touch the capital, as long as she stayed married. But they were also to police the provision that her husband could lay no claim at all to the money unless he matched it by settling on Judith lands of equivalent value (only if, as it was phrased, he 'do sufficiently assure unto her and the issue of her body lands answerable to the portion by this my will given unto her').

There followed a bequest of £20 and some of his clothes to his sister Joan, whom he also granted a life tenancy of the western portion of Henley Street for a peppercorn rent of 12d a year. Shakespeare could not remember the names of all her sons, his nephews; a blank space was left for one, duly filled in later as Thomas, to share £15 equally with his brothers William and Michael. To eight-year-old Elizabeth Hall went most of her grandfather's valuable plate (apart from Judith's bowl); and to his seven-year-old godson, William Walker, twenty shillings in gold. To 'the poor of Stratford' he left the handsome sum of £10.

To Thomas Combe, nephew of John, Shakespeare left his sword. Other local friends to benefit were lawyer Collins himself, to the tune of £13 6s 8d; and Thomas Russell, £5. Hamnet Sadler, William Reynolds and the Nash brothers, Anthony and John, were each left 26s 8d to purchase a memorial ring. The same amount, for the same affectionate purpose, he left to his three bosom friends from the King's Men, Richard Burbage, John Heminges and Henry Condell.

Susanna, of course, became chatelaine of New Place, inheriting all the contents not bequeathed to others, specifically 'all the rest of my goods, chattels, leases, plate, jewels, and household stuff whatsoever, after my debts and legacies paid and my funeral expenses discharged'. Shakespeare felt no need to remind his elder daughter in writing to care for her mother. Besides, he could assume that Anne was well enough provided for. English common law stipulated that a widow was entitled to one-third of her husband's estate, and continued residence in the family domicile, for life.

It would have been almost irregular for Shakespeare to specify any bequest to the former Anne Hathaway in his will. So understandable curiosity has ever since surrounded its most celebrated clause: 'Item: I give unto my wife my second-best bed.' This has long been interpreted as an insult, since it was first so read by an outraged Malone: 'To mark how little he esteemed her, he . . . cut her off . . . with an old bed.' But a modicum of research into Elizabethan and Jacobean custom and practice in fact suggests that the Shakespeares, like most well-to-do middle-class couples, would have reserved the best bed in their home, New Place, for overnight guests. Now, in turn, this would have passed to their older daughter, Susanna. The 'second-best' bed Shakespeare so famously specified in his will was, therefore, the marital bed he had shared with Anne – on and off, to put it mildly – for more than thirty years (and perhaps her own parents' bed before that). Far from signifying the rottenness of their marriage, the bequest suggests a specific (and rather touching) vote of thanks from a grateful husband, aware of his own shortcomings, for the long-suffering, dogged loyalty of a partner who had for years put up with a long-distance marriage, single-handedly brought up his children in his absence, and overlooked his own all-too-evident lapses when he did choose to put in the occasional appearance at home.

For as long as she lived (which turned out to be another seven years, to the age of sixty-seven), Anne would also enjoy the benefit of his overwhelmingly handsome bequest to the Halls. Not only did Susanna and her husband inherit the 'great house' of New Place, 'wherein I now dwell', but ownership of the Henley Street properties, 'all my barns, stables, orchards, gardens, lands, tenements, and hereditaments whatsoever . . . within the towns, hamlets, villages, fields, and grounds of Stratford upon Avon, Oldstratford, Bishopston, and Welcombe, or in any of them, in the said county of Warwick'.

As if that – plus 'all other my lands, tenements, and hereditaments whatsoever' – were not enough, Shakespeare also bequeathed to his more reliable older daughter, and her provenly worthy husband, his beloved Blackfriars gate-house, then occupied by the aforementioned tenant, John Robinson. This London connection was doubly important, not just symbolically, because his transfer to the Halls of all his 'leases' would in legal terms have signified his shareholdings in the Globe and Blackfriars theatres, with all the substantial posthumous revenue that would continue to accrue therefrom.

The Halls, had they been blessed with any sons, were 'made men'. After Susanna's death New Place, Henley Street, those unenclosed Welcombe 'yardlands' and all her father's other bequests – not least those London 'leases' – were to pass to her first son, and to that son's 'lawful heirs' and so on through the third, fourth, fifth, sixth and seventh sons, and their lawful heirs. Shakespeare was clearly hoping, even after his death, for a male grandchild to perpetuate his name. He was not to know it; but it was not to be. And he even made provision, however reluctantly, for that. 'And for default of such issue the said premises to be and remain to my said niece [a then common alternative for granddaughter] Hall and the male heirs of her body lawfully issuing. And for the default of such issue, to my daughter Judith and the heirs males of her body lawfully issuing . . .'

And so on, and so on. But there would never be any such male heirs; both Elizabeth Hall and Judith Quiney would die childless. For all his strenuous attempts to keep within the family the huge legacy purchased by his genius, Shakespeare's worldly goods would soon be disbursed amid a wide array of less than close relations, who, whether or not they perused his writings, would bless his memory for generations to come.

We who come later must bless the memory of John Heminges and Henry Condell, the King's Men who spent the next seven years gathering together the scattered texts of their friend and fellow-actor's

A CATALOGVE

of the seuerall Comedies, Histories, and Tragedies contained in this Volume.

COMEDIES.

He Tempest.	Folio 1.
The two Gentlemen of Verona.	20
The Merry Wiues of Windsor.	38
Measure for Measure.	61
The Comedy of Errours.	85
Much adoo about Nothing.	101
Loues Labour lost.	122
Midsommer Nights Dreame.	145
The Merchant of Venice.	163
As you Like it.	185
The Taming of the Shrew.	208
All is well, that Ends well.	230
Twelfe-Night, or what you will.	255
The Winters Tale.	304

HISTORIES.

The Life and Death of King John.	Fol. 1.
The Life & death of Richard the second.	23
The First part of King Henry the fourth.	46
The Second part of K. Henry the fourth.	74
The Life of King Henry the Fift.	69
The First part of King Henry the Sixt.	96
The Second part of King Hen. the Sixt.	120
The Third part of King Henry the Sixt.	147
The Life & Death of Richard the Third.	173
The Life of King Henry the Eight.	205

TRAGEDIES.

The Tragedy of Coriolanus.	Fol. 1.
Titus Andronicus.	31
Romeo and Juliet.	53
Timon of Athens.	80
The Life and death of Julius Cæsar.	109
The Tragedy of Macbeth.	131
The Tragedy of Hamlet.	152
King Lear.	283
Othello, the Moore of Venice.	310
Anthony and Cleopater.	346
Cymbeline King of Britaine.	369

Pages from the First Folio of Shakespeare's Collected Works (1623), cataloguing thirty-five of his plays and listing the principal actors who played them.

The Workes of William Shakespeare,

containing all his Comedies, Histories, and
Tragedies: Truely set forth, according to their first
ORIGINALL.

The Names of the Principall Actors
in all these Playes.

William Shakespeare.	Samuel Gilburne.
Richard Burbadge.	Robert Armin.
John Hemmings.	William Ostler.
Augustine Phillips.	Nathan Field.
William Kempt.	John Underwood.
Thomas Poope.	Nicholas Tooley.
George Bryan.	William Ecclestone.
Henry Condell.	Joseph Taylor.
William Slye.	Robert Benfield.
Richard Cowly.	Robert Goughe.
John Lowine.	Richard Robinson.
Samuell Crosse.	Iohn Shancke.
Alexander Cooke.	Iohn Rice.

plays, and checking and re-checking their embattled texts before publishing them in what we call the First Folio. 'Set forth according to their first originals' were not only the eighteen unpublished works but, 'now cured, and perfect of their limbs', the seventeen plays that had printed during Shakespeare's lifetime – those 'divers stolen and surreptitious copies, maimed and deformed by the frauds and stealths of injurious imposters'.

The volume, entitled *Mr William Shakespeare's Comedies, Histories and Tragedies*, was entered in the Stationers Register on 8 November 1623, and published by Edward Blount and Isaac Jaggard soon after. With a Shakespearean eye to the main chance, Heminges and Condell dedicated the book to potential future patrons, the theatre-loving William Herbert, third Earl of Pembroke, and his younger brother Philip, first Earl of Montgomery. Twelve years since the publication of the Authorised Version of the Holy Bible which he had himself commissioned, the reign of King James I had now seen the publication, barely a decade apart, of the two most important books in the English language.

Shakespeare never expected his works for the stage to outlive him; there was no precedent for the publication of a collection of plays. Later in the year of Shakespeare's death, 1616, Ben Jonson would become the first to enjoy such an accolade in his own lifetime, perhaps boasting about it at their 'merry meeting'; but that same year, ironically enough, the failure of his comedy *The Devil is an Ass* forced his temporary retirement from the stage. Seven years later, however, he was minded to pay handsome tribute to his great contemporary in a preface to his collected works, in the shape of the celebrated verses addressed 'To the memory of my beloved, the author Mr William Shakespeare, and what he hath left us'. Those who consider Jonson's tribute 'lapidary', or merely formulaic, or 'damning with faint praise', are confounded, surely, by its most celebrated lines:

> Soul of the Age!
> The applause! delight! the wonder of our stage!
> My Shakespeare, rise! . . .
> He was not of an age, but for all time!

Earlier in the volume, opposite the portrait of Shakespeare on its title page, Jonson had appended another short verse addressed 'To the Reader':

> This Figure, that thou here seest put
>   It was for gentle Shakespeare cut;
> Wherein the graver had a strife
>   With nature, to outdo the life:
> O, could he but have drawn his wit
>   As well in brass as he hath hit
> His face, the print would then surpass
>   All that was ever writ in brass.
> But since he cannot, Reader, look
>   Not on his Picture, but his Book.

This sound advice should not be taken as criticism of the portrait by the young Flemish engraver Martin Droeshout – a better likeness of Shakespeare, by all accounts, than the Chandos portrait (see the frontispiece on p. iv). Droeshout was only twenty-two when he executed the commission, and had yet to develop much mastery of scale; the head, which has been said by a medical man to have two right eyes, is horribly out of proportion with the trunk, the coat on which has been said by tailors to have two left sides.

But Droeshout's remains the only portrait of Shakespeare approved for publication by people who had known the dead poet well. To whatever extent it corresponds with our own private images of Shakespeare – 'to see his face', according to Burgess, 'we need only look in a mirror' – it feels more like him, to be sure, than the travesty of a bust by 'Gerard Johnson' (the Dutch stonemason Gheerart Janssen) on the north wall of the chancel of Holy Trinity, which makes the poet look like a 'self-satisfied pork-butcher'. Still, beneath many more coats of paint, it looks down incongruously on the tomb in which the poet's mortal remains were placed on 25 April 1616, two days after his death. To this day (if now in the shape of an eighteenth-century replacement) the tombstone carries an inscription to strike dread into the heart of the pilgrim come to Stratford to stand and pay his respects.

There seems no reason to disbelieve, as so many do, that Shakespeare wrote his own epitaph. Still haunted by that charnel-house of his youth, if so, this lapsed Catholic, humanist non-believer managed, for the first time in all of his miraculous writings, to mention the name of Jesus without (quite) taking it in vain:

GOOD FREND FOR JESUS SAKE FORBEARE,
TO DIGG THE DUST ENCLOSED HEARE:
BLESTE BE YE MAN THAT SPARES THESE STONES,
AND CURST BE HE THAT MOVES MY BONES.

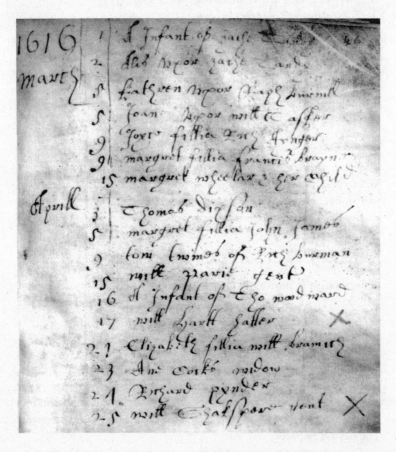

Shakespeare's burial entered in the Stratford-upon-Avon parish register.

APPENDICES

CHRONOLOGY OF
SHAKESPEARE'S WORKS

1587–92	1 Henry VI
	2 Henry VI
	3 Henry VI
	Richard III
	The Two Gentlemen of Verona
	Titus Andronicus
	[*contrib.* Edward III]
1592	Venus and Adonis
1593–94	The Rape of Lucrece
1593–1600	Sonnets [*published* 1609]
1593–94	The Comedy of Errors
	The Taming of the Shrew
	Love's Labour's Lost
1594–95	Midsummer Night's Dream
	Romeo and Juliet
	The Merchant of Venice
1595	Richard II
1595–96	King John
1596–97	1 Henry IV
1597	The Merry Wives of Windsor
1598	2 Henry IV

1598–99	Much Ado About Nothing
1599	Henry V
	Julius Caesar
	As You Like It
1600–1	Hamlet
1601	'The Phoenix and Turtle'
1601–2	Troilus and Cressida
	Twelfth Night
1602–3	All's Well That Ends Well
1603	[contrib. Sir Thomas More]
1604	Measure for Measure
	Othello
1605	King Lear
1606	Macbeth
1606–7	Antony and Cleopatra
1607–8	Timon of Athens
	Coriolanus
1607–8	Pericles
1609–10	Cymbeline
1610–11	The Winter's Tale
1611	The Tempest
1612–13	Henry VIII [with Fletcher]
1613	The Two Noble Kinsmen [with Fletcher]

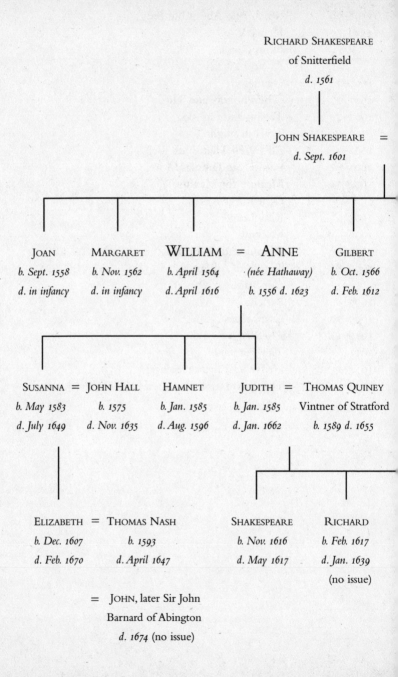

RICHARD SHAKESPEARE
of Snitterfield
d. 1561

JOHN SHAKESPEARE =
d. Sept. 1601

JOAN	MARGARET	WILLIAM =	ANNE	GILBERT
b. Sept. 1558	*b. Nov. 1562*	*b. April 1564*	*(née Hathaway)*	*b. Oct. 1566*
d. in infancy	*d. in infancy*	*d. April 1616*	*b. 1556 d. 1623*	*d. Feb. 1612*

SUSANNA = JOHN HALL	HAMNET	JUDITH = THOMAS QUINEY
b. May 1583 *b. 1575*	*b. Jan. 1585*	*b. Jan. 1585* Vintner of Stratford
d. July 1649 *d. Nov. 1635*	*d. Aug. 1596*	*d. Jan. 1662* *b. 1589 d. 1655*

ELIZABETH = THOMAS NASH	SHAKESPEARE	RICHARD
b. Dec. 1607 *b. 1593*	*b. Nov. 1616*	*b. Feb. 1617*
d. Feb. 1670 *d. April 1647*	*d. May 1617*	*d. Jan. 1639*
		(no issue)

= JOHN, later Sir John
Barnard of Abington
d. 1674 (no issue)

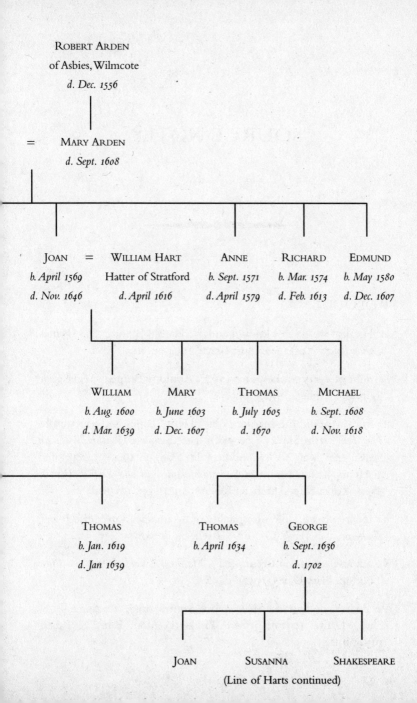

ROBERT ARDEN
of Asbies, Wilmcote
d. Dec. 1556

=   MARY ARDEN
d. Sept. 1608

JOAN	=	WILLIAM HART	ANNE	RICHARD	EDMUND
b. April 1569		Hatter of Stratford	*b. Sept. 1571*	*b. Mar. 1574*	*b. May 1580*
d. Nov. 1646		*d. April 1616*	*d. April 1579*	*d. Feb. 1613*	*d. Dec. 1607*

WILLIAM	MARY	THOMAS	MICHAEL
b. Aug. 1600	*b. June 1603*	*b. July 1605*	*b. Sept. 1608*
d. Mar. 1639	*d. Dec. 1607*	*d. 1670*	*d. Nov. 1618*

THOMAS	THOMAS	GEORGE
b. Jan. 1619	*b. April 1634*	*b. Sept. 1636*
d. Jan 1639		*d. 1702*

JOAN	SUSANNA	SHAKESPEARE

(Line of Harts continued)

SOURCE NOTES

PROLOGUE

'not because we do not know enough': Harold Bloom, *The Western Canon* (New York: Harcourt Brace, 1994), p. 61.

'the right of every Shakespeare-lover': Anthony Burgess, *Shakespeare* (London: Vintage, 1996), p. 9.

'the finer weapon, the sharper point': Henry James, introduction to *The Tempest* in Sidney Lee (ed.), *The Complete Works of William Shakespeare*, Vol. XVI (London: John Murray, 1906–9), reprinted in Henry James, *Essays on Literature: American and English Writers* (New York: New American Library, 1984), pp. 1219–20.

'the apparently boundless hospitality of his imagination': John Jones, *Shakespeare at Work* (Oxford: Clarendon Press, 1995), p. 12.

'We ask and ask': John Bryson (ed.), *Matthew Arnold, Poetry and Prose* (London: Hart-Davis, 1954), p. 32.

'We do not understand Shakespeare from a single reading': T. S. Eliot, 'Dante' (1929), *Selected Essays* (London: Faber & Faber, 1932), p. 245.

'We cannot know, by reading Shakespeare' ... 'he did not like lawyers': Harold Bloom, *Shakespeare: The Invention of the Human* (New York: Riverhead, 1998), pp. 7–8.

'If you read and re-read Shakespeare endlessly': Harold Bloom, *The Western Canon*, p. 53.

'We read, those of us who do': John Updike, *New York Review of Books*, Vol. XLVI, No. 2, 4 February 1999.

'everyone ... borrows from earlier writers': E. A. J. Honigmann, *Shakespeare: The Lost Years* (Manchester: MUP, 1985, revised 1998), p. vii.

I. STRATFORD: 1564–1569

'I loved the man': Ben Jonson, *Timber; or, Discoveries Made Upon Men and Matter*, written *c.* 1630, published in *Works* (London, 1640), pp. 97–8.

'in honour of her famous relation': De Quincey in Samuel Schoenbaum, *William Shakespeare: A Compact Documentary Life* (Oxford: OUP, 1987), p. 25.

'A Warwickshire antiquary': Edgar I. Fripp, *Shakespeare: Man and Artist* (London: OUP, 1938), pp. 79–80.

'able-bodied citizens': Schoenbaum, op. cit., p. 33.

'Can this be mere coincidence?': Eric Sams, *The Real Shakespeare: Retrieving the Early Years, 1564–1594* (New Haven, CT: Yale University Press, 1995), p. 20.

'very honest, sober, industrious': Schoenbaum, op. cit., p. 33.

'several intriguing questions': Ibid., p. 49.

'Three or four thousand or more of the Testaments': J. de Groot, *The Shakespeares and 'The Old Faith'* (1946), p. 88.

'clear their houses of all show of suspicion': Peter Milward, *Shakespeare's Religious Background* (London: Sidgwick & Jackson, 1973), p. 21.

II. CHILDHOOD: 1569–1579

'small Latin and less Greek': Ben Jonson, commendatory verses prefacing the First Folio of Shakespeare's *Collected Works*, 1623.

'pronouncing of letters, syllables, and words': Schoenbaum, op. cit., p. 64.

'To learne to wrytte dounc Ingglisshe': Burgess, op. cit., p. 29.

'the great commonplace': Schoenbaum, op. cit., p. 69.

'as well qualified in Latin': Stanley Wells, *Shakespeare: A Dramatic Life* (London: Sinclair-Stevenson, 1994), p. 13.

'all teachers of children': Ibid., p. 62.

'Quotations from . . . forty-two books of the Bible': Richmond Noble, *Shakespeare's Biblical Knowledge and Use of the Book of Common Prayer, as Exemplified in the Plays of the First Folio* (London: SPCK, 1935), p. 20.

'hardly a phrase of the story that has been missed': Ibid., p. 42.

'simple people': Schoenbaum, op. cit., p. 56.

'separates from the black clot': For this catalogue of Shakespearean blood, I am indebted to Eric Sams, *The Real Shakespeare*, p. 29.

'in the office of some county attorney': Edmund Malone, 'An Attempt to Ascertain the Order in Which the Plays Attributed to Shakespeare Were Written', in Shakespeare, *Plays and Poems*, ed. Edmund Malone (London: J. Rivington & Sons, 1790), Vol. I, Part 1, p. 307.

'The whole charm of Italy': Carl Elze, 'The Supposed Travels of Shakespeare', *Essays on Shakespeare*, translated by L. D. Schmitz (London, 1874), pp. 254–325.

'explored the inland waterways of Northern Italy': Schoenbaum, op. cit., p. 169.

'geographical accuracy': R. A. Foakes, Introduction to the Arden edition of *The Comedy of Errors* (London: Methuen, 1962), p. xxx.

'The author who ... makes a character depend': Duff Cooper, *Sergeant Shakespeare* (London: Hart-Davis, 1949), p. 14.

'A fight either takes place or is described': Ibid., p. 37.

'He had, by a Misfortune common enough to young Fellows': Nicholas Rowe, 'Some Account of the Life, &c., of Mr William Shakespear', in Shakespeare, *The Works of Shakespear* (London: Jacob Tonson, 1723), p. v.

'Such was his respect for Mr Shakespeare's genius': Shakespeare, *Plays and Poems*, ed. Malone, op. cit., p. 144.

'several old people' ... 'A Parliament member, a Justice of Peace': Shakespeare, *Works*, ed. George Steevens (London: Bathurst, 1778), Vol. I; *The Merry Wives of Windsor*, p. 223n.

'to the extreme end of ruin': 'William Shakespeare', entry in *Biographica Britannica* (1747–66), Vol. VI, Part 1, p. 3628, quoted in E. K. Chambers, *William Shakespeare: A Study of Facts and Problems* (Oxford: Clarendon Press, 1930), p. 287.

'Within this park is now standing a spot called Daisy Hill': Samuel Ireland, *Picturesque Views on the Upper, or Warwickshire Avon* (London, 1795), p. 154.

'They hid the buck in a barn': Eric Anderson (ed.), *The Journal of Sir Walter Scott* (Oxford: OUP, 1972), p. 454.

'fair game': Schoenbaum, op. cit., p. 106; 'Lucy thought papists fair game': Sams, op. cit., p. 46.

'enlightened and benevolent': Schoenbaum, op. cit., p. 107.

'put down abuses in religion': Sams, op. cit., p. 44.

'Forasmuch as that villainous traitor Parry': Clara Longworth de Pineton, *Shakespeare: A Portrait Restored* (London: Hollis & Carter, 1957), pp. 55–6.

'afterwards made an ale-house boast': Alice Fairfax-Lucy, *Charlecote and the Lucys: The Chronicle of an English Family* (London: OUP, 1958), p. 5.

'It is absurd to say we know *nothing*': Walter Bagehot, *Literary Studies*, Vol. I, p. 131, quoted in Cooper, *Sergeant Shakespeare*, p. 10.

'in some trouble with the authorities': Ibid., p. 31.

'excepting the three dates 1582, 1583 and 1585': Honigmann, op. cit., p. 1.

'normally went to university': T. W. Baldwin, *Shakespeare's 'Small Latine and Lesse Greeke'*, (1944), Vol. I, p. 487.

'How else could he have passed these years?': Honigmann, op. cit., p. 1.

III. THE 'LOST' YEARS: 1579–1587

No scholar has done more than E. A. J. Honigmann (*Shakespeare: The Lost Years*) to put flesh on the bones of an idea 'first suggested', as he concedes, by Oliver Baker's *In Shakespeare's Warwickshire and the Unknown Years* (London: Simpkin Marshall, 1937), 're-stated' by E. K. Chambers in 'William Shakeshafte', *Shakespearean Gleanings* (London: OUP, 1944), taken further by Alan Keen and Roger Lubbock in *The Annotator* (London: Putnam, 1954). Honigmann is endorsed cautiously by S. Schoenbaum (*Times Literary Supplement*, 19 April 1985, and in the 1987 edition of *A Compact Documentary Life*) and enthusiastically by Eric Sams (*The Real Shakespeare*). The argument was further advanced by Richard Wilson in 'Shakespeare and the Jesuits', *Times Literary Supplement*, 19 December 1997, and at 'Lancastrian Shakespeare', a conference held in part at Hoghton Tower under the auspices of Lancaster University's Shakespeare Programme, 21–24 July 1999.

'a schoolmaster in the country': Oliver Lawson Dick (ed.), *Aubrey's Brief Lives* (Harmondsworth: Penguin, 1962), p. 276.

'one of the premier families of Lancashire': Honigmann, op. cit., p. 8.

'to retain the Queen's Majesty's subjects in due obedience': J. Stanley Leatherbarrow, *The Lancashire Elizabethan Recusants* (Manchester, 1947), p. 55.

'especially the house of Richard Hoghton': *Acts of the Privy Council*, Vol. XIII, p. 149, quoted in Honigmann, op. cit., p. 10.

'Being taken from school': Sir Thomas Elyot, *The Boke Named the Governour* (London, 1531), quoted in Joseph Quincy Adams, *A Life of William Shakespeare* (London: Constable, 1923), pp. 61–2.

'highly unlikely': Honigmann, op. cit., p. 9.

'The Rufford connection ... Sir Thomas Savage': John Leslie Hotson, *Shakespeare's Sonnets Dated, and Other Essays* (London: Hart-Davis, 1949), pp. 128–9.

'Thomas Hesketh, my bastard son': Honigmann, op. cit., p. 36.

'If William Shakeshafte passed from the service of Alexander Hoghton': Chambers, *Shakespearean Gleanings*, op. cit., pp. 52–3.

'love for the one and lust for the other': Burgess, op. cit., pp. 53–4.

'unauthentic': Shakespeare, *Sonnets*, ed. Charles Pooler (London: Longman, 1918); ed. D. G. Mackail (London: Constable, 1930), quoted in Sams, op. cit., p. 49.

'Baker' for 'Barbar': J. W. Gray, 'Hathway or Whateley', *Shakespeare's Marriage* (London: Chapman & Hall, 1905), pp. 21–35.

'Luddington (three miles west)': S. W. Fullom, *History of William Shakespeare* (London, 1862), quoted in Sams, op. cit., pp. 87–8; and Schoenbaum, op. cit., p. 50.

'to celebrate his wedding-day': R. Phillips, *The Monthly Magazine*, Vol. XLV, No. 1, 1818, p. 152, quoted in Chambers, op. cit., p. 297.

'a little ale-house, some distance from Stratford': Wise, 'Letter from the Place of Shakespeare's Nativity', *British Magazine*, 1762.

'The people of Pebworth': Ireland, op. cit., p. 233.

'the branches had entirely vanished': Robert Bell Wheeler, *Collectanea de Stratford*, p. 202.

'close causal links among deer-stealing, pregnancy and marriage': Sams, op. cit., p. 52.

'When was she to have a house of her own?': Burgess, op. cit., p. 58.

IV. LONDON: 1587-1592

'favourite favourite': S. Schoenbaum, *Shakespeare: The Globe and the World* (New York: Folger Shakespeare Library/OUP, 1979), p. 40.

'multitudes of base tenements': John Stow, *A Survey of London Reprinted from the Text of 1603*, ed. C. L. Kingsford (Oxford: Clarendon Press, 1908), Vol. II, p. 368.

'gilt tower, with a fountain that plays': *Paul Hentzner's Travels in England During the Reign of Queen Elizabeth*, translated by Richard Bentley (London, 1797), p. 3.

'no longer a commodity': Burgess, op. cit., pp. 70-2.

'an indifferent actor': Shakespearean actors are fond of disputing this. 'You didn't get billing as a tragedian with the King's Men unless you could act,' insists one such, Peter O'Toole, who believes that Shakespeare was 'one of life's Mercutios'. (Author's conversation with O'Toole, 20 June 1999; Anthony Holden, 'Men Behaving Bardly', *Observer*, 11 July 1999.)

'Behold these sumptuous houses' . . . 'an evident token of a wicked time': T[homas] W[hite], 'A Sermon preached at Pawles Cross on Sunday the thirde of November 1577 in the time of the Plague' (London, 1578), p. 47, quoted in Chambers, *Elizabethan Stage*, p. 269; William Harrison, MS 'Chronologie', quoted in ibid.

'a butcher's apprentice would be useful': Sams, op. cit., p. 55.

'poor' . . . 'without money and friends': Ibid., p. 56.

'receiv'd into the Company': Nicholas Rowe, op. cit., p. vi.

'When Shakespeare fled to London': Shakespeare, *Plays*, ed. Samuel Johnson (London, 1765), i, p.c.

'first received into the playhouse as a serviture': Dowdall (1693), quoted in Schoenbaum, op. cit., p. 143.

'frets like a gumm'd velvet': Sams, op. cit., p. 56.

'first office in the theatre': Edmond Malone, *Supplement to the Edition of Shakespeare's Plays Published in 1778 by S. Johnson and G. Steevens* (London: Bathurst, 1780), p. 67.

'a perfect post for the aspiring young actor-playwright': Sams, op. cit., p. 57.

'one of the first actors in Shakespeare's plays': Seymour Pitcher, *The Case for Shakespeare's Authorship of 'The Famous Victories of Henry V'* (London: Alvin Redman, 1961), p. 175.

'The handwriting of his signature on the book suggests as much': Sir Edward Thompson, *Shakespeare's Handwriting: A Study* (Oxford: Clarendon Press, 1916); 'Special Transcript of the Three Pages', *Shakespeare's Hand in the Play of Sir Thomas More*, ed. A. W. Pollard (Cambridge: CUP, 1923), quoted in Sams, op. cit., p. 72.

'How it would have joyed brave Talbot': Thomas Nashe, *Pierce Penniless* (London, 1592).

'horror turns to pity': Herschel Baker, Introduction to *1–3 Henry VI* in *The Riverside Shakespeare* (Boston, MA: Houghton Mifflin, 1974), p. 592.

'It is very, very frightening . . . Tastes change': Arden edition of *Titus Andronicus*, ed. Jonathan Bate (London: Routledge & Kegan Paul, 1995), pp. 1–2.

'Edward III': See Eric Sams, *Shakespeare's Edward III* (New Haven, CT: Yale University Press, 1996).

'The cause of plague is sin': F. P. Wilson, *The Plague in Shakespeare's London* (Oxford: Clarendon Press, 1927), p. 52.

V. THE 'UPSTART CROW': 1592–1594

'subsistence through pleasing the public': Note to Sonnet 111, line 4, *The Riverside Shakespeare*, op. cit., p. 1769.

'turned out in force': Sams, op. cit., p. 58.

'About three months since died M. Robert Greene': Henry Chettle, 'To the Gentlemen Readers', epistle inserted into *Kind-Harts Dreame* (London, 1592).

'a great reckoning in a little room': See also Louis MacNeice's poem 'Suite for Recorders' (1950), *Collected Poems* (London: Faber & Faber, 1966), pp. 283–7.

'Marlowe was assassinated': The murky circumstances of Marlowe's murder are brilliantly investigated in Charles Nicholl's *The Reckoning* (London: Jonathan Cape, 1992).

'Fair Venus, queen of beauty and of love': Anon., *The Three Parnassus Plays, 1598–1601*, ed. J. B. Leishman (London: Nicholson & Watson, 1949), p. 192.

'Could but a graver subject him content': *The Return from Parnassus, Part 2*, quoted in Hallett Smith, Introduction to the Riverside *Venus and Adonis*, p. 1704.

'The younger sort takes much delight': *Gabriel Harvey's Marginalia*, ed. G. C. Moore Smith (Stratford-upon-Avon, 1913), includes a facsimile of Harvey's MS note, dated variously between 1598 and 1603, on Folio 394v of his copy of Speght's edition of Chaucer (London, 1598).

'Whoever she was, she enchanted the poet': Jonathan Bate, *Mail on Sunday*, 14 February 1999.

'You must believe in Mrs Florio': Jonathan Bate, *The Genius of Shakespeare* (London: Picador, 1997), p. 58.

'definitive . . . unanswerable': A. L. Rowse, *Shakespeare's Sonnets* (London: Macmillan, 1964, third edition 1984), pp. xix–xxv.

'a well known person . . . of superior social standing': Ibid.

'anonymous, even composite': Burgess, op. cit., p. 131.

'begotten between thought and mirth': Swinburne, quoted in Horace Howard Furness (ed.), *Love's Labour's Lost* in *The New Variorum Shakespeare* (Philadelphia, 1904), p. 363; also quoted in the Arden edition, ed. H. R. Woudhuysen (London: Nelson, 1998), p. 53.

'passages mean, childish and vulgar': Johnson, *Samuel Johnson on Shakespeare*, ed. H. R. Woudhuysen (London: Penguin, 1989), quoted in the Arden edition of *Love's Labour's Lost*, op. cit., p. 43.

'has come honestly by its enduring popularity': Anne Barton, Introduction to the Riverside edition of *The Taming of the Shrew*, p. 106.

'one of the worst of Shakespeare's plays': Charles Gildon, quoted in the Arden edition of *Love's Labour's Lost*, op. cit., p. 60.

'many features in common': Brian Morris, Arden edition of *The Taming of the Shrew* (London: Methuen, 1981), p. 60.

'Did Shakespeare attend the public execution': T. W. Baldwin, *William Shakspere Adapts a Hanging* (Princeton, NJ: Princeton University Press, 1931), quoted in the Arden edition of *The Comedy of Errors*, ed. R. A. Foakes (London: Methuen, 1962), pp. xv–xvi.

'deliverance from moral bondage': Arden edition of *The Comedy of Errors*, op. cit., p. 1.

'happy endings must, to carry conviction': Barton, Introduction to the Riverside edition of *The Comedy of Errors*, p. 81.

'an unconscious desire': A. Bronson Feldman, *International Journal of Psycho-Analysis*, Vol. XXXVI, 1955, quoted in the Arden edition of *The Comedy of Errors*, op. cit., n. 1.

'a fair description of some of the symptoms of syphilis': Burgess, op. cit., p. 198.

'my friend catches a venereal infection': John Kerrigan (ed.), *The Sonnets and a Lover's Complaint* (London: Penguin, 1986), p. 60.

VI. THE LORD CHAMBERLAIN'S MAN: 1594–1596

'A dear lover and cherisher': Thomas Nashe, dedication to *The Unfortunate Traveller* (London, 1594).

'disordered tumult and crowd': See *Gesta Grayorum: or, The History of the High and Mighty Prince Henry, Prince of Purpoole* . . . (London: W. Canning, 1688).

'the most complete man of the theater of his time': G. E. Bentley, *Shakespeare: A Biographical Handbook* (New Haven, CT: Yale University Press, 1961), p. 119.

'Few in any age have served the stage so variously': Schoenbaum, op. cit., p. 185.

'perhaps the most trivial verse': Stanley Wells and Gary Taylor (eds), *William Shakespeare: The Complete Works* (Oxford: Clarendon Press, 1986), p. 881.

'The gift is small': Ascription found in a manuscript compiled by Sir Francis Fane of Bulbeck (1611–80), now in the Bodleian Library, Oxford.

'the silliest stuff that ever I heard': Samuel Pepys, quoted in Anne Barton, Introduction to the Riverside edition of *A Midsummer Night's Dream*, p. 217.

'gossamer and moonshine': Ibid.

'Immature poets imitate; mature poets steal': T. S. Eliot, 'Philip Massinger', *Selected Essays* (London: Faber & Faber, 1932), p. 206.

'whip his bare arse with a rod' . . . 'as if they were precious metal': Burgess, op. cit., pp. 120, 126.

'appropriately limited place': Frank Kermode, Introduction to the Riverside edition of *Romeo and Juliet*, p. 1056.

'play of the hour': Sir Sidney Lee, *The Gentleman's Magazine*, February 1880, pp. 185–200, quoted in the Arden edition of *Romeo and Juliet*, ed. John Russell Brown (London: Methuen, 1964), p. xxiii.

'mythical beasts: strange, evil beings': Barton, Introduction to the Riverside edition of *The Merchant of Venice*, p. 250.

'internalized hero-villains': Bloom, op. cit., p. 11.

'a vice most odious': D. L. Thomas and N. E. Evans, 'John Shakespeare in the Exchequer', *Shakespeare Quarterly*, Vol. XXXV, 1984, pp. 315–18.

VII. 'MY ABSENT CHILD': 1596–1599

'dead from fever or blood-poisoning': Burgess, op. cit., p. 141.

'humanity and good nature': Rowe, op. cit., pp. xii-xiii.

'a ruffian-knight as all England knoweth': 'N.D.' (Robert Persons, under the pseudonym of Nicholas Dolman), *The Third Part of a Treatise, Intituled: of three Conversions in England* [etc.] . . . *by John Fox* (London, 1604), quoted in Chambers, op. cit., p. 213.

'a ruffian, a robber and a rebel': John Speed, *History of Great Britain* (London, 1611), quoted in Schoenbaum, op. cit., p. 193.

'Stage-poets have themselves been very bold': Thomas Fuller, *The Church-History of Britain: From the Birth of Jesus Christ Until the Year 1648* (London, 1655), Book IV, p. 168.

'Now as I am glad that Sir John Oldcastle is put out': Fuller, *Worthies of England* (London, 1662), p. 253.

'there is reason to believe': Wells and Taylor (eds), op. cit., p. 509.

'looked on approvingly': Schoenbaum, op. cit., p. 207.

VIII. THE GLOBE: 1599–1603

'went with my party across the water': Ernest Schanzer, 'Thomas Platter's Observations on the Elizabethan Stage', *Notes and Queries* (1956), p. 466.

'did riotously assemble themselves together': C. W. Wallace, 'The First London Theatre: Materials for a History', *Nebraska University Studies*, Vol. XIII, 1913, pp. 278–9.

'habits of business': J. O. Halliwell-Phillips, 'A Life of William Shakespeare', in Shakespeare, *Works* (1853–65), p. 151.

'So have I seen': Leonard Digges, 'Poets are born not made', commendatory poem affixed to *Poems: Written by Wil. Shakespeare, Gent.* (London, 1640), lines 41–6.

'I loved the man' . . . 'Many times he fell': Jonson, op. cit., pp. 97–8.

'I spurn thee like a cur out of my way': Arden edition of *Julius Caesar*, ed. T. S. Dorsch (London: Methuen, 1965), p. 65.

'Would he had blotted a thousand' . . . 'malevolent speech' . . . 'had an excellent fantasy': Jonson, op. cit., pp. 97–8.

'His mind and hand went together': The best discussion of Shakespeare's revision of his own lines is to be found in John Jones, *Shakespeare at Work* (Oxford: Clarendon Press, 1995).

'under the name of another': Thomas Heywood, *An Apology for Actors* (London, 1612).

'so old and out of use': Francis Bacon, *Declaration of the Practises and Treasons* (London, 1601), quoted in Schoenbaum, op. cit, p. 218.

'I am Richard II': Chambers, op. cit., pp. 326–7.

'that inflammatory tragedy': Burgess, op. cit., p. 174.

'Giants fought giants': Ibid., p. 161.

'voted the "masterwork" of the last thousand years': *Sunday Times*, 28 March 1999.

'Byrd's anthems, the Royal Exchange': Burgess, op. cit., pp. 183–4.

'His name is printed': Rowe, op. cit., p. vi.

'a much better poet': *Historia Histrionica: An Historical Account of the English Stage . . . in a Dialogue, of Plays and Players* (London, 1699), p. 4.

'Eternal reader, you have here': Prefatory epistle to *Troilus and Cressida* (London, 1609).

'to please the most diverse tastes': Barton, Introduction to the Riverside edition of *Troilus and Cressida*, p. 444.

'a difficult poem, but knowingly so': A. Alvarez, 'The Phoenix and the Turtle' in *Interpretations*, ed. John Wain (London: Routledge & Kegan Paul, 1955), pp. 1–6.

'the first night of *Twelfth Night*': See John Leslie Hotson, *The First Night of Twelfth Night* (London: Hart-Davis, 1954).

'in a laughing manner': Rowe, op. cit., p. xxxvi.

IX. THE KING'S MAN: 1603–1606

'played at court no fewer than 187 times': G. E. Bentley, 'Shakespeare and the Blackfriars Theatre', *Shakespeare Survey I* (Cambridge: CUP, 1948), p. 40.

'We have the man Shakespeare with us': *Extracts from the Letters and Journals of William Cory*, ed. Francis Warre Cornish (London, 1897), p. 168, quoted in Chambers, op. cit., p. 329, reports that in 1865 the Countess of Pembroke's descendant, Lady Herbert, told a visiting Eton master named William Cory that the family still possessed this letter; but it has never come to light.

'"somewhat insipid" French Senecan': Burgess, op. cit., p. 190.

'predominant harshness of tone': Barton, Introduction to the Riverside edition of *Measure for Measure*, p. 545.

'her teeth were made in Blackfriars': Ben Jonson, *Epicoene*, quoted in Schoenbaum, op. cit., pp. 260–1.

'did send and persuade one Mr Shakespeare': C. W. Wallace, 'New Shakespeare Discoveries: Shakespeare as a Man Among Men', *Harper's Monthly Magazine*, Vol. CXX, 1910, adds much new detail to E. K. Chambers's original account of this episode.

'a man among men': Wallace, ibid.

'quick snack, then back to work': Burgess, op. cit., pp. 195–7.

'Mary Mountjoy alained': Rowse, 'Secrets of Shakespeare's Land-lady', *The Times*, 23 April 1973.

'strange in their ways' . . . 'barbarians': Arden edition of *Othello*, ed. Honigmann (London: Methuen, 1997), p. 2.

'the medicinal gum of the Arabian trees': Kenneth Muir, *The Sources of Shakespeare's Plays* (London: Methuen, 1977), pp. 188ff, quoted in the Arden edition of *Othello*, op. cit., p. 5.

'more insistently time-bound': Arden edition of *Othello*, op. cit., p. 107.

'Choke the devil! Choke him!': A. C. Sprague, *Shakespeare and the Actors* (Cambridge, MA: Harvard University Press, 1945), p. 199.

'tactless': Burgess, op. cit., p. 200.

'echoes' . . . 'unconscious substitution': Arden edition of *Othello*, pp. 344–50; Honigmann, *The Texts of 'Othello'* (London: Routledge & Kegan Paul, 1996), also places the play earlier, at 1601–2.

'*King Lear* contains "echoes" of *Measure for Measure*': Kenneth Muir, Arden edition of *King Lear* (London: Methuen, 1955), pp. xxv-xxvi.

'monstrous burden' . . . 'Shakespeare and Burbage got drunk': Anthony Holden, *Olivier* (London: Weidenfeld & Nicolson, 1988), p. 376.

'discredit the values of absolute monarchy': Franco Moretti, *The Great Eclipse: Tragic Form as the Deconsecration of Sovereignty*, reprinted from *Signs are Taken for Wonders* (London: NLB, 1983), in John Drakakis (ed.), *Shakespearian Tragedy* (Harlow: Longman, 1992).

'Never did Shakespeare take a more deliberate': C. J. Sisson, quoted in Frank Kermode, Introduction to the Riverside edition of *King Lear*, p. 1251.

'as though Shakespeare were dispensing with the blossom': Note by A. Alvarez after seeing Ian Holm's Lear at the National Theatre, London, 1997, with the author; published here with his permission.

'From our particular vantage-point': Kermode, Introduction to the Riverside edition of *King Lear*, p. 1249.

'I would advise you, as you tender your life': Antonia Fraser, *The Gunpowder Plot* (London: Mandarin, 1997), p. 150.

'whether the imagination can produce real effects': Kermode, Introduction to the Riverside edition of *Macbeth*, p. 1308.

'beggars belief': Tony Tanner, Introduction to the Everyman edition of *Shakespeare, Tragedies, Vol. I* (London: Everyman, 1992), p. xcix.

X. THE 'ANTIQUE ROMAN': 1606–1608

'a great frequenter of plays': Sir Richard Baker, *Chronicles* (London, 1643).

'an admirer and lover of plays': Anthony Wood, *Athenae Oxonienses*, ed. P. Bliss (four volumes, 1813–20), especially Vol. III (1817), pp. 802–9.

'She supposeth herself with child': Mary Edmond, *Rare Sir William Davenant* (Manchester: MUP, 1987), p. 12.

'splenetic and melancholy': Ibid., p. 13.

'whether for the beautiful mistress of the house': Charles Gildon (ed.), *The Lives and Characters of the English Dramatick Poets . . . by Gerard Langbaine* (London, 1698), p. 32.

'In all probability he got him': Bodleian Library MS, Hearne Diaries.

'an old townsman' . . . 'There might be in the garden': Wood, op. cit.; Shakespeare, *Plays*, ed. Samuel Johnson and George Steevens (London, 1778).

'common in town' . . . 'seemed fond of having it taken for truth': Joseph Spence, *Observations, Anecdotes and Characters of Books and Men, Collected from Conversation*, ed. James M. Osborn (Oxford: Clarendon Press, 1966), p. 184.

'the features seem to resemble' . . . 'the want of a nose': William Chetwood, *A General History of the Stage* (London, 1749), p. 21n.

'just another of those rude Elizabethans' . . . 'Shakespeare might have done worse': Ian Hamilton, *Keepers of the Flame* (London: Pimlico, 1993), p. 22. Texts and analyses of Davenant's 'revisions' of Shakespeare's plays can be found in several volumes, notably *Five Restoration Adaptations of Shakespeare*, ed. Christopher Spencer (Urbana, IL: University of Illinois Press, 1965) and *Shakespeare Made Fit*, ed. Sandra Clark (London: Everyman, 1997).

'pretty certain that I shall be hanged' . . . 'Milton saved him from execution': Hamilton, op. cit., p. 18.

'a four-storey building' . . . 'a New College inventory': Park Honan, *Shakespeare: A Life* (Oxford: OUP, 1998), pp. 319–20, echoing Edmond, *Rare Sir William Davenant*, op. cit., pp. 19, 22–3.

'he liked to regard himself as Shakespeare's literary heir': Edmond, op. cit., p. 14.

'something recognisably filial': Hamilton, op. cit., p. 19.

'Antony and Cleopatra seem to us larger than life': John Wilders, Arden edition of *Antony and Cleopatra* (London: Methuen, 1995), p. 3.

'Cleopatra's Nile could be the Thames': Burgess, op. cit, p. 206.

'one of the most highly-wrought': Frank Kermode, Introduction to the Riverside edition of *Antony and Cleopatra*, p. 1343.

'incapable of adjusting himself to society': Ibid., p. 1443.

'turn his back on London': Burgess, op. cit., p. 209.

'overgrown schoolboys with "crazed" notions of privilege': Wyndham Lewis, *The Lion and the Fox*, quoted in Frank Kermode, Introduction to the Riverside edition of *Coriolanus*, p. 1392.

'Shakespeare's vocabulary': Max Müller, *Lectures on the Science of Language*, quoted in John Michell, *Who Wrote Shakespeare?* (London: Thames & Hudson, 1996), pp. 19–20.

XI. BLACKFRIARS: 1608–1611

'Joan for Joanna, Eleanor for Helen' . . . 'Someone of means': G. E. Bentley, *Shakespeare: A Biographical Handbook* (New Haven, CT: Yale University Press, 1961), p. 81.

'the depths of despair' . . . 'an elderly serenity': Edward Dowden, *Shakspere: His Mind and Art* (London, 1875), quoted in Kermode, Arden edition of *The Tempest* (London: Methuen, 1954), p. lxxxii.

'a serious illness' . . . 'a nervous breakdown': E. K. Chambers, *A Short Life of Shakespeare* (Oxford: Clarendon Press, 1933), p. 61.

'More nonsense has been talked and written': W. H. Auden, Introduction to the Signet Classic edition of *Shakespeare's Sonnets and Narrative Poems* (New York: New American Library, 1964), pp. xvii *et seq.*

'Shakespeare had been waiting for his mother's death': Honan, op. cit., p. 358.

'a fiendishly complex code': Nigel Hawkes, 'Codebreaker Names Bard's "Fair Youth"', *The Times*, 31 December 1997.

'too intimate' . . . 'eternity promised by our ever-living poet': Schoenbaum, op. cit., p. 270.

'Much scholarship has been devoted': See Leslie Hotson, *Mr W.H.* (London: Chatto & Windus, 1964).

'Play my song, Will Hewes': Anthony Holden, 'Oscar Wilde and Shakespeare's Sonnets', address at annual dinner of Oscar Wilde Society, 19 October 1996, published in abridged form, *The Wildean*, 10, Spring 1997, pp. 4–7.

'perhaps the mere effort to convert anyone': Oscar Wilde, 'The Portrait of Mr W.H.' (London: Penguin, 1995), p. 51.

'dazzlingly offered a theory': Richard Ellmann, *Oscar Wilde* (London: Hamish Hamilton, 1987), p. 280.

'shakes his furious Speare': Sams, op. cit., p. 102n.

'The form was good for Ben': Burgess, op. cit., p. 192.

'a royal exercise in negritude' . . . 'It was her Majesty's wish': Ibid., p. 193.

'The entertainment went forward' . . . 'Hope and Faith' . . . 'unmoved by declining standards at court' . . . 'collapsed early in the proceedings': *Chronicle of the Royal Family* (London: Chronicle, 1991), p. 206.

'among the tenderest lines in Shakespeare': Tennyson, quoted in J. M. Nosworthy, Arden edition of *Cymbeline* (London: Methuen, 1955), p. 177n.

'utilisation of good old reliable romantic motifs' . . . 'spectacular business': Hallett Smith, Introduction to the Riverside edition of *Cymbeline*, p. 1518.

'literalists of the imagination': Lines subsequently excised from the original version of *Poetry*, Marianne Moore, *Collected Poems* (London: Faber & Faber, 1951), pp. 266–7.

'a disposition of mutation': Cicero's *affectio* as defined in Cooper's Latin dictionary (1584 edition), quoted in Hallett Smith, Introduction to the Riverside edition of *The Winter's Tale*, p. 1565.

'philosopher of roguery': Ibid., p. 1566.

'a play of country hired shepherds': Fletcher, ibid., p. 1565.

'the survival into a new world': Kermode, Introduction to the Arden edition of *The Tempest*, p. lxxxiii, which also cites on this point A. Quiller-Couch, *Shakespeare's Workmanship* (London: Fisher Unwin, 1918), and J. Dover Wilson's published lecture, 'The Meaning of *The Tempest*' (1936).

'show us, in their very dullness' . . . 'Passed through his fire' . . . 'the correct pronunciation of Stephano' . . . 'Platonic, though never schematic': Ibid., pp. lxxi, lxx, lviii–lix.

'repeats . . . in miniature': G. Wilson Knight, *The Shakespearian Tempest* (Oxford: OUP, 1932), p. 247, quoted in Kermode, op. cit., p. lxxxiv.

'a necessary development': Kermode, op. cit., p. lxxxiv.

'whoring after strange gods of allegory': Ibid., p. lxxxi.

'a sacredness as the last work': Shakespeare, *Dramatic Works*, ed. Thomas Campbell (Paris, 1838), p. lxiv.

'The magus of *The Tempest*': Schoenbaum, op. cit., p. 278.

'For Milan, read Stratford': Burgess, op. cit., p. 226.

XII. 'A MERRY MEETING': 1611–1616

'I perceived I might stay': Halliwell-Phillips, *Outlines of the Life of Shakespeare* (seventh edition, 1887), p. 378.

'out of which he was accustomed to take his draught': George Steevens, note on Sir John Oldcastle, in Malone's *Supplement to the Edition of Shakespeare's Plays Published in 1778 by Samuel Johnson and George Steevens*, op. cit., pp. 369–70.

'How did the faculty so radiant': James, op. cit., pp. 1219–20.

'tedious' . . . 'worn out': Burgess, op. cit., p. 217.

'Those who believe that Bacon wrote Shakespeare': Michell, op. cit., pp. 11–12.

'heard I had some skill in words': Rudyard Kipling, 'Proofs of Holy Writ' (1932), in *Writings on Writings*, ed. Sandra Kemp and Lisa Lewis (Cambridge: CUP, 1996), pp. 99–110.

'If this is mere chance': Burgess, op. cit., p. 212.

'original manuscript' . . . 'an interesting curiosity' . . . 'several manuscripts': Wells and Taylor (eds), op. cit., p. 1341.

'the individual consciousness of each reader' . . . 'weak and disappointing': James Spedding, 'Who Wrote Shakespeare's Henry VIII?', *Gentleman's Magazine*, 1850, revised for the *Transactions of the New Shakespeare Society*, 1874.

'from normality and order' . . . 'the paradigm of Shakespeare's whole career': G. Wilson Knight, quoted in Herschel Baker, Introduction to the Riverside edition of *Henry VIII*, p. 979.

'drab and melancholy': *Chronicle of the Royal Family*, op. cit., p. 208.

'nothing did perish but wood and straw' . . . 'that would perhaps have broiled him' . . . 'certain chambers being shot off': Sir Henry Wotton, letter to Sir Edmund Bacon, quoted in Logan Pearsall Smith, *The Life and Letters of Sir Henry Wotton* (Oxford: Clarendon Press, 1907), p. 17; see also Chambers, op. cit., p. 153.

'an honest man sent to lie abroad': ('*peregre issus ad mentiendum Reipublicae causa*'), Sir Henry Wotton, *Written in the Album of Christopher Fleckmore* (London, 1604).

'No shower his rain did there down force': Chambers, *The Elizabethan Stage*, op. cit., p. 421.

'gone to the Globe, to a play' . . . 'rumours that the King himself' . . . 'each sharer was at first assessed £50 or £60' . . . 'while pruning' . . . 'this was a good time to sell': Schoenbaum, op. cit, p. 277.

'whatever Tom Stoppard would have us believe': In the penultimate scene of the Oscar-winning film *Shakespeare in Love* (Miramax, 1998, co-written by Sir Tom Stoppard), the Queen unexpectedly steps out from the audience at the Globe to sort out problems between Shakespeare, his beloved Lady Viola (Gwyneth Paltrow) and her equally fictitious husband.

'When God was pleas'd': Bodleian Library, Oxford; Rawlinson poet. 160, Folio 41, quoted in Chambers, op. cit., p. 551.

'dwelling-house or tenement' . . . 'great gate' . . . 'all and singular cellars': Conveyance dated 10 March 1613, quoted in Schoenbaum, op. cit., p. 273.

'my man Morris': Pearsall Smith, op. cit., pp. 32–3.

'*All* his plays are set in London': Author's conversation with Peter O'Toole, 1 April 1999.

'allegorical or mythological': Schoenbaum, op. cit., p. 272.

'so dark that their meaning': Chambers, op. cit., p. 153; Pearsall Smith, op. cit., p. 17.

'marked the end of his career': Burgess, op. cit., p. 228.

'scrap of paper' . . . 'considered for performance at court': Hallett Smith, Introduction to the Riverside edition of *The Two Noble Kinsmen*, p. 1639.

'pretty song' . . . 'Spalding carved the play up': Ibid., p. 1640.

'the communal tillage of open fields': C. M. Ingleby, *Shakespeare and the Enclosure of Common Fields at Welcombe* (Birmingham, 1885).

'my cousin Shakespeare coming yesterday to town': Thomas Greene, memorandum, Shakespeare Birthplace Trust Records Office, quoted in Schoenbaum, op. cit., p. 283.

'by tending to the ruin of the borough' . . . 'good football players' . . . 'set his heart at rest' . . . 'out of hope': Ibid., pp. 284–5. This account of the 'enclosure' episode gratefully draws, like Schoenbaum's, pp. 281–5, on the work of E. K. Chambers, J. O. Halliwell-Phillips, Edgar I. Fripp and especially C. M. Ingleby.

'The town wrote to him': Edward Bond, introduction to *Bingo* (London: Methuen, 1974), p. ix.

'less a rank than a role': Burgess, op. cit., pp. 229–30.

'preferring to pay the £10 fine': Schoenbaum, op. cit., p. 288.

'Shakespeare ate too many pickled herrings': Burgess, op. cit, p. 235.

'To mark how little he esteemed her': Malone, op. cit., p. 657.

'To see his face we need only look in a mirror': Burgess, op. cit., pp. 237–8.

INDEX

Page numbers in italics denote illustrations.